ENABLING INNOVATION AND DIVERSITY IN PSYCHOTHERAPY AND COUNSELLING

EDITED BY

YVONNE BATES

AND

RICHARD HOUSE

PCCS BOOKS
Ross-on-Wye

First published in 2003

PCCS BOOKS
Llangarron
Ross-on-Wye
Herefordshire
HR9 6PT
UK
Tel +44 (0)1989 77 07 07
enquiries@pccsbks.globalnet.co.uk
www.pccs-books.co.uk

**Ethically Challenged Professions:
Enabling innovation and diversity in
psychotherapy and counselling**

British Library Cataloguing in Publication Data.
A catalogue record for this book is available from the British Library.

ISBN 1 898059 61 6

Cover design by Jeannie Forbes
Printed by Biddles Ltd., Guildford, UK

CONTENTS

PART II ENABLING INNOVATION AND DIVERSITY

IIA: ENABLING ACCOUNTABILITY AND CO-OPERATION

IIB: ENABLING PRACTICE

IIC: WHITHER THERAPY?

DEDICATIONS

YVONNE BATES wishes to dedicate this anthology to her co-editor, Richard House, for making this opportunity available; for his confidence in her, his generosity of spirit, incredible work ethic and his commitment to always finding solutions which pleased us both! It is indeed a terrible blow for the field that Richard intends to leave counselling and psychotherapy in the not-too-distant future. Yvonne would also like to dedicate the book to Paula Bentley, for being her inspiration, and for her total support, patience, common sense, ever-pertinent suggestions and even a bit of typing!

RICHARD HOUSE wishes to dedicate this anthology to all of his peer-colleagues and friends in the British *Independent Practitioners Network* (IPN), who, since 1994, have been collectively pioneering a non-hierarchical, anti-bureaucratic approach to accountability and peer-ship which aims to take us beyond the tired and outmoded institutional authority structures which can only hamper a healthy and mature development of our occupational field in and beyond Late Modernity. In particular he wishes to thank and acknowledge his current and former 'Leonard Piper' IPN group colleagues: Jocelyn Chaplin, Tony Donaghy, Irene Galant, Jutta Gassner, Guy Gladstone, Juliet Lamont, Drue Nottage, Denis Postle, Annie Spencer and Maggie Taraz.

About the Contributors

'ROSIE ALEXANDER' is a whistle blower. She believes that no bad experience is wholly negative if it can be publicised in such a way as to reduce the likelihood of similar experiences happening to others. Her loudest whistle blast so far is *Folie à Deux — An Experience of One-to-One Therapy* (Free Association Books, 1995).

HARLENE ANDERSON is a founding member of the Houston Galveston Institute and Taos Institute, USA. She is renowned internationally for her contributions to the development and expansion of postmodern practices, including her *Collaborative Consultations approach*, which helps people and organisations enhance their creativities, strengths and resources. Harlene has authored and co-authored numerous professional writings, including her book *Conversation, Language and Possibilities: A Postmodern Approach to Therapy*. Among her many recognitions are the 2000 'American Association for Marriage and Family Therapy Award for Outstanding Contributions to Marriage and Family Therapy' and the 1997 'Texas Association for Marriage and Family Therapy Award for Lifetime Achievement'.

YVONNE BATES is a humanistic practitioner working with the Alexander Group, a telephone counselling association. She is Managing Editor of the independent journal *ipnosis* (see www.ipnosis.com or write to *ipnosis*, P.O. Box 19, Llandysul, SA44 4YE, UK for details). Yvonne is active in the struggle against the academic expropriation and professionalisation of practice, believing passionately that the clients and therapists 'at the coal-face' are in the best position to decide how their work is conducted. Yvonne can be contacted at ipnosis@aol.com.

ARTHUR C. BOHART, Ph.D. is Professor of Psychology at California State University, Dominguez Hills. He is also on the faculty at Saybrook Graduate School and Research Center. His interests are in the self-healing potential of humans and empathy in psychotherapy.

DHARMAVIDYA DAVID BRAZIER, Ph.D. is a Buddhist teacher and member of the Order of Amida Buddha. He is also a registered psychotherapist and author of books on Buddhism and on psychotherapy, including *Beyond Carl Rogers, Zen Therapy* and *The New Buddhism*. He can be contacted via www.amidatrust.com

VIVIEN BURR is Principal Lecturer in Psychology in the Department of Behavioural Sciences, University of Huddersfield, UK. Her earlier publications include *Invitation to Personal Construct Psychology* (with Trevor Butt), *An Introduction to Social Constructionism, Social Psychology and Gender* and *The Person in Social Psychology*.

TREVOR BUTT trained as a clinical psychologist before working at the University of Huddersfield, UK, where he is now Reader in Psychology. His teaching focuses on personality, psychological therapies and the individual in society. He has published in the areas of personal construct theory, existential phenomenology and psychotherapy.

PROFESSOR PETRUSKA CLARKSON is a Consultant Philosopher and Sexologist; Fellow of the BACP and BPS; Chartered Psychologist (Clinical, Counselling and Organisational); qualified Individual, Child, Couples, Sex and Group Psychotherapist; Recognised Psychodynamic and Integrative Supervisor, Management Consultant and Research Psychologist with 30 years' international experience, four Ph.D.s and more than 200 professional publications (in 23 languages), including the book *Ethics — Working with Ethical and Moral Dilemmas in Psychotherapy* (Whurr, 2002) She provides consultation, trainings and supervision at PHYSIS, 58 Harley Street, London. e-mail: petruska.c@dial.pipex.com. www.physis.co.uk.

COLIN FELTHAM is Reader in Counselling at Sheffield Hallam University, UK. A former co-editor of the *British Journal of Guidance and Counselling*, his publications include *Psychotherapy and its Discontents* (co-edited with Windy Dryden, Open University Press, 1992), *What is Counselling?* (Sage, 1995), *Controversies in Psychotherapy and Counselling* (Sage, 1999), *Taking Supervision Forward* (co-edited with Barbara Hawton, Sage, 2000) and *What's the Good of Counselling and Psychotherapy?* (Sage, 2002).

JOHN FREESTONE worked as a musician, jewellery designer, warehouseman and crofter until 1990, when his interest in health and philosophy led him to search, with the help of a hypnotherapist, for a new direction. He now works as a freelance counsellor, group facilitator, Reiki practitioner and relaxation/meditation teacher in North Yorkshire, UK.

NICKY HART, Ph.D., C.Psychol. is a chartered counselling psychologist currently working as course director of the D.Psych in Counselling Psychology at the University of Wolverhampton, UK. She has recently completed her doctoral research on the topic of power and ethics in therapeutic relationships.

JOHN HERON runs the South Pacific Centre for Human Inquiry in New Zealand. He founded the Human Potential Research Project, University of Surrey, UK, and was Assistant Director of the British Postgraduate Medical Federation, University of London. His books include *Feeling and Personhood*, 1992; *Co-operative Inquiry*, 1996; *Sacred Science*, 1998; *The Complete Facilitator's Handbook*, 1999; and *Helping the Client*, 2001.

DAN HOGAN received his doctorate in psychology and a law degree from Harvard University, where he served on the faculty for over ten years. While a Research Fellow there, he received a four-year grant to conduct research to determine how best to regulate the professions. In particular, he examined whether licensing laws were doing a good job in identifying competent professionals; and if not, what the alternatives might be. The results of his work appeared in the landmark 4-volume series *The Regulation of Psychotherapists*, published in 1979.

RICHARD HOUSE, Ph.D. has worked in diverse settings as a counsellor, supervisor and facilitator. An Independent Practitioners Network (IPN) participant since 1994, his many publications include *Therapy Beyond Modernity* (Karnac, 2003) and *Implausible Professions* (co-edited with Nick Totton, PCCS, 1997). A Steiner Kindergarten teacher, he edits Hawthorn Press's pioneering 'Early Years' series. His latest book *The Trouble with Education...* is in preparation.

JOHN KAYE is Senior Lecturer in Psychology at the University of Adelaide, South Australia, where he founded what is now the Masters in Clinical and Health Psychology programme. Convenor of the biennial Discursive Construction of Knowledge conference, John's teaching and research emerge from a post-foundational, critical/realist and discursive orientation — one which informs his work and ethic as a practising psychotherapist.

DR ARNOLD A. LAZARUS was one of the foremost pioneers of cognitive-behaviour therapy, and the founder/creator of Multimodal Therapy. He is Distinguished Professor Emeritus of Psychology at Rutgers University, New Jersey. Dr Lazarus has received numerous honours and awards, including the 'Distinguished Service Award' from the American Board of Professional Psychology, and he was the first recipient of the prestigious 'Annual Cummings PSYCHE Award'. In 1999 he received two Lifetime Achievement Awards, one from the California Psychological Association and the other from the Association for the Advancement of Behavior Therapy. He has maintained a clinical practice since 1959 and has authored or co-authored 18 books and over 300 articles and chapters.

IAN PARKER is Professor of Psychology in the Discourse Unit at Manchester Metropolitan University, where he is managing editor of the *Annual Review of Critical Psychology*. His books and articles in the fields of critical psychology, discourse analysis and psychoanalytic theory attempt to connect subjectivity with cultural processes and to possibilities of political change. He is also a member of the *Asylum* collective, a radical psychiatry magazine, and of *Psychology Politics Resistance*. His books include *Psychoanalytic Culture* (Sage, 1997) and *Critical Discursive Psychology* (Palgrave, 2002).

STEPHEN PATTISON is head of the Department of Religious and Theological Studies at Cardiff University, Wales, UK. A former consumer champion in the NHS and health and social welfare teacher at the Open University, his research interests lie in health-care ethics, management and the impact of inhabited world-views upon practices. He is a member of the Ethics Committee of the Royal College of General Practice. The author of *The Faith of the Managers* (1977) and *Shame: Theory, Therapy, Theology* (2000), Stephen is co-editor (with Roisin Pill) of *The Trouble with Professional Values* (forthcoming, 2004).

DENIS POSTLE is an artist, writer and musician who has had a counselling, coaching, supervision and psychotherapy practice in West London for over 17 years. He has co-run a variety of personal and professional development workshops and trainings focused around co-operative inquiry and facilitation. His approach to psychopractice seeks to help clients integrate politics, psychology and spirituality.

NIKOLAS ROSE is Professor of Sociology, Head of the Department of Sociology and Director of the LSE BIOS Centre for the Study of Bioscience, Biomedicine, Biotechnology and Society at the London School of Economics, UK. His most recent books are *Powers of Freedom: Reframing Political Thought* (Cambridge University Press, 1999); *Governing the Soul* (2nd edn, Free Association Books, 1999) and *Inventing Our Selves* (Cambridge University Press, 1996). His current research is on the social, political, legal and economic aspects of recent developments in biomedicine, especially in psychiatry and the brain sciences.

GAEL ROWAN is a psychosynthesis-trained therapist with a love of archetypal psychology. She works in private practice in Bristol and Dorset and has a teenage son.

'ANNA SANDS' lives in the country with her husband and two children. She writes textbooks for students of English as a foreign language. She has worked as an English teacher and teacher trainer in England and in France. She has a degree in Sociology and an M.Ed. in Language Teaching.

'NATALIE SIMPSON' is a mathematician who became interested in ethical issues in therapy after undergoing a disastrous course of psychoanalytical hypnotherapy in 1998. She is now half-way through a degree in psychology, but is certain that she will never desert her old friends *sin*, *cos* and *tan* for a career in psychotherapy.

DAVID SMAIL is a retired clinical psychologist and formerly Special Professor of Clinical Psychology at Nottingham University, UK. He is the author of a number of books looking at psychotherapy from a social perspective — most recently *The Nature of Unhappiness*. He maintains an informative website at www.djsmail.com/

ERNESTO SPINELLI is Professor of Psychotherapy, Counselling and Counselling Psychology at Regent's College, London. He practises as an existential therapist and lectures internationally on the approach. He is the author of numerous papers and books including *Tales of Un-Knowing* (Duckworth, 1997) and *The Mirror and The Hammer* (Continuum, 2001).

KAREN TALLMAN, Ph.D. earned her doctoral degree at the University of Southern California in 2000. She currently conducts research for Kaiser Permanente on physician-patient communication, barriers to the transfer of successful practices, successful practices in the physician work environment, and the role of interdependent teamwork in reducing stress and improving service quality in primary care medical centres.

BRIAN THORNE is Emeritus Professor of Counselling at the University of East Anglia, UK and a Co-founder of the Norwich Centre. He is an international figure in the world of person-centred therapy, and his latest book, *The Mystical Power of Person-Centred Therapy* (Whurr, 2002), is perhaps his most provocative.

GARI TOMKINS: With a background in integrative psychosynthesis, core-process psychotherapy, psychiatric art therapy and Jungian analysis, Gari's work places particular emphasis on the manifestation of individual uniqueness (or soul) in the world. His hobbies include making stained glass windows and furniture, and playing squash, football and pool. He has a particular liking for tropical beaches.

NICK TOTTON is a psychotherapist and trainer in private practice in Leeds, UK. He is the author of several books, most recently *Body Psychotherapy: An Introduction* (Open University Press), and editor of the *Psychotherapy and Politics International* journal (Whurr). Nick is part of the Burley Group, a prospective member group of the Independent Practitioners Network.

MICHAEL WHAN, MA is an analytical psychologist with the Independent Group of Analytical Psychologists. He lectures for various training bodies both in Britain and abroad. Background: NHS child, family and adult psychiatric services. His writings have been published in *Spring, Harvest, Dragonflies, Chiron*, the *European Journal of Psychotherapy, Counselling and Health* and the *Journal of Existential Analysis*.

FOREWORD

JOHN HERON

An ethically questionable degree of control characterises the current dominant world order: the control of commodities and services by large corporations; the control of valid knowledge by academic establishments; the legitimation of professional practice by statutory regulation; and so on. Such control is out of tune with the emerging values of what seems to be a new kind of civilisation, one that is essentially peer to peer. Peer-to-peer developments are afoot, notably on the internet; but also in manufacturing, in politics and social change, in psychological growth, in spiritual unfoldment, and in research and knowledge generation.

In all of these emerging fields, the interdependent values of personal autonomy and social co-operation are paramount; and hierarchy — thinking on behalf of, and proposing social structures and standards for, other people — is validated solely by its ability to enhance these prior values. A key distinction here is between hierarchy that controls autonomy and co-operation in a restrictive way, and hierarchy that provides forms for their liberation and continuous development.

This forthright book is poised very precisely on the leading edge of that distinction, exploring issues where controlling hierarchy and empowering hierarchy confront each other in the field of psychotherapy and counselling. This field provides a crucial test-bed for clarifying and enacting ethically appropriate ways of exercising empowering hierarchy.

I believe that this is the century of the spirit that is living deep within. The self-actualising tendency of growth psychology I see as a divine dynamic that is the ground of human motivation. Spiritual authority is found in the exercise of discrimination in depth, where human autonomy and divine animation marry, in those who associate with others similarly engaged. Nikolai Berdyaev, in the great tradition of European personalism, was on to this with his affirmation of human personhood as manifesting the creative process of spirit. For he defined spirit as self-determining human subjectivity engaged in the realisation of value and achieved in true community. He used the excellent Russian word *sobornost* to name such a community: it means diversity in free unity.

Translated into my world-view, Berdyaev's account means that living spirit emerges through autonomous people, each of whom I can identify their own idiosyncratic true needs and interests; each of whom can also think hierarchically in terms of what values promote the true needs and interests of the whole community; and each of whom can co-operate with — that is, listen to, dialogue with, and negotiate agreed decisions with — their peers, celebrating diversity and difference as integral to genuine unity. This creative and innovative dialogue among peers consummates the triadic process.

The autonomy of such people is not that of the old Cartesian ego, isolated and cut off from the world. Descartes sat inside a big stove to get at his 'cogito, ergo sum' — I think, therefore I am; and while his exclusively subjective self provided a necessary leverage against traditional dogmatisms to help found the modern world-view, it left the modern self alienated from the separated world it commands. The autonomy of those who flourish within *sobornost*, by contrast, is an autonomy that is grounded in and enriched by a profound kind of inner animation, that develops and flourishes only in felt interconnectedness, participative engagement, with other persons and with the biodiversity and integral ecology of our planet. What we are now about, I believe, is a whole regeneration of our world through co-creative engagement with the spirit that animates it and us.

I commend this book. It rigorously tills the ground, preparing for the kinds of psychotherapy and counselling, and their professional supporting structures, which honour the innovative authority of the spirit within each person in our emerging peer-to-peer reality.

INTRODUCTION

YVONNE BATES AND RICHARD HOUSE

Annie: Oh, you see an analyst?
Alvy: Y-y-yeah, just for fifteen years.
Annie: Fifteen years?
Alvy: Yeah, uh, I'm gonna give him one more year and then I'm going to Lourdes.

Woody Allen, 'Annie Hall'

Therapy is fertile ground for the comedian. It is a quirky, idiosyncratic phenomenon riddled with contradictions and inconsistencies.

Psychotherapy is, by its very definition, concerned with working with the soul, a scientifically unverified concept, yet the 'profession' seeks acceptance as scientific. Therapy is about listening to clients, yet its exponents don't seem to wish to listen to clients' opinions about therapy itself. Therapists want to help clients individuate and find their selfhood because that's the cultural and socio-political imperative of our time. Therapists want clients to trust them yet they impose an arguably alien, rigid set of boundaries and other ethical mandates, typically without explanation, that they have unquestioningly imbibed and passed on from their occupational/training bodies.

And here we are, the editors of *Ethically Challenged Professions*: we want to challenge the academic expropriation of counselling and psychotherapy, yet have produced a book full of academic chapters, academically supported and referenced, written by a host of distinguished doctors and professors. We want to challenge the orthodox scientific, modernist paradigm, yet need to be within it in order to be taken seriously enough to have our book published.

Postmodernism is a tremendously exciting, empowering and liberating concept. In its disputing of universal truths, it affords everyone's experience equal validity. There are huge areas where postmodern philosophy, humanistic psychology and feminist theory overlap - for example, equality, co-operation and mutual respect. Yet, sadly, at least for the present, postmodernism tends to be a cultivar in an academic cloche: writings on the subject are nearly always scholarly, at varying levels of inaccessibility, and off-putting to many people - and certainly to the vast majority of non-academics! Postmodernism, the approach that allows for the opinion of an unschooled person to be equally valid and *valued* compared to that of a professor, is the secret of an academic elite.

The editors and authors of *Ethically Challenged Professions* do not possess or profess easy solutions to ironies and contradictions such as these. What we have tried to do in this volume is to face up to them in many different ways. Perhaps wrestling with such dilemmas is, in any case, what is important, rather than resolving them. If so, we hope that this represents a step towards a truly postmodern or '*trans*modern' way of looking at therapy, that it is a book which will appeal to all counsellors and psychotherapists irrespective of their level of academic interest, and that it will provide a forum for the voices of clients to be heard by an increasing number of practitioners, and for the crucial dialogue between the two to gather pace.

THE FRAMEWORK OF THE ANTHOLOGY

The book falls into two parts. In Part I the contributions are concerned with challenging the assumptive base of what we, the editors, term 'professionalised' therapy. By 'professionalised' or 'profession-centred' therapy we are referring to the form that therapy has increasingly taken as the therapy professionalisation process in the UK has proceeded apace, and with increasing momentum, since the early 1990s. For us this is quintessentially an *ethical* issue (hence the title of the book) – but not, however, in the usual sense of codes of conduct based upon unquestioned assumptions of the 'profession'. Rather, the contributors to Part I variously challenge the very ethical base of therapy *qua* therapy itself. In the process, nothing is taken for granted, and profession-centred complacency and self-satisfaction receive very short shrift. As a result, the contributions to Part I serve to open up *a creative and innovative mental space* in which the reader, liberated from the constraining assumptions that dominate mainstream thinking in the field, can embark on the kind of 'clear-blue-sky' thinking about the fundamental nature of 'the therapeutic' which we believe to be essential for the long-term viability of counselling and psychotherapy in late-modern culture.

Part II moves on to consider ways in which the various challenges from Part I are beginning to influence thinking about and actual practices within the therapy field — influences which, we believe, are exciting, innovative, creative and, above all, enabling rather than subversive of all that is best in empowering therapy practice. Finally, two distinguished and influential radical commentators have contributed our Foreword and Afterword — namely, John Heron and Professor Ian Parker respectively.

In collecting together the following readings, we have tried to assemble the most incisive, intelligent writings available in the critical therapy tradition. Our initial searches revealed enough material to fill at least three volumes of this length, and we spent many hours of negotiation before finalising the contents of the current anthology. We would therefore like to take this opportunity to acknowledge the wealth of high-quality writings which we have — very regrettably — had to leave out due to constraints of space.

It is our hope and intention that *Ethically Challenged Professions* will make a significant contribution to the deepening and maturing of the debate about the place of therapy in modern culture; and to the extent that it does so, it will have more than served its purpose in the evolution of ideas on which the future healthy development of our field ultimately depends.

PART I:
CHALLENGING THE ETHICS OF PROFESSIONALISED THERAPY

IA: CHALLENGING ASSUMPTIONS

EDITORIAL INTRODUCTION AND COMMENTARY

Part I sets out a number of telling challenges to some of therapy's most hallowed and taken-for-granted assumptions. In Part IA there is a major recurring theme of *deconstruction*. Deconstruction as a critical practice is rooted in the insight that humanly constructed systems of all kinds are inevitably infused with unconscious influences and motivations of *power* and *fear/anxiety*. The problem is not necessarily that such fear and desire for power exist, but rather that they are systematically disowned, projected and unconsciously siphoned off into what inevitably become 'dysfunctional' human organisational-institutional and knowledge-producing practices. So one of the principal tasks of deconstruction, then, is to tease out and lay bare the hidden agendas of power, fear and anxiety that infuse human practices, such that those influences can be owned and integrated — thus enabling us individually and collectively to move towards greater *authenticity* and *honesty* in all our various human constructions and activities.

The therapy field is, of course, hardly immune from the manifold machinations of power and fear, as the following readings copiously reveal. What the readings in Part IA collectively illustrate is that *any* attempt to make therapy into a safe, linearly predictable and causally controllable 'child of modernity' is simply doomed to failure and to logical incoherence — with *the very attempt* being little more than an historically specific and transitory moment ('Late Modernity') in the evolution of human consciousness.

ARNOLD LAZARUS begins with a brilliant critique of the uncritical 'boundary-mindedness' which dominates therapy theory, and which, before Lazarus, pretty much no one had bothered ever to question — a classic example of professional therapy's constraining 'regime of truth'. The second chapter then offers an incisive client perspective on the seeking of professional help, specially written for this volume by the author of the recent book *Falling for Therapy* — 'ANNA SANDS'. Sands' transparently honest and non-mystifying description of the client position, and her own view of what makes for enabling therapy, will make engaging reading for all practitioners.

DAVID SMAIL then encourages us to question the wider place that therapy occupies in modern culture — and whether therapy, far from being a viable solution to human difficulties of living, may even render the 'origins of unhappiness' *more* rather than less opaque through a promotion of the belief that the source of distress lies within the individual, rather than within the culture which that individual inhabits. Writing from the sociological standpoint, NIKOLAS ROSE then takes us on a thought-provoking journey through some of the 'big questions' that any enlightened analysis of the psy-complex must address — not least, the kinds of power operating in psychotherapy, the influence of authority on therapy experience, and how deeper reflection on the wider ethics of the therapeutic can help us to understand the therapy phenomenon more fully.

STEPHEN PATTISON also challenges therapy's 'regime of truth' head-on, in daring to ask whether ethical professional codes *are*, in fact, ethical. Many of Pattison's examples are based on the old British Association for Counselling code. While the new British Association for Counselling and Psychotherapy (BACP) code is at least a cosmetic improvement on what it replaced, the majority of the convincing challenges Pattison launches still apply — indeed, they apply to most if not all of the codes of ethics of the major occupational bodies in the UK. COLIN FELTHAM's fearless challenge to the erstwhile sacred cow of therapy supervision deserves wide exposure and careful consideration. Feltham locates supervision as just one instance of the pervasive, 'control-freak' *surveillance culture* which has arguably saturated our public institutions in recent years, and which many believe to be doing untold damage to those institutions.

VIVIEN BURR and TREVOR BUTT then set out a detailed and explicitly *postmodern* perspective on the phenomenon of psychological distress, challenging the modernist psychopathologisation of everyday experience, offering some guidelines for a 'Postmodern Psychology', and outlining some associated implications for psychotherapy and counselling. In the penultimate chapter of Part IA, PETRUSKA CLARKSON demonstrates how the 'old paradigm' thinking of modernity has been comprehensively undermined by postmodern scientific developments — with profound implications for the very nature and assumptive base of psychotherapy and counselling as healing practices. Finally in this section, RICHARD HOUSE draws upon the important work of Ian Parker and Nikolas Rose to describe the threat to our field of a complacent professionalised therapy, whose self-justifying theoretical structures and precious clinical practices can all too easily serve the cause of professional self-interest far more than they do the clientele which professionalised therapy is claiming to assist.

In sum, if therapy is to move towards becoming a mature, client-centred healing practice at the death throes of modernity, then we maintain that the root-and-branch challenges represented in Part IA must not only be faced and engaged with, but their profound, often counterintuitive and paradoxical implications must become woven into the very foundational fabric of 'the therapeutic' — for anything less may ultimately precipitate the demise of all that is most empowering and enabling in the therapy experience.

1
How Certain Boundaries and Ethics Diminish Therapeutic Effectiveness

Arnold A. Lazarus†

In this chapter I argue that, when taken too far, certain well-intentioned ethical guidelines can become transformed into artificial boundaries that serve as destructive prohibitions and thereby undermine clinical effectiveness. Rigid roles and strict codified rules of conduct between therapist and client can obstruct a clinician's artistry. Those anxious conformists who go entirely by the book, and who live in constant fear of malpractice suits, are unlikely to prove significantly helpful to a broad array of clients. It is my contention that one of the worst professional/ethical violations is to permit current risk-management principles to take precedence over humane interventions.

Civilised interactions depend heavily on recognising and respecting boundaries. To violate a boundary, whether an entire nation or one individual, is to usurp someone's legitimate territory and invade his or her privacy by disregarding tacit or explicit limits. In quality relationships, people honour one another's rights and sensibilities, and are careful not to intrude into the other's psychological space. It is therefore not surprising that the literature on psychotherapy continues to dwell on this important issue from many different perspectives.

Ethical considerations are closely related to matters of personal and interpersonal boundaries. The revised ethical principles of psychologists (*American Psychologist*, 1992) spell out numerous specific boundaries that all professional psychologists are required to respect. Many of the ethical principles and proscriptions emphasise the avoidance of harassment, exploitation, harm and discrimination, and underscore the significance of respect, integrity, confidentiality and informed consent. Nevertheless, when taken too far, these well-intentioned guidelines can backfire. Furthermore, some psychotherapists have constructed artificial boundaries and tend to embrace prohibitions that often undermine their clinical effectiveness.

During my internship in the 1950s, I was severely reprimanded by one of my supervisors for allegedly stepping out of role (one type of boundary) and thereby potentially undermining my clinical effectiveness. (In many quarters, clearly demarcated client-therapist roles have been very strongly emphasised in recent years.) It had come to my supervisor's attention that at the end of a session, I had asked a client to do me the favour of dropping me off at a service station on

† This chapter first appeared in *Ethics and Behavior*, 4(3), 1994: 255-261 and is reprinted here with kind permission of publishers Lawrence Erlbaum Associates and the author.

his way home. My car was being repaired, and I had ascertained that the client would be heading home after the session and that I would not be taking him out of his way. My supervisor contended that therapy had to be a one-way street, and a client should not be called upon to provide anything other than the agreed-upon fees for service. Given my transgression, my supervisor claimed that I had jeopardised the client-therapist relationship. Interestingly, I recall that my rapport with the client in question was enhanced rather than damaged by our informal chat on the way to the service station.

The extent to which some clinicians espouse what I regard as *dehumanising* boundaries is exemplified by the following incident. During a couples-therapy session the husband mentioned that he had undergone a biopsy for a suspected malignancy and would have the result later that week. Our next appointment was two weeks away, so I called their home after a few days to ask about the laboratory findings. The husband answered the telephone, reported that all was well, and expressed gratitude at my interest and concern. The wife, a licensed clinical psychologist, had a different reaction. She told a mutual colleague (the person who had referred the couple to me) that she was rather dismayed and put out at what I had done, referring to it as the violation of a professional boundary. A simple act of human decency and concern had been transformed into a clinical assault.

A different boundary issue was raised in the columns of a state journal. A therapist was treating an adolescent and wanted to arrange a meeting with the boy's mother. A busy professional, the mother's schedule was such that the most convenient time was during a lunch break, and she suggested they meet to discuss the matter at a local restaurant. The position taken by various correspondents was that this would not only transgress various boundaries but constitute a dual relationship. I wondered whether meeting in the park, or at the mother's place of work, in a hotel lobby, or in a car would be similarly discounted. Or could the venue indeed be a restaurant if no food but only coffee were ordered?[1]

During more than four decades of clinical practice, I have emphasised the need for flexibility and have stressed the clinical significance of individual differences. Dryden (1991), in an interview with me that he aptly subtitled 'It Depends', clearly accentuated my contention that blanket rules for one and all often bypass important individual nuances that have to be addressed. With some clients, anything other than a formal and clearly delimited doctor-patient relationship is inadvisable and is likely to prove counterproductive. With others, an open give-and-take, a sense of camaraderie, and a willingness to step outside the bounds of a sanctioned healer will enhance treatment outcomes. Thus I have partied and socialised with some clients, played tennis with others, taken long walks with some, graciously accepted small gifts, and given presents (usually books) to a fair number. At times, I have learned more at different sides of a tennis net or across the dining-room table than might ever have come to light in my consulting room. (Regrettably, from the viewpoint of present-day risk management, in the face of allegations of sexual impropriety, it has been pointed out that such boundary crossings, no matter how innocent, will *ipso facto* be

---

1. It has been argued that meetings outside the office, followed by sessions during lunch, often lead to dinner dates, movies, and other social events, finally culminating in sexual intercourse (see Gabbard, 1989; Simon, 1989).

construed as evidence of sexual misconduct by judges, juries, ethics committees and state licensing boards.)

Out of the many clients I have treated, the number with whom I have stepped outside the formal confines of the consulting room is not in the hundreds, but give or take a few dozen. And when I have done so, my motives were not based on capriciousness but arose from reasoned judgements that the treatment objectives would be enhanced. Nevertheless, it is usually inadvisable to disregard strict boundary limits in the presence of severe pathology; involving passive-aggressive, histrionic or manipulative behaviours; borderline personality features; or manifestations of suspiciousness and undue hostility.

Some years back, I was treating a 'difficult' patient who was combative and contentious. He arrived early for his appointment one morning while I was still having breakfast. An intuitive whim led me to invite him to pull up a chair and have some toast and tea.[2] This was a turning point. The act of 'breaking bread' resulted in a co-operative liaison in place of his former hostility. Let me not be misunderstood. I am *not* advocating or arguing for a transparent, pliant, casual or informal therapeutic relationship with everyone. Rather, I am asserting that those therapists who always go by the book and apply predetermined and fixed rules of conduct (specific *do*'s and *don'ts*) across the board will offend or at the very least fail to help people who might otherwise have benefited from their ministrations.

For example, a psychiatric resident was treating a young woman who often asked him personal questions. 'How old are you?'; 'Where did you go to school?'; 'Do you enjoy the ballet?'; 'Are you married?'. In keeping with his supervisor's counsel, he studiously side-stepped all of these questions and asked about their intent. But the therapy was going nowhere, and he joined one of my supervision groups. 'I think the patient is about to drop out of therapy', he said. This matter was discussed at length, whereupon I advised him to apologise to his patient, to explain that he meant no disrespect but was merely following his previous supervisor's advice. I recommended that he answer each of her questions, even showing her the photo of his young son that he carried in his wallet. At the next supervisory meeting, he reported having carried out his assignment, and stated that their therapeutic alliance seemed to have been greatly enhanced; for the first time ever, real gains had accrued. The patient continued making progress.

There is something demeaning and hostile about having one's questions dismissed and answered by another question.

> *Client*: 'Have you seen the latest Tom Cruise movie?'
> *Therapist*: 'Why is this important?'
> *Client*: 'Is your car the blue Chevy with the white interior?'
> *Therapist*: 'Why do you want to know?'

It is even more demeaning when therapists simply dismiss straightforward queries:

> *Client*: 'Did you play hockey in high school?'
> *Therapist*: 'We are here to discuss you, not me.'

---

2. Except for a period of 5 years when I worked out of a professional office, my private practice has been conducted out of my home. This, for many, is in and of itself a transgression of a significant boundary.

Unless there are valid reasons for not being forthright, or unless the question goes beyond the bounds of propriety, why not answer it candidly and then inquire as to its significance? 'Yes, I was quite an avid hockey player in high school. Why do you ask?'

An example of what strikes me as an excessive boundary issue was related by one of my students. He was seeing a client who had written a short poem that she wished to share with him. According to my student, his supervisor was concerned that he may have taken the poem and read it, rather than having asked the client to read it to him. The supervisor had allegedly stated, 'It's best not to touch or handle clients' personal possessions'. This type of rigid professionalism is most unfortunate and seems likely to breed alienation and distance, and is apt to rupture the therapeutic relationship rather than foster it.

My thesis is that it doesn't hurt to temper rules and regulations with a touch of common sense. Thus, a colleague referred a couple to me. After two sessions, it seemed that their individual agendas took priority over their dyadic transactions, and I suggested to my colleague that she might want to work with the wife while I treated the husband. A few weeks later, I asked my colleague if she felt, as I did, that the marriage was probably bankrupt. 'I can't discuss this with you because I have not obtained [the wife's] permission to do so', she replied. Ethically, my colleague was certainly toeing the line, but to my way of thinking she exercised poor clinical judgement. My question was not an idle, voyeuristic attempt to pry into her client's privacy. It was geared towards a potentially helpful collegial exchange of information. Besides, having seen the wife myself, I was not a casual outsider, but someone who was concerned about and involved with the dyadic system.

By contrast, I was approached by a colleague who was treating one of my former clients and wanted specific information about him. Strictly speaking, I should first have obtained a written release from the client. Instead of wasting time, I simply told my colleague about traps and barriers that the client had erected that had undermined the therapy. I was able to alert her to various pitfalls that the client was likely to dig and into which she (like I) would probably fall unless she exercised due caution. She subsequently informed me that my caveats were of enormous clinical value in forestalling a self-sabotaging client from destroying his life. My motives behind this collegial interchange were obviously entirely in the client's best interests.

I have crossed many boundaries to good effect. I have even treated relatives and friends in addition to colleagues and acquaintances, and some of my closest friends are former clients. Nevertheless, my plea for flexibility and my defence of unorthodoxy are not completely heretical. I remain totally opposed to any form of disparagement, exploitation, abuse or harassment, and I am against any form of sexual contact with clients. But outside of these confines, I feel that most other limits and proscriptions are negotiable.

However, the litigious climate in which we now live has made me more cautious in recent years. I would not take certain risks that I gave no thought to in the 1960s. For example, I accepted two clients into my home (at different times). One lived with my family for several weeks, the other for several days. Both were men from out of state who had relocated and were looking for a place to live. Similarly, I would have thought nothing of offering a client our spare bedroom on a snowy night or furnishing a couple of aspirins if someone had asked for them. But like most of my colleagues, I have attended seminars on how to avoid malpractice suits that have made my blood run cold. It is difficult to come away from those lectures without viewing every client as a potential adversary or litigant. Fortunately, the effects tended to wear off after a few days, and I regained my spontaneity. But the ominous undertones remain firmly implanted and are reinforced by passages in books that explain how innocent psychologists can protect themselves against unwarranted lawsuits (Keith-Spiegel and Koocher, 1985). Consequently, being more guarded has rendered me a less humane practitioner today than I used to be in the 1960s and 1970s.

It is interesting that Freud gave some patients gifts, loaned them books, sent them postcards, offered a meal to the Rat Man, and even provided financial support in a few cases. Perhaps Freud's most striking boundary violation was the analysis of his own daughter, Anna. According to Gutheil and Gabbard (1993: 189), 'these behaviors are no longer acceptable practise regardless of their place in the history of our field'.

While reading a book on psychodrama by Kellermann (1992), I was particularly impressed with his account of a client who had participated in psychodrama groups for many years. When asked what she had found most helpful, the client stated,

> 'The most important thing for me was that I established a close relationship with Zerka,[3] a kind of friendship which extended beyond the ordinary patient-therapist relation. She took me to restaurants and on trips and treated me like my own mother had never done. That friendship had such a great impact on me that I can feel its effects to this very day!' (p. 133)

It is, of course, safer and easier to go by the book, to adhere to an inflexible set of rules, than to think for oneself. But practitioners who hide behind rigid boundaries, whose sense of ethics is uncompromising, will, in my opinion, fail to really help many of the clients who are unfortunate enough to consult them. The truly great therapists I have met were not frightened conformists but courageous and enterprising helpers, willing to take calculated risks. If I am to summarise my position in one sentence, I would say that one of the worst professional or ethical violations is that of permitting current risk-management principles to take precedence over humane interventions. By all means drive defensively, but try to practise psychotherapy responsibly — with compassion, benevolence, sensitivity and caring.

REFERENCES

American Psychologist (1992) Volume 47, no. 12

Dryden, W. (1991) *A Dialogue with Arnold Lazarus: 'It depends'*. Philadelphia: Open University Press

Gabbard, G. O. (ed.) (1989) *Sexual Exploitation in Professional Relationships.* Washington, D.C.: American Psychiatric Press

Gutheil, T. G. and Gabbard, G. O. (1993) The concept of boundaries in clinical practice: theoretical and risk-management dimensions. *American Journal of Psychiatry* 150: 188-96

---

3. Psychodrama was founded by J.L. Moreno (1889-1974). His wife Zerka, son Jonathan, and many enthusiasts have carried on and extended the overall tradition.

Keith-Spiegel, P. and Koocher, G. P. (1985) *Ethics in Psychology: Professional Standards and Cases*. New York: Random House

Kellermann, P. F. (1992) *Focus on Psychodrama*. Philadelphia: Jessica Kingsley

Simon, R. I. (1989) Sexual exploitation of patients: how it begins before it happens. *Psychiatric Annals* 19: 104-22

Acknowledgement
I am most grateful to Allen Fay, MD and Clifford N. Lazarus, Ph.D. for their criticisms of the initial draft.

2
SEEKING PROFESSIONAL HELP

'ANNA SANDS'

When we seek the help of a paid professional, we often lack a clear idea of what to expect, what our rights and responsibilities might be, and how best to achieve our desired outcome. In therapy, the diversity of approaches on offer, and the wide spectrum of clients or patients — from the 'worried well' to the psychopathic — add to the complexity of any proper discussion of its virtues and ills, and to the difficulty of saying much about it at all without the preface 'It depends...'. All we can say with any certainty is that therapy will have very different outcomes, and that the outcome will depend — far more, perhaps, than in other professions — on the behaviour and personality of the individuals concerned, and the chemistry kindled by their particular relationship. For me, the most pressing issue in any debate about therapy is how to avoid its causing us harm.

It has been suggested that '... formal training ... teaches us [therapists] how to use sophisticated techniques but gives us little or no guidance about how to appreciate and deal with the professional-client relationship' (Peterson 1992: 5). Yet in therapy, this relationship is a core ingredient. So what are the hallmarks of any 'professional' encounter, and how does this compare to what is offered in therapy? How professional are therapists and counsellors?

For Totton (2001: 21), 'It is ethically crucial for therapists to be clear about what they are offering'. Clarity is fundamental, but frequently lacking. Labels — psychoanalysis, psychotherapy, counselling and their myriad subheadings — do not always help prospective clients. Some — for example, 'practitioner in the field of the social unconscious' — seem designed to impress rather than inform. Semantic allusiveness and a misleading optimism too often characterise the way in which therapy is sold to the public. A poster for a psychodrama workshop, for instance, claims that 'healing can take place in impossible situations'.

A sense of clarity must also include a reasonable element of common ground between therapist and client regarding what is felt to be helpful. But research has found that the 'active ingredients' in the therapy process are often 'quite different from what any of the individual schools of thought had postulated' (Russell 1992). If it is, indeed, the case that 'consumers may often have quite a different take on therapy from that of their therapist' (Feltham 2002: 115), then this is not the most promising starting-point.

My first experience of therapy ended in a traumatic breakdown, though there followed later a positive experience with a different style of practitioner (Sands 2002). The literature I read, in my efforts to come to terms with what happened to me, often failed to appreciate or simply ignored the client's perspective. As Howe 1993: 1) has written,

> Though there has been a steady interest in the client's point of view, it is still unusual to begin … by looking at the world from the perspective of the client. Traditionally, one starts by describing the theoretical position of the therapist …'.

Do practitioners sometimes pay too much attention to the theory of therapy, thereby sublimating the experience of the clients who live it? If so, they may fail to realise that 'only by saying how the application of theory works in practice can questions about its justification have any relevance' (France 1988: 7).

Our behaviour in therapy is, in part, a reaction to the behaviour of the therapist — but that may not necessarily be a good measure of our responses in other, everyday situations. The orthodox, analytic 'blank screen' approach is certainly very different from the more spontaneous encounters of our daily life. The anonymous, aloof position which some practitioners adopt can confound our usual understanding of signals denoting friendliness and hostility, support and distance, courtesy and boorishness.

We expect a professional practitioner to treat us with courtesy and respect. Yet the literature at times suggests that the client in therapy be treated with what seems to me to be a lack of grace and tact. For example, a psychodynamic counsellor describes his response when his client brought him a book, as a gift (Jacobs 1998: 75). The counsellor puts the book on the table and asks the client what it is that the book says about him which he is unable to say himself — thus ignoring what the client has just done. In any other context, such behaviour would not only seem rude and insensitive, it would be extremely weird.

If it is to be beneficial, the therapy relationship has to make sense. If a therapist does not respond to us in ways which — within the norms of our particular culture — one might usually expect from a professional helper, it can feel very odd indeed. We endeavour to squeeze ourselves into a pattern of interaction which feels incongruous and artificial. The 'therapy' itself may then become a source of lasting disturbance.

Something which I found difficult was my analyst's silence, because I did not know what it signified. In theory, the practitioner's silence facilitates the client's free association and allows clients to 'be themselves' (Smith 1996). But the so-called 'blank screen' represents a concrete piece of behaviour which has social significance and associations. The 'empty space' is not 'empty' because there is another person in the room. If one has a naturally outgoing and friendly disposition, it can be particularly hard to feel at ease in such circumstances.

A counselling trainer describes how he made a point of remaining silent when his client arrived: 'I said nothing when they first came in, not even to introduce myself. I waited for them to start' (Jacobs 1998: 30). Yet many of us would find being greeted by silence when we walk into a room, particularly with someone we don't know, strange and unnerving. A friend described how her psychoanalyst routinely greeted her arrival with a stony silence, her eyes to the floor. She (the practitioner) was then curious to know why her client found this discomforting, and why the client 'needed' to end the session pleasantly and say thank you. There may be times when such behaviour is, indeed, indicative of other, relevant issues. But if the practitioner's behaviour causes the client to leave the therapy (as it did in this case), then an opportunity to explore, for example, a possible need for reassurance is lost in any case.

It has been suggested that clients, who are not 'insiders' (Spinelli 2001: 160), fail to appreciate the thinking behind such an approach. This is not always so and, in any case, I would argue that it is largely irrelevant. What matters is whether its effect is beneficial or damaging. Clients may feel disturbed not necessarily because they are recalling past traumas but by, for example, a succession of inappropriate — sometimes absurd — interpretations, a pathologisation of what the client says, a denial of one's own truth, an absence of response. Abrupt endings, too, can be upsetting and destabilising.

It is interesting that clients who wish to behave in a civil and friendly manner are seen by some therapists as 'needing' to be so, as if their behaviour is in some way inauthentic, a defence triggered by an underlying insecurity. Equally, the client may be seen as 'needing' to be in control when, in reality, s/he genuinely does have an assured and easy nature. A client's positive qualities can be undermined and distorted by this use of the concept of 'need'. When I tried to discuss with my analyst what I found difficult in our relationship, he suggested that I 'needed to hate him and say negative things about him', thus sidelining the more immediate problems which we really did need to discuss — but which he, perhaps, did not want to address or could not understand. This 'game playing' prevents the client from having a sense of ownership of or control over what is taking place, and is likely to be counter-productive.

The philosopher Simon Blackburn (1999: 274) points out that

> ...communication is often a matter of addressing one another's concerns. That is not done if one side has a concern, and the other regards that concern just as a kind of problem or obstacle in itself — something to be managed or cured.

Our concern is 'objectified', its acceptability is not acknowledged, and the reason for it is not considered. 'This point', Blackburn says, 'has vast repercussions in connection with the whole culture and industry of therapy' (ibid.).

Attempts to 'analyse' and 'treat' the client's reality may result in a failure to pay full attention to what is actually being said. In any professional relationship, we expect to be taken seriously, to be believed. If what we say is often refuted, or immediately 'interpreted', it is hard to feel that the therapist has any trust in us, and the trust that is so often cited as being the bedrock of good therapy must surely be mutual.

Richard House contends that there is a 'regime of truth' which therapy constructs, and which 'self-fulfillingly creates a framework which serves to guarantee its own legitimacy, and outside the confines of which it is often exceedingly difficult for clients or therapists to think ... therapy can, in and of itself, create difficulties which then provide material which gives therapy much of its *raison d'être*' (House 2001: 127). What is paramount is the attitude of the practitioner — whether there is genuine respect and integrity, an essential humility, and a willingness to point out that s/he may be wrong. 'The highest value should be placed on the ethic of care', writes Peterson (1992: 9) I wonder if all therapists truly care for and about their clients, or if some have chosen their profession for other, more questionable, reasons.

The tone of some case histories does not evoke the caring and compassionate attitude which we are led to believe underlies the practice of psychotherapy. 'When I make an interpretation he [the client] does not like, he immediately becomes defensive and mulish', explains one practitioner (Casement 1996: 99). A more open approach would be indicated, perhaps, by 'When I get things wrong

...' or 'When we disagree...'. Scott Peck decides for himself that a client is 'indulging in a subtle form of lying' and makes unilateral decisions about whether or not his clients were loved by their parents (Peck 1978: 61, 60). In a television programme showing extracts from therapy sessions, a therapist dismissively declares, 'I thought "rats"!' when discussing with colleagues something her client has said. Her attitude as she picked over her client's supposed delusions I, personally, found distasteful. Freud himself, it seems, frequently imposed his highly questionable theories on his patients, showing little respect for their point of view.

Misguided, and potentially destructive, suggestions can be made in any type of therapy. But many clients, I suspect, 'want it both ways' in some respects. We want our own truth to be recognised, but we expect our professional helper to provide us with a better way of seeing things:

> Most of us do not want to grow up and think for ourselves. Instead, we want to be released from doubt, ignorance and uncertainty, and we want someone else to do the job for us ... It is generally much easier to seek out someone else who may be only too willing to tell us who we are.
>
> (Howard 1996: 132)

The client who takes a responsible role is a 'co-analyst' rather than a 'patient', but this can only happen if the practitioner allows it to.

The pattern of a psychoanalyst's interventions may be very different from what the lay-person is used to; for example, they do not follow the conventions of 'turn taking' in normal speech. An analytic researcher who studied the transcripts of a series of therapy sessions suggests that impersonal, detached statements 'effectively eliminated the patient in a manner which seems quite inappropriate to a dyadic situation' (Dahl, cited in Malcolm 1980: 97). Dahl refers to the possibility of therapy then becoming 'psychological murder by syntax'. It is not hard to find examples of interchanges which border on the insane (see, for example, Sands 2000a: 203). So, if practitioners and their clients engage in these kinds of exchanges on a regular basis, how does it affect their perception of reality?

One of the most common criticisms I have heard from clients regarding 'bad' therapy is the absence of what Webster calls 'ordinary psychological insight' (Webster 1996). It seems that, at times, the practitioner lives in a world divorced from the reality of day-to-day living. France uses the term 'force feeding' when describing the many examples of interpretative clichés and unfitting stereotypes which she found in therapy texts and in her dialogue with other analysands (France 1988: 162). At times one senses in the literature an almost excessive zeal to interpret, dissect, connect and reconstrue — at the expense of acceptance, acknowledgement and empathetic understanding. This may be accompanied by a tendency to see all the client's behaviour in terms of the relationship with the therapist, suggesting a narcissism and grandiosity on the part of the practitioner which can then obscure the client's true perspective. In reality, it is often the more pressing concerns of our everyday lives which are at the forefront of our minds.

It is sometimes claimed that a strong emotional involvement is an essential part of any 'cure'. Becoming unduly dependent on, or attached to, the practitioner is something which, in my view, should be avoided rather than encouraged. A professional relationship is not usually intense or highly emotional and it can feel uncomfortable and inappropriate if it becomes so. But if the client chooses to finish therapy for this reason, s/he might be seen as 'fleeing' the therapy room because of a lack of courage or commitment.

A therapeutic approach which makes the concept of 'transference' its core is one that I would now be wary of — though at the outset of my therapy I was ignorant of its effect and its power. Regression, as I learnt to my cost, can be highly dangerous. If the relationship between the therapist and client is not sufficiently strong or enduring to sort out transference issues (and this is more than a remote possibility), they can rebound nastily, causing confusion, pain and even an eventual disintegration. The concept of transference can prevent proper discussion of the adult client-practitioner relationship, serving instead 'to protect [the therapist] from the consequences of his own behaviour' (Shlien 1984: 153). My first experience of therapy accentuated my accumulated insecurities and rubbed salt into old wounds, as well as adding some new ones. I had not bargained for the harrowing emotional baggage one carries in the aftermath of a failed therapy.

The effect of 'counter-transference' can be hurtful and harmful, and the client may become a 'blank screen' for *the practitioner's* negative projections. If this happens, it is the responsibility of the therapist to bring these issues to light, rather than hoping that the person on the receiving end has not noticed or will not be affected. Confusion and misunderstandings can only be sorted out if the practitioner is willing to be open and honest, and to deal with his client's questions in a clear and non-evasive way.

According to the United Kingdom Council for Psychotherapy (UKCP) Code of Ethics, the purpose of therapy is to alleviate suffering, and this probably accords with what most clients hope for from their professional helper. But bad therapy can be far worse than no therapy at all, and this is something which I — like many others, I suspect — failed to understand. The harm caused by therapy can be particularly difficult to recover from, because it is outside the realm of our day-to-day experience and understanding, and because its effects are so pervasive. Therapy provides 'a rich soil for creating deep and lasting misunderstandings, and even greater misery' (Masson 1992: 44).

A therapist commented to me that it is up to the client to get out of a therapy which isn't working. If the client cannot do that, he argued, then s/he should take responsibility for that fact, unless there was a clear offence. Yet the reality is more complex than that. For the client, it will not be easy to assess the competence of the practitioner. Therapists rightly emphasise the client's personal responsibility, but it must not be forgotten that s/he is paying (either directly or indirectly) in return for a service. If they wish to be seen as professionals, therapists cannot conveniently put aside the issue of their influence if the outcome of what they offer is negative. Some suffering is inevitable in therapy, but when the resulting anguish outweighs any gains, practitioners should be willing to be properly accountable.

A vital part of trying to heal some of the damage is for both parties to acknowledge what actually happened. But the practitioner may approach such a situation primarily from a fixed theoretical stance, rather than considering what constitutes intelligent and judicious behaviour. This is perhaps more likely if grievances are dealt with by a therapist's colleagues, and in my view complaints should be handled by a body which includes non-therapists. In a recent book on complaints and grievances, suggested model letters to complainants make no reference to the client's distress, showing little appreciation of how important such an acknowledgement is; and the views of 'service users' have not been sought (Palmer-Barnes 1998).

If a practitioner is trained to think that the feedback s/he receives from a client is what the client needs to work on, this can provide a convenient loophole when things go wrong: 'We have become victims of therapy and its good intentions - and the analyst can get off scot-free by ... ascribing the destruction of the involvement to the magic word "transference"' (Hillman 1992: 37). Psychotherapy is the only profession where the practitioner can be insensitive, evasive, patronising, arrogant, discourteous, self-righteous or just plain wrong, and where clients' observation of this can be taken to be an expression of *their* problems, evidence that what they really need is more of the same therapy.

My own experience of trying, and failing, to explore the impasse in which my first therapy ended, and to secure an acknowledgement that it had been damaging, is described elsewhere (Sands 2000b). My analyst's fellow practitioners could not 'comment on the work of a colleague', and my analyst was not prepared to attend a meeting with a mediator. But 'without the involved professional's help to sort out what happened between them, the client is left to struggle with the injury alone. His or her solo attempts to master the pain are ... undertaken at great personal cost' (Peterson 1992: 4).

The client is encouraged to believe that when we open the door to therapy, we step into a world of understanding and acceptance. Yet it is a world in which one practitioner refers to another as 'a helpless and traumatised child ... living in a perverse and faecal world' (Holmes, cited by Johnstone 1998: 211). Freud describes a critic as ' ... a demon, a brute, a retarded guttersnipe' and ' ... for daring to question Freud's authority Jung was, in effect, dismissed as being mentally ill' (Webster 1996: 381). John Sivyer suggests that therapy is often 'a profession of mistrustful people'. Complaints have a tendency to bring out the shadow side of many therapists '... rather like the manic-depressive or borderline personality who flips from one way of being to another' (Sivyer 2000: 15).

It is often emphasised that counsellors and therapists are human like the rest of us, and that clients need to realise they are fallible and make mistakes. I think it is important to remind clients of this, but it is not unreasonable to expect practitioners to have particular qualities and skills, just as we expect professional teachers, airline pilots and heart surgeons to have particular qualities and skills in order to perform their work competently. When we open up to someone and put our trust in them, we give them the power to hurt us deeply. Such power should not be given to those who cannot use it wisely.]

The question of accountability is at the core of any occupation that wishes to be seen as a profession. Yet how can therapists be held to account unless there is some agreement over what constitutes unethical or incompetent behaviour? Responses to those who challenge therapy vary so dramatically that it is difficult for a client to sense any consistency on the part of the profession as a whole. For example, my book has, generally speaking, been well received by therapists. But, whilst many reviewers suggest it 'should be core reading for all counselling and psychotherapy training courses' (Fitzgerald-Pool 2001: website review), another describes me as having 'no humour, insight or self-reflection', and claims that I 'blamed my analyst relentlessly', accepting no responsibility for what happened (Martin 2001: 16). A third therapist felt Martin's assessment was 'appalling, vitriolic and totally misplaced' (personal communication). So if the response of the professional to the client's expressed experience depends primarily on his or her personal reactions, where does that leave us?

What concerns me about Ms Martin's article is not so much that I have been criticised but, rather, that someone who works as a counsellor (and in this case also trains counsellors) misreads — or has not read thoroughly — what has been said, and then jumps to erroneous conclusions over a situation which she actually knows very little about. If I am as she describes, why did therapy fail to have any impact on me? And how helpful is it to repeat the familiar (but, in my view, erroneous) contention that, if one is angry, this invalidates the arguments one is putting forward?

The therapist Lena Davis wrote a facile and sneering review of another client account of therapy, *Folie à Deux* by Rosie Alexander (who contributes the final chapter to this anthology). When challenged, she claimed her review was 'informative and entertaining' (Davis 1996: 30) — as if the author of the book (who had suffered greatly) were some kind of dancing bear. It could be argued that this is simply the view of one therapist, but the editor of the journal in which it was published claimed: 'We stand by the review ... counselling is a broad church' (*Counselling News*, 1996: 17) So is the profession in which I work, English as a foreign language; but if I were to write a book review in a similar tone for a professional journal, I suspect it would never see the light of day.

The nastiness of Davis's review illustrates an absence not only of professionalism, of respect and compassion, but also of understanding. She and her colleagues show a worrying lack of intelligence and seem to have completely missed the point. Alexander would not have written her book if her behaviour during psychoanalysis had been similar to the way she behaved in her day-to-day life. No one was more shocked by the strength of feeling, and the effect of therapy on her, than Alexander herself.

That effect, though more extreme, was not dissimilar to the way I felt as a result of my first therapy. It was only when I read Alexander's and Ann France's books that I realised that others had suffered from 'therapy-induced lunacy', and these accounts, paradoxically perhaps, helped me to regain a sense of my own sanity. Letters from clients who have read my own book convey a similar message: 'At last I have found someone who understands how I feel.' The therapist Ernesto Spinelli refers somewhat scathingly to 'a developing category of psychotherapeutically focused texts written by ex-clients: the 'read how psychotherapy messed me up and how awful (or evil) it is' genre' (Spinelli 2001: 161). But to those for whom therapy has been iatrogenic, the insights that are offered in such texts can be a life-line in a sea of professional ineptitude. Clients continue to be damaged by therapy, and find it hard to get effective help to understand and recover from such experiences.

Nathan Field takes an informative look at the 'weirder' dimensions of therapy, concluding that 'the breakdown of the ego is obviously a dangerous business ... and can result in permanent damage to the personality' (Field 1996: 20). Field describes, for example, the trance-like state that he and his patients sometimes go into, where it is 'impossible to determine where one ended and the other began'. This is what I experienced, and I felt profoundly disturbed by it because I could not understand what was happening. My analyst suggested I 'needed to relive my negative experiences', but the hallucinogenic state I was in had no recognisable connection to the past. Field 'never had the courage' to discuss with his supervisor the more bizarre occurrences in his therapy room, in case she thought he was 'psychologically abnormal'. That is how I felt with my analyst. I thought I had gone permanently mad, and it terrified me. If practitioners are ill-equipped to handle such phenomena, then this serious gap in their expertise should be attended to.

Despite what many see as a changing climate, client feedback still seems to be viewed as something of a novelty. For example, a journal article bears the title 'The importance of considering client's perspectives in psychotherapy research' (Lacran et al. 1999), as if the point is debatable. A published letter supportive of my book states, 'I greatly admire your decision to publish the article about Anna Sands' experience' (Palmer 2001: 21). Is it, then, an uncharacteristic and courageous act to talk openly about therapy's flaws and failures? A friend recently commented that 'a lot of ground has been gained recently in getting dialogue between therapists and clients'. Maybe so, but it is nevertheless an extraordinary statement, considering that dialogue between therapist and client is supposed to be the essence of therapy.

In my experience, there is considerable scepticism amongst the general public about the sanity of much 'therapeutic' practice. And when arrogance and insensitivity are apparent in the work of therapists, it is, because of the nature of that work, particularly chilling. So perhaps therapy needs to grow up, become more intelligent and more truly professional. Peterson points out that 'professionals tend to identify and describe boundary violations in terms of content … [This] eclipses the more fundamental injury, the injury to the core of the professional-client relationship itself' (1992: 3). I would argue that this relationship has to be based on sound ethical principles rather than on tenets of psychological theory.

We will not be best helped while the attitude of the practitioner is that s/he has the ability to 'explain to patients what is wrong with them' (Jacobs 1998: 28). In my view, only when the emphasis shifts towards the view of therapy expressed, for example, by Thomas Moore will progress be made: 'Be present … Each person is a mystery. The response to a mystery should be entirely different from that to a problem' (Moore 1997: 182). And if we use our collective ignorance and confusion to move forward collectively, then let us hope that, ultimately, everyone will gain.

REFERENCES

Alexander, R. (1995) *Folie à Deux*. London: Free Association Press

Blackburn, S. (1999) *Think*. Oxford: Oxford University Press

Casement, A. (1996) Psychodynamic therapy: the Jungian approach. In W. Dryden (ed.), *Handbook of Individual Therapy*. London: Sage

Davis, L. (1996) Review of Alexander's *Folie à Deux*. *Counselling News* March: 30

Feltham, C. (ed.) (2002) *What's the Good of Counselling and Psychotherapy?* London: Sage

Field, N. (1996) *Breakdown and Breakthrough: Psychotherapy in a New Dimension*. London: Routledge

Fitzgerald-Pool, Z. (2001) Review of Sands' *Falling for Therapy*. Counsellingbooks.com

France, A. (1988) *Consuming Psychotherapy*. London: Free Association Books

Howard, A. (1996) *Challenges to Counselling and Psychotherapy*. Basingstoke: Macmillan/Palgrave

Hillman, J. (1992) *The Myth of Psychoanalysis*. San Francisco: Harper Perrenial

House, R. (2001) Therapy on the couch? — a client scrutinizes the therapy phenomenon. *European Journal of Psychotherapy, Counselling and Health* 4(1): 123-36

Howe, D. (1993) *On Being a Client*. London: Sage

Jacobs, M. (1998) *Psychodynamic Counselling in Action*. London: Sage (orig. 1988)

Johnstone, L. (1998) 'I hear what you're saying': how to avoid jargon in therapy. *Changes* 16 (3): 209

Lacran, S. and others (1999) 'The importance of considering clients' perspectives in psychotherapy research'. *Journal of Mental Health* 8 (4)

Malcolm, J. (1980) *Psychoanalysis: The Impossible Profession*. New York: Viking

Martin, L. (2001) Opinion. *Counselling* 12 (1): 16

Masson, J. (1992) *Against Therapy*. London: Fontana

Moore, T. (1997) *The Re-Enchantment of Everyday Life*. London: Hodder & Stoughton

Palmer, E. (2001) Letters. *Counselling* 12 (1): 21

Palmer-Barnes, F. (1998) *Complaints and Grievances in Psychotherapy: A Handbook of Ethical Practice*. London: Routledge

Peck, S. (1978) *The Road Less Travelled*. London: Arrow Books

Peterson, M. R. (1992) *At Personal Risk*. New York: W. W. Norton

Russell, R. (1992) *Report on Effective Psychotherapy*. New York: Hilgarth Press

Sands, A. (2000a) *Falling for Therapy: Psychotherapy from a Client's Point of View*. London: Macmillan/Palgrave

Sands, A. (2000b) Locking the stable door... *Self and Society* 28 (3): pp. 22-6

Sands, A. (2002) Consumers' views of the benefits of counselling and psychotherapy. In Feltham, C. (ed.), *What's the Good of Counselling and Psychotherapy?* (pp. 120-7). London: Sage

Shlien, J. M. (1984) A countertheory of transference. In R. Levant & J. Shlien (eds), *Client Centred Therapy and the Person Centred Approach* (pp. 153-81). Westport, CT: Praeger. Reprinted in J.M. Shlien, *To Lead an Honorable Life: Invitations to think about Client-Centered Therapy and the Person-Centered Approach* (pp. 93-119). Ross-on-Wye: PCCS Books, 2003

Sivyer, J. (2000) Complaints: the search for restorative justice. *Self and Society* 28 (1): 15

Smith, D. (1996) Psychodynamic therapy: the Freudian Approach. In W. Dryden (ed.), *Handbook of Individual Therapy* (pp. 19 -39). London: Sage

Spinelli, E. (2001) *The Mirror and the Hammer*. London: Continuum

Totton, N. (2001) Book review: *Falling for Therapy* by Anna Sands. *Ipnosis* 2: 21

Webster, R. (1996) *Why Freud was Wrong*. London: Fontana Press

3
PSYCHOTHERAPY, SOCIETY AND THE INDIVIDUAL

DAVID SMAIL[†]

There is no doubt that psychotherapy can be — perhaps usually is — a very powerful experience. Like many other kinds of experience, however, its power — the weight of conviction it imposes — is no guarantee of its validity.

There are, of course, many kinds of psychotherapy, frequently radically incompatible with each other, theoretically irreconcilable and technically mutually inconsistent. And yet nearly all share one crucial characteristic: they involve an on going — often indeed protracted — closely intimate relationship between two people. (Group therapy is quite a different kettle of fish, and I'll not be talking about it for present purposes.) It is this relationship, technicised by the psychoanalysts as 'transference' and 'counter-transference', which gives psychotherapy its experiential power. It's really quite difficult to spend many hours of your life cooped up in the consulting room of someone who is intently trying to understand you without emerging with the feeling that something momentous has happened.

It's very nearly impossible to discount the conviction of significance which our personal feelings so often carry with them. An example which may be familiar to people here who haven't experienced psychotherapy may be that of writing. Many professional writers speak with awe of the magical experience of writing, of the way it seems to take place *through* them, almost as if their words were being written by the hand of God. Portentous accounts of creativity have been grounded on this experience. Indeed, I have experienced it often myself, and can vouch for its capacity to leave one feeling deeply moved.

It wasn't until a man I knew told me how his short stories came to him that I began to get an idea of what this experience is about. His eyes misting with emotion, he told me how his stories seemed eerily to write themselves, how they poured themselves from the end of his pen faster than he could control the muscles of his hand. He positively glowed — humility and pride in equal proportions — that the mystery of the creative act should have been vouchsafed to him. The trouble was, his were without question the worst short stories I have ever seen committed to paper. Chaotically constructed, banal, misspelt and ungrammatical, they were in fact barely literate.

What this reveals, I suspect, is merely that for anyone, creatively gifted or not, writing tends often to carry with it a different kind of experience from talking,

† This chapter was originally delivered as a talk to the 'Ways with Words' festival of literature, Dartington, Devon, UK, 12th July 1999, and is reproduced here with the kind permission of the author.

without the same kind of illusion of control: one is more aware, with writing (rather perhaps as with dreams), that the ego is not as central as we often take it to be. That's all.

The experience of psychotherapy is rather like this. No matter what the content of what passes between client and therapist, the relationship generates in both a conviction of profundity and significance which leads not only to a (most often) erroneous belief that fundamental changes have taken place in the client, but also a widespread certainty in the truth of the theory employed and the efficacy of whatever technique the therapist claims to have used. Once you've experienced this, you are more than likely to be hooked. Perhaps this is why (though probably not consciously) so many schools of psychotherapy insist on their acolytes going through the therapeutic experience themselves. Most religions and cults make the same kind of requirement. The power of personal experience is not to be underestimated, and (as well, of course, as more noble human sentiments and achievements) prejudice and bigotry depend upon it.

If we take a step back from personal feelings, difficult though that may be, we are likely to get a more sober view of the significance and efficacy of psychotherapy. Taking this kind of step back is, of course, precisely what science is supposed to be about; and although the social sciences can scarcely be considered as a unified and uncontentious field (if it wasn't such a cliché, I'd say they were riven with dissent), it is still true that over half a century of intense scientific examination of psychotherapy, producing countless volumes – indeed libraries – of evidence, provides little support for the confidence most therapists, as well as many of their clients, have in their procedures.

So far as a scientific consensus is possible, we might be able to agree that the helpfulness of therapy, such as it is, has more to do with the personal qualities of the therapist than with any particular theory or technique; that such personal qualities are not a matter of training, so that many people who are not 'qualified' therapists are likely to be as good or better at it than people who are; that fairly obvious forms of common-sense inquiry and advice (ponderously baptised 'cognitive-behavioural') are likely to be more effective in alleviating psychological distress than are the more recondite procedures of, for example, 'dynamic psychotherapy'.

The best course of action for psychotherapists faced with this kind of evidence is to look around for grounds for dismissing it. Human ingenuity being what it is, that is not too difficult, especially in 'postmodern' times when the whole boring nature of so-called 'positivistic' science is discredited at some of the highest intellectual levels. But that's not what I want to do – not least, no doubt, because my own experience of around 40 years as a clinical psychologist accords rather well with the scientific evidence (and of course I am as vulnerable as anyone to personal conviction!).

What seems to me important is to understand why psychotherapy is not as effective as people feel it to be and, more important, to develop a more satisfactory idea of how psychological distress comes about and how it might best be dealt with.

I am making some assumptions here which need to be spelt out if misunderstanding is to be avoided. I am assuming that the principal aim of psychotherapy is to alleviate distress and that the question of its effectiveness may legitimately be raised. These assumptions are, I think, linked; that is to say, the question of its effectiveness can be raised only if psychotherapy is seen as a technical procedure for the relief of psychological or emotional distress.

Many psychotherapists, especially of the 'psychodynamic' variety, reject the idea that what they do constitutes a form of 'treatment', preferring to characterise it as a procedure of inquiry and self-understanding. This is fair enough in my view, but puts psychotherapy in the same camp as religion, say, or astrology. The procedure is self-justifying, and one need seek endorsement for it no further than the participants' own feelings. If, for example, you want to spend 15 years, five days a week (and several thousand pounds) coming to understand yourself and your conduct in the terms set out by Sigmund Freud, without necessarily expecting it to make any significant or observable difference to your personal suffering or the way you conduct your life and relationships, that is entirely your business and that of your (in this case) psychoanalyst.

Though I wouldn't choose it for myself or particularly recommend it to others, I am not, as a great believer in freedom, against this kind of activity; it may even have some things to be said for it. One thing most forms of therapy do is champion the individual and his or her personal feelings and experience: that is to say, they privilege subjectivity. Indeed, I suspect that this is one of the main secrets of the success of psychotherapy as an enterprise: from its outset, psychotherapy challenged objectifying forms of authority which sought to impose on people explanations for and meanings of their conduct which resided outside of their own experience and potential control. This is not to say that psychotherapy itself doesn't in many of its aspects quickly become just such an objectifying authority; but at best it furthers at least an illusion of subjective, personal freedom and responsibility.

Even this, though, has its own attendant set of dangers: a defence of subjectivity and celebration of individuality can quickly develop into a pervasive orgy of interiority in which people become so exquisitely sensitive to their own feeling-states, intuitions and so on, that they are virtually removed from the public world of spontaneous social action. Absolutely nothing is more boring and futile than focusing to the exclusion of almost everything else on the quality and finer meaning of one's own sensations and experiences — not to mention dreams. Therapy junkies can easily find themselves in that kind of condition, and spend far more time than is good for any of us writing about it.

But I think what most people understand by 'psychotherapy' is precisely a form of treatment for psychological disturbance; and certainly by far the majority of the practitioners of the myriad forms of therapy available today at least imply that that is indeed the nature of their game, even if they don't openly claim it. In other words, what most psychotherapists are offering, at least tacitly, is a *professional* service involving established and validated procedures for the relief of distress. In this situation, it seems to me perfectly legitimate to ask for evidence that such procedures do indeed exist, and that they work. And it is precisely here, of course, that psychotherapies become unstuck in a big way.

Now I don't at this point want to get embroiled in a dispute about 'evidence' and what may legitimately be said to constitute it: social scientists can (and will — nothing is more certain) go on squabbling about that kind of thing for ever. Pretty well everyone not having directly vested an interest in a particular therapeutic brand name is agreed that the evidence for the effectiveness of therapy is, overall, weak. What I do want to do is suggest some reasons why this isn't such an outrageous or dismaying circumstance as some may feel it to be. In fact, it's pretty well to be expected.

Psychotherapy is, when one comes to think about it, a curious phenomenon: one very much of the twentieth century and indeed particularly suited to these supposedly 'postmodern' times — which is perhaps why it is currently booming as never before. We have become so familiar with the ideas explicit and implicit in psychotherapy, it chimes in so harmoniously with the *Zeitgeist* — indeed, in part it is definitive of that *Zeitgeist* — that it becomes quite a struggle to see how curious a phenomenon it is. But what it does, I would suggest, is something quite radical — even violent — to the nature of our personhood and our relations with the world. To be more specific: it *disembodies* us and it *dissociates* us.

Through its focus on the individual, and its limitation for the most part of its analysis to the individual's relations with (a) his or her family and (b) the therapist, psychotherapy lifts the person out of the physical and social contexts which actually shape and maintain him or her *as* a person. It simply ignores the main factors and influences which make us the people we are. The aim, of course, is to free us, to give us power over our lives and the ability to change their course when things go badly. But it is an illusory freedom, and one which in the long run does us much more harm than good. In fact, if only it could speak for itself, the consensual core of psychotherapeutic thinking would find much to agree with in Margaret Thatcher's dictum that there is no such thing as society, only individuals and families. It might even go further in maintaining that, its 'all being in the mind', there are no such things as bodies either. Let me just take the factors of disembodiment and dissociation one at a time.

DISEMBODIMENT

In nearly all of its varieties, psychotherapy tends to think of bodies as unproblematic, as secondary to mental influence; in many respects the mind is seen as *constitutive* of physical structures. This is seen at its most extreme in the view that, through the operation of 'imaging', a person can organise a kind of biological attack on pathogenic physical processes such as the production of cancer cells. (Apart from its absurdity, this kind of thinking can lead to very unfortunate consequences, for what starts out as a half-baked notion of the magical power of thought ends up in people feeling *responsible for* their inability to cure their cancer.)

The privileging of the mental is rarely as extreme as this, but is still widespread in psychotherapeutic thinking. Psychoanalysis, of course, gives colossal power to 'the Unconscious' and its ability to shape our bodily experience and reactions, and ideas like that of 'psychosomatic' illness can quickly slide into a view that psychological events *cause* physical ones. Such ideas may be harmless enough — even quite fruitful — as a kind of rhetorical counter to an unthinking biological mechanism, but they too easily come to underpin a received — and utterly erroneous — notion of the power of mind over matter.

In run-of-the-mill therapeutic work, the factor of disembodiment is encountered most frequently, albeit somewhat indirectly, in the pervasive notion of 'insight'. At first glance, the idea that we can act freely on the basis of what we see to be the case, and that the identification of misconceptions is enough to enable us to change our ways, seems innocent enough, and indeed forms one of the principal pillars of everyday ways of thinking. Psychotherapy is built around this idea. In order to change their neurotic ways, people have to see into their reasons, conscious and unconscious, for clinging on to them, and having done so will be able to take a different course.

'What's the matter with that?', you may say. Well, the matter is that our learned patterns of thought and action are not merely *mental* acquisitions, but are embodied. It is no easier for people, for example, to throw off anxiety and lack of self-confidence merely through having seen into its history than it is for them to speak anything other than their mother tongue simply by being given an account of how they came to speak it. Psychotherapy tends in this way to represent our personal characteristics and conduct as matters of *choice*, as though we were, from infancy onwards, disembodied wills, selecting (even if unwisely or unconsciously) what suited us from a kind of hypermarket of possibilities.

But experience is embodied. Wired in. If we are lucky, we may be able to an extent to choose our influences (good parents will do this for us as we grow up, and the more resources they have at their disposal the more successfully they will be able to do it); but we cannot choose whether or not to be influenced, or to become uninfluenced once we have been influenced. As I've found myself saying over and over again to people, you can't choose to forget how to ride a bike. The same is true with so-called 'psychological' influences: you can't just divest yourself of their consequences merely because it now suits you (having gained 'insight') to do so.

DISSOCIATION

Because psychotherapy focuses almost exclusively for the derivation of its theory and practice on the two occupants of the consulting room, looking beyond for the most part only to the members of the patient's immediate family, the result is a dissociation (social dislocation) of the individual which has profound implications for the understanding of how, among other things, psychological distress comes about. A world is created in which it seems as though persons are made solely through the interplay of wilful action among those with whom they are most intimately involved — that is to say, in the 'proximal' relations with their family and some others with whom they have close, intense relations, including of course their psychotherapist. It is their relations with the latter which are seen as crucial to their psychological transformation. Left unanalysed in this situation, and very possibly not considered at all, are the influences of the wider culture and social environment.

In mainstream psychotherapeutic thinking there is nowhere to look for the meaning of action beyond the actors themselves, and so the potent factors in the process of becoming a person and the struggle to change are likely to be seen as intention, will, desire — those factors which in fact all of us in our day-to-day lives take for granted as the sources of our conduct. However, because it is every therapist's experience that people cannot change merely because they intend to or want to, another dimension has to be added to the equation to explain their apparent recalcitrance, and that of course is the dimension of the 'Unconscious' which becomes a repository for intentions and desires of which the person is unaware. What you then end up with is a kind of voluntarism at one remove, where therapists can hint at what people 'really' (unconsciously) desire and intend, and chide them (though obliquely) with a kind of concealed moralism: 'Now you've seen what you're really up to, don't you think you'd better change your ways?' As an account of human conduct this really is extraordinarily inadequate.

In many areas of our lives, we are in fact shaped by forces well beyond the reach of our will and even, in some respects, of our understanding. Very significant parts of what we take to be our personal individuality are quite literally culturally determined. Socio-economic influences affect us as intimately and as uncontrollably as the weather. As people we are locked into a network of social power-relations, which sets the strictest limits on what we are able to achieve purely through the action of our own will. (It was of course Michel Foucault's particular achievement to elucidate the nature of this apparatus of social power.) What aspects of our personal and interpersonal conduct may be controlled by powers which we cannot even see, let alone influence, is far from clear, largely because our individual-centred psychology has for the most part failed to pay them any attention. However, what is clear, I think, is that the influence upon us of such 'distal' powers is far, far greater than we have so far been able to understand, and severely limits what can be achieved through such 'proximal' undertakings as psychotherapy.

We are through and through social creatures, and our happiness and unhappiness are conditioned by our relations with each other, not just as face-to-face individuals but through highly complex networks of social organisation. And that organisation is above all structured by power. How much we are able to alter our circumstances, and so perhaps affect the balance of our happiness and unhappiness, will depend not on our being able to tap sources of 'will power', hitherto perhaps buried in our unconscious, but on what forms of social power are available to us from without.

Please let me remind you at this point that I am not trying to say that psychotherapy as an undertaking or as a vocation (to use Paul Gordon's term[1]) is intrinsically invalid. What I am saying is that in its guise as technical procedure of change, the disembodiment and dissociation of human beings which psychotherapy so easily brings about ends up inevitably in a — very probably unrecognised — belief in magic, for the material means of causality have been removed from the picture. We are not the kind of self-creating, self-changing entities that psychotherapy so often assumes us to be. Our conduct is shaped and given meaning by a social world and mediated by biological structures which we cannot change simply by seeing the necessity for doing so or desiring to be otherwise. There is in fact no such thing as 'will power': if we are able to will an action it is because the power is available to us to perform it, and that availability of power originates from without, not from within. We can transcend the reality of social power (of its facilitating as well as of its constraining effects) and of the capacities and limits of our own biological structure only in our imagination; and when it comes to affecting the circumstances of our lives which cause us pain, imagination is not the most potent instrument.

I am not saying anything new with this. I'm sure that to many it seems, as it does to me, so obvious as to verge on banality. What I am doing is taking a side in a debate which runs right throughout the history of culture. In view of this, it always surprises me how upset some people seem to get with what I'm saying. Apart from sheer abuse from some fellow professionals (for example, that I'm suffering from 'clinical depression'), the most frequent accusation aimed at me is that I am depriving people of hope. But this is the case only if the version of

---

1. Paul Gordon, *Face to Face: Psychotherapy as Ethics*, London: Constable, 1999.

psychological suffering and its 'treatment' offered by the therapeutic paradigm is the only valid possibility. I am indeed saying that 'psychotherapy' as a technique or set of techniques for the treatment of psychological distress can only be of limited value (not that it is value*less*). This is because by far the greater part of psychotherapeutic theory has failed to progress beyond the most naïve psychology of personal development and essentially magical ideas of change. I don't see anything particularly hopeful about reliance on magic as a cure for distress. Hope lies in other directions. Perhaps I should take just a little time to give an indication of what kind of other direction might be worth following.

From a psychological point of view, the twentieth century has been a colossal diversion (certainly in the West) from an examination of the way individuals are created and maintained by their environment. The quality of thought Plato gave in his *Republic* to the kind of cultural diet most suitable for its future leaders is barely conceivable now, where about the most we get is cursory studies or literature reviews to show, for example, that television has no influence on violence. Our emphasis, as I have already indicated, is very heavily on the *inside*, on mental factors such as choice and will, and moral factors mostly seen as personal, such as 'responsibility'. Because of this, our gaze is diverted from the social world around us and our preoccupations are with self-transformation of the personality rather than political transformation of the society beyond the boundaries of our skin.

The logical culmination of this — one whose lineaments are already clearly discernible — is that our world becomes virtual rather than actual, and in place of a materially created reality we are immersed in an ideality which is spun by its various doctors into all manner of marketed wishfulness. At the political level, exhortation and the avowal of 'values' come to be seen as an acceptable substitute for material action.

The costs of pretending that we are immaterial beings capable of self-transformation into shapes and conditions of our own choosing, as essentially free of the limitations of the body as of the constraints of society, are, I believe, already to be seen in the forms taken by the psychological afflictions of the young, some of whom have become prey to a kind of anxiety in which they are panicked by, for example, the experience of their own bodies; they have simply not been taught what it is to be a human being and do not recognise feelings which are the common lot of ordinary mortals.

We have come absolutely to depend on the notion that it is possible to change aspects of ourselves we find inconvenient, to erase the inscription upon us of the environmental influences which surround us. Rather than accepting that experience marks us for good and all, we wish to insist — indeed, have come to expect and demand — that its effects can be counselled away.

But would it really be so terrible if psychotherapy didn't work in the way we seem to expect it to? Perhaps if we were shaken out of our bewitched fascination with imagination and 'virtuality', the wishful invention of interior worlds which have no embodied substance, we might come to see that paying sober attention to the realities of social structure and of our relations with each other as public, not simply private, beings is an option. A difficult one certainly — not so easy as dreaming and wishing — but at least a real one. What this would entail is a recognition that maybe prevention is more possible than cure; a down-grading of psychology in favour of an up-grading of politics.

Where, though, would this leave individuals? Would we not, for example, be in danger of depersonalising ourselves and risk becoming part of a grey, undifferentiated mass, prey to totalitarian solutions of the kind too often experienced already in this now dying century? I really don't see why this should be. Politics doesn't *have* to be dishonourable. There is no reason in principle why we shouldn't be able to resurrect a politics whose central concerns are with such things as liberty, justice and equality. Very difficult, certainly; naïve, Utopian, idealistic, I can't deny. But at least not, like the psychology of self-creation and self-transformation, impossible.

Our disillusion with and widespread rejection of what passes for politics these days — that is, for the most part, the acquisition and manipulation of power by large interest-groups — leave us exposed to ideologies at least as dangerous as those recognised as political. For the marketed ideology of interiority, the world of 'third ways' where public opposition is supposed to be at an end and the interests of all can be reconciled, where exhortations to 'personal responsibility', 'naming and shaming' and other forms of sanctimonious moralising take the place of government, all these take us into a realm of make-believe where there is only an *illusion* of control, and where the real, material principles of social reality threaten to run riot.

I hope it is clear from what I've said that I am absolutely not meaning to suggest that the lives, interests or feelings of individuals be sacrificed to some idealised political notion of the common good. Perhaps psychotherapy's greatest contribution (though by no means always and everywhere) has been, as already suggested, to support and sustain individual subjectivity, to respect individual feelings and to respond compassionately to individual pain. But these humane aims and impulses did not originate with psychotherapy and are in fact not realisable by it in any other context than that of a personal relationship. That is to say, psychotherapy is incapable of bringing about change on a wider social scale if only because it hasn't the powers available to it to do so. The kind of moral aim which underlies the best psychotherapy cannot be achieved by a procedure of personal transformation or 'cure' (on an analogy with medicine), but by constructing a context of 'taking care' which, as I argued in an earlier book,[2] can be furthered only politically, i.e. as a collective social undertaking.

Even the respect for individuals which lies at the heart of the best psychotherapy can too easily become submerged in a pernicious moral and aesthetic prescriptiveness by no means dissimilar from political totalitarianism. For it is easy for therapists to slide from a compassionate interest in how people *are* into a superior judgement of how they *ought* to be. In part it is this phenomenon which feeds the whole culture of personal 'change' to which psychotherapy is so prone. It is impossible to be exposed for long to the privileged insights which the role of psychotherapist offers without becoming aware of the darker and more depressing sides of human experience and conduct, and so hard to resist an impulse to moral exhortation (in however veiled a form) and to holding up to people a model of 'normality' or 'being' to which they should strive to conform. But this is just another form of tyranny, disguised victim-blaming in which people are asked to do the impossible. Impossible because the vast majority haven't in fact got the powers available to them to effect the changes considered necessary.

---

2. David Smail, *Why Therapy Doesn't Work*, London: Constable and Robinson, 2001.

We would do better, I think, to see that the kind of changes which might improve our lives are matters of social, not personal concern and action. If we need to change anything, it is the social environment in which we are all located and embodied. This leads to a very different psychology from the one we are used to, a very different way of conceiving experience and action (ways that, unfortunately, I haven't the time to develop now, but which I touch on in my books *The Origins of Unhappiness* and *How to Survive Without Psychotherapy*).[3]

It leads also to a very different way of conceiving of ourselves and each other, but not one which is totally unfamiliar to us. Rather than seeing ourselves as free agents, able in principle to pick and choose the ways we want to be, we could, I suggest, see ourselves as *characters*, not unlike characters in novels (I should probably say some novels): fixed, predictable, often caught tragically on paths not of our own making and from which diversion is not an option. Characters we can identify with, whether through love, pity or fear, but also characters created by sets of circumstances and worlds which perhaps it would have been possible to influence, characters whose experience *means* something by virtue of pointing to ways in which sets of circumstances and worlds could be. Characters, that is to say, who exist not just for themselves, but for a future.

3. These books are available in the combined volume, David Smail, *The Nature of Unhappiness*, London: Constable and Robinson, 2001.

4

POWER AND PSYCHOLOGICAL TECHNIQUES

NIKOLAS ROSE[†]

What does it mean to talk of power in psychotherapy? I approach this question with a certain trepidation. My trepidation is not because what I am going to say is going to be so critical of the ills of the therapies, but the reverse. It may appear too mild, too benign. But I think the value of the radical gesture is exhausted. To understand how the therapies operate and how they have achieved such a wide influence on those who go to them and on those who practise them, we need to abstain from denunciation. Of course, we may need to come to judgements about what therapies do to their subjects, or about the role they play in society. But in order to reach such judgements, it is helpful first to be descriptive and diagnostic.

The French philosopher and historian of science, George Canguilhem, gave a lecture about 40 years ago at the Sorbonne entitled 'What is psychology?' (Canguilhem 1980). In this lecture, he examined the peculiar nature of those types of knowledge that call themselves psychology or psychotherapy, knowledges that the French tend to call simply 'psy'. After a provocative dissection of these disciplines, showing the hybrid elements from which they were put together, he ended his talk with a little metaphor. When psychologists take the exit from the Sorbonne on the *rue Saint Jacques*, he said, they can either go up the hill or down the hill. If they go up the hill they end up at the Pantheon, where, as everybody knows, the philosophers rest along with the great and the good. If they go down the hill, whichever route they take, they are bound to end up at the Prefecture of Police.

Now this is a rather nice metaphor. Unfortunately, however, it is a little misleading. It suggests that we can think about the psy knowledges in terms of a kind of opposition between a benign philosophical sort of knowledge and a malign controlling sort of knowledge. Clearly, what Canguilhem wants to do is to urge those who are involved in the psy business to take the path up the hill rather than the path down the hill. Something similar seemed to underpin many criticisms of psychoanalysis and the psychotherapies in the 1970s and 1980s. Critics argued that, of course, in contemporary, racist, capitalist, patriarchal societies, the therapies were clearly instruments of normalisation and control. But in accepting such a normalising role, or failing to challenge it, what had happened was that the radical potential of therapeutic theory — psychoanalysis

† The original version of this chapter was presented at the annual Universities Psychotherapy and Counselling Association (UPCA) Conference, London, on 'Power and Influence in Psychotherapy', November 1997. An earlier version appeared in *The Review of the UPCA*, 2, 2001, pp. 50–66. It is reproduced here with kind permission of the author and the editor of the Review.

in particular — had been 'recuperated'. In this kind of criticism, it appeared that there was, or there could be, a 'pure' psychotherapy, a 'pure' psychoanalysis that would be culturally critical and indeed, which had radical and liberatory potentialities. Radical critics had to free this pure potentiality from all the deformations that it had undergone through being taken up in normalising practices designed to produce docile and obedient individual.

I take a different view. I do not think that the theories of therapy and the practices of therapy are distinct and external to one another. In fact, I think it is better to begin the other way round. Rather than seeing actual practices of psychotherapy as in some way or other an 'application' or 'misapplication' of therapeutic theory, I would start from the reality of actually existing therapeutic practices as they function today. The question would then be how the concepts, theories and explanations of the various therapeutic schools make these practices possible and operate within them. Of course, in talking about actually existing therapeutic practices, one is talking about a motley assortment, ranging from five days a week, 50 minutes a day, potentially interminable psychoanalysis, through brief psychotherapy, cognitive therapy, behavioural therapy, rational emotive therapy, and a whole variety of other therapeutic practices and sites from radio phone-ins to the use of therapeutic techniques in hospitals, in prisons, in schools, and so forth. It would be foolish to pretend that the power relations in all these practices are the same. But for the purposes of my argument here, I am going to use the word 'psychotherapy' rather indifferently to refer to all these psychodynamically or psychologically informed practices for what I shall call — for reasons that I think will become obvious later on — the cure of souls.

Therapists don't really need a sociologist to come along and point out the power relations in these practices, because in many ways they are obvious — which doesn't mean to say they are not important. Let me just list some of these obvious kinds of power in psychotherapy, in no particular order.

First, psychotherapy is a relations of clienthood. What is clienthood? The dictionary gives a number of senses. In the early seventeenth century, the term could refer to one who uses the services of a professional, a customer; by the nineteenth century it was also used for a person assisted by a social worker. But there is an older meaning, going back to late middle English, to around the fourteenth century, in which a client is one who is under the protection and patronage of another, a dependent. In the psychotherapies, it seems, all three senses are combined: the client uses services of a professional, and is the subject of a kind of assistance, but is also in a relation of subordination and dependence. This is so, however much the individual relation may strive to be egalitarian. For example, in order to enact this activity called therapy, one person characteristically travels to another person's place of work. One person controls the time, the frequency, the physical location, the layout of the room in which the activity occurs. These features of the situation already establish certain vectors of power. Of course, there are some cases when the psychotherapist travels to the patient, but that is usually when the patient is in confinement in a mental hospital or in a prison.

Second, money usually changes hands. Therapy is not freely given as the help of one person for another who is suffering. Care is contractualised. There is a lot that could be said, and indeed has been said, about the role that money and the financial exchange plays within the psychotherapeutic relationship. There is a whole literature which argues, in different ways, that the exchange of money has a value in the therapy. And there is another whole literature that argues that the financial relation disguises a relation of inequality and power, if not exploitation. I only want to make one point here. In our current climate, the exchange of money is often seen as a liberating phenomenon, one that liberates the individual doing the paying from dependency, giving him or her power over the other who provides a service in return for the payment, and establishing legitimate expectations as to the nature and quality of that which is provided, the time scale, and so forth. The contract, especially over the period of the 1980s in Britain and the United States, was seen as a mechanism that established equivalence between two parties. The classical legal notion of a contract is of an exchange freely and mutually entered into by equals, which is binding on both parties, and specifies that certain goods or services should be provided by one party in exchange for a specified price or other consideration.

A moment's thought, I think, is sufficient to indicate that the contract in therapy is not of that sort. It is a pseudo-contract. Certainly there is a financial exchange involved, but it would be difficult to regard the patient or the client as a customer in the way in which the passenger on the railways is now supposed to be a customer able to chose between Virgin Express and Great Western and entitled to a certain level of service, with legal redress if this is not delivered. Actually, the relation is more tutelary than contractual: the therapist is more like a tutor than a plumber and the recipient of therapy more like a ward than a purchaser. This shapes the whole structure of the encounter. One person is in charge, one person isn't. One person establishes the pace, the direction, the structure, the sequence, the etiquette, the language of the encounter. The other has only limited capacity to influence any of these things. Of course, I am not saying that it is a simple one-way relationship. No doubt, no relationship between master and disciple or teacher and pupil is entirely one way. But it would be foolish to deny that, in therapy, tutelage infuses and underpins the contract.

Some have argued, powerfully, that the contract is indeed a liberating device and that the movement to contractualisation in the social services and the helping professions is a move away from relationships of dependency and a means of empowering the user, the client. I think that psychotherapies don't actually fit in to that pattern very clearly. And indeed, although therapies are mostly thought to be voluntary and contractual, sometimes they are not voluntary and contractual even in the sort of pseudo-voluntary and pseudo-contractual sense that I have mentioned. For example, there is an increasing use of therapeutic techniques as a condition of probation or in the prison service or in psychiatric hospitals. And in some jurisdictions, more in the United States than in the United Kingdom, I suspect, entry into a therapeutic relationship is the condition for having some more severe punishment suspended — for example, a mother may be required to go into some form of therapy if her child is not to be taken into care.

Third, therapy involves a kind of power that might be termed priestly. One person confesses and is known. The other does not, remains secret, mysterious, merely hears the confession. This kind of relation involves what Pierre Bourdieu terms 'symbolic violence'. One person is a person of knowledge, and the other person isn't. One person has the capacity to reshape the meanings through which the other makes sense of their life and their actions. I'm going to have more to say about this later.

Last, in this rough and ready catalogue of dimensions of power in therapy, is the aspect that has been the basis of a long-standing critique. This is the argument that psychotherapies turn public and social ills into private woes. This type of criticism was very powerful in the 1960s and 1970s, where it centred in particular on the depoliticising effect of psychoanalysis. Therapies take problems that are the consequence of the damage wrought by social and political disadvantage, by familial and sexual pathologies, by cultural or ethnic discrimination or oppression, and construe them, intentionally or unintentionally, as private, individual difficulties amenable to solutions by working upon the damaged individual rather than the things doing the damage. In so doing, they are condemned to be apologists for these wider ills, or to admit their impotence to change them, or to actually support and legitimate those ills by treating adaptation to the existing state of affairs as if it were progress. I am less sure about this line of criticism. Many would argue that it is entirely possible to have therapy that does not normalise — for example, ending in female clients getting married and having a baby. Others would say that the therapist, in his or her professional practice, has no option but to work with the individual in front of them, whatever they may do in other parts of their life to act politically on the wider ills of our society.

Of course, even if one terms these 'dimensions of power', that is not necessarily to be normative and critical. Power certainly can involve relations of coercion, repression, exclusion and denial. Power can also involve relations of tutelage, mastery and subservience. But power can also create things. Power, as Michel Foucault suggested, is best seen as action on the action of others (see Foucault 1986: 331ff). Power relations are ways of shaping the conduct of others, the action of others, their intention and their decisions, which nonetheless leave the other party free, free to act. Power works most powerfully, works most effectively if it works by shaping the way in which individuals enact their freedom. And what I want to suggest is that the most interesting way of looking at this question of power and influence in psychotherapy is to examine the ways in which the therapist shapes the way in which human beings enact their freedom.

This is not to deny that there are some forms of power in psychotherapy which we can adjudge bad without requiring fancy sociological analysis or ethical expertise to advise us. It is easy enough, for example, to condemn therapies where they involve impropriety, charlatanism, exploitation, sexual abuse or even, perhaps, where they involve disbelief or the discrediting of certain versions of events. But these ways of being bad aren't particularly exclusive to psychotherapy. Garage mechanics can take money under false pretences, builders can be charlatans, child-care workers can sexually exploit the children in their care, police can and do disbelieve and discredit.

In the psychotherapies, it is usual to use the term 'ethics' to talk about the way in which the professional conduct of the therapists is regulated so as to ensure that these malign effects are reduced, if not excluded altogether. I don't want to deny the importance of this sense of ethics in the internal governance of the therapeutic professions. But I think we can take ethics in a different and in a more interesting sense. Ethics, in this different sense, has to do with the ways in which human beings lead their lives, the ways in which they make decisions as to how to live, what to avoid and what to strive for, the relative weight accorded to different values, the criteria of judgement of what are good or bad, wise or foolish, vicious or virtuous ways to proceed. I think that we can link ethics, in this different sense, to the idea that I proposed earlier of power as action upon action, the shaping and enactment of individual freedom. This is what I want to try to do in the rest of this chapter.

EXPERTS OF LIVING?

Max Weber gave a famous lecture in 1918 called 'Science as a vocation' (Weber 1948). In that lecture he made reference to a remark made by Tolstoy, or rather a judgement made by Tolstoy. 'Science is meaningless', said Tolstoy, 'because it gives us no answer to the only question that is important for us, what shall we do and how shall we live?'. Well of course, whether or not you agree with Tolstoy and Weber depends on what you are prepared to call science, and if you are willing to put the therapies in this category. Weber himself has harsh words for psychologists and psychotherapists; in fact, he agrees with Friedrich Nietzsche. Nietzsche was witheringly critical of psychologists and therapists (Nietzsche 1956). He called them 'those last men who invented happiness'. He has contempt for a way of life and a type of person that thinks that happiness can be achieved by scientific or rational techniques for the mastery of life. Indeed, Nietzsche and, I think, Weber have a profound contempt for happiness, or even contentment, as an ethic of existence. They regard it as a kind of slave morality; the nature of the human being is to suffer and to overcome, not to be content.

Well, we may well agree with their normativity here. Some would argue that Freud himself shared this view, and his well-known therapeutic pessimism was linked to a pessimism about the prospects or the attractions of happiness and contentment. Nonetheless, I think it is useful to defer our judgement for a while about the ethical worth of the life offered by the psychotherapies and to see that they do, in some non-trivial fashion, relate to Tolstoy's question, and do claim a certain kind of 'expertise' in this regard. With the rise of psychological knowledges and therapeutic theories and techniques over the course of the last century, there is a certain sense in which science *has* tried to address Tolstoy's question: 'What shall we do and how shall we live?' The psy knowledges have addressed the questions of 'How shall we live?', 'What shall we do?', 'What kind of people are we?', 'How shall we conduct our existence?'. Even if these sorts of questions cannot be resolved by science, they are addressed and understood on a dimension of positive knowledge. By positive knowledge I do not mean anything evaluative. I do not mean that positive knowledge is either good or true. But I do mean that it is truthful.

Georges Canguilhem, whom I quoted earlier, argued that scientific knowledges may not be true, but they were truthful, veridical — that is to say, they were internally organised around a norm of truth and error; and through a constant attention to the issue of error, they subjected themselves to critical correction (for an introduction to Canguilhem's work, see Canguilhem 1994 and Osborne and Rose 1998). They were to that extent open. Now, we know that many writers, Karl Popper being the most notable, denied this status to psychoanalysis. Popper argued that psychoanalysis was a closed knowledge, not correcting itself through its errors but constantly reassuring itself of its truth. Reading the actual history of the therapies, however, I think it is possible to see something different. The therapies have embraced, perhaps disingenuously, the apparatus of the positive knowledges, including learned journals, conferences, presentation of results, research, evaluation and so forth, together with a whole apparatus of training and credentialing of practitioners.

So the claim of the therapies is that, in this sense at least, it is possible to have expert knowledge, it is possible to have expert technique, it is possible to have experts who can address this fundamental ethical question of who we are and how we should live, or at least who can provide the spaces and the tools through which this question can be addressed. The line of division between the ethical and the scientific is not so clear as Weber thought. And I want to suggest that with the emergence of these therapeutic knowledges and techniques over the course of the twentieth century, this question of how to lead a life has entered the domain of positive knowledge and it has entered the domain of expertise. New forms of authority, therapeutic authority, have emerged over how to lead a life. And there has been a kind of therapeutic transformation of a whole range of other types of authority. A whole range of governors of conduct in our own culture — social workers, nurses, even prison officers — give their authority legitimacy because it has undergone a kind of therapeutic mutation. They exercise a therapeutic authority, and this gives it a new ethical basis, a way of legitimating itself at a time, and in a climate, in which all authority has to justify the authority which it wields.

CONDITIONS

The rise of therapeutic authority did not take place in a vacuum. It was intertwined with some significant transformations in the nature of the life that was led and the kinds of people humans thought themselves to be in the twentieth century. If these conditions transform again, it is likely that therapies will lose their cultural and ethical significance.

There is a well-known journalistic argument that the psychotherapies have undermined and replaced religion and theology in our moral codes and in our ethical practices: therapies have taken the place of religion; the visit to the therapist has taken the place of confession; the therapist has assumed the role of the priest. That is a simplistic argument, I think. But it does point us in the direction of some interesting features of the relationships between the therapies and power.

The first is the actual organisation of psychotherapy itself. The therapies have moved from what one might describe as a sect-like structure, based on the charismatic leadership of a few great men and women, to a Church-like structure, regulated bureaucratically, with career structures, attempts to regulate professional status via training and initiation rituals of various sorts, hierarchies granting licences to practise, inter-school rivalries, strategies to expend social influence, and so on. To that extent the analogy between 'the therapeutic complex' and 'the religious complex', if I can use those two phrases, is not entirely far fetched.

But I want to focus on a different sense. This is the relation of therapies to practices of 'spiritual guidance'. I have suggested that we can think of 'ethics' in terms of the practical systems, types of judgement, languages and exercises which people use in order to shape and direct their own conduct under the guidance of others. Now since the Greeks there have been more or less systematic ethical doctrines and ethical practices designed to shape conduct, systems which have guided people in their choices as to what to do and what not to do, how they should do what they do, why they should not do what they should not do, how they should avoid vice, how they should become virtuous and so forth (Hadot 1995; Leites 1988). Each of these ethical practices has depended in some way or another on a certain understanding of the person whose conduct is to be shaped, the person who is to be the subject of ethics. That is to say, they have been based on some understanding of who the person is who is being instructed, what kind of person is the bearer of these ethical codes, as a man, as a woman, as a master, as a slave, as a child, as a freeman, as a serf and so on.

From this perspective, I think we can trace a line between psychotherapeutic practices of the self and these ancient spiritual exercises. For example, Benjamin Nelson has argued that Freud was also central to the invention of a whole novel scheme for the direction of souls (Nelson 1965). Therapy here has to be seen, then, in terms of the invention of an array of new ways in which human beings can take themselves as the object of their own thought and their practice, act upon themselves in the name of their mental health. To that extent, therapies are continuous with, and not a radical break from, a whole series of other techniques of spiritual guidance. Indeed, before Freud there was a range of other quasi-psychological techniques of spiritual guidance, such as those of Mesmer; and many of the practices that Freud adopted, such as his early use of hypnosis, had a longer history in the practices of the nerve doctors of the nineteenth century.

Why, then, in our own culture have the therapies come to replace, or at least to displace, these older religious techniques of spiritual guidance? Well, I suggest that the psychotherapies, like the psychological knowledges, are bound up with the transformation of the very kinds of people that human beings are considered to be. The modern self is considered — in a rather historically unusual way — to be autonomous, to be free, to be an agent. This modern form of human being is thought to become a self most fully when he or she is able to choose, is able to make a life for themselves in their everyday existence, to become the actor in their own narrative. This notion of the self that is free to choose is not simply an abstract cultural notion; it is embodied in a whole series of practices throughout our society. Most notable are the practices of consumption, where we human beings define the kind of self that we are through the choices that we make, through the books that we buy, the clothes that we wear, the car that we drive around in. Each of these goods both *realises* or *materialises* our personality in the choice we make, and casts a kind of glow back on the kind of person that you are. Thus, the self in our society is not merely free to choose; the self is *obliged* to choose, obliged to make his or her life meaningful, as if it were the outcome of a series of choices. Marriage or not marriage, children or not children, how many children, to work or not to work if you are a mother, what to wear, how to lead your life, what football team to support, whatever. Each decision is seen to realise a certain aspect of the personality and you make it intelligible to yourself and to others as if it was an expression of some underlying feature of your personhood. You are to take responsibility for the happiness or the sadness of your own existence. You are to be the actor in the drama of your own existence.

Now at the most general level, I suggest that the rise of the psychotherapies as techniques of spiritual guidance is intrinsically bound to this injunction that the self must become the subject of choice in its everyday life, in order to realise its potential and become what it truly is. Therapies are sought out by individuals when they feel unable to bear the obligations of choice. Or individuals are directed to therapy where others consider them to be unable to exist as responsible choosing selves. Even those therapeutic systems that claim not to be normative give a particular value to this notion of the autonomous, choosing self. Their watchwords are self-control, self-direction, autonomy, self-worth, be self aware, become yourself, realise the sort of person that you are. So I want to suggest that, at the very least, the ethics of personhood espoused by the therapies are entirely consonant with the new regimes of the self that have come into existence over this century. A stronger claim, which I would actually want to make, but cannot justify here, is that the therapies, their languages, techniques and types of authority, have actually played a significant role in making us up as certain kinds of self. The kind of persons that we now take ourselves to be are tied to a kind of project of our own identities: we are to live, and to discover our identity as a matter of our own freedom.

Thus far, this probably seems a rather airy cultural critique, of the type that pleases sociologists but is less relevant to practitioners. But I would like to suggest that this argument can be followed through at a rather micro-level. So let me try and change the scale, as it were, of the investigation.

ASSEMBLING

Bruno Bettleheim contributed the Afterword to a moving autobiography by Marie Cardinal (Cardinal 1984). This book was called *The Words to Say It*, and was a narrative of her experience of schizophrenia and psychoanalysis. In his Afterword, Bettleheim writes this:

> once the inner freedom to be truly herself was added to the outer freedom
> of running her own life as she saw fit, which she gained during her years of
> analysis, she no longer needed the help of an analyst... she has become a
> stranger to her analyst, but not a stranger to psychoanalysis. Psychoanalysis
> will remain with her all her life.

What does he mean by this? And what is meant by the title of Cardinal's book: *The Words to Say It*? Well, actually, for Cardinal, 'It' is bound up with a complex set of beliefs, which I don't want to go into. But at a fairly obvious level, the title suggests that the place to start might be with words. And as we all know, therapies are, in large part, a matter of the exchange of words. So what of the words of therapy?

It is commonplace to say that therapy is our response to an age-old injunction: know thyself. In late antiquity, St Augustine urged his contemporaries to 'return to yourself, it is in the inner man that truth dwells' (Hadot 1995: 65). But this inner man that Augustine and his contemporaries sought was a very different character from the psychological self we are urged to discover as our truth today. And at least in part that different character of the inner person who we are urged to discover, if we are to 'know ourselves', has to do with language. The birth of psychological languages of description of persons and their conduct hollows out certain kinds of self, locates certain zones or fields within that self which are significant, requires us to speak about ourselves in particular vocabularies, to evaluate ourselves in relation to certain norms, to narrate our experience to one another, and to ourselves in a psychological language:

traumata, emotional deprivation, depression, repression, projection, motivation, desire, extroverts and introverts. We now have a whole psychological vocabulary to describe ourselves — or rather a family of divergent vocabularies; and whatever the origins of these languages of the self, they are indispensable to the ways in which we can make ourselves the objects of our own reflection. They are indispensable, that is to say, to the ways in which we 'know ourselves'.

In equipping human beings with a new language of the self, we make it possible for us to experience ourselves and to act as particular kinds of human beings. Ian Hacking argues that we can experience ourselves as certain types of creatures only because we do so under a certain description (Hacking 1995). It is only because we can describe ourselves in certain ways that we are able to reflect upon ourselves and act. When new languages of description are brought into existence for human beings, Hacking suggests that we actually bring into existence what he calls new 'human kinds'. He calls this 'the looping effect of human kinds'.

Let me give you one example: the word 'trauma' — an example that Hacking himself uses. Trauma, he points out, was originally a surgeon's word, a word for a wound of the body. Over a period of about 100 years it has become fully psychologised. It was extended first to the idea that head injuries could cause loss of memory and other psychological symptoms without manifest neurological damage; then, by Janet, to the notion that horrifying experiences alone were sufficient to produce hysterical symptoms without any physical assault on the body which could be treated by hypnosis; and then, by Freud, to the idea that repressed memories of past events were enough to generate hysterical symptoms. Once it has been psychologised in this way, we can think of any number of events and experiences as traumatic — not in terms of the damage that they do to our flesh, to our bones, to our limbs, to our head, or even our brain, but of the damage that they do to some inner personality, to development, to self-esteem. In early life traumatic events, such as bereavement, now appear to cause irreversible psychological damage. In the case of adults, involvement in road traffic accidents, or witnessing a fire or a riot, are sufficient to cause 'post-traumatic stress disorder'. According to the most recent version of the *Diagnostic and Statistical Manual* of the American Psychiatric Association, post-traumatic stress disorder has lifetime prevalence rates of up to 14 per cent, and up to 58 per cent amongst combat veterans and others at risk (1994: 426). So not only is there now a whole specialist literature on the aetiology, diagnosis, treatment and prognosis of different kinds of trauma, but we can all have our own experience of trauma. No wonder we are 'depressed' after splitting up with our partners, having a job interview, taking an exam, because these, naturally, are all incredibly traumatic events.

Applying new languages to ourselves as human beings makes it possible for us to experience things in new ways, to form new intentions, and to do new kinds of things — for example, to go into counselling, have different relations with our lovers. It also makes it possible for new kinds of person to come into existence, and for us to become such types of person. For instance, there was once cruelty to children and there were people, sometimes cruel, sometimes evil, sometimes merely callous or misguided, who beat or injured children. But we now have a different way of speaking about this: not people who are cruel, which anyone can be, but 'child abusers' who are specific human types, with particular personalities, psychic formations and so forth. Anyone can be cruel to children, but the child abuser is what Hacking would term a certain 'human kind'.

Language, then, is important in this matter of power and influence in psychotherapies. But psychotherapies are more than just language. They are, if I can use this term, 'technologies'. They are ways of working on ourselves in a rather practical kind of way. Michel Foucault took confession, the confession as it operated within the apparatus of priestly power in the Catholic Church, as a rough model of the type of technology in the therapies (Foucault 1979). Confession, Foucault argued, was a practice of subjectification. In confessing, one was subjectified by another, because one confessed in the actual or in the imagined presence of a figure who prescribed the form of confession, who appreciated, who consoled, who understood. Confession was also subjectifying because in the process of confession one constituted oneself. He had in mind the reflexive nature of the speech one brings forth in the confessional context: the 'I' that speaks identifies itself with the 'I' that is the subject of that speech, of the acts confessed. This is an act of *identification*. One identifies oneself with the 'I' of which one speaks, one identifies oneself with and through the language which one brings forth in this confessional situation. Through the obligation to produce words that are in some way true to an inner reality, through the self-examination that precedes and accompanies the speech, one is made a subject for oneself.

For Foucault, confession was a diagram of a certain kind of power. It was a diagram of a kind of power that binds us to others, to those to whom we confess and to those who originate the language within which we confess, at the very moment as it binds us to our own identity. So when I use these words — trauma, stress, neurosis, self-esteem — it is not simply a matter of words and meanings. It is not just that I am telling myself stories in a certain vocabulary about my experience, and in so doing coding it and classifying it in particular ways and giving aspects various kinds of positive and negative valuations. I am also activating a whole 'regime of truth', an array of authorities who stand behind this language and guarantee it, a complex of practices and procedures.

If we turn again to the question of spiritual exercises for a moment, we can see that this diagram of power is not, in essence, particularly novel. I have already referred to Pierre Hadot's research on the history of these spiritual practices (Hadot 1995). He has suggested that the whole ethics of self-government can best be understood within this field of spiritual exercises, the instruction and practice of particular techniques for the therapeutics of the passions, of the mind, of the body and of the will. For Hadot, the meaning of philosophy in antiquity was bound up with these kinds of practices. The philosopher was not one who pursued a particular academic discipline, but one who pursued a practical ethical discipline in their everyday life. The Stoics were exemplary in this regard for Hadot, but many of the principles and practices were common to the Epicureans and others. One who would lead a philosophical life must practise self-examination, a constant vigilance and presence of mind, must cultivate attention to the present moment, devote oneself to duties, cultivate indifference to indifferent things, keep certain things before one's eyes, practise exercises to curb anger, gossip, curiosity, meditate first thing in the morning, write things down last thing at night, utilise rhetoric and imagery, mobilise the imagination. All these kinds of things were spiritual exercises which the philosopher undertook to craft themselves as a certain kind of person with a certain kind of ethical relation to themselves.

Now of course, the spiritual exercises amongst the Greeks were exercises for an elite. They sought to reshape the soul of a very small group of individuals who were concerned with a kind asceticism, a cultivated practice of the art of living. But these practices of spiritual exercise and spiritual guidance did not die with the ancient world; they were the organising principles of early Christian communities. From the twelfth century onwards, a new practice of Christian administration of 'the cure of souls' made advances across Europe: 'After 1215, when annual confession became the obligation of all Christians, these treatises became the guides to Christian souls everywhere' (Nelson 1965: 64; cf. Leites 1988). It is a well-known and familiar sociological argument that with the rise of Christianity, these practices for the cure of souls spread themselves to all Christian persons. Max Weber, who I have already mentioned, famously pointed to the way in which Protestantism universalised Christian asceticism and then enjoined it on each pious individual in the mundane world (Weber 1976). And by the nineteenth century in Europe and the United States, elements of religious exercises for the formation and administration of an inner and personal conscience were incorporated within a whole range of secular practices — notably those of schooling — for the inculcation and administration of habits of life and modes of self-scrutiny and vigilance (Hunter 1988).

So this is another sense, it seems to me, in which that tired old analogy between the therapies and religion can be given a bit of a new life. The techniques of psy, and the therapies that have been promulgated by rival schools from psychoanalysis to behaviour therapy and from humanistic counselling to family therapy, can be understood, I suggest, as the contemporary successors to these spiritual and Christian exercises for the cure of souls. And they have disseminated a whole variety of procedures by means of which individuals, on their own or in groups, can use techniques, elaborated by psychological experts to act on their bodies, their emotions, their beliefs and their forms of conduct, in order to transform themselves. Such technologies set up a certain kind of relationship that the self has with itself, and give us certain procedures for deciphering ourselves, for examining ourselves, for judging ourselves and for rectifying ourselves.

ETHICS

Let me now turn to look more directly at some of the ways in which these kinds of reflections on ethics might help us understand the psychotherapies. I want to look at these along four dimensions: ethical scenarios; ethical materials; ethical techniques; and ethical goals. The terms should not be taken too seriously — they are rather pretentious names for things that are really quite mundane.

By *ethical scenarios* I mean the way in which a whole range of problem spaces have been transformed through the application of therapeutic knowledges into kinds of therapeutic issues. I have discussed a number of these in more detail elsewhere. The first is *the subjectification of labour*. Issues such as where one works, how one works, one's satisfaction in one's work, one's choice of work — all are now understood in subjective terms: as having subjective determinations affecting choice, having subjective characteristics that can be assessed to ensure that one is best matched to one's work, as having subjective consequences for one's life outside work. We have come to believe that work is crucial, as much for its psychological as for its financial benefits: we realise our potential and discover ourselves, at least in part, through work. Thus, issues of labour and the whole complex of relations around it have become saturated with therapeutic languages and have become profoundly psychological affairs.

Second, there has been a *psychologisation of the mundane*. A whole range of everyday matters have been made into psychological affairs — that is to say, matters which are discussed and understood in a therapeutic language. It is not just the rise of counselling in general, or even marriage-guidance counselling, or sex counselling. There is counselling for debt, for diet, around reproduction, childbirth and a whole array of matters which are to do with the minutia of how one leads a life. These have become rephrased in therapeutic languages and judgements, which have permeated way beyond the consulting room, on to television, radio, into the newspapers and magazines: into the everyday discourse of everyone (more women than men, perhaps, more the 'haves' than the 'have-nots' — the epidemiology needs further study).

Third, there is a new *therapeutics of finitude*, by which I mean a therapeutic engagement with all the implacable limits of human existence: illness, bereavement and death. These aspects of human finitude have become very fertile grounds for the generation of psychological knowledges and techniques. This is not simply because of the rise of specialist psychological and psychotherapeutic sub-professions like bereavement counselling, but also because of the ways in which these issues of our limits, of our loss, of our ending have become infused with a therapeutic language outside the therapeutic situation and a psychodynamic significance within the therapeutic situation.

So this is what I mean by the proliferation of ethical scenarios which are framed in a therapeutic way: the kinds of issues in our society that have become rendered problematic in a therapeutic vocabulary, have therefore entered the domain of therapy, both because they move into the routine practice of therapy and because they become the object of therapeutic problematisation by other experts and by lay people themselves.

The second dimension of ethics is what I have called the *ethical material*. By this I mean simply the aspects of the self that are given ethical significance, that are valued, that are problematised, that have to be worked upon. When one casts one's gaze upon oneself, what is it in oneself that one takes to be of significance? For many, the rise of psychoanalysis in its Freudian form was exemplary. Psychoanalysis seemed to show that, for all the therapies, what one took to be of significance in one's ethical substance was desire — sexual desire. It appeared that sexuality was the truth that had been hidden within us in order to be discovered in therapy, in order to be made the principle according to which one lived one's life. And, of course, psychoanalysis was criticised for giving that sexuality a particular form and for valorising in its theory one particular type of domestic arrangement: Daddy, Mummy and baby.

But I think that this focus on sexuality, the assumption that sexuality and desire is the only kind of material that the therapies work upon, is misleading. More significant, I suggest, is the way in which autonomy and identity, the autonomy of the self and the self-possession of our own identity, of who we really are, have become the central terms in the organisation of therapeutic discourses. Our identity, the discovery of our identity, the release of our identity, the capacity to be who we truly are has been fabricated as the truth that we must discover, that we must proclaim, that we must have recognised by others. We must find the person within, we must release our potential, we must become who we are.

Of course, the therapeutic valorisation of the autonomy and identity of the individual is only one part of a much wider cultural celebration of autonomy, individuality and identity in our own society, and perhaps even more in the United States, where the politics of recognition of identity has become so absolutely powerful and producing both good and rather problematic consequences. The critiques of therapeutics in the 1970s focused upon this aspect of their cultural significance (Lasch 1980). But perhaps the most interesting thing that has occurred over the last 25 years or so has been the emergence of an understanding of the self as a kind of complex of acquired competencies and habits. This is the ethical material presupposed by behavioural therapies: the emergence of the self as a composite of skills of life conduct that can be taught and can be learnt.

One of the things that has been least recognised in the literature on therapeutics is the way that, in the proliferating practices of clinical psychologists, of social workers, of health visitors and others, the psychotherapeutic and psychodynamic languages that used to be so dominant have been displaced (Baistow 1997). There are a whole series of reasons for this, which I cannot discuss here; but the consequence is the prominence of forms of analysis that have a much more direct concern with the conduct of the individual. These behavioural and cognitive therapies take the superficial conduct of the individual as that which is problematic and as that which is to be reformed. In the simplest of these kinds of therapeutic techniques, conduct is broken down into a series of problematic areas: in each of those areas, targets are identified, homework is set for the individual to practise, and the goal is to achieve those targets. The individual goes away, and practises the little habits necessary to achieve those targets on their own — particular ways of dealing with provoking situations, for example, or of calming a distressed child. These are techniques which are not all that dissimilar from the spiritual exercises I discussed earlier: the person seeks to learn techniques and to internalise them within themselves as habits, in order to achieve a better life. The ethical material here is behaviour itself, in the form of social skills and capacities to cope: therapy here is a matter of the cultivation of competencies.

There is a whole story to be told about why competencies have come to supplant other kinds of objectives in so much of the therapeutic work of social workers, doctors, clinical psychologists, health visitors and nurses. It is partly because competencies can be specified and measured, and thus converted into targets, outputs, throughputs and the like. It is partly because competencies promise to be achieved in a short period of time, thus becoming amenable to audits, monitoring and evaluation. It is partly because the therapists themselves can feel some satisfaction in producing a noticeable change. It is partly because the therapists can feel that their clients are being given something to take away when they leave the consulting room, which is important within contemporary client-centred and customer-centred professional ethics.

It seems to me that we have here an example of something which is rather difficult to evaluate in terms of power. In fact, those who practise these forms of cognitive and behavioural therapy frequently use the language of power themselves. What they say is that these techniques are empowering. They are giving people the power and the skills to live their own lives, unlike the forms of psychotherapy which, they believe, set up an endless, an interminable relationship of tutelage, between a disciple — the client or patient — who will never know enough, and a powerful person — the therapist — who will know more, control more, be more. Now it is easy to be cynical, and to say that the belief that these forms of therapy are empowering is self-serving, self-aggrandising and self-deluding. But perhaps cynicism would be misplaced, in part at least. These techniques of living, of actively and consciously sculpting a self, of deliberately fabricating the competencies, capacities and presentations of the self one wants to be and the life one wants to lead, are not themselves new. They have been the prerogative of the privileged, of aristocrats, bohemians and dandies through the ages. We may query the values embodied in these contemporary therapeutic programmes of self-shaping. We may query the means employed. We may query the problems around which these kinds of concerns are developed. We may ask questions about the extent to which these new forms of self are actively chosen by their recipients, or imposed coercively. Nonetheless, the thought that one can shape the kind of person one is by practical exercises, and the generalisation of this beyond an elite, doesn't seem to me something that should simply be mocked.

Thirdly, let me say a bit about *ethical techniques*. The technique side of things which I have alluded to in relation to these behavioural therapies seems to me to be extremely significant. Therapies do not merely equip people with a certain language. They do not merely equip people with a certain way of disclosing and accounting for their inner world and confessing it or making it hearable in certain ways. They do not merely provide people with a certain way of understanding their sorrows. They also equip them with certain techniques for acting upon themselves in order to reform themselves. Now, of course, some therapies, psychoanalysis in particular, deny that they do provide such techniques. Psychoanalysts refuse to see themselves as merely technicians of the soul, giving people a few little techniques which might help them lead their lives in a more contented manner. But even psychoanalysis, by providing people with certain ways of reflecting upon themselves, enjoining people to reflect upon themselves, to interpret their actions, their conduct and their words in particular ways and to bring them forth in particular situations, is giving people a 'mental technology' for acting on their life in thought, and so perhaps in action.

I have suggested elsewhere that we could make a four-fold inventory of these ethical techniques:

- Techniques of *engaging with the self*: an epistemological mode, for example, which searches for past determinants of present states; an interpretative mode in which the word or act is understood in terms of its significance in relation to other parties to the interaction; a descriptive mode which seeks to fix attention on conduct dissected into micro-competencies such as grooming, bathing, eating and eye-contact, which can be recorded, normalised and made the subject of pedagogies of social skills.
- Techniques of *disclosing the self*: ways of speaking not only in the consulting room, but to children, bosses, employees, friends and lovers. We do not merely have 'confessional' styles, but a whole range of other ways of putting the truth of the self into discourse, making it hearable, seeable, inscribable — and hence manageable, manipulable. And we have a proliferation of

sites within which human beings are required to reflect upon themselves in psychological terms and render this into speech, from the doctor's surgery to the radio interview.
- Techniques of *evaluating the self*, diagnosing its ills, calibrating its failings and its advances in terms of the norms of the intellect or the personality propagated by psychology, the repertoires of feelings and emotions disseminated by the therapies, the forms of normality certified by the proponents of cognitive and behavioural systems.
- Techniques of *reforming the self*: the purgative effects of speaking out, the liberating effect of understanding, the restructuring effect of interpretation, the little practices for the re-training of thoughts and emotions, the techniques one should adopt to raise self-confidence and to maximise self-esteem. As I have already said, of particular importance here has been the invention of new methods for the therapeutics of behaviour and cognition, versatile micro-procedures which can be taught by a variety of professionals and utilised by individuals in order to reshape their psychological self to 'take control of their lives' within an ethics of 'empowerment'.

ETHNOGRAPHIES

Now it would be nice to say that these rather abstract remarks could be confirmed by empirical evidence on the actual practice of psychotherapy. But unfortunately we lack detailed ethnographies of the way in which the psychotherapies work. If one could observe in practice the ways in which the psychotherapies work, it would then be possible to support or even to deny the kinds of approach that I have tried to outline about the way in which certain kinds of things are brought into existence in the therapeutic situation.

Sociologists, over the last 15 or 20 years, have carried out a whole series of studies of other kinds of enterprises — in particular, scientific enterprises. We have a number of very detailed ethnographic studies of what goes on in scientific laboratories (Latour and Woolgar 1986). These ethnographic studies of what goes on have shown the way in which scientific laboratories bring certain phenomena into existence that did not exist before. The facts that science theorises are actually forced into existence through the experimental apparatus and procedures of science. Ethnographic studies of even the most apparently 'hard-nosed' sciences, such as astrophysics, have shown the labour involved in making up scientific facts, and the theory-laden nature of even the apparently most objective or real fact. It is not so much that these scientific facts — the measurements, observations, inscriptions on graphs and the like, which are produced through complex manipulation of scientific apparatus, measuring devices and inscription mechanisms — are true or false. What they produce is a kind of 'irreal' world, the world of scientific reality. Scientists seek to conjure up in reality — through their observations, measurements, inscriptions and so forth — the things they have already conjured up in thought, in their concepts, theories and explanatory forms.

I think that one can regard psychotherapeutic situations in somewhat similar ways. If we look, for instance, at Bion's descriptions in *Experience in Groups*, you can see the way in which, in the forced 'hot-house' atmosphere of the groups that he deliberately produces, certain phenomena pertaining to the relations between individuals which are invisible in other situations are forced into existence (Bion 1961; cf. Miller and Rose 1994). They are rendered visible through a kind of intensification of effects that is entirely analogous to that intensification that is deliberately produced in a scientific laboratory to make the invisible visible. This is why I think that therapeutic situations are like laboratories: they force certain things into existence. And, in the same way as scientific experiments, they force those things into reality which have already been dreamed up in the minds of the therapists.

Now, of course, like the scientist, the therapist can't force *anything* into existence. Despite what is sometimes said by critics of 'recovered memories', it is seldom a case of simple suggestion or implantation of ideas or beliefs from the therapist to the patient or client. But the way in which an entity is brought into existence is made visible, is made hearable, is then described, is then made to operate, to do certain things, seems to me a characteristic of those kinds of therapeutic situations and one of the ways in which they realise their effects. This is the way in which the 'irreal' reality of the therapeutic encounter is produced.

If one did have detailed ethnographies of what went on in therapeutic situations, I think one would begin to observe the way in which, in a complex and subtle way, through the joint labour of the therapist and the patient or client, the problem is shaped up according to certain grammars, repertoires or frameworks. For example, Ian Hodges has been looking at a rather particular kind of therapeutic situation: radio phone-in therapy (Hodges 1995, 2001). This is very interesting because it is a very, very intense two- or three-minute condensation of something which goes on at a slower pace, and in a manner that is more difficult to discern, in other therapeutic contexts. In these radio phone-ins, within a matter of two or three exchanges between the caller and the counsellor, the person doing the counselling has transformed the problem that has been brought to them by the caller. It has been made amenable to therapy; it has been transformed into therapeutic terms. For example, the caller may have phoned in with a problem with a recalcitrant husband, and this is transformed into a problem of the difficulty that the caller has with authority or with showing love. This is a process of *shaping up the problem*: the caller, or more generally the client, needs to become a 'good subject of therapy' by representing their problem in a particular psychotherapeutic form, as a matter of the relation between inner world and outer conduct, or inner world and felt emotion or will.

Thus, through a series of conversation encounters — because all there is, is words — the problem gets shaped up through the use of a small number of discursive techniques. Further, one can describe the ways in which an individual is identified as a certain kind of person from a particular therapeutic repertoire of persons: this is a diagnostic moment even in the least explicitly diagnostic therapies. And one can see the way in which the caller is given instruction in certain ways of conducting self, or, at the very least, a valuation of certain norms of conduct and speech and a classification of others as suitable for treatment, requiring work, working on oneself.

Now of course, sophisticated therapists have long known this, although they tend to ascribe this to others rather than themselves. In *The Basic Fault*, Michael Balint has some unkind things to say about what he calls 'the Klein School' (Balint 1968). Balint says that the Kleinians have developed 'a very characteristic, though somewhat peculiar, "mad" language, but nevertheless the patients learn to adopt this language if it is consistently applied.... As a result of the interaction between a consistent analyst and his conforming patient', Balint writes, 'an atmosphere is created in which certain events will inevitably happen'. He goes on to say that the interpretations that are made of these events 'create the impression of originating from a confident, knowledgeable and perhaps even overwhelming analyst, an impression apparently shared by their patients'. Balint continues,

> If this is true, this attitude of the analyst might be one of the reasons why on the one hand so much aggressiveness, envy and hatred emerges in their patients' association-material and, on the other hand, why they seemed to be concerned so much with introjection and idealisation. These are the two most frequently used defence mechanisms in any partnership in which an oppressed weak partner has to cope with an overwhelmingly powerful one.
> (Balint 1968: 106–7)

As those who know Balint's work will know, he also suggests that general practitioners shape up the problem that is brought to them, transform it. He thinks that general practitioners have an irresistible urge to organise their patients' complaints into an illness and that this produces, in the patients, a compulsion to organise their own condition into a 'clinical illness' which may have little to do with their original dis-ease. So the lines of approach I have been suggesting do not really say anything that would not be quite familiar to the many therapists who are attentive to the microstructure of the analytical situation.

Many people might say that this is all very well, but what has it got to do with power? Well, as I said at the very beginning, I felt rather hesitant about my presentation here. It is not a grand denunciation of the evils, abuses, manipulations, patriarchal powers, exploitation that some claim characterises the therapies. It is a rather mild attempt to describe some of the things that go on within the situations of therapy and a culture in which therapeutic situations abound. Nonetheless, if one construes power in terms of 'action upon action', one can see the ways in which, through the kinds of mechanisms I have sketched out, therapeutic language, therapeutic techniques, therapeutic scenarios, the proliferation of the therapeutic through our culture, have a role in fabricating us as certain kinds of persons: certain human kinds who attend to ourselves in certain ways, value particular aspects of ourselves, take certain things as our truths — whether these be our desire or our identity or our skills — and act on those things in order to lead our own lives.

The therapeutic situation, even in Britain, is a relatively rare experience. But unlike many other professionals, psychologists in general, and psychotherapists in particular, are incredibly generous. They give their knowledge away, they give their language away, they give their techniques away. Through this 'generosity' of the therapists, many other authorities of human conduct, engineers of the human soul, have had their ways of working, their styles of practice, transformed. This generosity of psy is on one condition only: that these other technicians of the psyche adopt a therapeutic language, therapeutic techniques, therapeutic norms, values and objectives. This therapeutic transformation can give their authority a kind of ethical cast. Whether it be as a social worker, as a nurse, as a probation officer or as a prison guard, these authorities can understand their authority as a matter of doing good for others. And part of the significance of the therapeutic, for these authorities, is that, in giving them a kind of ethical basis for their work, it actually 'authorises' authority, it gives authority a basis which is more than simply brute power or dominion — it is democratic and therapeutic, it is in the interests of those over whom it is exercised, and hence it is a virtuous vocation for those who will exercise it.

I think part of the attraction of the therapeutic is indeed this ethical characteristic. Hence, if one were looking at the powers of therapy in more detail, one would want to look not merely at ethics in terms of the transformation of the client or patient, but the kind of ethical transformations of the therapists themselves. A certain amount of ethical work on yourself is not just a characteristic of what the therapist gives to the client, but also a characteristic of what the therapists get for themselves. Perhaps this accounts for some of the seductiveness and the proliferation of psychotherapies in our culture.

REFERENCES

American Psychiatric Association (1994) *Diagnostic and Statistical Manual of Mental Disorders, Fourth Edition (DSM–IV)*. Washington, D.C.: American Psychiatric Association

Baistow, K. (1997) 'Behavioural Psychology as a Social Project: From Social Engineering to the Cultivation of Competence'. Unpublished Ph.D. thesis, Goldsmiths College, University of London

Balint, M. (1968) *The Basic Fault: Therapeutic Aspects of Regression*. London: Tavistock

Bion, W. (1961) *Experiences in Groups*. London: Tavistock

Canguilhem, G. (1980) What is psychology? *Ideology and Consciousness* 7: 37–50

Canguilhem, G. (1994) *A Vital Rationalist: Selected Writings of Georges Canguilhem*, ed. F. Delaporte. New York: Zone

Cardinal, M. (1984) *The Words to Say It*. London: Picador

Foucault, M. (1979) *The History of Sexuality. Vol. 1: An Introduction*. London: Allen Lane

Foucault, M. (1986) *A Foucault Reader*, ed. P. Rabinow. London: Penguin

Foucault, M. (1988) Technologies of the self. In L. H. Martin, H. Gutman and P. H. Hutton (eds), *Technologies of the Self* (pp. 16–49). London: Tavistock

Hacking, I. (1995) *Rewriting the Soul: Multiple Personality and the Sciences of Memory*. Princeton: Princeton University Press

Hadot, P. (1995) *Philosophy as a Way of Life*, Oxford: Blackwell

Hodges, I. (1995) Changing your mind: therapeutic discourse and Foucault's ethics. In I. Lubek, R. van Hezewijk, G. Pheterson and C. Tolman (eds), *Trends and Issues in Theoretical Psychology*. New York: Springer

Hodges, I. (2001) A problem aired: radio therapeutic discourse and modes of subjection. In J. Morss, N. Stephenson and H. Van Rappard (eds), *Theoretical Issues in Psychology*. MA: Kluwer

Hunter, I. (1988) *Culture and Government: The Emergence of Literary Education*. London: Macmillan

Lasch, C. (1980) *The Culture of Narcissism*. London: Abacus

Latour, B. and Woolgar, S. (1986) *Laboratory Life: The Construction of Scientific Facts*. Princeton: Princeton University Press

Leites, E. (ed.) (1988) *Conscience and Casuistry in Early Modern Europe*. Cambridge: Cambridge University Press

Miller, P. and Rose, N. (1994) On therapeutic authority: psychoanalytic expertise under advanced liberalism. *History of the Human Sciences* 7 (3): 29–64

Nelson, B. (1965) Self-images and systems of spiritual direction in the history of European civilization. In S. Klausner (ed.), *The Quest for Self Control*. New York: Free Press

Nietzsche, F. W. (1956) *The Genealogy of Morals*, trans. Francis Golffing. New York: Doubleday

Osborne, T. and Rose, N. (1998) The Normal and the Pathological: Special Double Issue of *Economy and Society* in Honour of Georges Canguilhem. *Economy and Society* 27 (2–3)

Rose, N. (1985) *The Psychological Complex: Psychology, Politics and Society in England, 1869–1939*. London, Routledge

Rose, N. (1990) *Governing the Soul: The Shaping of the Private Self*. London: Routledge

Rose, N. (1996) *Inventing Our Selves: Psychology, Power and Personhood*. New York: Cambridge University Press

Weber, M. (1948/1918) Science as a vocation. In H. Gerth and C. W. Mills (eds), *From Max Weber*. London: Routledge and Kegan Paul

Weber, M. (1976) *The Protestant Ethic and the Spirit of Capitalism*. London: Allen and Unwin

5

ARE PROFESSIONAL CODES ETHICAL?

STEPHEN PATTISON[†]

Over recent years, codes of ethics and practice in health and social care professions have proliferated (BASW 1996; COT 1997; UKCC 1992). The former British Association for Counselling (now the British Association for Counselling and Psychotherapy) produced its own Code of Ethics and Practice for Counsellors (1997) which is constantly reviewed and revised. I do not intend to review in detail the content of the various codes, the circumstances that have brought them into being, or the fascinating and often inexplicable differences between them. Rather, I want ask the basic question, 'Are professional codes ethical?'. To put it more specifically, 'Do ethical codes such as that produced by the BAC(P) actually foster and elicit ethical awareness and behaviour?'.

I ask this question from the perspective of a lay person who has made extensive use of counselling and psychotherapy over the years and who is an academic applied ethicist. I believe it may be of interest to counsellors, not only because of the wide range of ethical issues that they may have to cope with on a day-to-day basis, but also because it raises issues about professional identity and responsibility, and the broad intellectual and social context of counselling practice and theory. While I shall refer fairly often to the 1997 BAC code to illustrate my argument, I do not provide a comprehensive critique of it. Furthermore, I believe it may help counsellor readers to gain a better sense of perspective on their own code if I make reference to the codes of other professions. I hope that this chapter will encourage counsellors and others to think more carefully and more widely about the nature, scope and content of their ethical and practice codes, as well as about professional responsibilities and training needs in relation to ethics.

THE MEANING OF ETHICS

Are professional codes ethical? Do they promote ethical behaviour and awareness? To the casual observer, these questions might seem otiose. Some codes, like that of the British Association of Social Workers (BASW 1996), overtly describe themselves as codes of ethics, or as codes of ethics and practice (BAC 1997). They proscribe and prescribe particular moralities, together with certain actions and attitudes in professional practice. The presumption must therefore be that such codes promote ethical behaviour and awareness.

---

† The original version of this chapter appeared in *Counselling* (BAC), 10 (5), 1999: 374-80, and is reprinted here with kind permission of the author and of the British Association for Counselling and Psychotherapy.

If ethics is understood to be synonymous with the inculcation of a particular morality, my questions are largely absurd. If, however, the realm of the ethical is understood to be larger and more critical than the laying down of particular principles by a certain group that has an interest in promoting conformity among its own members for reasons that might only be partly ethical and moral, they become more interesting and important. Their significance can best be discerned if I outline an ideal vision of what I take ethical behaviour and judgement to be. I will then look in detail at what might be considered to be some of the ethical limitations of professional codes.

An ideal vision of the 'ethical practitioner'

For better or worse, the majority Western philosophical tradition has put at its centre the notion of the rational agent with free will and choice of action (Singer 1991). Within this understanding, the ethically responsible person is one who rationally assesses courses of behaviour and action having regard to salient factors and, particularly, to the needs and interests of other morally significant beings. Such a person might adopt a utilitarian or a deontological stance in assessing situations and deciding upon actions. Thus, they might choose to weigh the balance of pleasure versus pain that might result from a particular course of action, or they might choose to employ some version of the Golden Rule: 'Do unto others what you would that they should do unto you.'

It is also possible that they might adopt some rules and foundational principles that have been found over time to be useful in structuring moral life. Thus, they might adopt principles of seeking justice, equality and liberty for all, or those of respect for persons and their autonomy, or beneficence and non-maleficence. The important point is that any espoused ethical principles and approaches should be freely adopted. Moral agents must also be able to provide some kind of rational account for their adoption and application in particular circumstances.

From this broad philosophical perspective, the ideal 'ethical' person is one who has regard to others, uses their own rational judgement, and freely assents to and adopts a course of action, albeit that the chosen course of action might in fact be to conform to certain social rules and conventions if these are thought to promote well-being, good and the avoidance of harm within the moral scheme adopted.

This ideal 'ethical' person should not be regarded as a detached free spirit or atomised individual who only follows their own lights and interests. That would be contrary to the notion of paying attention to the universality of reason, taking into account the needs and interest of others, and being able, in principle, to give an account of one's actions and choices as other-regarding and reasonable. However, neither should such a person be seen as a mindless conformist. Being 'ethical' requires one's critical reason, making up one's own mind, freely adopting a particular principle or course of action, and then being able to account for this publicly using words and arguments that other rational beings will be able to understand and evaluate.

If this 'ideal-type' of the ethical person is concretised in practice, an ethical counsellor, say, would be someone who understood and took seriously the rules and conventions governing society generally and counselling practice in particular. If these were sensible, this person would tend actively to assent and conform to them. However one would also expect such a person to have the capacity to make their own judgement about the applicability of rules and conventions in particular situations. One might hope that this hypothetical counsellor would have regard not only to professional rules and conventions, but would also on occasion have an eye to the larger principles governing human existence and behaviour. So, for example, if his or her practice were being used to support or sustain situations of abuse, harm or the violation of human rights, one would hope that she would exercise her own judgement and autonomy (for which she would surely be held to account) to desist from the offensive practice, and to protest against it, perhaps by whistle-blowing or by making some other kind of disclosure.

This idealised vision extrapolates from a fairly normal vision of the kind of human behaviour that is commonly characterised as ethical. It posits an actively discerning practitioner who uses reason to identify and pursue the good and to avoid doing harm. This person uses their own judgement freely to exercise choice and evaluate choices against reasonably universal human ethical principles such as beneficence, non-maleficence, a respect for autonomy, and justice (Beauchamp and Childress 1994). Because this practitioner freely adopts attitudes, practices and ways of acting or not acting, he or she can be held responsible for his or her actions as a moral agent. If practitioners simply obey rules determined and endorsed by others, theirs may not be a truly ethical stance. They may very well not be held responsible for their actions, except in so far as they had assented to obeying the commands and strictures of others. If they have been coerced into certain kinds of actions against their own reason and will, then they cannot be held responsible for what they have, or have not, done. The ethical practitioner is a person who actively chooses, questions and judges, not a mindlessly conforming automaton, albeit that the acts of a mindlessly conformist automaton might be judged as good in their effects by others.

I suggest that it is this kind of thoughtful, autonomous practitioner who possesses a measure of independent critical judgement and practical wisdom, together with having regard to a hinterland of wider human values and principles, that both professionals and consumers of services would hope to meet to work within care arenas. But do professional codes actually promote the existence of such professionals, or might they in fact in some ways militate against their emergence? Worse, could it be that codes even inadvertently promote unethical or immoral attitudes and practices among professionals? It is my contention that, in many ways, professional codes can be unwittingly antipathetic to the kind of ethical practice and ethical practitioners that I have characterised above. In what ways, then, might codes engender the 'unethical'?

THE 'UNETHICAL' IN PROFESSIONAL CODES

As an ethicist, my main anxiety about professional codes is that they do little to develop or support the active independent critical judgement and discernment that should be associated with true moral responsibility and, indeed, good professionalism. They may engender confusion, placidity, apathy and even immorality — the antithesis to ethical discourse and responsibility. This regrettable conclusion eventuates from consideration of the cumulative effects of the ethical defects and inadequacies of many codes which I shall now outline.

Terminological confusion to ambiguities

To be fair to some of the code-makers, most significantly the UK Central Council for Nursing, Midwifery and Health Visiting (UKCC), they do not all label their products as codes of ethics. The BASW does label its professional code, which includes principles for practice, a 'code of ethics', while the former BAC entitled its document 'a code of ethics and practice'. Whether or not the word ethics is used in the title, all codes prescribe certain practices, values and attitudes in greater or lesser degrees of detail. In this sense, all of the codes outline practical moralities. Thus, in common parlance they can be described as ethical, ethical being understood to mean anything to do with prescribing behaviour and outlining *do*'s and *don't*s. Furthermore, their authors would doubtless hope that nothing in them actually encourages people to do wrong or avoid being good in commonsensical terms. In this sense the codes embody at least a basic moral orientation and a broadly ethical outlook upon practice.

The problem here is that the concept of the 'ethical' is not discussed, nor are its different uses, ambiguities and understandings explored. The clear implicit understanding of all the codes is that if people conform to them, they may well be acting, to all intents and purposes, ethically. In this context, 'ethical' basically means conforming to professionally chosen and mediated values and norms of practice rather than exercising rationally informed autonomous choice and judgement. Conformity to a code is not necessarily the same thing as acting ethically in the broad philosophical sense discussed above. Indeed, if conformity is uncritical it may actually be unethical. The danger is not recognised in the codes I have read, though most at least implicitly allow for a measure of individual interpretation and judgement.

Doubtless, the re-titling of codes as 'codes of morals and practice', or 'codes of habits, values and commands' would be rejected in a 'helping' profession because it might sound heavy, moralistic and judgemental. It might, however, be more honest and less ambiguous. Most codes do not set out to help people to act ethically in the broadest sense, but to outline norms and exact a degree of fairly narrow conformity. There is nothing necessarily wrong with this as long as authors and users understand what is going on. Here it might usefully be pointed out that honesty, clarity and exactitude are much prized as virtues that obviate needless and possibly damaging confusion in philosophical ethical discourse.

Arbitrary values and principles

Confusion about ethical terminology in codes is amplified by the fact that they do often adopt some high, universal moral principles that would be recognised as such by any audience. So, for example, the UKCC Code of Professional Conduct makes its first stipulation that nurses shall act in such a manner as to 'safeguard and promote the interests of individual patients and clients', a duty that clearly derives from respect for the dignity and autonomy of service users. This code also requires nurses to serve the interests of society — representing a muted appeal to notions of justice and equality, perhaps. The BASW bases its Code of Ethics upon notions of the citizenship and rights of both service users and workers, while the former BAC postulated the values of integrity, impartiality and respect as the basis for ethical practice in counselling.

There is not necessarily anything wrong with the selected principles in themselves. However, there is an element of arbitrariness in their selection. Why should nurses not work within broad notions of citizenship and rights if social workers do? Why should not counsellors have to pay attention to the universally important value of justice as part of the framework for their activity? And why does no professional code enshrine the principle of truth-telling or honesty — surely an important basis for trusting relationships of all kinds — as a basis for working with members of the public?

Such broad, reasonably universal principles might be held to be relevant to all caring work, indeed to living in general. In some cases they might provide a much-needed point of reference and critique of professional norms of behaviour when important moral dilemmas arise. Would integrity, impartiality and respect provide any kind of moral challenge for counselling practice within a totalitarian regime, or justify the moral protests of those who objected to the social effects of that regime, for example? A broad, inclusive framework of moral principles that would be recognised as important and acceptable by a general audience of citizens might be a useful addition to most codes if they are naturally to promote ethical behaviour in professionals in its widest and proper sense.

Ethical intelligibility and coherence

Arbitrariness and the selection of principles are compounded in a number of codes by an apparent failure to understand, or at any rate satisfactorily explain, the nature and status of components of the code, and how, in fact, these relate to each other and to wider ethical methods and themes in a rationally coherent and defensible way. The now-replaced 1997 BAC code, for example, appears significantly defective in this regard.

This document started with a statement of the fundamental values of counselling (integrity, impartiality and respect) and then claimed that six principles arise from these (responsibility, anti-discriminatory practice, confidentiality, contracts, boundaries and competence). These six principles then formed the basis for the subsequent code of practice in counselling.

The defects of this way of proceeding are apparent. First, no rationale is advanced for the adoption of the three basic values out of the many others that might have been adopted. We are simply told that these are in fact 'Counsellors' basic values' (BAC 1997: A). This immediately raises the problem of whether these are values to which counsellors aspire (aspirational values), whether they are, in fact, manifest in the practice of all counsellors all the time (observable normal values), or whether there is a mixture of both kinds of value (partly normal, partly aspirational) (Pattison 1998).

Moving on from the question of what sort of values these might be, there is then the question of what the words 'integrity, impartiality and respect' mean, and to whom they apply. The code provides no definitions or explications.

From the 'is' of the code's value normativity we are then invited to see the arising 'ought' of six action-guiding principles. Here again, the code left out reasoning and explanation. This meant that it was actually rather difficult to see on ethical grounds why these particular six principles as opposed to six others were advocated and held to arise from the fundamental values. I have particular difficulty in seeing how 'integrity' informs any of them, but since I do not understand what integrity means in the first place in this context, that is not surprising.

Interestingly, the code moved straight from values as goods to be promoted and sought, to principles of practice. These were then characterised as 'ethical principles' (BAC 1997: B). However, no attempt was made to justify this claim to moral status, or to relate them to the discipline and practices of academic ethics and moral philosophy, even at a basic level. Within ethical discourse, it would be more usual, and often more helpful, to move from the vision of the moral good broadly understood, through some consideration of general ethical principles pertaining to the attainment of that good (e.g. promoting justice, truth-telling), and only then to consideration of particular practices and habits. This intermediate stage of moral discourse that brings ethics to practice was missing. Effectively, the former BAC code moved from the generalities of high moral vision to everyday pragmatics in one line space! In this sense, it might be argued that it is not a code of ethics at all in any philosophically recognisable way, but rather a statement of values and principles for practice.

Moving beyond the opacity of the basic values and their connection to principles that dangle from them in the BAC code, the moral voice in this document also raised problems of coherence and intelligibility. At some point this voice appeared to be indicative and descriptive but, confusingly, sounded as if it was really trying to be normative and prescriptive. We are told, for example, that 'the counsellor-client relationship is the foremost ethical concern' (BAC 1997: B1.1). At other times it was straightforwardly prescriptive and imperative: 'Counsellors must not exploit their clients financially, sexually, emotionally, or in any other way' (BAC 1997: B1.3.2). Sometimes the voice was exhortatory and advisory. In relation to conflicting ethical priorities, for example, counsellors were simply 'urged to consider the particular situation in which they find themselves and to discuss the situation with their counselling supervisor and/or other experienced counsellors' (BAC 1997: B1.6.3). None of these usages of voice are necessarily inappropriate. However, a certain unevenness and lack of explanation for different usage added to a measure of intellectual incoherence that characterised this particular code among others. In particular, ambiguously conflating description with prescription and 'is' (the case) with 'ought' (to be the case) cannot easily be seen to contribute to ethical clarity and responsibility in professional guidance and practice.

MIXING ETHICAL AND OTHER NORMS

The problem of the arbitrary selection of reasonably universal principles and values is compounded by mixing them with norms and principles that emerge from other concerns. In the UKCC code, for example, the foundational principles of safeguarding and promoting the interests of individual patients and clients, and serving the interest of society, are clearly important, morally derived and altruistic principles of the first order (UKCC 1992). They would be recognised as valuable by most people. However, alongside these, and apparently equal to them, are the principles of acting so as to 'justify public trust and confidence', and to 'uphold and enhance the good standing and reputation of the professions'.

It is certainly desirable that people should adhere to these latter principles, particularly from the profession's point of view. It can be argued that they maintain the capacity of the profession to be useful to clients and patients, which may be seen as a good (Koehn 1994). Unfortunately, I do not think it can really be argued that these latter principles are of the same moral standing as the first two. In so far as they might be seen to be mainly self-interested and so protective rather than altruistic, they might even be regarded as unethical. They appear to invite practitioners to take the upholding of the reputation of the profession with the same degree of seriousness that they take safeguarding the interest of individual patients or clients.

There seems to be here, as in other codes, an unfortunate and misleading elision of principles of different types and weights which might lead practitioners to believe that they are acting ethically in the general sense, when in fact they are acting mainly in the interest of the profession. So it proves in practice when nurses follow the Code of Professional Conduct by failing to whistle-blow, i.e. to publicise practices that threaten the interests of individual patients, once they have reported their concerns to 'an appropriate person or authority' (Hunt 1995). It is doubtful that any group of lay people would ever think that protecting the reputation of the profession is in any way morally equivalent to preventing the abuse and neglect of individual service users by all possible means. In the same way, it is doubtful whether any group of lay people would ever think that 'the counsellor-client relationship' is a greater or equivalent ethical principle to that of 'ensuring that the client suffers neither physical nor psychological harm during counselling sessions' (BAC 1997: B1.3.1).

The point here is that important ethical and lesser, specifically professional principles of practice should be kept separate: the latter should be firmly subordinated to the former. Mixing the two types of principle indiscriminately lends an aura of moral authority and force to what are properly subordinate professional principles. This they should not be allowed to enjoy.

Failure to prioritise and arbitrate between values and principles
Many codes do not discriminate between different levels and kinds of principles. Furthermore, they do not rank or prioritise them in any way. Nor is any guidance given as to how to moderate between principles if they clash or contradict one another, as is common in the delivery of any kind of care. The most unfortunate and limp example of this occurs in the 1997 BAC code. Having suggested that practitioners who find themselves in difficulties over fundamental conflicts between ethical priorities should consider their situation and discuss it with their counselling supervisor or other experienced counsellors, the code rather feebly concluded its all-too-brief desiderations on this subject with a truism: 'Even after conscientious consideration of the salient issues, some ethical dilemmas cannot be resolved easily or wholly satisfactorily' (BAC 1997: B1.6.3). So much for helping practitioners to become effective managers of their ethics, values and choices.

LACK OF REAL ETHICAL GUIDANCE

Substantial ethical dilemmas arise for many care professionals on a daily basis. Curiously, however, professional codes stop short of giving the kinds of detailed guidance on such dilemmas that would really be of practical use. At the same time as giving very specific guidance about professional matters such as gifts, fees and sexual relationships with clients, some codes seem to go out of their way actually *not* to show and demonstrate their relevance to a large number of common ethical issues that cause professionals moral pain (Sawyer 1989). So, for example, the UKCC code does not give guidance on the appropriate actions, or the kind of moral reasoning that might be appropriate, in evaluating nursing participation in, say, abortion or the administration of Electro-Convulsive Treatment, and much less on the nature and role of conscience in nursing practice.

The 1997 BAC code did not give guidance upon the nature and place of conscience in practical decision-making either. Furthermore, it did not, for example, explore the ethical problems that might arise in couple counselling where there may be competing individual interests. Nor did it suggest what might happen when a counsellor becomes aware of relevant facts that are obtained about a client or third party inadvertently, e.g. due to informal social relationships. Crucially for individuals who often work on their own in private practice outwith an institutional setting, it made no suggestions about what should happen when a counsellor feels so embarrassed about a case that they choose not to bring it to the attention of their supervisor. In this particular instance, the client effectively loses any protection that supervision might afford in the counselling relationship, a situation made all the more dangerous by the fact that it is often in such 'embarrassing' cases that real mistakes may have been made or personal boundaries breached.

None of the codes that I have examined impose on professionals the obligation to consider, audit and learn about the ethical issues that they confront. Ethical sensitivity, knowledge and ongoing development is not specified as a specific professional competence. If case studies or examples were used as illustrations of implementing principles and values, and pertinent specific questions were asked around them, it is possible that practitioners would be in a much better position to evaluate situations and the ethically responsible actions that would be appropriate to them. Thus, they might become more competent, autonomous ethicists, as well as better interpreters of the professional code in practice. Instead, codes often exist at a level of principle that is so abstract and general that they are open to being either misinterpreted or ignored.

The exclusion of ordinary moral experience

Codes often fail to address and give guidance on approaches to common but very important ethical problems and dilemmas. Similarly, they appear to give little value to the moral experience and judgement of professionals – and more specifically, that which emerges from their experience of living and developing within the moral community which forms society.

Edgar points out that implicit in most codes is the notion that the professional world is a different, very particular world into which professionals need to be socialised (Edgar 1994). Part of their socialisation is to acquire the notion that the beliefs, values and experiences that they bring with them into their professional work are of little or no value. They must be subordinated to the values and strictures embodied in the professional code of conduct. The consequences of this kind of myopia can be personally emasculating and morally disastrous. Quite apart from the fact that many people will find it impossible to 'forget' what they know and think as ordinary human beings with a lifetime of experience upon which to draw, if they do succeed in doing so they may find themselves acting entirely unethically. Edgar cites evidence to show that most whistle-blowers who attempt to expose real evils are usually not members of professions which oblige them to follow a code of practice. He infers from this that faithful obedience to a code of practice may actually blunt ordinary moral sensibilities. Thus, professionals collude with, or remain silent about, what would widely be thought to be unethical behaviours and practices.

The effects of codes in practice

At the beginning of this chapter, an ideal-type of the reasonable, critical, autonomous 'ethical' practitioner who strives to make life-respecting and life-enhancing choices amid the confusion and ambiguities of everyday professional life was described. Is seems reasonable, even desirable, that professional codes of practice should promote, or at least not make less likely, the existence of such practitioners. By the same token, it seems reasonable to ask what practical effects codes of practice actually have. Do they achieve the benefits of enhancing the lives of professionals and their clients? Or might they harm and narrow the lives of these people?

At one level, these questions cannot be answered. As far as I know, no one has ever properly evaluated the effects of codes upon the actual behaviours and attitudes of professionals, nor the uses to which codes are put in practice. This might suggest that it is possible that codes have no effect either for good or ill. If so, it could be argued that they are literally not worth the paper they are written on. In a world where resources of professional care are often in short supply, it could be suggested from an ethical perspective that the effort put into compiling and propagating codes could be more reasonably deployed elsewhere.

I suspect that whatever their good effects in terms of clarifying standards, expectations, accountability and so on, codes contain considerable potential for harm and limiting ethical awareness. By failing directly to consider and include many ethical principles and dilemmas that members of the general public as well as professionals would think directly relevant to the provision of care, codes may narrow the sensibilities and responsibilities of professionals.

In so far as codes exact unswerving adherence to their own narrow field of vision and regulation from professional members, they may discourage them from developing and exercising appropriate autonomous ethical judgements. By including an undifferentiated mixture of professional and broader, more philosophical ethical norms, codes may induce a false sense in professional members that, when they are following and obeying the code, they are in fact automatically acting ethically. This, too, might lead to a suspension of individual judgement.

In that codes require obedience to some clear norms and precepts, they may encourage professions to be passive and legalistic rather than actively morally discerning. Related to this is the fact that it is possible for some people to work down to overtly expressed standards and practices rather than these forming the basis for positive, thoughtful action. Codes can easily become a narrow cage rather than a springboard for responsible, ethically informed action.

In so far as codes may be used to evaluate professional behaviour within a professional disciplinary system or a legal system — for example, if complaints or crimes are identified — they may become normative in a way that requires professionals to behave in a legalistic, self-preserving and defensive way which may be inimical to acting ethically. All of which might lead to the conclusion that codes have the potential to be actively ethically disempowering for professionals.

It would be possible to identify further ethical problems with codes, not least the fact that they are mostly created by professional groups with their own interests at heart. This raises questions about their public legitimacy and acceptability. One suspects that many codes are not the product of extensive, effective public consultation. They are certainly not couched in terms that members of the public could easily understand. However, it is now time to conclude.

CONCLUSION

Professional codes of practice and ethics have evolved to articulate, maintain and perhaps raise standards of care as conceived by the professions who formulate them. In this chapter, I have tried to show that while the principles and language of ethics are often to be found in codes, there are considerable problems with these documents from an ethical point of view. Generally, they have a narrow and confusing view of ethics that may be misleading or even downright harmful. They are unlikely to engender or promote the emergence of ethically competent, responsive and responsible professionals who exercise autonomous, rational critical judgement and choice in the light of universally important moral principles and concerns. This is particularly so because they are largely unaccompanied by the kinds of commentaries, case studies and detailed explanations which would provide for active induction and pedagogy into the critical world of ethics.

I recognise the rights of professions to require certain behaviours and attitudes of their members, whether or not these are directly related to ethical norms and principles of a philosophical ethical kind. However, if professional codes are basically codes of behaviour that may or may not have much to do with ethical norms and principles as they appear in philosophy, they should be overt and clear about this. This would allow their status and authority to be discerned and evaluated more adequately by professional members and by the wider moral community of the general public.

Furthermore, there seems to be no good reason why professional codes should not situate themselves within a broad ethical framework and relate themselves to it (Berwick 1997). It might be illuminating to see all codes relating themselves directly to principles such as liberty (promoting autonomy), equality (promoting justice) and fraternity (promoting mutual responsibility), to notions of citizenship and rights (the basis of the BASW Code of Ethics), and to important universal declarations such as the Declaration of Human Rights. This would place professional work on a much broader canvas. It would probably relativise the interests, conservatism, self-protectiveness, narrowness and defensiveness of particular professions. It would also provide a built-in mechanism of self-criticism, and appeal for those who do see the importance of broad ethical responsibility and judgement.

Beyond this, it would be appropriate for professions to nurture positive individual ethical awareness, choice and responsibility in their members, such as that attributed to my ideal-type 'ethical practitioner'. Part of being a professional is to accept responsibility and to account for one's own judgement and choices. Aiming to produce professionals who are confident in their own ethical judgement would obviate the dangers of blind, possibly unethical obedience to a code of practice. It might also increase the competence of those professionals in such a way as to enhance their senses of responsibility accountability, trustworthiness and even enjoyment. Virtuous attitudes and practices based on truly ethical principles and approaches might thus be internalised and routinised rather than being confined to the pages of a document, one of whose principal present uses may be to threaten and coerce people rather than helping them positively to develop creative, life-enhancing professional practice.

REFERENCES

Beauchamp, T. & Childress, J. (1994) *Principles of Biomedical Ethics*. Oxford: Oxford University Press

Berwick, D. (1997) An ethical code for everybody in health care. *British Medical Journal* 315: 133–4

British Association for Counselling (BAC) (1997) *Code of Ethics and Practice for Counsellors*. Rugby: BAC

British Association for Social Workers (1996) *The Code of Practice for Social Workers*. Birmingham: BASW

College of Occupational Therapists (COT) (1997) Code of ethics and professional conduct for occupational therapists. *British Journal of Occupational Therapy* 60(1): 33–7

Edgar, A. (1994) The value of codes of conduct. In G. Hunt (ed.), *Ethical Issues in Nursing*. London: Routledge

Hunt, G. (ed.) (1995) *Whistleblowing in the Health Service*. London: Edward Arnold

Koehn, D. (1994) *The Ground of Professional Ethics*. London: Routledge

Pattison, S. (1998) Questioning values. *Health Care Analysis* 6: 352–9

Sawyer, L. (1989) Nursing codes of ethics: an international comparison. *International Nursing Review* 36(5): 145–8

Singer, P. (ed.) (1991) *A Companion to Ethics*. Oxford: Blackwell

United Kingdom Central Council for Nursing, Midwifery and Health Visiting (UKCC) (1992) *Code of Professional Conduct*. London: UKCC

6
A SURVEILLANCE CULTURE?

COLIN FELTHAM[†]

Counselling and psychotherapy supervision is a valued and established practice, professional requirement and, increasingly, theoretical and research topic in its own right. Supervision training courses, workshops and conferences continue to increase too. Some reservations about the unquestioned expansion of the supervisory domain have been expressed (Feltham 2001; Lawton and Feltham 2000), but much more needs to be said about the shadow of supervision and its possible alternatives.

I have argued in the above texts that there are problems with supervision,

- falsely reinforcing practice traditions and becoming an empty ritual;
- not being capable of dealing with the challenges of our many differing theoretical orientations;
- stifling autonomy via mandatory mechanisms;
- having no known empirical support for its effectiveness;
- not necessarily protecting clients;
- not necessarily serving the needs of experienced practitioners; and
- too easily becoming a social-psychological and sociological blind spot for the profession.

The very surveillance function that counselling supervision carries, if with embarrassment, makes it difficult to question without arousing suspicion among colleagues.

PROFESSIONAL AUTONOMY

We argue that counselling and psychotherapy are dedicated to increasing self-determination and resourcefulness in clients, yet in the UK we have decided as a profession that there are real limits to practitioners' autonomy and resourcefulness. Supervision is, for British Association for Counselling and Psychotherapy (BACP) members, mandatory; and for accredited members there are mandatory requirements relating to amount, frequency, boundaries and so on. While strong arguments have been put forward for the ostensibly universal and lifelong necessity of supervision, a certain deafness seems to befall most of us when strong counter-arguments are put forward. Let me put

† This chapter first appeared in *CPJ: Counselling and Psychotherapy Journal*, 13 (1), 2002: 26–7, and is reprinted here with kind permission of the author and the British Association for Counselling and Psychotherapy.

the counter-arguments in a nutshell: the requirement that we all must engage in something identified as supervision denies professional self-determination. (I'm using the term 'professional' to refer to what we do in practice, not to discriminate against unpaid practitioners.)

While it seems prudent to require all trainees and new practitioners to engage in ongoing formative supervision, and it may seem reasonable to suggest that everyone, no matter how experienced, might gain from it, there is no evidence — empirical or logical — that supervised experienced practitioners practise more effectively, creatively or safely that unsupervised experienced practitioners. Indeed, within the BACP no such comparison can be made (no control group could be made available), since everyone must be supervised.

We could argue that mandatory lifelong supervision is so important as to put into second place concerns for full professional autonomy; we might say that mandatory supervision can somehow go hand in hand with professional autonomy; or we might accept that there are real limits to supervision, and possible alternatives to be considered. It is this latter possibility that I wish to dwell on here.

POSSIBLE ALTERNATIVES

If we take seriously the capacity of most practitioners for creative reflective practice, and the finiteness of our available time and money, it makes sense to consider trusting experienced practitioners (however so defined) to select options from a menu of alternative means of continuing professional reflection and development. Some of these are:

- supervision as optional or sporadic, tailored to caseload and experience, used intermittently with other forms of professional reflection, enrichment and retraining;
- 'holidays' from supervision, whereby for various reasons practitioners might be able legitimately to compare practice with and practice without supervision;
- radical professional autonomy, in which the risk is taken that some practitioners may practise best without supervision, or might better develop their practice given the opportunity to rely entirely on their own resources;
- meaningful forms of self-supervision, possibly facilitated or supported by participation in professional reflection and development groups and networks;
- varieties of accountability mechanisms, from occasional peer review to periodic 'inspections' and regular pro forma completion;
- investing in research to determine the comparable benefits of no supervision, regular supervision, more personal therapy and less supervision, more targeted retraining and less supervision, or targeted and individual supervision, and so on; and
- simply scrapping supervision as a requirement beyond, say, five to ten years of practice.

This list is by no means exhaustive or commended, but simply illustrative. We do not *have to* continue practising as we do — we have choices. Much of the support for traditional mandatory supervision relates, I believe, to a combination of uncritical emotional attachment to the idea of a permanent state of supervisory security, lack of imagination regarding alternatives, and fear of being perceived as opposing the valued status quo.

DANGERS AND LIMITS OF SUPERVISION

It is easy to argue that unsupervised practitioners may become complacent, arrogant, dangerous or whatever. But it is just as logical to argue that supervised practitioners may become complacent, arrogant and dangerous, perhaps in unwitting collusion with their supervisors. (A highly experienced supervisor trained in Approach X and supervising a supervisee trained in Approach X may be useless or worse in cases where the client is simply not helped by Approach X, for example.) There is a superficial logic to the idea of supervision, but it falls down when we realise the absurdities and costs involved in this infinite chain of supervision. We have tacitly adopted a safety-in-numbers philosophy of practice accountability in practitioner support, and without any serious consultation we have made the assumption that the majority, at least, of practitioners are never to be trusted as fully autonomous professionals.

We might have learnt from Foucault and others the dangers of a surveillance culture. Resist it as we might, supervision is at least partly a form of surveillance and is associated with professional bureaucracy. There are limits to the consultative, supportive, collegial aspects of supervision. By its very nature, supervision creates micro-cultures of conformity and mediocrity. Anecdotally, there is ample evidence of supervisees feeling cowed, de-skilled and wary in relation to supervision, however skilled and ethically competent the supervisor. This is a because supervision is an institution in which we are at risk of infantilisation. We like to applaud the concept of autonomy, creativity and use of the self (Wosket 1999), but we do not in fact 'trust the process' sufficiently to see where these might lead us: beyond the limits of everlasting surveillance.

REFERENCES

Feltham, C. (2001) Supervision: critical issues to be faced from the beginning. In M. McMahon and W. Patton (eds), *Supervision in the Helping Professions*. Pearson Education Australia

Lawton, B. and Feltham, C. (eds) (2000) *Taking Supervision Forward: Enquiries and Trends in Counselling and Psychotherapy*. London: Sage

Wosket, V. (1999) *The Therapeutic Use of Self: Counselling Practice, Research and Supervision*. London: Routledge

7

CITRINITAS — THERAPY IN A NEW PARADIGM WORLD

PETRUSKA CLARKSON[†]

A Necessary Autumn Inside Each
You and I have spoken all these words
but as for the way we have to go,
There is no getting ready,
other than grace.
My faults have stayed hidden.
One might call that a preparation!
I have one small drop of knowing in my soul.
Let it dissolve into your ocean.
There are so many threats to it.
Inside each of us, there's continual autumn.
Our leaves fall and blown out
over the water. A crow sits
in the blackened limbs and talks
about what's gone.
Then your generosity
returns: spring, moisture, intelligence,
the scent of hyacinth and rose and cypress.
Joseph is back!
And if you don't feel in yourself
the freshness of Joseph,
be Jacob!
Weep, and then smile.
Don't pretend to know something
you haven't experienced.
Very little grows
on jagged rock.
Be ground.
Be crumbled
so wildflowers will come up
where you are.
You've been stony for too many years.
Try something different.
Surrender.

(Rumi 1991: 61)

† This is an edited version of Chapter 7 of Clarkson, P. (2002) *The Transpersonal Relationship in Psychotherapy: The Hidden Curriculum of Spirituality*. London: Whurr. It is reprinted here with kind permission of the author and the publishers.

What I call 'the *citrinitas* phase' in psychotherapy has to do with the 'stuck places', the 'impasses', the disappointment, disillusionment — and difficulties, the yellowing or maturing of the earlier '*albedo* phase' (for a detailed elaboration of this framework, see Clarkson 2002). It has also earned the epithet 'the greater dark night'. Accepting that common factors account for much of therapeutic change does not mean, however, that suddenly a 'model*less*' or technique*less* therapy should be advocated. As part of the family of curative factors shared by all therapies, models and technique do have something to offer. A therapy informed by an understanding of the common factors, therefore, incorporates and actively uses all of the elements or ingredients that have been found to facilitate change (Hubble et al. 1999: 408).

Since comparisons of therapy techniques have not demonstrated differential efficacy, it follows that theories, techniques and models can obstruct effective therapy or they can inspire confidence, hope and credibility. (Witness the claims made for eye-movement desensitisation.) According to Kottler, 'That the procedures are not in and of themselves the causal agents of change matters little' (quoted in ibid.: 418). The research literature displays considerable evidence that hope and positive expectations — being 'possibility focused' — in one's clinical work enhances the likelihood of clients changing in beneficial ways (Frank and Frank 1993). I have referred to this elsewhere as creating a 'conceivable self' (Clarkson 1995a: 118).

De Shazer (e.g. 1985) also points out that when clients can describe themselves in *the future*, it facilitates achievable changes in *the present*. It is of course not necessary to ask directly — usually the client will spontaneously bring out their hopes for the future. Then the therapist can join in and support this theme within the client's frame of reference and in the client's language.

I believe that psychotherapy, psychology and all their associated disciplines need to take on the challenges of the new contexts in which we find ourselves — not to be learnt by rote, but to be held in the mind as a constant resource. Otherwise they may become a symptom of those conditions which called them into being. Can it be that the other professions have not fully responded to the call of our time, since no-one else, including any established church, seems fully to have answered it?

A discipline such as psychology in its particular British shape, then, does not appear to be responding to the fragmentation and chaotic complexity of our postmodern era (cf. Burr and Butt's Chapter 8, this volume), which is moving at exponentially increasing speeds. The problems facing the world on a macroscopic scale, as well as psychologists on a microscopic scale, have become too complex for psychologists or counsellors to have unbridled faith in singular solutions, or to insist on imposing such singular solutions on their trainees or colleagues. We must learn to listen to each other, no matter what our differences of opinion or seniority. There are three requirements for all associated helping professions: that we be willing to move with our times, that we move with our art/science, and that we move with each other.

In the turbulent and troubled psychological waters at the end of an old century and the beginning of a new one, communication may become more important than certainty, effectiveness more important than positivistic elegance for its own sake, and intellectual and moral questioning of our basic assumptions more important than adherence to a single way of integration:

> Believe it or not, the existing ethical codes of the three largest nonmedically oriented health provider organizations ...[in the USA] mandate that therapists neither practice effectively not even subject their practices to any systematic or ongoing assessment of outcome ... Instead all that is required is that therapists practice 'within the boundaries of their competence and experience' ... As strange as it may sound, however, a therapy can be administered competently and still be ineffective.
>
> (Hubble et al. 1999: 438)

Furthermore we all know people whose years of experience consist of practising the same mistakes over and over again! Another strand of this incredibly rich tapestry of changing paradigms and collapsing realities is the momentous event which MacPherson reported happening in April 1992: ' ... a robot spacecraft "heard" the very birth pangs of the creation of the universe from almost unimaginable depths of space and time' (1992: 17).

Evidence has now been found that galaxies and stars, and ultimately humans therefore, condensed from a violent explosive fog of radiation and elementary particles more than 14 thousand million years ago. The universe was thus born from an infinitesimal point — out of nothingness. Even as the boundaries of our knowledge expand in this way, many more scientists are acknowledging some form of ultimate consciousness which can be understood as God. I like to think of this as *physis* (Murray 1955). First named by the pre-Socratic Greeks, it is defined as a generalised creative force of Nature which eternally strives to make things grow and to make growing things more perfect. It was conceived of as the *healing* factor in illness, the *energetic* motive for *evolution*, and the driving force of *creativity* in the individual and collective psyche.

Paul Davies, in MacPherson (1992), concerning the Big Bang evidence, suggests that there is a purpose and design to the universe and that we, as intelligent and conscious human beings, are necessary to its functioning. Perhaps we are more intelligent than we know in continuing to try to make sense and meaning of a seemingly chaotic universe — often with too few or too many clues. And perhaps this is why we continue to try to make sense and meaning of our own lives, and live them to a fulfilment that goes beyond the mere satisfaction of physiological, even psychological needs, but that reaches towards the transcendent, the transpersonal, the ultimate wholeness. I believe that psychology, psychotherapy, counselling, supervision and organisational work need also to acknowledge the final mysteries — the end of our knowledge and the beginning of nothingness.

CHANGES IN OUR SCIENTIFIC CONTEXT

Another important change in our conceptual environment is, of course, in the area of science, particularly quantum dynamics and human systems of psychoanalysis and psychotherapy. The scientific context is particularly concerned with quantum dynamics in human systems on the one hand, and chaos theory on the other. Zohar (1990: 13) describes the process in modern physics thus:

> Quantum field theory takes us even further beyond Newton's dead and silent universe, giving us a vivid picture of the dynamic flux which lies at

the heart of an indeterminate being. Here, even those particles which do manifest themselves as individual beings do so only briefly ... [It gives a] graphic picture of the emergence and return, or the beginning and ceasing, of individual subatomic particles at the quantum level of reality [which] holds out deep implications of our way of looking at the nature and function of individual personalities or the survival of the individual self.

Rumi (1991: 22) says:

This
that we are now
created the body, cell by cell,
like bees building a honeycomb.
The human body and the universe
grew from this, not this
from the universe and the human body.

What is often referred to as 'the new physics' (being already almost an octogenarian, it is not so 'new') has hardly been addressed in any of the major systems of psychoanalysis and psychotherapy. Apart from the Jungian literature, there is only an occasional paper in Jungian and Gestalt journals. Yet the implications of quantum physics for psychology are potentially enormous. Thus, for example, the Cartesian dualism between mind and matter is called into question in a radical and fundamental sense. (It is only from such a dualistic and causal perspective that *vitalism* can be so termed or criticised. 'Vitalism is the notion that life cannot be any sort of function or characteristic of exclusively material objects' — Flew 1971: 161. It is thus obviously based on an untenably strict division between the living and the material.)

Such simplistic dualisms have virtually been transcended in modern physics. With it has disappeared many *pseudo-problems* such as trying to find the means whereby 'the body' influences 'the mind' or vice versa, and what the 'first cause' was. Perhaps the notion of causality itself is limiting. In the mean time, most recent findings from physics and artificial intelligence (as well as the most ancient myths) point to a finding to the effect that *Life is self-causing*. That is the meaning of *auto-poeisis*, i.e. physis. Such findings have already potentially invalidated the classical or positivist ideal of an 'objective' description of nature; the goal of traditional academic psychology. For all practical purposes, however, it seems that many psychologists and psychotherapists have not yet quite noticed these seismic tremors to our conceptual universes.

As in postmodernism, the new physics makes it untenable to consider an objective or value-free scientific approach. It also postulates the co-existence of apparently contradictory views of reality, for example in the words of Sir William Bragg, 'Elementary particles seem to be waves on Mondays, Wednesdays and Fridays, and particles on Tuesdays, Thursdays and Saturdays' (quoted in Zohar 1990: 10). The whole idea of uni-directional causality (that past conditions cause future conditions) is thus also up for rethinking. Many of our psychological theories, for example, are based on the idea that early childhood influences affect adult life choices and patterns. This could mean that, if we were to consider the human being as a quantum system, such an idea of 'past causes' may become quite invalid and unhelpful in effecting changes for the future. It is equally possible, according to the new paradigms, that we live in a *teleological universe* where the future is determining the present (see, for example, de Chardin 1966).

I do not think we should rule out the possibility of a Copernican revolution in psychotherapy, and I do think we should pay attention to the almost automatic knee-jerk mental reflex by which we may reject such revolutionary and 'upsetting' ideas.

QUANTUM DYNAMICS IN HUMAN SYSTEMS

Quantum physics is 'the physics of that tiny micro-world within the atom, it describes the inner workings of everything we see and, at least physically, are' (Zohar 1990: 4). Naturally, human beings also 'contain' such micro-worlds, and at some levels will obey different laws from the ones that rule the macro-universe. Quantum physics is also an invitation for the psychologist to think about possibilities.

There are aspects of the so-called quantum physics that operate, according to some theorists, only at certain quantum levels. Others (such as the controversial author Dina Zohar) believe that human beings also operate on psyche and soma levels (or many more), and that these constitute quantum systems. Their smooth interaction constitutes *health* — on all levels and quantum dynamics.

> The whole world of matter, including our own bodies, is made up of atoms and their even smaller components, and the laws which govern these tiny bits of basic reality spill over into our daily lives. A single photon, or 'particle' of light, affects the sensitivity of the optic nerve. The uncertainty principle that rules the behaviour of electrons plays a role in the build-up of genetic mistakes that contribute to the ageing process and the development of certain cancers, and the process of evolution itself is thought to be similarly influenced.
>
> (ibid.: 4)

Playwrights and novelists have long exploited this fractal effect, by which the whole is fully present in any fragment of it (Atlas 1992). Psychotherapy, in common with some art forms, is the art and craft of promoting growth and/or healing in human beings. However, our most usual paradigm for it is that of client and therapist in a one-to-one, individual relationship. Group or even community therapy is less popularised. (See, however, Clarkson and Clayton on new paradigms of group dynamics, in Clarkson 1995b.)

In 1948, Foulkes, arguably the father of group analysis, already wrote that:

> From a mature, scientific point of view, each individual — itself an artificial, though plausible, abstraction - is basically and centrally determined, inevitably, by the world in which he lives, by the community, the group, of which he forms a part. Progress in all the sciences during the last decades has led to the same independent and concerted conclusion; that the old juxtaposition of an inside and outside world, constitution and environment, individual and society, phantasy and reality, body and mind and so on, are untenable. They can at no stage be separated from each other, except by artificial isolation.
>
> (1983: 10)

At one level one can differentiate these artificial opposites; at other levels they cannot be differentiated in any sense-able way. From scientific biology, some decades later, new information and new models for human behaviour, particularly the relationship between individuals and the community, are being discovered and developed which continue to support Foulkes' views. Studies of slime moulds (Elliott and Williams 1991) are being used as analogies to human communities. Cellular slime moulds are a group of soil inhabitants that live as single-celled amoebae. When conditions are adverse, however, they aggregate to form a cellular collective based on mutual communication, specialisation of tasks, and co-ordination.

As in postmodernism, the notion of the individual as separate from others as an aspect of received consciousness may bite the dust, and what seems to be remaining are the encodings of life in terms of relationships. Zohar (1990: 113), for example, doubts that this perspective has yet been adequately addressed:

> Klein, like Freud, Sartre and Heidegger, has no model for genuine two-way relationship of the sort that leads to intimacy. None can discriminate between the way we relate to other people and the way we might relate to a machine because for them all both machines and people share the quality of being objects.

Interestingly, as Rogers (1986) pointed out in the 1960s, an emphasis on groups, genuine encounter and mutuality of relationships tends to be construed by right-wing governments and right-wing climates as revolutionary and subversive. This is, of course, not unusual since the group is the most powerful fulcrum for individual or social change. It is the family or cultural group which sometimes appears to create most benefit or to do most damage. It is the group that scapegoats the Jew, the crowd that crucifies Christ, and the mob that lynches a black man in Alabama. It is also a feature of the time at which I am writing that right-wing governments and neo-Fascist or fundamentalist groups are in the ascendant in many places in, for example, Asia, Africa and Europe.

After much analysis of separate parts, relativity and quantum mechanics have brought scientists to the inescapable acceptance that the world cannot be analysed into separate and independently existing parts. Every whole is a part. All parts are wholes. Each part involves all the others in some way, contains or enfolds them (Bohm 1980). The implications of this, taken seriously, could herald the end of empiricism, or at the very least give equal weight to other possible perspectives such as phenomenology.

> Freudian psychoanalysis, too, largely influenced by Descartes and Newton and in turn so responsible for the way so many ordinary people see themselves, has no conceptual framework for interpersonal relationships ... As the author of *The Dictionary of Psychoanalysis* puts it, 'This is because psychoanalysis is a psychology of the individual and therefore discusses objects and relationships only from the point of view of a single subject' [Rycroft 1968: 101].
>
> (Zohar 1990: 112)

The fact that there is, in some senses, no 'other' to observe or with whom to interact has remarkable implications for psychotherapy and supervision. For example, and as already mentioned, perhaps a traditionally understood uni-linear causality limits and restrains rather than enhances our understanding of, and effectiveness in, the therapeutic and supervisory relationship (see, further, Chapter 10 of Clarkson 2002). From the perspective of the new physics and particularly from that of complexity science, uni-directional causality becomes a highly dubious notion in explaining physical (or psychological) illness, or many comparatively ordinary phenomena (whatever psycho-languages are used to describe them) in the therapeutic relationship. According to Field (1996: 41),

> I think we must recognise that projective and introjective identification, especially in its embodied form, has all the characteristics of a paranormal phenomenon. The fact that it occurs routinely in the therapeutic situation does not make it any less extraordinary.

From these additional perspectives, it becomes very difficult, if not impossible, to determine for certain whether the client, frightened of being harshly judged by the therapist, seeks out a therapist who judges him- or herself harshly, or interacts with such a therapist in such a way that brings about, or at least obviates, the resolution of a similar pattern in the client. How is it that our clients sometimes bring us the very problems which we now need to deal with in our own personal work? We have all noticed occasions when, after dealing with, say, a parent symbolically in therapy, the real-life parent changes. There is much that is unexplained. Or as a client recently observed: 'There is more that we don't know than we know.' *In particular, complexity science and the new physics underlines again the vitality of the relationship field and its crucial importance for the future.*

> Walking one evening along a deserted road, Mulla Nasrudin saw a troop of horsemen coming towards him.
> His imagination started to work; he saw himself captured and sold as a slave, or impressed into the army.
> Nasrudin bolted, climbed a wall into a graveyard, and lay down in an open tomb.
> Puzzled at this strange behaviour, the men — honest travellers — followed him.
> They found him stretched out, tense and quivering.
> 'What are you doing in that grave? We saw you run away. Can we help you?'
> 'Just because you can ask a question does not mean that there is a straightforward answer to it', said the Mulla, who now realised what had happened. 'It all depends upon your viewpoint. If you must know, however: *I* am here because of *you*, and *you* are here because of *me*.'
>
> (Shah 1985: 2)

RELATIONSHIP

Epistemologically, the things we see (people, objects etc.) exist only in relationship and, when analysed microscopically, they too are best viewed as relationships. It is no secret in physics (Capra 1976, 1983) that the closer we analyse some 'thing' the less it appears as a thing and the more it appears as a dynamic process (things in relationship). Consequently, relationships become a primary source of our knowledge of the world. This can be taken to the ontological extreme by stating that things do not exist ... that, in fact, things ultimately *are* relationships.

(Cottone 1988: 360)

The development of technology and communications has led to a situation where 'For the first time ... all humanity has the technological means to sit round the same planetary hearth and listen to each other's stories' (O'Hara 1991: 73). The ecological connectedness of our world has been dramatically brought to our attention by the way in which, for example, the damage to the ozone layer can affect people in all parts of the world. In the same way, the fall-out of Chernobyl can affect sheep in Wales. According to Chaos Theory (Gleick 1989), even the fluttering of a butterfly's wings in South America can affect weather conditions in Europe.

There are many thinkers whose work more and more supports the notion that the planet Earth is a whole. One of the most ingenious of these is Lovelock (1989), who postulates the idea that the life of the Earth functions as a single organism which actually defines and maintains conditions necessary for its survival. It has become famous as the 'Gaia' hypothesis. It can no longer be said that one part of the planet can be assumed to exist separately from any other part. Our planet is moaning from the assault of pollution in the seas, the deforestation in South America, and the extinction of rare and beautiful species of animals, all of which add up to the equivalent for the planet of cancer in a body. For too long, man has attempted to control nature, as opposed to connecting or co-operating with nature; and yet, according to Rinzler (1984: 236): 'Our human malaise of disconnection from natural sensation, our symptoms of violence on all levels, our lack of compassion for our home, the earth, our incomprehension of the connectedness among all the things of the earth, of the universe, are curable — if we are willing.'

A RELATIONAL ETHICS

The co-existence of what we experience as evil and what we experience as beauty (or good or truth) is the relational nature of *ananke* (necessity). The virus which attacks our immune system shares the same life force as the blood cells which overcome or become defeated by it. They are also always in relationship.

I explored our moral interrelationship with 'our others' and our world in my 'Byestander' book (Clarkson 1996). Bauman (1993) was a major inspiration for it. For example, he writes (p. 230):

The excuse 'I did not know', 'I did not mean it', is not an excuse which moral responsibility at whatever level would accept ... Whether inside the circle of proximity or beyond, I am morally responsible for my ignorance — in the same way and to the same degree in which I am morally responsible for my imagination, and for stretching it to limits when it comes to acting or refraining from action.

It has become more and more difficult to 'know for certain' what is 'good' and what is 'bad' in any permanent way. The foundations of our moral certitudes are constantly being challenged, undermined and sometimes shaken to the core. *Moral and ethical behaviour* can therefore no longer be formulated and prescribed in stone tablets; *it is more like a continually renewing creative co-engagement in our relationships:*

> There is a need for new relations between man and nature and between man and man. [And woman and man]. We can no longer accept the old a priori distinction between scientific and ethical values. This was possible at a time when the external world and our internal word appeared to conflict, to be nearly orthogonal. Today we know that time is a construction and therefore carries an ethical responsibility.
>
> (Capra 1983: 312)

FIVE ETHICAL RELATIONAL MODES

My book on working with ethical and moral dilemmas in psychotherapy (Clarkson 2000) brings together a variety of ways of appreciating that a *relational ethics* affirms that no one can act or not act without mutually affecting and being affected by other people, creatures, the planet itself. Neither can there be an end to this engagement.

- In any encounter the *working alliance* dimension specifies, overtly or not, what can be reasonably expected from one another, and carries an implicit warning about what would constitute a violation of these expectations.
- In any encounter the *transference/distorted* relational dimension refers to the multitude of ways in which the working alliance can be distorted, often to the detriment of all concerned. However, such distortions always contain information from which valuable learning about self, others or life can arise.
- In any encounter the *developmentally needed or reparative* relational mode refers to the multitude of ways in which ethically sound relationships can heal previous relational wounds or develop us as persons or as a collective.
- In any encounter the *person-to-person or dialogic* aspect of relationship can strengthen bonds of affection and respect and/or can bring individual needs into uncomfortable and painful, but authentic conflict with self or others. This may sometimes mean that choices have to be made which have implications for all the other aspects of a relationship. However, from such conflict, different and perhaps more complex kinds of ethics can arise.
- In any encounter the *transpersonal* is the relational mode which emphasises our ultimate values, knowing that the human condition often falls short of our dreams. We appear to be forever entangled with each other and the world in the quantum sense of relationship. An ethical questioning of the transpersonal aspect of a relationship is concerned with our ultimate ideals and even notions such as grace. It implies that ethical relationships are in essence inspirational and aspirational.

I believe Physis is the name people have been looking for to describe the life force. It's what I believe is a phenomenon of growth and healing prior to Eros and Thanatos. Life and Death there are, yes; but really, between those boundaries lies the wonder that we grow, we develop, we evolve, we connect, we strive for greater and greater perfection, we move towards 'the good'. Perls, Hefferline and Goodman were in agreement that 'man does not strive to be good; the good is what it is human to strive for' (1951: 335). In these words they are articulating a philosophical position similar to that of the Stoics who were grappling with this idea thousands of years ago:

> A good bootmaker is one who makes good boots, a good shepherd is one who keeps his sheep well, and even though good boots are in the Day-of-Judgement sense entirely worthless and fat sheep no whit better than starved sheep, yet the good bootmaker or good shepherd must do his work well or he will cease to be good. To be good he must perform his function; and, in performing that function, there are certain things that he must 'prefer' to others, even though they are not really 'good'. He must prefer a healthy sheep or a well-made boot to their opposites. It is this that Nature, or Physis, herself works when she shapes the seed into a tree or the blind puppy into a good hound. The perfection of the tree or the blind puppy is in itself indifferent, a thing of no ultimate value. Yet the goodness of Nature lies in working for that perfection ... For the essence of Goodness is to do something, to labour, to achieve some end; and if Goodness is to exist, the world process must begin again ... Physis must be moving upward, or else it is not Physis.
>
> (Murray 1955: 43)

We are part of an Order, a cosmos, which we see to be infinitely above our comprehension ... But in the rest of the world, we can see a moving Purpose. It is Phusis [Physis], the word which the Romans unfortunately translated 'Nature', but which means 'growing' or 'the way things grow' — almost what we call Evolution. But to the Stoic it is a living and conscious evolution ... The direction was towards the perfection of each thing or species after its own kind ... If a man is an artist, it is his function to produce beauty.

> Or if one is a bootmaker — to make good boots. On the Day of Judgement it hardly matters whether you made good boots, or you're chic, or fat or starving. But it matters that you were doing it well.
>
> (ibid.: 126)

(And the same goes for counsellors, psychoanalysts and psychotherapists.)

TRANSPERSONAL PSYCHOTHERAPY IN PRACTICE

Sad to say, clients have not been highly regarded in most therapeutic systems. Called maladjusted, disturbed, regressed, neurotic, psychotic and character-disordered (to name just a few of the terms used), a reasonable person might conclude that therapists have nothing good to recount about the very people who support their livelihoods. This is no fault of therapists, but it does strongly speak to the professions' traditions. As Held (1991) pointedly observed, 'most theories of therapy are, in reality theories of psychopathology ... No matter how many unfavourable ways clients are classified in professional discourse, the practice of therapy is not about nosology. It is about change' (quoted in Hubble et al. 1999: 409).

Building on and applying the wisdom of therapy's most influential scholars, Duncan and others (in ibid.: 427) view the client's theory as containing most, if not all of the trappings of any psychological theory. It encompasses aetiology, treatment and prognosis, and includes clients' thoughts, attitudes and feelings about their problems and how therapy may best address their goals. They view the client's theory of change as not only having the values that most affect the client's participation in therapy but also as holding the keys to success despite the method or technique used by the therapist.

There is a story of a Zen master who was found scrabbling on the pavement under a streetlight in the dirt. 'What are you looking for master?', asked a passer-by. 'I'm looking for my key', said the Teacher. Many more passers-by joined him in looking for his key. After some hours someone asked: 'Are you sure you lost your key here Master?'. The Master said: 'No, I lost it in my house.' 'So why are you out here looking for your key?' The teacher said: 'Because there's more light here.'

> Just as the discovery of Deinonychus [a dinosaur] dramatically changed how dinosaurs were viewed, converging empirical evidence − regarding the importance of clients and their perceptions to positive outcome − is transforming how clients are treated and therapy is conducted. Specifically, the shift is encompassing changes in perspective from (a) clients are slow-witted plodders (or pathological monsters) to resourceful motivated hunters of more satisfying lives; (b) the clinician as the leading character in the drama of therapy to the client as the star of the therapeutic stage; and (c) the omnipotence of the therapist's theory of therapy to the prominence of the client's theory of change.
>
> (ibid.: 425)

Ask the person who had the key to tell you where he lost it.

The following list of possible questions are added to and adapted from Hubble et al., 1999: 410, 412 and 432:

- *What brought you here?*
- *Did you notice any changes before making your first appointment and our first session?*
- *How do you understand your problem?*
- *What do you think will help?*
- *What ideas do you have about what needs to happen for you to get through this stuck place?*
- *Tell me about previous times when you've succeeded in getting through stuck places?*
- *What ideas do you have about what needs to happen for further improvement to occur?*
- *Many times people have a pretty good hunch about not only what is causing a problem, but also what will resolve it. Do you have a theory of how change is going to happen here?*
- *In what ways do you see me and this process being helpful to attaining your goals?*
- *How does change usually happen in your life?*
- *What do you and others do to initiate change?*

- *What was happening at those times? (Obtain a detailed description of what is helping.) What difference will that make to you tomorrow?*
- *How will your day go better? The day after that?*
- *What have you tried to help the problem/situation so far?*
- *Did it help?*
- *How?*
- *What's your idea about why it didn't help in the way you wanted?*
- *Please tell me about a time when you felt confident and secure in yourself?*
- *Who or what helped you then?*
- *How did you do that?*
- *What was different then that you used those resources?*
- *Which people, places or situations do you use to comfort yourself when things are rough?*
- *What will be different when (your anxiety, drinking, feuding with your spouse etc.) is behind you?*
- *What would be the smallest sign that the (_____) is getting better?*
- *What will be the first sign?*
- *When you are no longer (e.g. fighting, in trouble with the law, drinking, etc.), what will you be doing more of instead?*
- *Who will be the first person to notice that you have achieved a victory over this?*
- *What will that person notice different about you that will tell him or her that the victory is achieved?*
- *Where do you suppose you will be when you first notice the change?*
- *What will have happened just before those changes that will have helped them happen?*
- *What will happen later that will help maintain them?*
- *What do you think may go wrong once you leave psychotherapy?*
- *What could we do to prevent that or cope with it in a better way than you did in the past?*

CASE STUDY: THE *CITRINITAS* PHASE — 'THE GREATER DARK NIGHT'; THE I-YOU ENCOUNTER

...Then tragedy struck. '*Citrinitas*' is characterised by the loss of illusions. During the client's annual medical check-up, prostrate cancer was suspected. At first he just couldn't believe it and denied it by not making another doctor's appointment — until I made it a condition if he wanted to keep coming to see me. He was angry with me. Surely it was his right to make decisions about his own life. He should have committed suicide while he was still in control. I was a psychologist. It wasn't me that was dying. Anyway he didn't trust doctors. I held my ground. We started arguing in sessions as often as we did other good work together. But this was also 'good' work. He challenged me about my views on various matters that came up — British intervention in Bosnia, a modern art exhibition, whether adult children should live at home.

The cancer was malignant and fast spreading. He was sinking. Emotionally he became even more depressed than earlier, but now he was also angry, irritable and full of rage. Why had God let this happen to him? Just as he was truly ready for a fulfilling life during his autumn years, a life which had meaning and joy as well as feeling that he could cope with almost anything Life could throw at him. He couldn't cope with this. He felt betrayed. Why now? If he hadn't changed, then perhaps this wouldn't have happened. Or it wouldn't matter so much. Years ago he would have welcomed death — any death; *now was the wrong time.*

He was struggling in quicksand. The more he fought, the deeper he sank. Everybody was to blame — including himself. He should have done this, done that, the coils of a big snake which was suffocating the life out of him. He knew it was unreasonable but couldn't help feeling that I should have warned him. Why had I not warned him? Periods of intense rage interspersed with paralysing depressions — just like Churchill's 'black dog'. Treatment, chemotherapy and radiation were attempted, but failed — although he lost all his hair and several stones in weight. I was angry too and told him so. Alternative therapies were tried and found ineffective. All our good work threatened by death. How cruel life can be. How helpless was I.

The Bible says: 'It rains on the just and the unjust'. It's just not fair. I remembered an old Chinese acupuncturist I once knew. He stuck needles in sick people's bodies, but he was actually a famed spiritual healer in his region — often achieving miraculous cures. But even for him, there were some people he couldn't cure. So, every morning between 4 and 7 a.m. he would burn incense, meditate and offer them up by name to the Divine, yielding the healing and decisional power to whence it came. But I am not that holy all the time. It's only sometimes I feel like that.

Then I remembered Job and the unreasonableness of the Old Testament God. But Isaac, Job and Jonah were delivered in the end! My supervisor told me that in Islam they say: 'Allah has a thousand hearts.' Apparently it means that God can answer our prayers or not. It's a mystery as to why some get favoured and others not, some prayers get answered and others not. WHY? Surely after all the pain and suffering and healing Jeder had gone through, he deserved to live, not die.

I told him a joke: There was a man hanging by his fingernails over a terrible abyss. He couldn't even look down, it was so terrible. So the man shouted: 'Is there anybody out there?' And God answered: 'Yes, my son'. So the man said: 'Please tell me what to do!' And God said: 'Let go my son.' The man considered this for a minute, then he cried out: 'Is there anybody else out there?'. Jeder laughed.

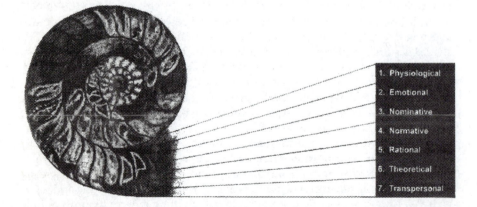

1. Physiological
2. Emotional
3. Nominative
4. Normative
5. Rational
6. Theoretical
7. Transpersonal

References

Atlas, J. (1992) Review of Nicholson Baker's 'Vox'. *Vogue*, March

Bauman, Z. (1993) *Postmodern Ethics*. Oxford: Blackwell

Bohm, D. (1980) *Wholeness and the Implicate Order*. London: Ark

Capra, F. (1976) *The Tao of Physics*. London: Fontana

Capra, F. (1983) *The Turning Point: Science, Society and the Rising Culture*. London: Fontana

Clarkson, P. (1995a) *The Therapeutic Relationship in Psychoanalysis, Counselling Psychology and Psychotherapy*. London: Whurr

Clarkson, P. (1995b) *Change in Organisations*. London: Whurr

Clarkson, P. (1996) *The Byestander (an End to Innocence in Human Relationships)*. London: Whurr

Clarkson, P. (2000) *Ethics: Working with Ethical and Moral Dilemmas in Psychotherapy*. London: Whurr

Clarkson, P. (2002) *The Transpersonal Relationship in Psychotherapy: The Hidden Dimension of Spirituality*. London: Whurr

Cottone, R.R. (1988) Epistemological and ontological issues in counselling: implications of social systems theory. *Counselling Psychology Quarterly* 1 (4): 357–65

de Chardin, T. (1966) *Man's Place in Nature*. London: Collins

de Shazer, S. (1985) *Keys to Solution in Brief Therapy*. New York: Norton

Elliott, S. and Williams, K. L. (1991) Modelling people using cellular slime moulds. *Australian Natural History* 23 (8): 609–16

Field, N. (1996) *Breakdown and Breakthrough*. London: Routledge

Flew, A. (1971) *An Introduction to Western Philosophy*. London: Thames and Hudson

Foulkes, S. H. (1983) *Introduction to Group-analytic Psychotherapy: Studies in the Social Integration of Individuals and Groups*. London: Maresfield (orig. 1948)

Frank, J. D. and Frank, J. B. (1993) *Persuasion and Healing: A Comparative Study of Psychotherapy*. Baltimore: Johns Hopkins University Press

Gleick, J. (1989) *Chaos: Making a New Science*. London: Heinemann

Held, B. S. (1991) The process/content distinction revisited. *Psychotherapy* 28: 207–18

Hubble, M. A., Duncan, B. L. and Miller, S. D. (eds) (1999) *The Heart and Soul of Change: What Works in Therapy*. Washington, D.C.: American Psychological Association

Lovelock, J. (1989) *Gaia: A New Look at Life on Earth*. Oxford: Oxford University Press (orig. 1979)

MacPherson, A. (1992) Does this give God his P45? (interview with P. Davies). *The Mail on Sunday* 26th April: 17

Murray, G. (1955) *Five Stages of Greek Religion*. Garden City, New York: Doubleday Anchor

O'Hara, M. (1991) Horizons of reality: demystifying postmodernism (book review). *Networker* July/August: 71–4

Perls, F., Hefferline, R. and Goodman, P. (1951) *Gestalt Therapy: Excitement and Growth in the Human Personality*. New York: Julian Press

Rinzler, D. (1984) Human disconnection and the murder of the earth. *Transactional Analysis Journal* 14 (4): 231–6

Rogers, C.R. (1986/1951) *Client-centred Therapy: Its Current Practice, Implications and Theory*. London: Constable

Rumi, J. (1991) *One-handed Basketweaving.* Athens, GA: Maypop (versions by C. Barks)
Rycroft, C. (1968) *A Critical Dictionary of Psychoanalysis.* Harmondsworth: Penguin
Shah, I. (1985) *The Exploits of the Incomparable Mulla Nasrudin.* London: Octagon Press
Zohar, D. (1990) *The Quantum Self.* London: Bloomsbury

8

PSYCHOLOGICAL DISTRESS AND POSTMODERN THOUGHT

VIVIEN BURR AND TREVOR BUTT[†]

In recent times, we have witnessed a marked rise in the discovery of numerous psychopathologies and syndromes. A wide variety of psychological difficulties and problems is now recognised as constituting identifiable symptoms or characteristics of syndromes previously unheard of. Premenstrual syndrome (PMS), battered woman syndrome and attention deficit disorder are just some of the disorders lately 'discovered' and offered up for public attention. Alongside this increase in the discovery and categorisation of these types of problems is a parallel rise in the provision of counselling and therapy. Of course, if these syndromes are indeed unmitigated discoveries, the rise in therapy provision is an unambiguous blessing. However, it can be argued that the therapy industry, like any other, creates as well as serves a need.

The proliferation of named syndromes and pathologies, we argue, is part of the more general phenomenon of the *pathologisation of everyday life*. More and more aspects of our lives are becoming problematic. We are now used to feeling and expressing doubt about our performance as parents, as lovers, as workers, and we scrutinise our thoughts and feelings for signs of some developmental flaw, perversion or personal inadequacy. In turn, the problems we reveal to ourselves are viewed as the proper concern of therapists and counsellors.

An important feature of this process of pathologising is its inherent 'psychologisation' — that is, the casting of difficulties and problems into psychological frameworks and therefore locating them at the level of the individual. Once this is achieved, the onus for change and the moral responsibility for the problem are placed upon the person. For example, despite the availability of alternative, more social explanations (e.g. Parton 1985), child abuse continues to be seen as rooted in the pathology of the individual abuser, and not in social and political contexts. Furthermore, dyslexia and some learning disabilities may be seen as socially constructed outcomes of inegalitarian educational systems. Anorexia nervosa, too, may be fruitfully seen as the product of the common, gendered patterns of cultural life. A variety of women's problems in particular may be regarded as constructions that shore up patriarchal society. In each case, locating the problem at the level of the individual draws attention away from the social conditions — poverty, capitalism, patriarchy — which might provide the contextual backdrop that is intrinsic to individual experience.

---

† This chapter first appeared in Fee, D. (ed.) (1999) *Pathology and the Postmodern: Mental Illness as Discourse and Experience.* London: Sage, and is reprinted with kind permission of the authors and publishers.

In addition, this psychologisation is often implicitly reductionist, frequently appealing to biological elements as the 'real' underlying causes. For example, in disparate circles, genetic coding has recently been suggested as the cause of schizophrenia, alcoholism, criminality and, once again, homosexuality. Such reductionism has considerable implications for the individual, who is often caught in various contradictions and double binds when conceptualising and treating his or her condition.

It is not our intention to suggest that the problems and distress experienced by people are illusory. We may be doing no more than recognising as patterned and systematic the problems and distress that have always been experienced by people. Or it may *really* be the case that psychological difficulties of one kind or another are on the increase in contemporary Western societies. After all, a social causation view of mental illness has been convincingly argued. Social isolation and poverty have long been found to predict greater incidence of schizophrenia (Faris and Dunham 1939), and Brown and Harris (1978) have shown how poverty can lead to depressive illness. Perhaps intense stress and illness do result from the particularly complicated lives we lead within contemporary social structures.

Nevertheless, regardless of whether and why psychological distress might be on the increase, it is our contention that social constructionism can go beyond the question of causation through examining the conditions under which experiences themselves become constructed as 'problems' in particular instances. Such analysis places the psychologisation and pathologisation of everyday life into a broader historical analysis of cultural change and social control. Furthermore, it invites us to see counselling and therapy as possibly complicit in the construction of the psychological problems that they have been called upon to address.

Social constructionists are of course not the first to question psychological and medical accounts of distress. Those associated with labelling theory (Goffman 1961; Rosenhan 1973; Scheff 1966) maintained that, under certain social conditions, non-normative or deviant behaviour comes to be seen as a symptom of mental illness. The person is thus labelled as 'mentally ill' — a label which then determines how future behaviour will be perceived and addressed. This label is internalised by the person, whose identity and behaviour become defined by his or her illness — a process Wilkins (1971) refers to as 'deviancy amplification'.

Furthermore, mental health industries have previously come under attack from various directions. Proponents of the anti-psychiatry movement in Britain and North America such as Laing (1959, 1967) and Szasz (1961, 1970, 1971) were highly critical of the personal and political intrusiveness of psychiatry. Szasz argues that psychiatry inappropriately adopted the metaphor of illness as a way of framing unacceptable behaviour. He draws a distinction between real, physical illness (disease) and mental illness, which he regards as simply deviations from moral and ethical norms. Szasz, however, has no specific objection to contractual psychotherapy — that is, therapy undertaken by people freely and volitionally. Sedgwick (1982), on the other hand, is in some ways nearer to contemporary social constructionist views, since he regards all illness, whether physical or mental, as social constructions having no objectively definable ontological basis. However, he regards the illness metaphor, or the 'sick role', as a facilitative one for the person suffering psychological distress.

Current social constructionist attention to mental health and psychotherapy issues (e.g. Parker et al. 1995) has often been heavily influenced by Foucault, and has involved a renewed radical questioning of the values and practice of the mental health professions. We believe that a broadly Foucauldian framework can fruitfully be used to understand the increasing psychologisation and pathologisation of everyday life just described. However, we shall argue that such an understanding demands that we do more than simply question the desirability of therapy and counselling: it requires that we both reassess the status of individual distress, and strive to develop more appropriate conceptions of therapy and counselling.

THERAPY AND DISCIPLINARY POWER

Foucauldian analyses of mental illness and the contemporary mental health professions have often drawn upon the historical account given by Foucault in *Madness and Civilization* (1965). However, in our argument we will draw directly upon Foucault's later work (1976, 1977) and upon Rose (1989, 1990), who uses a similar style of analysis. These perspectives are organised around the concepts of discipline, supervision, confession, normalisation and the individual.

The rise of discipline
Foucault argues that demographic change and changes in the mode of production in the eighteenth century brought about a radical shift in the organisation and management of the population, especially at work. First, there was an increase in the size of the population, with consequent problems in housing and public health and, more specifically, an increase in the floating population – those persons who in various ways were pursuing a nomadic existence. Secondly, there was the growth and development of the capitalist mode of production, which was becoming more difficult and more costly to manage. Foucault argues that these two problems – the population changes, and the need to organise production more efficiently and profitably – could not be addressed by the existing cumbersome feudal arrangements. Instead, they were effectively managed by the broad adoption of *discipline* as a form of social organisation and practice.

'Discipline' organises, structures and categorises human activity by the use of timetables and hierarchies; increases the differentiation of tasks (divisions of labour); and makes specific use of supervision and surveillance to ensure the smooth running of the whole. Through these means, the factory, the military, the school and the hospital alike ensured the docility, control and productivity of individuals within them. In addition, the use of hierarchical structures with clear distinctions between one category of person and another, for example by rank or job status, ensured that the opportunities for solidarity among individuals were minimal, thus reducing the risk of resistance or revolt:

> That is why discipline fixes; it arrests or regulates movements; it clears up confusion; it dissipates compact groupings of individuals wandering about the country in unpredictable ways; it establishes calculated distributions. It must also master all the forces that we formed from the very constitution of an organised multiplicity; it must neutralize the effects of counterpower that spring from them and which form a resistance to the power that wishes to dominate it: agitations, revolts, spontaneous organizations, coalitions – anything that may establish horizontal conjunctions.
>
> (Foucault 1977: 219)

Disciplinary power

For Foucault, the supervisory and surveillance features of discipline mark an important shift in the exercise of power and in social control. He sees this shift as a move away from the use of what he calls 'sovereign power' to the much more effective and efficient 'disciplinary power'. Sovereign power operated through the threat of what the sovereign (or the sovereign's representative) could do to the person who infringed the law, but as a form of social control it was inadequate to deal with the increasing size and complexity of the changing Western societies of the eighteenth century. By contrast, disciplinary power operates through the voluntary subjection of people to the regulations and norms of the hierarchical institutions that they inhabit: it is literally *self*-discipline.

The control and regulation of persons, whether in the factory, the army or the school, are characterised by a proliferation of rules governing required behaviour and their reciprocal punishments and rewards. But the effects of surveillance make the person effectively self-regulatory. This is epitomised by the invention of Bentham's Panopticon, a circular prison which houses the prisoners in cells around the periphery, where they can be watched by a single guard placed at the centre. The Panopticon's efficiency and innovation is that prisoners — who live with the constant knowledge that their behaviour might at any moment be scrutinised — come to internalise 'the gaze' of the guard and thus incorporate this monitoring and control into their own selves. Disciplinary power is therefore a feature not only of prisons but of all institutions and organisations which control their members through hierarchies, divisions, norms and surveillance. It could be argued that disciplinary power has infiltrated modern societies to such an extent that no one is beyond its reach. Some writers (Parker et al. 1995; Sarup 1988) even see Panopticism at work in the organisation of cyberspace and the computer monitoring of individuals.

Confession

This self-surveillance and self-discipline develops and is perpetuated through various practices that can essentially be seen as 'confession'. In the Middle Ages, monks were required to control their sinful desires by confession — a detailed recollection and description of sinful deeds, words and thoughts. At this time, confession was not widespread amongst the general population, but during the seventeenth century it expanded greatly in the Catholic Church, and ordinary people were required regularly to examine their behaviour and desires — especially those of a sexual nature — and to confess them.

In the context of the increasing need to regulate the population, the confessional played a central role in the construction and emergence of numerous categories of sexual abnormality and perversion. Self-scrutiny and surveillance through the confessional could channel the sexual behaviour and desires of the population along lines favourable to the effective management and regulation of society. Thus, birth rates, age of marriage, legitimacy or illegitimacy of births and so on could be effectively controlled through self-discipline and confession. Rose (1989) points out that with the rise of Protestantism, the confessional came to be replaced by *self*-inspection, since the person has the right to make him- or herself accountable to God, without the mediating actions or directions of priests or confessors.

The trend towards categorisation, scrutiny, surveillance and self-inspection continued and expanded, so that in the nineteenth century it took the form of a burgeoning sexology literature. This represented a proliferation in the classifications and divisions of sexual normality and abnormality, the detailing of perversions, and the endless dividing and sub-dividing of categories of sexual dysfunction. Foucault argues that the modern-day gatekeepers of this knowledge are no longer the clergy, but doctors, psychiatrists, psychologists, therapists and other mental health practitioners. These are the people for whom we are now required to inspect and scrutinise our actions, wants and secrets, and to whom we confess them. Confession has thus become a way of life:

> The confession has spread its effects far and wide. It plays a part in justice, medicine, education, family relationships, and love relations, in the most ordinary affairs of everyday life, and in the most solemn rites; one confesses one's crimes, one's sins, one's thoughts and desires, one's illnesses and troubles; one goes about telling, with the greatest precision, whatever is most difficult to tell. One confesses in public and in private, to one's parents, one's educators, one's doctor, to those one loves; one admits to oneself, in pleasure and in pain, things it would be impossible to tell to anyone else, the things people write books about ... Western man has become a confessing animal.
>
> (Foucault 1976: 59)

Normalisation

The effectiveness of disciplinary power lies in the fact that it relies not upon coercion but on the willingness — even desire — of people to submit to it. It is invisible in its workings, since signs of conflict or resistances do not betray it. The rewards for submitting oneself to disciplinary power are inherent in the system of hierarchical organisation and regulation itself. The different ranks, statuses and divisions of inmates in the military, schools, hospitals and prisons form the conditions for an extensive set of rules, norms and expectations attached to each position. As a member of a category or holder of a particular status, one becomes subject to a set of normative expectations of conduct, thought, dress and so on. Adherence to these brings acceptance and validation from others, as well as, importantly, confirming to the person that he or she is reassuringly average or normal:

> Like surveillance and with it, normalisation becomes one of the great instruments of power at the end of the classical age. For the marks that once indicated status, privilege and affiliation were increasingly replaced — or at least supplemented — by a whole range of degrees of normality indicating membership of a homogeneous social body but also playing a part in classification, hierarchy, and the distribution of rank. In a sense, the power of normalisation imposes homogeneity; but it individualises by making it possible to measure gaps, to determine levels, to fix specialties, and to render the differences useful by fitting them one to another.
>
> (Foucault 1977: 184)

The 'examination' is a key concept for Foucault. It captures all the factors of scrutiny, surveillance, judgement and normalisation that he sees as central to modern disciplinary power, and demonstrates — through its use in widely differing contexts such as the doctor's consulting room and the school-room — the degree of infiltration of such practices into everyday life.

Such normalising practices are not only the preserve of institutions such as schools and the military. Disciplines such as Psychology have had a major role to play in extending this normalisation to more and more areas of life. A great part of the business of psychologists has explicitly involved developing measures of various human capacities, generating the means or 'technologies' through which individuals can be compared with one another and with the average or norm. This began with the development of tests of intelligence, but psychometrics soon included a multitude of aspects of personality, masculinity and femininity, attitudes and so on:

> The power of psychology lay in its promise to provide inscription devices that would individualise such troublesome subjects, rendering the human soul into thought in the form of calculable traces. Its contribution lay in the invention of diagnostic categories, evaluations, assessments, and tests that constructed the subjective in a form in which it could be represented in classifications, in figures and quotients. The psychological test was the first such device.
>
> (Rose 1990: 109)

Furthermore, this trend has not stopped at the boundaries of academic psychology. The appeal of the normal distribution is such that it has reached a wide audience through media, such as magazines which often feature quizzes and questionnaires inviting readers to assess their own personalities in some way.

The individual
The rise of the modern individual is intimately connected with the processes of normalisation and confession. Rose (1989) argues that the act of confession — whether to doctors, therapists, teachers, parents or lovers — produces the subjectivity and sense of self that is fundamental to our concept of the individual (cf. Rose's Chapter 4, this volume). The person *becomes* an individual through this process. We confess, and the other consoles, understands and judges: more than being subjectified by the other, we become subjects for ourselves. The very act of describing and speaking of the self simultaneously *creates* it as an object for inspection: 'In the act of speaking, through the obligation to produce words that are true to an inner reality, through the self-examination that precedes and accompanies speech, one becomes a subject for oneself' (Rose 1989: 240).

Rose argues that confession also involves an incitement to self-regulation according to some moral code. The self must be monitored, tested and improved. With specific reference to psychotherapy, Rose states that

> psychotherapeutics is linked at a profound level to the socio-political obligations of the modern self. The self it seeks to liberate or restore is the entity able to steer its individual path through life by means of the act of personal decision and the assumption of personal responsibility
>
> (ibid.: 253–4)

So, through the combined forces of discipline, normalisation and confession, the modern individual emerges as a person having a sense of self, a sense of difference from other selves, and a conviction of moral responsibility for that selfhood.

The social construction of everyday pathology

The argument here is that the 'discovery' and isolating of syndromes and pathologies — and the provision of therapy and counselling as a response — is the latest phase in a long process of the development of disciplinary power in Western societies that has been going on at least since the eighteenth century. The practice of confession has been passed down to those experts and professionals — psychiatrists, psychologists, psychotherapists and counsellors, among others — who are thought to be the appropriate monitors of our psychological well-being. Foucault (1977) referred to all the sciences having the prefix psy- or psycho- as the 'psy-complex,' and argued that they are all fundamentally concerned with the supervision, monitoring and regulation of individual functioning. Through the constant incitement to confess, our sense of ourselves as individuals is to some degree created and maintained. Images of normal sexuality, relationships, parenting, family life, social adjustment, and so on, surround us: and the social sciences have provided us with every means of inspecting and assessing ourselves — of comparing ourselves to others and to the norm, and of finding ourselves wanting.

The moral obligations to inspect, regulate and improve one's self set us on a path to a goal we can perhaps never achieve. As Rose writes, 'the self that is liberated is obliged to live its life tied to the project of its own identity' (1989: 254). This project — this search for the truth about ourselves, the search for the autonomous self — is carried out in what Rose calls the 'passage through the therapeutic'. He argues that many popular therapies have this search at their root, in one form or another. The Client-Centred Therapy of Carl Rogers, for example, exhorts the person to drop façades, to accept his or her own feelings, to cherish close relationships, and to move towards more intimacy and openness. Gestalt therapy seeks to recover wholeness, to find growth and maturity, to develop the person, to become oneself; while self-direction and self-control are the aims of Transactional Analysis. The task is to discover who we 'really are,' and to believe that the attainment of that goal is in our own hands.

This passage through the therapeutic, however, is not confined to the private consulting room. Many encounters may take alternative therapeutic forms, such as the interview with the personnel officer, the ward group of the psychiatric hospital, or even the radio phone-in:

> Psychotherapeutic language and advice extends beyond the consultation, the interview, the appointment: it has become a part of the staple fare of the mass media of communication, in the magazine advice column and in documentaries and discussions on television. No financial exchange need be involved, for on live radio phone-in programs we may confess our most intimate problems for free and have them instantly analysed — or eavesdrop on the difficulties that so many of our fellow citizens appear to have conducting the business of their lives.
>
> (ibid.: 214)

Psychotherapy has thus extended its gaze into hitherto unexplored corners of our lives, which Rose describes by four processes: *the subjectification of work*, whereby our working lives have become suffused with issues of identity and personal fulfilment; *the psychologisation of the mundane*, whereby routine daily life has been transformed into a series of life events which need to be analysed, understood, managed; *a therapeutics of finitude*, whereby all kinds of loss and frustration become reframed as healthy or potentially pathological; and *a 'neuroticisation' of social intercourse*, in which our relationships (and in particular their deficits) are seen as the roots of many personal and social ills. (Cf. Rose's Chapter 4, this volume.)

The rise in the therapy and counselling industries, then, can be seen as an expansion of the activities of the psy-complex; and the problems and pathologies to which these industries are being addressed are part of that very expansion. Confessor and confessant together — through surveillance, psychologisation and normalisation — ensure the voluntary regulation and social control of the population. As more areas of our lives become psychologised — framed in terms of our private skills, capabilities, traits, desires, repressions, attitudes — there is a correspondingly greater potential for dissatisfaction and distress in our lives. We want to be 'normal' — a term that has latterly acquired a meaning more akin to 'healthy'. Thus, in recent times, the desire to be normal is utilised as a claim to psychological health and well-being.

Social constructions, personal lives

Although the power of such social constructionist arguments may be convincing, they leave us in a problematic position. We may agree that the myriad of syndromes, pathologies and neuroses affecting us are socially constructed, and that the therapists and counsellors to whom we appeal for help are the (albeit unwitting) figureheads of an extensive system of social control through disciplinary power. Nevertheless, the distress and misery experienced by people, framed though it is in terms of personal inadequacy and pathology, cannot be ignored, morally or empirically.

Although providing often brilliant historical analyses of contemporary life, writers such as Foucault and Rose have not broached the issue of what our response, if any, should be at the level of the individual. Indeed, post-structuralist analyses have tended to regard the level of the social or of 'discourse' as the only appropriate one. These approaches have described what is termed the 'death of the subject', and have invalidated attempts to analyse phenomena at the level of the individual, which is itself revealed as a social construction (Kitzinger 1992; Sampson 1990). The 'strong' constructionist approach of Foucault suggests that all this psychopathology is a production of society. Indeed, the individual agent is an invention of the Enlightenment. Through the medium of language, we have invented the self and encouraged introspection by developing a vocabulary of confession.

The writings of Foucault have been criticised by Sedgwick (1982) and Habermas (1986) on the grounds of their anti-humanism. Walzer (1986) adds that it is impossible to see what Foucault envisages as an alternative to the rise in disciplinary power he attacks. On the face of it, he appears to advocate any local resistance that neutralises discipline, but elsewhere criticises those prison reformers who follow the implications of his argument. He is, in fact, unimpressed with any alternatives at all, believing that to envisage any alternatives is merely to participate in the present system along with its disciplinary power that he abhors.

Rorty (1989) endorses these criticisms. Like Habermas and Walzer, he wants to give more credit to democratic societies, and sees disciplinary power as better for humankind than sovereign power. His view is that the rise in disciplinary power, with all its restraints, is more than compensated for by the decrease in pain and suffering that ensues. Unlike modernist critics, however, he applauds what he terms Foucault's 'ironism'. The ironist is a person who accepts that all their views and beliefs — including their most cherished values — are in the end constructions, accepting that their starting-point is always historically and socially contingent. There is nothing deep inside us except that which is laid down through social processes; and there is no intrinsic human nature: the self and subject are indeed social productions. Unlike Foucault, Rorty thinks that the modern subject, encumbered as s/he is with self-examination and self-criticism, is better off than the pre-modern one. He agrees with much of Foucault's analysis, but believes that it leaves us paralysed and without hope. What is needed, perhaps, is an understanding of how people are constructed as sufferers and recoverers, and what can be done to help them.

Our argument here is that therapy and counselling do not in any simple way create problems, as a Foucault-inspired analysis might claim. Disciplinary power may, as Rorty asserts, have produced better citizens. The self-reflective person should be more aware of the rights of both him- or herself and others. However, therapeutic vocabularies have over-sensitised people to their faults and misfortunes, and helped them to be defined as such — and this must be addressed. In order to do so, we need a psychology which takes a broadly social constructionist theoretical framework, but which at the same time allows us legitimately to address the experience of the contemporary individual. However, this examination of psychological experience must be done without sliding back into a modernist search for essentialist truths.

A POSTMODERN PSYCHOLOGY

Rorty (1989) generally equates a postmodern position with an ironical stance. He identifies two strands of ironists in philosophy: American pragmatists like James and Dewey, and European existentialists like Nietzsche and Heidegger. In the sketch of a postmodern psychology that follows, we will draw on a number of psychologists who reflect these two traditions in some way. We have found the ideas of personal construct theorists and existentialists to be particularly rich. Our aim is to outline the main features of a postmodern psychology, and to show how it can conceptualise the experience of psychopathology in helpful ways. We will contrast modernist and postmodernist understandings of psychopathology using the four interrelated themes that Polkinghorne (1992) identifies as characterising postmodern thought.

Foundationlessness
Modernist approaches presuppose an objective world that we come to know through the expansion of scientific knowledge. Academic psychology seeks indisputable truths about humankind that often transcend time and culture. Rorty (1982a) applauds the aims of the Enlightenment project, with its intention to free humankind from the prevailing religious dogma and to replace it with a humanist ethic and scientific inquiry. But science, too, can enshrine a dogma, and people come to expect it to rescue them in the same way that God was once supposed to.

In contrast, postmodern thought emphasises the local and contextual nature of knowledge. There is no universal human nature to be discovered. We have no original sin, nor are we basically good beings who violate their basic nature when cruel to others. Our values are laid down by society, and the nuggets of truth psychologists have collected, like Oedipal feelings and actualising tendencies, only reflect local moral orders, and not human essences. Accordingly, language is no longer seen as a transparent medium used to describe the objective world. Indeed, even the term 'medium' is seen as misleading. It is not something used to express the thoughts and feelings of some deep, inner self, but a tool with which we constitute the world. Rorty (1989) cautions us that we should never assume we have reached a final description of the world; we can never speak 'nature's own language'. The world may be 'out there', but truth is not. 'Truth' comprises descriptions of the world, and anything can be re-described; everything is changed through re-description, and can be made to look either good or bad.

Earlier concepts of mental illness saw constitutional factors and individual temperament as reasons for illness. In the re-descriptions of life offered by the current objective, reality-orientated scientific knowledges of stress and abuse, blame is shifted to the environment. To define one's self as 'abused' or 'neurotic' is not to arrive at a value-free description; it is to take a new perspective on events, to reconstrue them. To 'get in touch with your feelings' today is not a matter of discovering a truth that was not clear yesterday. In the therapeutic encounter, Kelly (1969b) contends that 'insights' occur when the client adopts the perspective or story of the therapist. Indeed, he was suspicious of insight and of the truth it was supposed to herald, and claimed that it is what the client is left with when stripped of his or her imagination (ibid.: 347).

Fragmentariness

The Enlightenment project encouraged a search for an ordered and unified view of the world. In psychology, this has led to the metaphor of 'depth' of a person. In psychoanalysis, which is predominantly a structural and modernist approach, 'deeper' and invisible layers of the person are seen as incorporating more truthful statements about him or her. 'Surface' behaviours are caused by deeper unconscious motives. When 'in touch with our feelings', we have discovered the causes of our affects and behaviours. A postmodern approach to psychology sees depth as merely a spatial metaphor applied to the person; and the attribution of causality to deeper layers is seen as misleading.

Modernist thought penetrates our everyday thinking when we 'discover' how we 'really feel' about someone or something. Perhaps we find that we are in love with someone, or that there is something fundamentally wrong with our current relationship. Object-relations theory (see Bott-Spillius 1988), a dominant variant of psychoanalysis, sees ambivalence towards our objects as resulting in 'splitting', a defensive manoeuvre to avoid anxiety. Although used to some extent by everyone, it carries overtones of psychopathology. 'Splitting' implies an ego that was naturally whole to begin with, and 'defence' assumes a deep or core self that is being defended, presumably, at some cost.

Postmodern thought accepts and even celebrates plurality. The spirit of 'both/and' rather than 'either/or' predominates, without a need to reconcile what we *really* think or feel. The rhetorical model of humankind proposed by Billig (1991) shows how we take up positions in argument in response to the positions adopted by others. We may appear as radicals to our parents and conservatives to our friends as we position ourselves in discursive space. Potter and Wetherell (1987) demonstrate how the same person can produce both apparently racist and anti-racist opinions, and thus how the concept of 'attitude' lying somehow behind our behaviour does not explain our deeds and actions. Similarly, persons take up different positions with respect to their own lives: 'Are you *really* happy in your marriage?'; 'Is your life empty?'. The meaning of such questions becomes unstable and contingent, as there is no static, fundamental layer of experience to be contacted.

From an existentialist perspective, Spinelli (1995) suggests that we think of consciousness as having vertical splits in it rather than horizontal ones. Psychoanalysis proposed horizontal splitting, with conscious material at a surface level repressed into deeper unconscious levels where it motivates surface behaviour. Following Sartre (1958), Spinelli proposes that we do not need the concept of repression, that unconscious material was never conscious in the first place. Our action in the world is naturally pre-reflective, or unconscious, and is only made conscious through reflection and the use of language. Like Fingarette (1969), he sees consciousness as a skill, an ability to spell things out. However, a person may be not only unable but also unwilling to spell something out, since doing so may produce a conflict of feelings or interests. This is dissociation rather than repression. Vertical schisms in consciousness endow no single fragment with inherent importance. In narrative terms, we could see this process as an ability or willingness to elaborate a particular story-line. Coaxers and available media may facilitate the telling of a certain story: 'Once I loved my parents, but now I realise they abused me'; 'I thought I was happy in my marriage, but now I realise I am unfulfilled'. Alternative stories lead parallel lives, and there is no final and truthful story or account of our selves or our experience.

Once we have spelled out and committed ourselves to a new story, it often acquires the status of an insight, and yesterday's tale seems like a self-deception. The theme of foundationlessness insists that there is no story that ever captures the whole truth. Perhaps we are never so dangerous — both to others and ourselves — as when we are certain, when we crusade, when we are utterly convinced by our own case.

Constructivism
Modernist psychologies posit an objective world that is revealed to us through our senses. There is a split between this objective world and our subjective reality, which mirrors the objective world in consciousness. Postmodern thought proposes that we will never be able to penetrate 'the real' with our imperfect perceptions and constructions. Although we have no basic human nature in terms of content, we are naturally sense-making beings, who interpret events and confer meanings upon things. The perceived world is not a more or less perfect replica of objective reality; we produce constructions that serve our purposes and help us in our projects.

This stance echoes the work of the existential phenomenologists, who prefer to talk of 'the lived world' rather than the objective world and subjective representations of it. Merleau-Ponty's *Phenomenology of Perception* (1962) is an attempt to show that neither empiricism nor intellectualism — the research programmes of realism and idealism, respectively — can succeed in understanding human beings. Although radically different from each other, they both commit the error of positing an objective world that is entirely separate from a disembodied *cogito* that attempts to represent it in consciousness. We cannot understand the lived world through this dualism. The world we experience is *between* subject and object: it is both made and found. Similarly, here there is an emphasis on the interpersonal rather than the *intra*personal; it is the interaction *between* people — the conversations, the gestures and symbols, and the negotiated accounts — that should be psychology's starting point. Kvale (1992) comments that Merleau-Ponty's psychology was in many ways a forerunner of postmodern thought, and for 50 years was marginalised within mainstream psychology.

Shotter (1992), building on Merleau-Ponty's analysis, addresses the realism/constructionism issue in comparing empirical and hermeneutic methodologies. On the one hand, realism has produced an empirical method of investigation; it is affordances in the world that allow us to talk about that world in certain ways. Our ways of representing it are grounded in nature. On the other, idealism, in its current guise of textualism (see Rorty 1982b), advocates a hermeneutic method. Here, our ways of talking about the world determine what we will find there. Shotter argues that, paradoxically, we must assert that both of these competing claims are true. We are limited both by events in the world and by our constructions of them. Indeed, following Derrida (1978), he claims that each approach — couched as it is within a systematic discourse — gives credibility to the other through its absent presence.

So we make our worlds, but what we can make is always regulated by what the world affords, which exerts a resistance to our constructions. Individual psychopathologies are both found and made. An interesting illustration might come from the perception of body odour. We can imagine that a century ago, most people smelled strongly. Now, with the advent of plumbing, central heating and, moreover, an industry devoted to clean, fresh fragrances, we have the opportunity and the motivation to present ourselves as odour-free. We readily identify and are repelled by body smells. This has been accompanied by a general sensitisation to smells. Just a decade or two ago, the smell of cigarette smoke was everywhere. Now it is seen not only as a threat, but also as offensive, and associated with disease and ill-health. This sensitisation surely represents both the making and the finding of a problem; the smells are there, but they always have been. Like a palate becoming educated to the taste of fine wine through a language rich with metaphor, the language of smells becomes elaborated to pick out what was once merely background. Similarly, we have become sensitised to our feelings, our inner lives, our psychological states. The discourse in which it is elaborated is primarily psychiatric/psychological. The modernist framework of psychoanalysis has been exported into everyday life, with its notion of a deep unconscious and early hidden traumata that are responsible for current unhappiness.

Polkinghorne (1992) makes the point that these three themes together — foundationlessness, fragmentation, constructivism — comprise a negative epistemology. They appear to call into doubt — even to scorn — humanitarian advances occasioned by the Enlightenment. The charge of relativism or perspectivism, where, in the absence of a truth standard, one perspective seems as valid as any other, has been made against postmodern approaches (Burman 1990; Parker 1992; also see Hollinger 1994). It is Polkinghorne's fourth theme, 'neo-pragmatism', which makes for an affirmative aspect to postmodern thought. If the three themes leave us with no criteria for action in the world, pragmatism provides this purchase.

Pragmatism

Following William James, Rorty (1989) defines truth in terms of 'what is good by way of belief'. In our imperfect construction of reality, we can never assume that we have arrived at a final and definitive description of it. We can never use nature's own vocabulary. It is a mistake to think that the world will constrain us into speaking the truth. A real world exists independent of us, but constructions of it are our property, our responsibility.

Kelly (1955) built his psychology of personal constructs on what he called the philosophical position of 'constructive alternativism'. This holds that there is no ultimately correct way of construing anything, and constructions cannot be evaluated in terms of their truth. Yet one perspective is *not* as good as another. Some ways are certainly more useful than others; and what makes them more or less useful is their ability to help us to anticipate the world, to beat the world to the punch. This pragmatic principle accepts that any construing has to take into account a 'real world' of events; you cannot whimsically make anything you want of things. Yet events in the world are never perceived in the raw, so to speak: they are always served up, 'cooked' by our constructions.

Our constructions, then, are to be judged not in terms of their truth, against some answer in the back of nature's book, but in terms of their usefulness. Does a particular vocabulary help us in our project, or is a new one called for? Is an atom best conceived of as a particle or a wave when we have a particular aim in view? It doesn't matter that two incompatible pictures of reality result from these conceptions. From a pragmatist stance, we should not ask whether a particular theory is correct. A more interesting question is: does this theory do its job?

Too often, the dominant stories of psychopathology do not do the job. For one, they can reduce people to helpless victims. Van Deurzen-Smith (1994) points out that the concept of sexual abuse is now used so widely that it makes it more difficult to focus on those real and dreadful cases of abuse that need urgent attention. If it is true, she writes, that one-third of women have been sexually abused by the age of 18, then 'abuse' has been defined so broadly as to become meaningless. Certainly, people who feel abused need understanding and recognition for the distress caused to them; but this is only part of the therapeutic task. The pragmatic approach would pay less attention to syndrome-criteria, and — emphasising the practical context of action — more to the meanings that would allow the individual to create new action-possibilities.

Kelly (1969a) recommends that we apply philosopher Hans Vaihinger's 'as if' philosophy in psychology. The indicative mood in our language shapes our thinking and leads us to confuse things in the world with our constructions of them. For example, I conclude that I am an introvert, suffering from stress, unable to form close intimate relationships. Instead, Kelly advocates the use of an 'invitational mood' that makes our constructions explicit and highlights their pragmatic value. Suppose I construe myself as if I were oppressed, abused or stressed — or, perhaps, as resilient, able to resist, or empathise with others under oppression. The casting of language in the invitational mood leaves people open to extend themselves — elaborating possibilities, instead of being stuck in unhelpful definitions which make them impermeable to change. The over-emphasis on *definition* is what Sartre (1958) criticises as living in bad faith. His insistence that we must recognise our freedom is, of course, not a denial of how circumstances in the world impose limits upon us. But, following from Kelly, we are free to reconfigure that which we cannot deny.

We will now return to the issue of the experience of psychopathology, and show how narrative psychology — which broadly draws upon the four features outlined above — can be used to understand the proliferation in psychopathology as it is manifested at the level of the individual.

NARRATIVE AND THE APPROPRIATION OF PSYCHOPATHOLOGY BY INDIVIDUALS

We naturally 'story' our experience. The constructivist approach sees the person as putting together events in a way that makes sense to him or her. So in remembering the past, we do not simply recall events as they happened; rather, we selectively recall, narrating a story of the past that makes sense to us. The 'facts' of the past are not like mushrooms, waiting to be collected; they are picked out within shifting narrative searchlights. When a new story emerges, new facts are remembered. Sarbin (1986) has made a convincing case that narrative 'emplotment' is ordinarily used by people to read meaning into events confronting them. Once we have adopted the tales of, say, abuse, events from the past suddenly make sense within this story. Memory is thus not a simple matter of accuracy, but one of construing afresh in the present. As Kelly (1955) contended, the person is not determined by his or her autobiography, but rather by the way he or she writes it.

Story-telling is not a simple individual-level phenomenon, however. The stories we inhabit belong to a particular time and social context. Plummer (1995) considers the proliferation of 'sexual stories' in late modernity, and why it is that a particular type of story appears to 'have its time'. Following the symbolic interactionism of Blumer (1969), he argues that stories are good examples of 'joint action' — they are not principally individual productions. Though they require a basis in the lives of tellers, they also need encouragement and the articulation of others to produce them. It is also necessary to have audiences willing to accept them, and perhaps recognise their own experiences within them. The psychopathological stories of stress, abuse and survival tell not only of lived experience — the traces in individuals' lives that are woven into narratives — but also of therapists who 'coax' them, and 'readers' who accept them as plausible.

White and Epston (1990) point out that in 'storying' our experience, we have to draw on the discourses available to us. Following Foucault (1980), they suggest that these discourses will reflect those 'objective,' scientific knowledges that make universal truth-claims. Here, White and Epston are referring to the power/ knowledge coupling, a site where the therapy industry now figures prominently. The complaints presented to therapists are, expectedly, couched in therapeutic languages (often before any tangible encounter), validating and reproducing therapeutic discourses — a process similar to what Gergen (1989) calls the 'warranting voice of therapy.'

Therapy is the child of Enlightenment-based Psychiatry and Psychology, and its stories often reflect interventionist narratives of illness and passivity. The very term 'patient' means one who passively suffers. The 'patient's' experience is one of discovery rather than invention: he or she 'now realises' that s/he has been abused, suffers from stress, has this or that syndrome. From the modern, realist world-view, one would evaluate memories and realisations in terms of their truth-value: 'Was she really abused by her father?'; 'Am I really suffering from depression?'.

A constructivist account, by contrast, would see these revelations as constructed narratives, an inseparable mixture of construction and event. They have been subject to what Spence (1986) terms 'narrative smoothing': facts that fit the new theory or story emerge and are reinterpreted; those that do not are forgotten. Accounts must therefore be judged in terms of narrative truth rather than historical truth. Within narrative theory, mental illness becomes a framework in which to interpret experience, rather than the surface expression of real underlying disease entities. The 'patients' have used the prevailing vocabulary of illness to weave together their stories. From our standpoint, to ask about the truth of these stories is to ask a silly question: rather, one should ask whether these stories make sense. Do they do justice to the person's experience?; And are they helpful to people?; Can going over the past, examining their relationships, wondering what is wrong with them, lead to their living their lives in a more satisfactory way?

Many modernist tales, with their assumptions of progress and emancipation through scientific discovery, see therapy as empowering in this way. Where there was id, there shall be ego; where once we were driven, we shall take up the reins of our lives. Through insight and reflection, we will become the masters of our own ships. Although notoriously difficult to evaluate, meta-studies of therapy effectiveness show a definite therapeutic effect (Smith and Glass 1977) — but there seems to be a high price to pay. We have a proliferation of syndromes from which we are suffering. In the view of Hillman and Ventura (1992), we are a 'society of recoverers'. Individuals, sensitised to their suffering, feel helplessness, rage and despair. The modernist faith in cures and progress has led to a blurring of Freud's distinction between 'common unhappiness and neurotic misery'. Kovel (1976) notes that whereas the aim of therapy — initially a short-term enterprise — was to relieve neurosis, to reduce it to common unhappiness, the therapeutic target is now discontent and unhappiness at large. 'Growth' is the promise of many humanistic therapies — developing the self, perhaps even creating a new self. Discussing psychology's 'sanction for selfishness', Kvale comments that, with modernity, the soul has evolved into the self or psyche, an entity cut off from its social and historical context, and bent on its own 'actualisation' (1992: 43). It is worth asking whether or not this has ironically led to — at least in part — an apparent increase in unhappiness.

THE IMPLICATIONS OF A POSTMODERN PSYCHOLOGY FOR THERAPY AND COUNSELLING

The implications of postmodern thought, as it has been outlined here, are quite radical in terms of the status, practices and purposes of psychotherapy and counselling.

First, the status of the therapist or counsellor as 'in possession' of expert knowledge is questioned under a postmodern psychology — and thus the therapist-client relationship comes under new scrutiny. Traditional, modern forms of clinical practice connote oppression, signifying power relations that operate to the disadvantage of the pathologised client.

The status and power of the mental health professions has already been challenged by a number of initiatives in the USA, Britain and Italy (see Parker et al. 1995) which have attempted to empower mental health service users. In the practice of therapy and counselling, attempts should be made to deal with the power differential between client and therapist. As Bannister (1993) argues, a differential in power is inevitable in the therapy situation, but the nature of the therapeutic expertise should be more clearly defined. Within a postmodern framework, the therapist does not have, in mystified form, an enclosed view of what is natural or good for clients. He or she does not speak from any position of essential knowledge, and does not see things in terms of skills that the client ought to acquire. He or she does not have a patent on what is rational, and does not encourage any sort of therapeutic dependency. For Bannister, there are various metaphors of the therapeutic relationship that he rejects as inappropriate. These include doctor/patient, priest/penitent, trainer/trainee and friend/friend. He follows Kelly in advocating a research-supervisor/research-student model. This positions the client as a researcher who always knows most about his or her project, and who takes ultimate responsibility for it. The therapist or supervisor has a general eye for how different sorts of projects might be approached.

Secondly, practitioners need to examine the way in which the prevailing constructions of sanity and insanity, normality and deviance, pathological and healthy, inform interactions between themselves and their clients in ways that actively construct their clients as particular kinds of people. Harper (1995) describes how, in his own clinical interview with a client, his questions subtly construct the client as 'paranoid'. Practitioners might actively seek to offer their clients new and more liberating ways of constructing experience. For example, the Hearing Voices Network aims to help people to redefine their experience in ways which do not reduce their status to that of victimised patient (see Parker et al. 1995; Romme and Escher 1993).

Thirdly, practitioners must therefore question their usual normative framework and recognise the extent of human diversity in experience and behaviour. This diversity exists not only between people, but also in the apparent inconsistency and fragmentary quality of individual experience. Social constructionism rejects the unitary, consistent self of liberal humanism. There is no deep, real self to be mined, no true inner feelings to be contacted. Social constructionism exhorts us to recognise the truly situated and relational nature of human experience and conduct. If we do not possess true selves, we must learn to live with and, further, see opportunities in our fragmentation. Mair (1989) has put forward a model of self as a community, and suggested that one task of therapy is to allow the different voices of this community to be heard.

Fourthly, language is not primarily a medium through which we express ourselves; rather, language speaks through and constitutes us. There is nothing inside us that is isolated from social practices and language, but there is no reason to believe that our 'vocabulary' of self cannot be changed. Seemingly indisputable accounts of others and us are, in fact, disputable. We can encourage the elaboration of 'subjugated knowledges' that might better reflect our lived experience than the dominant discourses. We are not determined by our past — we write and rewrite it. Just as history may be written from many perspectives, so many personal autobiographies are equally possible. It is *the way* we construct the histories that is important. We must experiment with different narratives, searching for those that best empower us in dealing with our circumstances. A postmodern psychology can help construct new vocabularies through which to construct new worlds of meaning and relationship (Gergen 1992).

Fifthly, we are pre-reflective beings, whose action and experience arise jointly out of interaction with others. We cannot always expect to find individual causes and reasons for our conduct. Traditional psychology individualises problems and locates them in intrapsychic processes, but this is already being questioned by the rise of such approaches as family therapy, which, even with its own epistemological difficulties, privileges the social system in which individuals are enmeshed. Many of the problems that people experience may be better understood as products of the identities that they are unable to resist within the context of their family, social group or society. Accordingly, our attempts to help should focus on providing effective strategies for resisting the debilitating constructions of themselves and their discursive positions (Burr and Butt 1993).

CONCLUSION

We have argued that a social constructionist analysis of the current rise in therapy and counselling offers a penetrating account of how, through surveillance and disciplinary power, they may serve the purpose of social control. However, we have argued that such analyses often stop short of making recommendations for change, particularly at the level of individual subjectivity. We believe that a postmodern psychology is capable of doing so without abandoning a social constructionist framework, and we further believe that there is much that can be done to address these needs within the current framework of therapy and counselling.

Rorty (1982c) argues that the aim of the social sciences should be to act as interpreter for those who, for one reason or another, cannot speak for themselves. Like the novelist, the psychologist, faced with conflict and cruelty, makes lives intelligible to others, thereby enlarging the human community. A specifically postmodern psychology, we think, can also make people more intelligible to themselves — without the search for any foundational self. Rather, they might be enabled to produce self-narratives which allow them to live at peace with themselves.

REFERENCES

Bannister, D. (1983) The internal politics of psychotherapy. In D. Pilgrim (ed.), *Psychology and Psychotherapy* (pp. 139–50). London: Routledge

Bilig, M. (1991) *Ideology and Opinions.* London: Sage

Blumer, H. (1969) *Symbolic Interactionism.* Englewood Cliffs, NJ: Prentice-Hall

Bott-Spillius, E. (ed.) (1988) *Melanie Klein Today.* London: Routledge

Brown, G. and Harris, T. (1978) *The Social Origins of Depression.* London: Tavistock

Burman, E. (1990) Differing with deconstruction. In I. Parker and J. Shotter (eds), *Deconstructing Social Psychology* (pp. 208–20). London: Routledge

Burr, V. and Butt, T. W. (1993) Personal and social constructionism. Unpublished paper/mimeo, University of Huddersfield

Derrida, J. (1978) *Writing and Difference.* Chicago: University of Chicago Press

Faris, R. and Dunham, H. (1939) *Mental Disorders in Urban Areas*. Chicago: University of Chicago Press

Fingarette, H. (1969) *Self Deception*. London: Routledge

Foucault, M. (1965) *Madness and Civilization: A History of Insanity in the Age of Reason*. New York: Vintage

Foucault, M. (1976) *The History of Sexuality, Vol. 1*. Harmondsworth: Penguin

Foucault, M. (1977) *Discipline and Punish: The Birth of the Prison*. London: Allen Lane

Foucault, M. (1980) *Power/Knowledge: Selected Interviews and Other Writings, 1972–1977*, ed. C. Gordon. New York: Pantheon

Gergen, K. (1989) Warranting voice and the elaboration of self. In J. Shotter and K. Gergen (eds), *Texts of Identity* (pp. 70–81). London: Sage

Gergen, K (1992) Towards a postmodern psychology. In S. Kvale (ed.), *Psychology and Postmodernism* (pp. 17–30). London: Sage

Goffman, E. (1961) *Asylums*. Harmondsworth: Penguin

Habermas, J. (1986) Taking aim at the heart of the present. In D. Couzens Hoy (ed.), *Foucault: A Critical Reader* (pp. 103–8). Oxford: Basil Blackwell

Harper, D. J. (1995) Discourse analysis and mental health. *Journal of Mental Health* 4: 347–57

Hillman, J. and Ventura, M. (1992) *We've Had a Hundred Years of Psychotherapy and the World is Getting Worse*. New York: Harper Collins

Hollinger, R. (1994) *Postmodernism and the Social Sciences: A Therapeutic Approach*. London: Sage

Kelly, G. A. (1955) *The Psychology of Personal Constructs*. New York: Norton

Kelly, G. A. (1969a) The language of hypothesis: man's psychological instrument. In B. Maher (ed.), *Clinical Psychology and Personality: The Selected Papers of George Kelly* (pp. 147–62). New York: Wiley

Kelly, G. A. (1969b) Epilogue: Don Juan. In B. Maher (ed.), *Clinical Psychology and Personality: The Selected Papers of George Kelly* (pp. 333–52). New York: Wiley

Kitzinger, C. (1992) The individual self-concept: a critical analysis of social constructionist writing on individualism. In G. Breakwell (ed.), *Social Psychology of Identity and the Self-Concept* (pp. 221–50). London: Surrey University Press in association with Academic Press

Kovel, J. (1976) *A Complete Guide to Therapy*. Harmondsworth: Penguin

Kvale, S. (1992) Postmodern psychology: a contradiction in terms? In S. Kvale (ed.), *Psychology and Postmodernism* (pp. 31–57). London: Sage

Laing, R. D. (1959) *The Divided Self*. London: Tavistock

Laing, R. D. (1967) *The Politics of Experience*. Harmondsworth: Penguin

Mair, J. M. (1989) *Between Psychology and Psychotherapy: A Poetics of Experience*. London: Routledge

Merleau-Ponty, M. (1962) *Phenomenology of Perception*. London: Routledge and Kegan Paul

Parker, I. (1992) *Discourse Dynamics: Critical Analysis for Social and Personal Psychology*. London: Routledge

Parker, I., Georgaca, E., Harper, D., McLaughlin, T. and Stowell-Smith, M. (1995) *Deconstructing Psychopathology*. London: Sage

Parton, N. (1985) *The Politics of Child Abuse*. London: Macmillan

Plummer, K. (1995) *Telling Sexual Stories: Power, Change and Social Worlds*. London: Routledge

Polkinghorne, D. (1992) Postmodern epistemology of practice. In S. Kvale (ed.), *Psychology and Postmodernism* (pp. 146–65). London: Sage

Potter, J. and Wetherell, M. (1987) *Discourse and Social Psychology*. London: Sage

Romme, M. and Escher, S. (eds) (1993) *Accepting Voices*. London: MIND

Rorty, R. (1982a) The world well lost. In R. Rorty (ed.), *Consequences of Pragmatism* (pp. 3–16). Hemel Hempstead: Harvester Wheatsheaf

Rorty, R. (1982b) Nineteenth-century idealism and twentieth century textualism. In R. Rorty (ed.), *Consequences of Pragmatism* (pp. 139–59). Hemel Hempstead: Harvester Wheatsheaf

Rorty, R. (1982c) Method, social science and social hope. In R. Rorty (ed.), *Consequences of Pragmatism* (pp. 191–210). Hemel Hempstead: Harvester Wheatsheaf

Rorty, R. (1989) *Contingency, Irony and Solidarity*. Cambridge: Cambridge University Press

Rose, N. (1989) *Governing the Soul: The Shaping of the Private Self*. London: Routledge

Rose, N. (1990) Psychology as a social science. In I. Parker and J. Shotter (eds), *Deconstructing Social Psychology* (pp. 103–16). London: Routledge

Rosenhan, D. (1973) On being sane in insane places. *Science* 179: 250–7

Sampson, E. E. (1990) Social psychology and social control. In I. Parker and J. Shotter (eds), *Deconstructing Social Psychology* (pp. 117–26). London: Routledge

Sarbin, T. (1986) The narrative as a root metaphor in psychology. In T. Sarbin (ed.), *Narrative Psychology: The Storied Nature of Human Conduct* (pp. 3–21). New York: Praeger

Sartre, J.-P. (1958) *Being and Nothingness*. London: Methuen

Sarup, M. (1988) *An Introductory Guide to Post-Structuralism and Postmodernism*. Hemel Hempstead: Harvester Wheatsheaf

Scheff, T. (1966) *Being Mentally Ill: A Sociological Theory*. Chicago: Aldine

Sedgwick, P. (1982) *Psycho Politics*. London: Pluto

Shotter, J. (1992) Getting in touch. In S. Kvale (ed.), *Psychology and Postmodernism* (pp. 58–73). London: Sage

Smith, M. and Glass, G. (1977) Meta-analysis of psychotherapy outcome studies. *American Psychologist* 132: 152–70

Spence, D. (1986) Narrative smoothing and clinical wisdom. In T. Sarbin (ed.), *Narrative Psychology: The Storied Nature of Human Conduct* (pp. 211–32). New York: Praeger

Spinelli, E. (1995) The Unconscious: an idea whose time has gone? In H. Cohn and S. du Plock (eds), *Existential Challenges to Psychotherapeutic Theory and Practice* (pp. 217–47). London: Society for Existential Analysis

Szasz, T. S. (1961) The myth of mental illness. *American Psychologist* 15 (February): 113–18

Szasz, T. S. (1970) *Ideology and Insanity: Essays on the Psychiatric Dehumanization of Man*. New York: Doubleday

Szasz, T.S. (1971) *The Manufacture of Madness*. London: Routledge and Kegan Paul

van Deurzen-Smith, E. (1994) Questioning the power of psychotherapy: is Jeffrey Masson on to something? *Journal of the Society for Existential Analysis* 5: 37–44

Walzer, M. (1986) The politics of Michel Foucault. In D. Couzens Hoy (ed.), *Foucault: A Critical Reader* (pp. 51–68). Oxford: Basil Blackwell

White, M. and Epston, D. (1990) *Narrative Means to Therapeutic Ends*. New York: Norton

Wilkins, L. (1971) The deviance-amplifying system. In W. Carson and P. Wiles (eds), *The Sociology of Crime and Delinquency in Britain, Vol. 1: The British Tradition* (pp. 252–60). London: Robertson

9

LIMITS TO COUNSELLING AND THERAPY: DECONSTRUCTING A PROFESSIONAL IDEOLOGY

RICHARD HOUSE[†]

> ... this historical period of therapy ... that [tries] to fix what we do not understand.
>
> (Hillman 1997: 81)

INTRODUCTION

> there exists precious little about therapy that we can say with any certainty ... therapists really don't know what they're doing — even if they insist upon pretending ... they are 'experts'.
>
> (Spinelli 1996: 56, 59)

In 1977 Ivan Illich published a seminal book, *Limits to Medicine*, in which he made a radical counterintuitive case for the cultural institution of professional medicine being deleterious to societal health. In this chapter I will make the equally radical suggestion that the professionalised institution of 'Therapy' is also in danger of perpetrating net harm at the cultural level.

Despite decades of research that point to the unifying, so-called 'non-specific' or 'intangible' factors being what really matter in a therapeutic encounter (Frank and Frank 1991; Shepherd and Sartorius 1989), the all-too-common internecine warfare between different therapeutic approaches (e.g. Hugill 1998; King and Steiner 1990), and the commonly observed emphasis that specific approaches give to difference rather than to factors of commonality, suggest that such parochial preoccupations may have far more to do with practitioners' own insecurity-driven need to self-define and self-justify themselves as a 'professionals' than they do with any disinterested 'objective' perspective on what the therapeutic experience consists in.

What if, we may justifiably ask, the 'non-specific' healing factors triggered within a therapeutic experience occur *despite* rather than because of any particular distinctive characteristics of the various therapeutic approaches? And what, furthermore, if there were no demonstrable, statistically significant difference in outcome between the therapeutic help offered by highly trained 'professionals' and that of very lightly trained 'para-professionals', as a great deal of empirical

† This chapter first appeared in the *British Journal of Guidance and Counselling,* 27(3), 1999: 377-392, and appears here by kind permission of the author and the *BJGC.*

research (well summarised in Bohart and Tallman 1996 — reproduced as Chapter 27, this volume) seems to indicate? Perhaps these counterintuitive findings aren't so outlandish when seen in the context of Smail's view that 'we are all highly skilled and experienced psychologists who have spent a lifetime developing ways of living in a world which contains other people, observing the regularities of their conduct, and conducting ourselves in accordance with our observations' (1983 18; cf. Parker 1998b). Of course, any 'professional' is likely defensively, even desperately, to resist such uncomfortable possibilities (House 1997: 104), because their acceptance would throw into considerable doubt the legitimacy of therapy as a 'professional' practice. To be blunt, the whole edifice of 'professionalised' therapy would immediately be thrown into very severe question. As Kalisch (1996: 46) has challengingly put it, 'The behaviour of the "profession" is the next bit of resistance that needs looking at'!

In what follows, I hope to show that many of therapy's most taken-for-granted conventional 'wisdoms' have far more to do with the creation of a self-serving, self-justificatory (and typically self-deluding) ideology than they have to do with authenticity and 'truth' in the healing encounter. (These arguments are developed at far greater length in House 2003.) It must be stressed that this chapter is largely confined to considering therapy at the level of its (predominantly) individualised practice and discourse. As a consequence, I have not addressed the political and cultural effects of the therapy phenomenon — which have been penetratingly detailed by a number of authors (e.g. Albee 1990; Cloud 1998; Cushman 1995; Pilgrim 1992, 1997; Smail 1996). One of the dangers, of course, is that in a therapy culture, 'there is an obsession with persons at the expense of social relations. Politics degenerates into the struggle for self-realisation not social change' (Kennard and Small 1997a: 214); and an accompanying tendency, perhaps, tacitly to sanction a normalising ideology which 'reinscribe[s] individuals into the very social relations that produced their "illnesses"' (Cloud 1998: xv). There is also the question of material self-interest in any professional field: for Cloud (ibid.: 20), for example, 'the therapeutic comprises a set of discourses which are linked ... to a particular historical moment and to the interests of those who benefit from the perpetuation of a therapeutic society'. Certainly, this literature has made no little contribution to the arguments I develop below; and any thorough-going critique of therapy must take account of its possibly deleterious consequences at the level of culture — and not least, its increasingly pervasive institutionalisation within Western culture.

It has been argued that the price we are paying in the course of therapy's institutional professionalisation is the loss of therapy's soul (Edwards 1992); and if she is right, then some pretty swift 'New Paradigm' footwork (or rather, *heart*work) may well be required if the fundamentally beneficial impulse that surely underpins therapy is to be rescued from the deadening hand of self-serving professionalisation, and thereby preserved in some organically healthy and culturally enabling form. Such heartwork, however, is not the prime concern of this chapter; rather, I set myself the far more limited task of *using old-paradigm thinking against itself*: that is, I use the language and style of the old paradigm to show how its own ideological discourse and associated therapeutic practices contain inherent self-contradictory elements which render it self-refuting and in urgent need of transcendence (cf. House 2003). Finally, my own project is not, of course, without its own tensions and contradictions — to which I return briefly at the end of the chapter.

THE IDEOLOGY OF PROFESSIONALISATION

> It is fear that has, in my experience, characterised the response of
> psychotherapists to the whole political process of professionalisation. They
> fear loss of livelihood, loss of status and recognition, loss of legitimacy.
> And in this fear I detect a strong element of transference itself.
>
> (Heron 1990:18)

It is highly sobering to read a prominent therapist writing the following: 'perhaps
too many therapists have as their *raison d'être* a need to see themselves as
extraordinarily powerful, virtually omniscient healers. Consequently, *they have
a penchant for infantilising and overpathologising their patients*, viewing them as
extraordinarily fragile' (Lazarus 1994: 301, my emphasis — see his Chapter 1,
this volume; cf. Mowbray, 1997) — with consequences for therapeutic practice
which, I will argue below, are in danger of being intrinsically abusive and
unethical. That is, I make the strong claim that client/patient abuse is intrinsically
inscribed into the very form increasingly taken by professionalised therapy.

A further effect of institutionalised professionalisation is the rigidification
and rendering legitimate of what some might call the precious, often mystifying
language and procedures of the therapy world-view. Nearly 20 years ago
Hinshelwood described how different therapeutic schools 'protect themselves
by arcane terminologies', with insecurity being dealt with 'by inculcating each
other ... into a system of mutual confirmation of the grouping's theoretical ideas'
(1985: 16). More recently, Hart (1998) cites Habermas's work on communicative
distortion (1978, 1982) to make the point that power is often exercised through
the manipulation or distortion of communication (cf. her Chapter 23, this volume,
and Parker's views on discourse and deconstruction, below), and that therapy
has become a dominant cultural discourse which threatens to 'direct
communication towards the achievement of [therapists'] own ends'.

Below I will outline some concrete examples of how power is arguably being
abused through the intrinsic nature of what I will call the Professionalised Therapy
Form (hereafter, the PTF). This is a convenient short-hand term to connote the
increasingly commodified and professionally boundaried form which
psychoanalysis, and the so-called 'new professions' of psychotherapy and
counselling, have been taking in recent years, as professionalisation gathers steam.

Perhaps it is possible to trace the flawed project of professionalised
commodified psychotherapy right back to the very origins of psychoanalysis
itself. For as Frosh points out, Freud was

> far less interested in psychoanalysis as a therapeutic system than as an
> instrument of knowledge [about individual and society]. Freud's project
> was ... to develop a system of ideas that could make sense of people ...
> psychotherapy was a secondary project, *undertaken to make a living*.
>
> (Frosh 1987: 211, my emphasis)

In his highly revealing clinical diary, Ferenczi is even more blunt in recounting
how, for Freud, 'patients are only riffraff. The only thing patients were good for
is to help the analyst make a living and provide material for theory' (quoted in
Rowe 1990: 19; see also Dupont 1995: 93). Kurtz (1989) has similarly pointed to
the less than auspicious historical origins of the therapeutic/analytic form: he

painstakingly shows how 'The narcissistic and psychotic ... layers of Freud's personality entered profoundly into his creation of the psychoanalytic situation and its manifestation in space ... *every analyst to some degree recreates that office in the Berggasse*' (ibid.: 28–9, my emphasis).

If the very framework in which therapy is 'delivered' is in principle antithetical to what really matters in a therapeutic experience, then the professionalised, commodified direction which therapy is increasingly taking may well be doing a kind of violence to the foundational values from which the healthy and fundamentally good therapeutic impulse no doubt springs (cf. Bracken and Thomas 1998).

THE DUBIOUS ETHICS OF PSYCHOTHERAPY AND COUNSELLING

> ... a setting which, infused with ambiguity, encourages the development of an insatiable love in both therapist ... and patient ... Once attained, these affective states ... then become the prime focus for the psychoanalytic process of government ...
>
> (Kendall and Crossley 1996: 192)

Heron (1990) has referred accusingly to therapy's exploitation and abuse of the transference: 'psychoanalysts in particular were hypocritical in wanting to protect the public from transference abuse [in their professionalisation strategies], when their own therapy was riddled with this very phenomenon'! (ibid.: 17, describing the behaviourists' response to the 1972 Foster Report). Perhaps the very way in which therapy as a PTF is structured (rather than the particular features of psychoanalysis *per se*) may actually encourage and if not *actively produce* client infantilisation and dependency through the unconscious(?) dynamics triggered by the PTF, and often buttressed by the assumptive framework typically embraced by the professional therapist (cf. McDougall 1995). As one of the ex-clients in Alexander's book *Folie à Deux* remarks, 'it doesn't seem to matter whether the therapist encourages [dependence] or discourages it. It's just there, like the weather' (Alexander 1995: 145). On this view, then, the PTF may be self-fulfillingly constructing a framework which then guarantees the conditions of its own existence.

Hinshelwood (1997), a leading psychoanalyst, has bravely outlined some profound ethical dilemmas encountered by the analytic project. Chief among these is 'the prior-agreement argument' (ibid.: 101–2), an unavoidable ethical aspect of which is that:

> The patient does not have the capacity to conceive, at the outset, what will befall him [in analysis] ... The unconscious cannot be explained to the patient to any useful degree. The nature of the [analytic] process ... cannot really be understood prior to treatment at all. We cannot rely on the patient consciously to understand what his unconscious will do ... [The consent to analysis] is not a fully informed consent.
>
> (ibid.; cf. Pilgrim 1997: 117)

It follows from this that the analyst cannot but take up a paternalistic stance in relation to 'patients' who necessarily (it is assumed) cannot make informed decisions about entering analysis, and therefore need the analyst to take responsibility for knowing what is in their best interests.

But it gets worse still ... for:

> patients become immobilised, as if transfixed, upon the couch until the end of each session ... For periods, the patient in psychoanalysis may subjugate himself ... And this lasts until *these unconscious processes that deplete the patient's personality* have been adequately dealt with in the process of the treatment.
>
> (ibid.: 103, my emphasis)

In other words, the PTF of psychoanalysis actively encourages a particular psychic state within patients, which then requires extensive 'treatment' to cure! The self-serving, ethically dubious nature of such an 'enterprise' (I use the term advisedly) is relatively clear for all to see — except for the 'patient' in analysis, of course!

The tell-tale opposition to the politicisation of therapy by those 'who regard "the clinical" as an untouchable, privileged category, on the basis of its contribution to the alleviation of human suffering' (Samuels 1993:6) is suggestive of a rationalised, therapist-centred professional self-interest. Yet of course, the 'individualising' of distress is in many ways necessary to legitimate psychoanalysis — and much of therapy — as a form of treatment (cf. Parker's arguments, below); and this in turn constitutes another dimension of the self-serving PTF ideology.

Hinshelwood's frank discussion surely throws a very long shadow over the ethical basis of not only psychoanalysis, but over any (and conceivably, every) therapeutic practice in which such relational dynamics are tacitly or explicitly encouraged, or can be triggered. As Kovel (1976: 82) argues, 'Transference wishes are stirred up willy-nilly, whether the therapist cultivates them or not'. Thus, I maintain that therapeutic approaches (like many humanistic and cognitive-behaviour therapies) which claim to offer an open and unmystifying description of their procedures may be no less immune from these ethical difficulties than are the more purist versions of psychoanalysis and analytic therapy — and not least through the degree of practitioner self-delusion typically involved! (House 1998). Thus, therapists never really 'know what they're doing' in any comprehensive, 'objective' sense (Frank and Frank 1991; Spinelli 1996). And it could conceivably be that the boundaried PTF itself and the 'therapeutic frame' (relatively ubiquitous as it is across the generality of therapeutic approaches) *actively encourage* client infantilisation, dependency and associated processes through the deep ('unconscious') dynamics that are precipitated in the therapeutic encounter, irrespective of theoretical approach. In House (2003, Chapter 3) I elaborate in detail on what I call the '"material"-generating nature' of the PTF: as France put it, 'Psychotherapy ... can merely be the replay of past traumata ... which lead to nothing ... It creates an artificial situation ... *which could lead to ... the artificial creation of [problems]* (France 1988: 139, my emphasis). And Freud himself, arguably the 'father' of therapy, made no secret of his therapeutic intention: 'it remains the first aim of the treatment to attach [the patient] to [the treatment] and to the person of the doctor' (1913: 139).

The way in which culturally legitimated therapeutic discourse structures both client and therapist subjectivities is a major focus of the next section.

THEORY, TRUTH AND POWER

> Certain categories of experience can never occur unless elicited and maintained by the actions of another.
>
> (Daniel Stern, quoted in Arden 1998: 84)

Professions typically legitimate their existence by claiming privileged access to a body of expert (typically theoretical) knowledge or theory, which is seen as being indispensable to their professional practice. Here is David Smail (1996: 56):

> There is, of course, a constant struggle within society for certain professional groups to mystify and monopolise 'truth', but it is still perfectly possible to clarify the reasons for our unhappiness without recourse to a professional psychotherapist. In many respects, it may even be easier.

No-one involved in the field will have missed the extraordinary and intemperate stampede into the 'academicisation' of therapy training and practice which has accompanied professionalisation (House 2001; Parker 2001). Clearly, if an activity is to become sedimented into a legitimate 'profession', then it must find a way of claiming that what it has to offer to clients is distinctive, 'specialistic' and broadly undeliverable in any other way — here is Smail again in his classic 1983 paper:

> When professional claims are made, expectations established among clients, and money changes hands ..., it becomes important to establish a solid justification for psychotherapy as a discipline ... Ever since the beginnings of psychoanalysis, psychotherapists have been desperately anxious to establish the validity of their credentials ... in order, no doubt, to justify their professional (fee-taking) status.
>
> (1983: 7–8)

There is certainly no general agreement about what it is that therapists do (cf. Spinelli's epigraph at the start of this chapter), and the field has repeatedly been described as being in a state of (theoretical) disarray (e.g. Erwin 1997: 2). And more generally still, some commentators have been starting to challenge the epistemological relevance of theory (and its associated form of 'technical' knowledge) to the healing practice of therapy (Craib 1987; McDougall 1995: Riikonen and Smith 1997), as 'New Paradigm' epistemologies begin to challenge head on the ideology of modernity and its narcissistic preoccupation with ego, control, technocratic science and the material (cf. House, 2003 and Chapter 26, this volume).

As Burman points out, 'mainstream' psychotherapy is — or pretends to be — a quintessentially rational, modernist enterprise which 'rehearses the modern condition of western, split subjectivity wedded to singular truths and linear histories' (1997: 126). But what if, as Smail maintains, 'the technical rhetoric of psychotherapy has ... more in common with magic than with a truly scientific spirit of enquiry' (1987: 34; cf. Frank and Frank 1991)? In the highly contrasting New Paradigm, postmodern world-view of Chaos, complementarity and participative consciousness (Skolimowski 1994; cf. Clarkson's Chapter 7, this volume), our very foundational notions of 'explanation', 'understanding' and 'truth' are 'up for grabs' — which situation, of course, has very profound implications indeed for the practice of any healing art.

There exist a number of modernity-transcending '"theories" [sic!] of truth' (e.g. the coherence theory, the participative theory and the congruence 'theory of truth' — e.g. Lacan 1965; Skolimowski 1994; Alcoff 1996; Heron 1996 — see House 2003: 190–1), which challenge quite fundamentally the aridity of the epistemologically dubious 'correspondence' theory that has tended to dominate Western analytic philosophy and the modernist world-view of positive science since the Enlightenment (Tarnas 1991; cf. Burr and Butt's Chapter 8, this volume). Parker's important work on the 'discursive complex' (1996, 1997a, b, 1998a), discussed below, points to how notions of truth within therapeutic discourse can themselves actively structure subjectivity — with the implication that 'we must be attentive to the power of the therapist as a ... part of the regime of truth that defines what subjectivity must be like' (Parker 1996: 459). And ultimately, 'the subject does not know what the truth is; nobody knows ...' (ibid.).

Parker et al. (1995: 135) have written that '"theories" about distress masquerade as "Truth" ... that truth is relentlessly forced upon people'. The question of 'theory as abuse' has also recently been courageously addressed by Ernesto Spinelli, who argues that therapist reliance on interpretations derived from theory can become 'more abusive than anything else ... Many of the assumptions we take for granted don't really have any basis to them ... we might hold [them] because at the very least they keep us employed, or they provide employment for our trainees' (Spinelli and Longman 1998: 181, 183,).

All this, of course, ultimately leads quite naturally into questions of power. It is a sobering and highly revealing fact that, with a few notable exceptions (Guggenbühl-Craig 1971; Embleton Tudor and Tudor 1994), the issue of power is scarcely discussed in the therapy field (Hart 1998; see also Chapters 4 and 23, this volume). The real substance of power is never really fearlessly and fundamentally addressed. Perhaps we can all convince (delude?) ourselves into complacently thinking that we've dealt with therapy's thorny power issues by simply repeating the word a few times, like some sort of mantra. Yet as some commentators have either suggested or implied (Masson 1988; Hart 1998), 'power' probably constitutes one of therapy's most embarrassing can of worms.

Hart (ibid.) maintains that it is illusory to believe that clients are free to explore their inner worlds in therapy, for 'the boundaries and rules, like the vocabulary, are as fixed as they ever were in the psychiatric world of the fifties and sixties': all that has changed is that we now *pretend* that the client has power, and that we as therapists do not use a normalising and subtly impositional discourse. And as is repeatedly argued in this book, 'Therapy can never be value free ... It happens within a context and someone has set the agenda' (ibid.).

In psychoanalysis (possibly generalisable to therapy in general), Hinshelwood (1997) does concede that the patient's 'lack of conscious knowledge of his unconscious does put him [sic] at some disadvantage. It makes him consciously helpless in the search for his knowledge' (ibid.: 167). Moreover, the extent to which patients operating within a therapeutic milieu (and all that goes with it in terms of both individual and cultural dynamics) are free to exercise full conscious consent may well be significantly compromised (ibid.; cf. House 2003: 110–11, 232–3). All this can routinely lead to a kind of power-imbalanced Laingian 'knot' in which the therapist 'knows [or *thinks* s/he knows — RH] a great deal, but also *knows* that he [sic] knows a great deal and *knows* that his client does not know much ...' (Hinshelwood 1997: 168, original emphases). For Hinshelwood, this power imbalance can be carried through 'to a degree that distorts both identities. Professional relationships based on this redistribution of knowing will result in the expert enhancing the depletion of the personality of his more vulnerable clients' (ibid.).

It seems to me that abuses such as these are ones to which the 'professions' of therapy are by their very nature peculiarly and intrinsically susceptible. And in the light of this we would do well to follow family therapist Lynn Hoffman's injunction that 'therapists of all kinds must now investigate how relations of domination and submission are built into *the very assumptions* on which their practices are based' (quoted in Hart 1998, my emphasis). Below, I will propose that therapy must routinely and ongoingly embrace a radical deconstruction of its theories and practices (cf. Parker 1999), paradoxically entailing a continual undermining of its own conditions of existence, if it is to avoid the kinds of abuses which are, I believe, intrinsic to the PTF as currently practised and culturally legitimated.

THE DISCOURSE OF THERAPY AND ITS CRITICAL DECONSTRUCTION

> any system of therapeutic talk conveys an enigma to the subject, and positions the subject in a regime of truth. Then it may not be good to talk.
> (Parker 1996: 459)

> the therapeutic as a modern ideological, strategic discourse ... has as its ultimate effects the privatization of social experience and the disciplining of private subjects into a regime of self-blame and personal responsibility.
> (Cloud 1998: xxi)

The so-called discursive, deconstructionist approach to therapy typically views language and discourse, and the power relations intrinsic to them, as actively constituting notions of '(psycho)pathology' (Parker et al. 1995), aspects of psychic 'reality' and so on. By extension, moreover, our associated subjective experiences are themselves seen as being deeply structured through the culturally sanctioned discourse which is available to us. Thus, 'Language ... is not a reflection of another world, but an implement of construction for the world we now occupy' (Gergen and McNamee 1997: viii, my emphasis). It follows that words are always far more than merely 'labels for objective things' (Riikonen and Smith 1997: 3). And such a perspective is so crucial to therapy and human relationship more generally because 'our conceptions of language and words have a close connection to the kinds of relationships which *can* exist between people' (ibid.: 7, original emphasis).

Ian Parker (who has contributed the Afterword to this volume) has made a very considerable contribution to the discursive deconstructionist line of thinking. He explores 'the way meaning is transformed and reproduced in culture, rather than trying to find the sources of meanings inside individuals alone' (1997a: 9). More specifically, he maintains that psychoanalytic concepts (particularly around intellectualisation, transference and trauma) have increasingly infiltrated cultural discourse such that it becomes difficult for people to think about their experience outside of this discourse (e.g. Parker 1997a, b).

On this view, then, Western culture is actively structured by psychoanalytic notions which 'saturate and support cultural phenomena' (1997a: 258); and '"regimes of truth" ... make it difficult for participants to challenge the "realities" [a discourse] refers to ... [and] govern what can be spoken about ...' (ibid.: 7). Laplanche expresses a similar view: 'psychoanalysis *invades the cultural*, not only as a form of thought or a doctrine, but as a *mode of being*' (1989, quoted in Parker 1996: 449, original emphases). What Parker calls 'discursive complexes' structure subjectivity, 'so that when we speak within them they provoke certain types of emotional response, certain notions of what it is to be a self' (1996: 451). For current purposes, what is most relevant is the way in which specifically psychotherapeutic discourse actively 'structures the way a person, as therapist or patient, participates in the therapeutic enterprise' (Parker 1997a: 256; see also Parker, 1996: 458). Thus, for example, it is arguable that the very way in which the notion of 'transference' has surreptitiously penetrated cultural discourse makes it more likely that transference dynamics will be created within therapeutic relationships (particularly when the therapist is also expecting to find 'transference'! — cf. McDougall 1995: 234, 236).

All this clearly has very considerable implications for the ways in which the self-experienced identity of 'clients' and 'patients' is actively constructed by a psychotherapeutic discourse which is culturally sanctioned, and buttressed by a massively influential ideological framework of professionalisation. Thus, people with 'personal problems' will tend immediately to think of themselves as potential therapy 'clients' — thereby positioning themselves within therapeutic discourse — precisely because that discourse constitutes a dominating set of values and culturally legitimated practices that circulates within the culture and actively helps to constitute subjective experience.

In a very real sense, then, it can be argued that the psychotherapeutic world-view actively and self-servingly creates the cultural conditions that guarantee its own existence and perpetuation — erecting, as with any ideological apparatus, 'a system of defences and discursive operations which guarantee its place in a regime of truth' (Parker 1997b: 489). Pilgrim (1997: 141) agrees:

> The gaze of professionals constructs both normal and abnormal subjectivity and leaves little space for ordinary people to speak for themselves in ways which are unmediated by the inscriptions and conceptual filters of experts. Moreover, professionals control not only the language associated with the technologies of the self but also the style and even the occurrence of these representations.

This situation surely places an enormous ethical imperative upon therapists continually to deconstruct their own therapeutic practice, such that therapy continually revolutionises its own theories and practices — actively subverting itself whenever there is any whiff of complacent self-satisfaction — rather than conservatively (like Ted Hughes' roosting hawk) 'keeping things like this' through overly rigid, self-serving and institutionalised 'professional' procedures which demonstrably have far more to do with therapist self-interest than with client well-being.

Parker seems to be saying something quite similar when he writes of 'a "deconstructing psychotherapy" as [being] a practice that is always *in process* rather then something fixed, a movement of reflexive critique rather than a stable set of techniques' (1999: 2, original emphasis); and that 'We must be attentive to the power of the therapist as ... part of a regime of truth that defines what subjectivity must be like' (1996: 458).

Clearly, there are crucial issues of power and control at work here:

> The issue of control — on a grandiose, omnipotent scale — permeates the analytic situation. It is always the analyst ... who establishes the rules that govern behaviour in this primal space. However much these rules may be constructed to enable the patient's cure, the analyst is their maker and enforcer.
>
> (Kurtz 1989: 27–8)

Nor are these features unique to psychoanalysis alone.

Is there anything special and distinctive about the healing properties of the PTF *qua* PTF, over and above its coercive ideological and discursive effects on clients/patients, and which could not be found elsewhere in other cultural forms, outside of the confines of the discrete commodified PTF? Following the kind of arguments outlined above, perhaps therapy might be 'no more than another ideological stance, an "as if" way of relating to the world which provides relief from confusion and personal emptiness because it happens to be relatively coherent' (Frosh 1987: 220).

Elsewhere (House 2003: Chapters 3–4) I critically deconstruct what I see as some of the more pernicious self-serving categories and assumptions of therapeutic discourse — including 'resistance', 'the frame', 'boundaries', 'holding', and the infantilisation intrinsic to the PTF and its associated relational dynamics. In that work I reach the conclusion, unpalatable as it will be to many, that there may well be far more examples of routine client abuse *stemming directly from the Professionalised Therapy Form itself* than there are the kinds of overt abuse against which the therapy institutions so assiduously attempt to legislate.

FINAL REFLECTIONS

> I merely wish to invite ethical reflection upon the nature of a society in which the provision of love becomes increasingly a matter for paid professionals.
>
> (Smail 1987: 36)

Despite first appearances, this is not an anti-therapy chapter, but an anti-*profession-centred* therapy chapter. For although I do see therapy as an historically specific and ultimately transitory cultural phenomenon, it must necessarily be serving an important evolutionary function; and to this extent I think it crucial to rescue what is the essentially 'good baby' that exists in therapy from the professionalising bathwater, and its accompanying ideology of late modernity, that in my view threatens to engulf it. Needless to say, therefore, I do not agree with Craib's assertion that 'if we decide we want the baby, we *have to* swim in the dirty bathwater' (Craib 1992: 244, my emphasis).

Heron (1997) and Totton (1997), among others, have both made a strong case for the activity of therapy being far more akin to *a spiritual practice* than to a medicalised 'treatment' for so-called 'psychopathology'. For Totton (ibid.: 138–

9), for example, 'psychotherapy ... functions as a deconstructive spiritual and political practice rather than as a form of medicine or social work'. Similarly, in a wise editorial in the former British Association for Counselling's *Counselling* magazine, the then-editor Judith Longman referred to 'knowing [being] false understanding, truth being beyond language, and the sensibility of the mystic or the poet perhaps being at least as effective as the practitioner-scientist' (1998: 82; see also House 1998: 175). Views such as these clearly have profound implications for the question of whether counselling and psychotherapy can, with validity, be viewed as 'professions' in anything like a conventional sense.

I hope I have shown in this chapter that as soon as we embrace the ideology of professionalisation (rigidifying institutionalisation, commodification, a scientific 'treatment' mentality and so on), then we quite possibly do a terminal violence to those very intangible, 'non-specific' 'being'-qualities that are in my view what makes at least some therapeutic experiences worth having. On this view, if our culture does continue to demand some form of help for those struggling with what Peck calls 'the necessary pain of living' (Peck: 1993), then it behoves us bravely and fearlessly to embrace the full implications of Samuels' (1992: xi) statement that what we do 'cannot even be named', and perhaps to find a paradoxical 'anti-form' of 'deconstructive therapy' which is foundationally and ongoingly deconstructive of its own appropriately precarious conditions of existence, such that we minimise the danger of its becoming a commodified, institutionalised, self-reproducing set form — a form that is necessarily reproductive of the modernist status quo, rather than a force for transcending it. As Smail so aptly puts it, 'the foremost obligation on power is to "deconstruct" itself' (quoted in Rowe 1990: 22).

If professionalised, individualised therapy as currently constituted is part of the problem rather than part of the solution to our malaise, then we surely need *cultural-level* transformations to support people in their 'difficulties of living' (cf. House, 2003), remembering in the process what the therapy 'profession' might well wish us to forget — that 'the process of healing can be brought about by other kinds of relationships than psychotherapy ...' (Arden 1998: 85). Such practices would presumably challenge the individualised commodified therapeutic practices which only tend to mimic the ideology of modernity, and which can therefore surely only exacerbate the spiritual malaise of modernity rather than ameliorating or transcending it (cf. Burr and Butt's Chapter 8, this volume). For Smail (1983: 16), many clients entering therapy 'have been mystified and crippled by the bludgeon of objectivity' (and modernity — RH) — which places an enormous moral and ethical responsibility on therapists not to reinforce and compound their 'bludgeoning' still further through dogmatic and ideological professional practices.

In a typically far-sighted paper written over a decade ago, Smail warned that 'through becoming unthinkingly over-extended, [psychotherapy] is in danger of being ethically misused or abused. In order to guard against such misuse, psychotherapists must beware of slipping into the role of established and technically sound professional expert' (1987: 43). And as if anticipating Smail's objections, describing the American situation in 1973, Carl Rogers wrote:

> if we did away with ... the 'certified professional' ..., we might open our profession to a breeze of fresh air, a surge of creativity, such as it has not known for years ... Can psychology find a new and a better way? Is there

some more creative method for bringing together those who need help and those who are truly excellent in offering helping relationships?

(Rogers 1990: 366)

Perhaps this latter is one of the most urgent — and most challenging — questions facing the therapy *Weltanschauung* as we enter a new millennium.

CODA: PARADIGMS, PARADIGMS ...

... any system of logic is unable to prove its own logical consistency.

(Michael Guillen 1983)

If Guillen (and Godel's famous 1931 theorem) are anything like right, then of course I am on very shaky ground if I pretend to claim any kind of universal truth-status for the ideas set out in this chapter. For I would certainly be comprehensively hoisting myself with my own petard if I tried to replace one 'regime of truth' with my own! And while it is arguably legitimate to demonstrate how the old paradigm's most cherished values and procedures are self-refuting from within its own discourse, we must always remain alert to the seductive strength of the old paradigm — how easy it is to delude ourselves that we've transcended it when we're still inextricably and unawarely still caught up in it! (cf. House 1996).

In their book *Re-Imagining Therapy*, Riikonen and Smith write, 'Will this book be a systematic, single-voiced text which argues against systematic single-voiced texts? Will it present yet another set of well ordered truths as it argues against well ordered truths?' (1997: 7). In the writing of their book the authors clearly realised that in order for their

> re-imagining' of therapy to have credibility, it was crucial that they transformed and transcended the traditional language and style of conventional, modernist 'therapy' — which they achieved by 'speak[ing] differently, metaphorically, even strangely ... We have to use different styles ... We have to exaggerate and use wrong words (*and lose at least some of our academic respectability*). In addition to this, we have to disrupt the automatic and even flow of ideas ...

(ibid.: my emphasis)

Alas, I have not been nearly so brave in this chapter: for I have simply challenged conventional therapy from within the (for me) safe terrain of academic rigour, a third-person (and distanced) 'detachedness', and careful, intellectually dominated rationalist analysis. Such an approach seems very double-edged: on the one hand, it shows how the old paradigm can be used against itself, and that it contains within it the seeds of its own transendence; but on the other, if my (albeit critical) use of old-paradigm procedures is valid, then the danger is that this self-refutingly undermines the veracity of my very challenge to that self-same paradigm!

These are very difficult philosophical issues (particularly around relativism) which I cannot pursue here; suffice to say that, first, I do not present these ideas as *the* Truth about therapy, or as being a better 'regime of truth' than the one it challenges — for I see the very ideology of 'Truth' as being even more problematic than whatever particular content a regime of truth contains. A quarter-century ago, George Steiner graphically wrote of 'the drug of truth': 'The quality of the obsession is clear from the start. The search for truth is predatory. It is a literal hunt, a conquest' (1978: 42).

I agree with the Derridean view that it is a fundamental error of the (ironically named) 'Enlightenment' project to expect humanly built systems of Truth to lead to reliable, 'objective' accounts of 'reality' (Tarnas 1991). Rather, my own particular 'truth' is unavoidably 'local', based on my own unique experiences of therapy as client, trainee, practitioner, supervisor and trainer — and upon my best endeavours to interrogate the therapy phenomenon as openly and in as presuppositionless a way as I have been able. I further believe that views such as these are never anyone's personally 'owned' property or creation, but have in some mysterious sense been channelled through the writer from the culture; and in this particular case I happen to be the person who has channelled and expressed them. Whether what I have written proves to have any credence or mileage will depend upon whether it finds a resonance within the evolving culture of therapy, and not on whether it is in some sense 'objectively true' in any naïve 'Correspondence Theory of Truth' sense.

It might also be objected that there is some personal disappointment about therapy fuelling the arguments in this chapter. Kennard and Small (1997b: 161) write that 'It may be that many of psychotherapy's critics criticise ... [because] they feel let down that it doesn't have all the answers' (David Kalisch has made a similar point to me in a personal communication). My response is that although there is some truth in this in my own case, it does not follow that critical arguments are therefore *ipso facto* invalid. That is, and as Masson (1992) has also implied, whether an argument is plausible or realistic is logically independent of its emotional rootedness or drivenness. Indeed, I believe that *all* of the positions we take and the belief systems to which we adhere — including 'pro' and 'anti' therapy positions — have crucial emotional roots; and this chapter will have more than served its purpose if it leads those with (emotionally rooted) pro-therapy views to examine more deeply their own particular belief systems, assumptions and clinical practices.

References

Albee, G. W. (1990) The futility of psychotherapy. *Journal of Mind and Behavior* 11 (3–4): 369–84

Alcoff, L. M. (1996) *Real Knowing: New Versions of the Coherence Theory*. Ithaca, NY: Cornell University Press

Alexander, R. (1995) *Folie à Deux: An Experience of One-to-One Therapy*. London: Free Association Books

Arden, M. (1998) *Midwifery of the Soul: A Holistic Perspective on Psychoanalysis*. London: Free Association Books

Bohart, A. C. and Tallman, K. (1996) The active client: therapy as self-help. *Journal of Humanistic Psychology* 36 (3): 7–30; reprinted as Chapter 27 of this volume

Bracken, P. and Thomas, P. (1998) Limits to therapy. *Open Mind* 93: 17

Burman, E. (1997) False memories, true hopes and the angelic: revenge of the postmodern in therapy. *New Formations* 30: 122–34

Cloud, D. L. (1998) *Control and Consolation in American Culture and Politics: The Rhetoric of Therapy*. Thousand Oaks, CA: Sage

Craib, I. (1987) The psychodynamics of theory. *Free Associations* 10: 32–56

Craib, I. (1992) Reply to Pilgrim. In W. Dryden and C. Feltham (eds), *Psychotherapy and Its Discontents* (pp. 243–9). Buckingham: Open University Press

Cushman, P. (1995) *Constructing the Self, Constructing America: A Cultural History of Psychotherapy*. Reading, MA: Addison-Wesley

Dupont, J. (ed.) (1995) *The Clinical Diary of Sandor Ferenczi*. Cambridge, MA: Harvard University Press

Edwards, G. (1992) Does psychotherapy need a soul? In W. Dryden and C. Feltham (eds), *Psychotherapy and Its Discontents* (pp. 194–224). Buckingham: Open University Press

Embleton Tudor, L. and Tudor, K. (1994) The personal and the political: power, authority and influence in psychotherapy. In P. Clarkson and M. Pokorny (eds), *The Handbook of Psychotherapy* (pp. 384–402). London: Routledge

Erwin, E. (1997) *Philosophy and Psychotherapy*. London: Sage

France, A. (1988) *Consuming Psychotherapy*. London: Free Association Books

Frank, J. D. and Frank, J. B. (1991) *Persuasion and Healing: A Comparative Study of Psychotherapy*, 3rd edn. Baltimore: Johns Hopkins University Press

Freud, S. (1913) On beginning the treatment... In *Standard Edition* (pp. 123–44). London: Hogarth Press

Frosh, S. (1987) *The Politics of Psychoanalysis: An Introduction to Freudian and Post-Freudian Theory*. New Haven: Yale University Press

Gergen, K. J. and McNamee, S. (1997) Foreword. In E. Riikonen and G. M. Smith, *Re-Imagining Therapy: Living Conversations and Relational Knowing* (pp. vii–ix). London: Sage

Guggenbühl-Craig, A. (1971) *Power in the Helping Professions*. Dallas: Spring Publications

Guillen, M. (1983) *Bridges to Infinity*. Los Angeles: Tarcher Publications

Habermas, J. (1978) *Communication and the Evolution of Society*. London: Heinemann

Habermas, J. (1982) *The Theory of Communicative Action*. London: Heinemann

Hart, N. (1998) Discourses of power within the therapeutic relationship. Paper presented at the British Association for Counselling Research Conference, Birmingham (mimeo)

Heron, J. (1990) The politics of transference. *Self and Society* 18 (1): 17–23; reprinted in R. House and N. Totton (eds), *Implausible Professions* (pp. 11–18). Ross-on-Wye: PCCS Books, 1997

Heron, J. (1996) *Co-operative Inquiry: Research into the Human Condition*. London: Sage

Heron, J. (1997) A self-generating practitioner community. In R. House and N. Totton (eds), *Implausible Professions* (pp. 241–54). Ross-on-Wye: PCCS Books

Hillman, J. (1997) *The Soul's Code: In Search of Character and Calling*. London: Bantam Books

Hinshelwood, R. D. (1985) Questions of training. *Free Associations* 2: 7–18

Hinshelwood, R. D. (1997) *Therapy or Coercion? Does Psychoanalysis Differ from Brainwashing?* London: Karnac Books

House, R. (1996) Conference review: Beyond the Brain, Cambridge, August 1995. *Self and Society* 23 (6): 30–1

House, R. (1997) Training: a guarantee of competence? In R. House and N. Totton (eds), *Implausible Professions* (pp. 99–108). Ross-on-Wye: PCCS Books

House, R. (1998) Counselling: performance or quality of being? *Counselling* 9 (3): 175

House, R. (2001) Psychotherapy professionalization: the post-graduate dimension and the legitimacy of statutory regulation. *British Journal of Psychotherapy*, 17 (3): 382–90; reprinted in *Ipnosis: An Independent Journal for Practitioners* 5, 2002: 28–9 and 7, 2002: 26–7

House, R. (2003) *Therapy Beyond Modernity: Deconstructing and Transcending Profession-Centred Therapy*. London: Karnac Books

Hugill, B. (1998) Analysts in trauma over identity crisis. *Observer* newspaper, 22nd March

Illich, I. (1977) *Limits to Medicine*. Harmondsworth: Penguin

Kalisch, D. (1996) Registration — who is asking the right questions? *The Therapist* 3 (4): 46

Kendall, T. and Crossley, N. (1996) Governing love: on the tactical control of countertransference in the psychoanalytic community. *Economy and Society* 25 (2): 178–94

Kennard, D. and Small, N. (1997a) Living together in uncertain times. In D. Kennard and N. Small (eds), *Living Together* (pp. 202–20). London: Quartet Books

Kennard, D. and Small, N. (1997b) Commentary: Cold comfort. In D. Kennard and N. Small (eds), *Living Together* (pp. 160–3). London: Quartet Books

King, P. and Steiner, R. (eds) (1990) *The Freud–Klein Controversies, 1941–45*. London: Routledge

Kovel, J. (1976) *A Complete Guide to Therapy*. New York: Pantheon Books (Penguin edn quoted)

Kurtz, S. (1989) *The Art of Unknowing: Dimensions of Openness in Analytic Therapy*. Northvale, NJ: Jason Aronson

Lacan, J. (1965) *Écrits*. Paris: Seuil

Laplanche, J. (1989) *New Foundations for Psychoanalysis*. Oxford: Blackwell

Lazarus, A. A. (1994) The illusion of the therapist's power and the patient's fragility: my rejoinder. *Ethics and Behavior* 4 (3): 299–306

Longman, J. (1998) Editorial. *Counselling* 9 (2): 82

McDougall, J. (1995) *The Many Faces of Eros: A Psychoanalytic Exploration of Human Sexuality*. London: Free Association Books

Masson, J. (1988) *Against Therapy*. Atheneum (London: Fontana/Collins, 1990)

Masson, J. (1992) The tyranny of psychotherapy. In W. Dryden and C. Feltham (eds) *Psychotherapy and Its Discontents* (pp. 7–29, 36–40). Buckingham: Open University Press

Mowbray, R. (1997) Too vulnerable to choose? In R. House and N. Totton (eds), *Implausible Professions* (pp. 33–44). Ross-on-Wye: PCCS Books

Parker, I. (1996) Postmodernism and its discontents: therapeutic discourse. *British Journal of Psychotherapy* 12 (4): 447–60

Parker, I. (1997a) *Psychoanalytic Culture: Psychoanalytic Discourse in Western Society*. London: Sage

Parker, I. (1997b) Discourse analysis and psychoanalysis. *British Journal of Social Psychology* 36: 479–96

Parker, I. (1998a) Constructing and deconstructing psychotherapeutic discourse. *European Journal of Psychotherapy, Counselling and Health* 1 (1): 65–78

Parker, I. (1998b) Paper presented to British Association for the Advancement of Science conference, Cardiff; reported in: Psychology a fake science that abuses public, says expert. *Daily Telegraph*, 12th September: 14

Parker, I. (1999) Deconstruction and psychotherapy. In I. Parker (ed.), *Deconstructing Psychotherapy* (pp. 1–18). London: Sage

Parker, I. (2001) What is wrong with the discourse of the university in psychotherapy training? *European Journal of Psychotherapy, Counselling and Health* 4 (1): 27–43

Parker, I., Georgaca, E., Harper, D., McLaughlin, T. and Stowell-Smith, M. (1995) *Deconstructing Psychopathology*. London: Sage

Peck, M. S. (1993) Salvation and suffering: the ambiguity of pain and disease. *Human Potential* Summer: 15, 17, 24–6

Pilgrim, D. (1992) Psychotherapy and political evasions. In W. Dryden and C. Feltham (eds) *Psychotherapy and Its Discontents* (pp. 225–43, 249–53). Buckingham: Open University Press

Pilgrim, D. (1997) *Psychotherapy and Society*. London: Sage

Riikonen, E. and Smith, G. M. (1997) *Re-Imagining Therapy: Living Conversations and Relational Knowing*. London: Sage

Rogers, C.R. (1990) Some new challenges to the helping professions. In H. Kirschenbaum and V. L. Henderson (eds), *The Carl Rogers Reader* (pp. 357–75). London: Constable (orig. *American Psychologist*, 28 [5], 1973: 379–87)

Rowe, D. (1990) Foreword. In J. Masson, *Against Therapy* (pp. 7–23). London: Fontana/Collins

Samuels, A. (1992) Foreword. In W. Dryden and C. Feltham (eds), *Psychotherapy and Its Discontents* (pp. xi–xv). Buckingham: Open University Press

Samuels, A. (1993) *The Political Psyche*. London: Routledge

Shepherd, M. and Sartorius, N. (eds) (1989) *Non-Specific Aspects of Treatment*. Toronto: Hans Huber

Skolimowski, H. (1994) *The Participatory Mind: A New Theory of Knowledge and of the Universe*. London: Penguin/Arkana

Smail, D. (1983). Psychotherapy and psychology. In D. Pilgrim (ed.), *Psychology and Psychotherapy: Current Trends and Issues* (pp. 7–20). London: Routledge and Kegan Paul

Smail, D. (1987) Psychotherapy and 'change': some ethical considerations. In S. and G. Fairbairn (eds), *Psychology, Ethics and Change* (pp. 31–43). London: Routledge and Kegan Paul

Smail, D. (1996) *How to Survive Without Psychotherapy*. London: Constable

Spinelli, E. (1996) Do therapists know what they're doing? In I. James and S. Palmer (eds), *Professional Therapeutic Titles: Myths and Realities* (pp. 55–61). Leicester: British Psychological Society, Div. Couns. Psychol., Occasional Paper 2

Spinelli, E. and Longman, J. (1998) Counselling and the abuse of power. *Counselling* 9 (3): 181–4

Steiner, G. (1978) Has truth a future? *The Listener* 12th January: 42–6

Tarnas, R. (1991) *The Passion of the Western Mind: Understanding the Ideas that Have Shaped Our World*. New York: Ballantine

Totton, N. (1997) Not just a job: psychotherapy as a spiritual and political practice. In R. House and N. Totton (eds), *Implausible Professions* (pp. 129–40). Ross-on-Wye: PCCS Books

Acknowledgement

I am very grateful to my colleagues and friends Jutta Gassner and David Kalisch for their (as always) detailed and incisive comments on an earlier version of this chapter, which helped me significantly to improve it.

1B: CHALLENGING PROFESSIONALISATION

EDITORIAL INTRODUCTION AND COMMENTARY

From the broad landscape of ethical dilemmas painted in Part 1A, Part 1B narrows the focus to one key issue — that of professionalisation. Implied in that general title is also accreditation, registration and statutory regulation (and henceforth in this introduction the word 'professionalisation' will be used to represent all of these). These issues are, of course, intimately linked, yet each provides its own particular challenges and bones of contention.

The editors consider this anthology to be something of a sequel to the acclaimed 1997 anthology *Implausible Professions*, which assembled very many powerful arguments against professionalisation. It is highly noteworthy, even startling, to find that in the six years since *Implausible Professions'* publication, further crucial questions and arguments have emerged which seem to further strengthen the anti-professionalisation case. Some of those questions and arguments are posed in this section. There is in this anthology some degree of reiteration of the challenges raised in *Implausible Professions*, but it is felt that until those advocating institutional professionalisation are able to provide coherent and convincing responses to these manifold concerns, it is essential that concerned practitioners continue to bring them forward.

This entire book could have been filled with penetrating and incisive anti-professionalisation articles that have appeared since 1997. The selection that follows draws together some very diverse examples. YVONNE BATES' 'Still whinging' provides a useful and succinct catalogue of many of the arguments against professionalisation. NICK TOTTON's 'The baby and the bathwater' looks at the hierarchical 'pyramid selling scheme' that is emerging due to professionalisation, and the associated demise of local knowledge systems. MICHAEL WHAN argues brilliantly that any attempt to professionalise or legislate working with the soul is oxymoronic, and makes it even harder for the soul to re-emerge in Western culture. One of the central arguments of RICHARD HOUSE's 'The statutory regulation of psychotherapy' is that the 'closed shop' which is emerging through professionalisation tends to drive out the very practitioners who bring crucial freshness of energy to our occupation. BRIAN THORNE's personal appeal to the British Association for Counselling and Psychotherapy (BACP), which first appeared in the pages of that body's journal the Counselling and Psychotherapy Journal, is no less powerful for its brevity, and is surely one of the most moving and bravely honest pieces that has been written on the subject to date. This part's final chapter by ARNOLD LAZARUS offers an horrific insight into the nightmarish situation in the USA, where rigid statutory licensing is already in place. Since it is by no means 'too late' in the UK, it is hoped that Lazarus' chapter will help to raise awareness that the disasters which some predict will befall us if we do not act to stop licensing are not ungrounded pessimism; they can be seen in all-too-stark reality across the Atlantic.

10

STILL WHINGEING: THE
PROFESSIONALISATION OF THERAPY

YVONNE BATES[†]

The 1990s may well be remembered as 'the professionalisation years' in
counselling. Setting ourselves up as a profession and installing compulsory
registration has been a major concern. So much has been written about the subject
that some people are tired of hearing about it. In a letter to the editor of the
British Association for Counselling's *Counselling* magazine in February 1999,
Graham Wilson (1999: 3) asks:

> Do you think we could stop publishing the whingeing and drawn out
> criticism about the BAC's approach to improving standards? This stuff is
> really getting tedious ...Outside I know of no one who would dispute the
> need and many ridicule the minimal standards required.

This chapter will focus on why that 'whingeing' is still continuing, and indeed
why anyone would be against counselling gaining respect as a profession and
proving its worth through research and well-policed registered practice. It would
seem futile to 'whinge' in any case since it is claimed that European law will
enforce these changes on us, both by making it illegal to practise if not on the
register (Frankland 1996) and by bringing UK law into line with other European
Community (EU) countries, making it illegal to offer any service for remuneration
unless it has been approved as legal (thus preventing people calling it something
other than 'counselling' and continuing to practise) (Wasdell 1992). It should be
noted, however, that Mowbray (1995a) argues that (certainly up to the mid-
1990s) neither the UK nor the European government has shown any interest in
initiating legislative changes.

Even ignoring the spectre of the EU, many counsellors (e.g. Feltham 1995;
Lefébure 1996) feel that the professionalisation process is inevitable and that we
should just surrender to it despite our reservations. Counselling has been widely
adopted in the public sector and by general practitioners, and so is being seen
more as a medical instrument. Counsellors are thus subject to demands for cost-
justification (via scientific research) and cost-effectiveness (via the adoption of
short-term models) by these major employers. As the professionalisation process
gathers pace, counsellor training is incorporated more and more into university
curricula, rendering it more academic and encouraging the scientific and research

† This chapter first appeared in *Changes: An International Journal of Psychology and
Psychotherapy,* 18(2), 2000: 91-9, published by PCCS Books, and appears by kind permission
of the author.

elements being demanded by employers. This is compounded by the fact that academics find it easier to get books and articles published, and so have kudos and credibility, have the opportunity to persuade, occupy prominent positions in the professional organisations, and have a vested interest (Postle and Anderson 1990) in fostering the professionalisation, 'scientification' and 'academicisation' of counselling. A former chair of the UK Council for Psychotherapy (UKCP), Emmy van Deurzen-Smith (cited in Postle 1998) said in a keynote address to the UKCP in 1996 that, 'We have to transform what used to be a craft or an art based on moral or religious principles into a scientifically based accountable professional expertise', and stating that this is necessary in order to secure more research funding.

Another major influence on the process has been a seemingly constant flow of media criticism of counselling, the most prominent of which was BBC TV's 'Watchdog' programme on 26th February 1996. Such criticism seems to have provoked a rather defensive response which seems to have fuelled the push towards professionalisation and licensing (House 1996c; Thorne 1997).

So given the apparent inevitability of professionalisation and licensing, the power behind it and the idea that it is in the client's best interests, we might ask why the whingeing, as Dr Wilson puts it, continues. Some (e.g. Frankland 1996: 56) implore the whingers to view accreditation as 'a suitable challenge, a step in professional development and a learning opportunity in its own right'. Some would argue that the 'whingers' are counsellors who are simply not prepared to put in the work required to get accredited. It will be contested in this chapter that far from this being the case, the 'whingers' represent a substantial, rapidly growing but relatively voiceless proportion of Britain's counsellors who are concerned that where we are going is *not* in the client's best interests, and fear that in fact it will be quite harmful to the client.

As this new era of professional counselling dawns, it may be useful to project the current trends into the future in order to predict what the client will get from counselling.

First, *the client will get the illusion of security*. By introducing a register of approved counsellors who have all been trained in a certain way to a certain 'standard', we may be offering the client false reassurances that this will reduce the likelihood that she will be damaged by the counsellor. As Wasdell (1992) points out, such confidence would be misplaced. It may encourage her to drop her natural guard, in the same way that someone might let a police officer through their front door late at night but would not do so for someone without credentials. There is simply no evidence to suggest that a registered counsellor will be any less damaging than a non-registered one (House 1996a; Pilgrim 1997; Postle 1998). As Carl Rogers (cited in Mowbray 1995: 113) states, 'There are as many certified charlatans and exploiters of people as there are uncertified'. Moreover, the increasing number of statistics (via scientific research) which seem to vouch for its effectiveness also reassure the client that counselling is a scientifically proven discipline practised by carefully screened professionals. It appears to be a treatment which promises to 'cure' clients.

There are several problems with sending out messages like this. First, as Heron (1990: 17) points out, it 'legitimises psychotherapists taking money under the pretence of offering a service that did some good'. Research has *not* demonstrated unequivocally that counselling works, and it certainly has not demonstrated how or why it works, or what aspects of it work and in what ways (Erwin 1997; Feltham 1995; Thorne 1997). Our fear of ridicule or accusations of quackery lead us to clutch at straws, claiming 'research proves it works' when it does no such thing. 'Self-interest impels therapists to pretend to knowledge they do not possess' (Masson 1993: 285). It is even debatable that scientific research can ever give the answers to what is an essentially non-scientific question (House 1996a, b; Szasz 1995). Counselling is not a thing, out there, to be measured; it is a word used to describe a relationship, and as such we might just as well ask questions like 'Do relationships work?', 'Which types of relationships work better than others?' and so on.

Another issue around accepting a medicalised, scientific status is that *the client will get the message that counselling is for people who are not functioning properly.* Szasz (1995) notes that 'the degeneration of psychoanalysis — and of psychotherapy in general — is an exorable consequence of the medicalisation of life, that is, of the tendency to regard despair and deviance as diseases and talking as treatment'. The use of counselling as a tool for personal growth will become more and more marginalised. It is also possible that as medical research throws out statistics which claim that counselling is a cure that works in, say, 80 per cent of cases, *the client will believe either that his own investment is irrelevant or, conversely, that if he does not feel better, it is his own fault* since 80 per cent of people do improve. Statistics such as those currently being demanded are dangerous weapons for authorities, convenient defences for counsellors, and of no apparent use to clients.

We live in an extremely materialistic society where people are under both temporal and financial pressure. A huge part of what counselling is about is to help the client to not lose sight of what is important and meaningful to his innermost self. To do this we need to acknowledge the constraining effects of our materialistic, cost-efficiency-driven society, rather than collude with and conform to it (O'Hara 1997; Thorne 1997). Sadly, the purse-strings for counsellors who are not in private practice are often held by bureaucrats and civil servants who demand the very materialism and cost-efficiency against which counselling seeks to shelter us. The result is that *the client will get a materialistically driven package from the materialistic world from which she may want or need to distance herself.* Kalisch (1990: 27) notes that humanistic psychology plays the role of a 'social sanctuary' and warns that 'by surrendering the historical rebel role ... we project the rebel elsewhere, tighten ranks against him/her, and alienate him/her to other, perhaps more dubious causes'.

The drive towards high efficiency is encouraging the use of brief, time-limited counselling solutions (House 1996b) and therapeutic approaches which lend themselves to both easier research and cost justification (ibid.; O'Hara 1997). In practice this means predominantly, if not exclusively, cognitive-behavioural approaches (Thorne 1999). Some would argue that this is the emergence of 'conveyor-belt counselling' where clients' thinking is quickly reprogrammed as the perpetual waiting-lists are fed through the system. The popularity of cognitive-behavioural therapy with the 'powers that be' can be seen clearly in the USA, where of the first 20 clinical treatments to be endorsed by the American Psychological Association's task force on 'practical guidelines', 19 were cognitive-behavioural (O'Hara 1997). In short, *the client will get a ration of six sessions or less, and will get a much narrower choice of approaches — predominantly cognitive-behavioural.*

The choice of approaches even in private practice will diminish, since private practitioners will have to go through the same registration/licensing procedures, which will involve more and more university-run, homogenised training courses focused on the market demands of the public sector. As journalist Melanie Phillips (1996, cited in House, n.d.) writes, people are 'being funnelled towards qualifications which mask their vocational deficiencies by increased social status'. Therefore *the client will get a counsellor who has been blinkered in her professional development and whose innovation has been stifled.* Feltham (1995) observes that many claim that scientifically trained practitioners are 'handicapped' as counsellors because they have too narrow a focus and are over-mechanical.

Such restrictions will act as a deterrent to innovative and creative people who are considering a career as a counsellor. Postle and Anderson (1990: 27) ask, 'Isn't the professionalisation of psychotherapy denying one of the lessons of its own history, that the trapping of expertise in professions leads to defensive monopolies that legislate against innovation and change?' *The client will get counsellors who tend towards conformity and who may not really believe in what they are doing.* Masson (1993: 296) warns that 'professional loyalty means subordinating human impulses to what is considered most advantageous to the profession'. Thorne (1997: 158) believes this is a fundamental incongruity for a person-centred counsellor, and that 'the harsh truth is that person-centred therapists who fall victim to conditions of worth which alienate them from their own essential wisdom are no longer capable of being therapists'. For the client, working with a counsellor in this position will feel incongruent at best, and at worst, he might be encouraged into collusive conformity or even be encouraged to rebellion either through projection or (counter-)transference on the part of the counsellor-in-denial (Wasdell 1992). As Heron (1990: 18) writes, 'One can scarcely have much confidence in psychotherapists whose need to have their management of transference government approved is itself a sign of unresolved transference material'.

At present in the UK (i.e. as of *circa* 1998), it is just about possible for a counsellor to develop her own learning scheme rather than follow a formalised training programme, since counsellors are eligible for accreditation with little or no formal training as long as they have seven years of supervised experience. It seems unlikely that this will continue to be a viable route to accreditation (and therefore registration) for very long. If compulsory registration is introduced, it will become extremely difficult to gain seven years' experience without being on the register in the first place. The likelihood is that trainee counsellors will only be allowed to gain experience in a registered practice/ organisation, and these, as discussed above, are most likely to offer time-limited cognitive-behavioural counselling, and expect their counsellors to train in that approach. The result will be that in order to become a counsellor, it will be necessary to undergo an extensive 3–5 year academic training programme, predominantly through a university, whilst working for minimal (or no) wages on a placement, possibly whilst incurring regular supervision and personal counselling fees (depending on the generosity of the employer). One would have to have substantial financial backing and confidence in one's academic ability to undertake such a venture. Many potentially excellent counsellors will be prevented from being able to fulfil their potential, as the former chair of the BAC, Judith Baron, concedes (Baron 1996). *The client will have fewer counsellors from which to choose.*

The often fearful forces that would 'tighten up' and professionalise the art, above all the craft, of listening, might, if we are not careful, endanger the work of the common counsellor, who has the expertise, the sense of knowing and feeling how to be with a client, but not necessarily the academic ability or compliance to pass tests successfully and thus become, in the eyes of others and even self, an expert.

(Sivyer 1995: 276)

The client will have access only to privileged, affluent and academically gifted counsellors. Not all clients would choose a counsellor with that general background. The cost of training and the tilting of the balance towards demand exceeding supply will drive counselling prices up — *the client will have to pay more for counselling,* and it will become even less accessible to those on low incomes (House 1995). The increase in counselling fees will be reflected in increased supervision fees, and the combined effect of these increases may be cumulative in successive generations of practice.

It does not require a great leap in imagination to predict that the development of such an elite, narrowly focused set of 'professionals' will give rise to some of the problems observed in other professions — the traditional medical profession, for example. Few would dispute that there is an imbalance of power between patients and doctors, that the profession tends to 'protect its own' when dealing with complaints, and that too many of its members have a dogmatic certainty that their own views represent the 'right way' or truth. This may be in part (or wholly) due to the elitist structure of the profession, its prescriptive and academic route to registration, and to its hierarchical and patriarchal nature, all of which can be seen developing in counselling (House 1996a), and all of which mitigate against egalitarian ideals and philosophical freedom. Pilgrim (1997: 114) notes that 'psychotherapists can be found making statements *implying* expert certainty, which are unfounded and can border on the ridiculous'. Clients will be treated less as equal humans and more as objects; and as Laing writes,

one has to be able to orientate oneself as a person in the other's scheme of things rather than only to see the other as an object in one's own world ... one must be able to effect this orientation without prejudging who is right and who is wrong.

(Laing 1969: 26)

In short, *the client will encounter more closed-minded, dogmatic counsellors claiming to be experts* (Postle 1998; Thorne 1997) and ironically, *the client will have less access to protection and justice* when ranks are closed.

The professionalisation process seems also to be giving rise to practices which seem humiliating and punitive. It is not obvious whose benefit such practices are serving. One example is the ghoulish pillorying of complainees in the pages of the former BAC's *Counselling* magazine and its supplements. One could be forgiven for thinking of Stalin's show trials when seeing these pages. O'Hara (1997) also points to examples of out-group discrimination in the USA. It is hard to believe that this is the best that can be offered by a professional body of an occupation whose role is to promote self-esteem and to empower people.

A friend of one of my clients said that I was not really his friend because he has to pay for my time. He replied that we all pay for friendship in different ways. The Chambers' dictionary definition of friendship is 'Attachment from mutual esteem; friendly assistance', and these seem to be words which could also describe counselling. Rogers (1967: 201) notes: 'I enter the relationship not as a scientist, not as a physician who can accurately diagnose and care, but as a person, entering into a personal relationship.' There are special boundaries to the friendship, and part of the counsellor's commitment to it is to learn as much as she can about effective ways of helping, theories of human development and potential, what she brings to relationships, and ways in which she can work most effectively within this particular relationship. Whilst she might use skills training, theory training, personal counselling and supervision (respectively) to meet those objectives, there are many other ways in which she could meet them.

It seems extremely disempowering to foist a particular set of rules on someone as to how they should learn to conduct relationships. This is all in the name of protecting the client from dubious, ineffective or unscrupulous counsellors, but in practice it will have the opposite effect, for many of the reasons discussed above. Still, the professionalisation bandwagon rolls on, colluding with the public's fear of being hurt, and claiming to be able to protect the client from the risks involved in entering a relationship. As Szasz (1972: 173) writes, 'We must scrutinise ... all therapeutic attitudes traditionally ascribed to benevolence, keeping always in mind that such manoeuvres on the part of the therapist may serve only to depreciate and subjugate the patient' — or as Heron (1990: 19) puts it, 'In the guise of protecting their clients from the unqualified, they will oppress them'.

Perhaps the response to Bernard Manning's membership of the BAC should have been 'Yes, of course he can call himself a counsellor, but who would choose to employ him as one?'. As Mowbray (1995b) points out, *the client is being insulted that she cannot judge for herself whom to take a risk in trusting, and she is being given insufficient and inappropriate information on which to base her choice*. We should not attempt to choose relationships for other people, which is effectively what we are doing. Masson (1993: 288) points out that 'if anyone ever developed the ability to make the "match" [of client to counsellor] .. there would be no divorce'. If the client is given a portfolio containing details of the counsellor's relevant developmental/learning processes of a theoretical, practical and personal nature, together with a statement of professional philosophy and some indication of practice (in other words, what Schultz [cited in Postle 1998] calls 'full disclosure' — see Postle's Chapter 17, this volume), he would then be able to make an informed, adult choice about whether he feels that this particular counsellor would suit him.

Counsellors who feel that arguments such as those articulated in this chapter are merely scaremongering, or the result of the author's unresolved unconscious conflicts, or simply over-pessimistic, need only look to the emerging pattern in the USA to observe the decay of the profession there (Mowbray 1995; O'Hara 1997). Frankland (1996) suggested that the debate has now moved on to one of which system of professionalisation is best. Perhaps to his surprise, and to the further irritation of Graham Wilson (1999), there are many 'whingers' like myself who are determined to keep this debate alive, and who are committed to protecting the interests of the client, not by elevating their own status, but by climbing down from their ivory towers and entering into a genuine human encounter with an equal human being.

REFERENCES

Baron, J. (1996) The emergence of counselling as a profession. In R. Bayne, I. Horton and J. Bimrose (eds), *New Directions in Counselling* (pp. 16–24). London: Routledge

Erwin, E. (1997) *Philosophy and Psychotherapy*. London: Sage

Feltham, C. (1995) *What is Counselling*. London: Sage

Frankland, A. (1996) Accreditation and registration. In R. Bayne, I. Horton and J. Bimrose (eds), *New Directions in Counselling* (pp. 25–36). London: Routledge

Frankland, A. (1997) Professional recognition: accreditation and reaccreditation. In P. Wilkins (ed.), *Personal and Professional Development for Counsellors* (pp. 50–64). London: Sage

Heron, J. (1990) The politics of transference. *Self and Society* 18(1): 17–23 (source: G.O.R.I.L.L.A Web Site; also reprinted in R. House and N. Totton (eds), *Implausible Professions* (pp. 11–18). Ross-on-Wye: PCCS Books)

House, R. (1995) The dynamics of power: why Mowbray is right about professionalisation. *Counselling News* 20: 24–5

House, R. (1996a) The professionalization of counselling: a coherent 'case against'? *Counselling Psychology Quarterly* 9 (4): 343–58

House, R. (1996b) The dynamics of professionalism: a personal view of counselling research. *Counselling* 8 (3): 200–4

House, R. (1996c) In the wake of *Watchdog*. *Counselling* 7 (2): 115–16

House, R. (n.d.) Professional vs. vocational training in counsellor development (source: Internet *http://lpiper.demon.co.uk/*)

Kalisch, D. (1990) Professionalisation: a rebel view. *Self and Society* 18 (1): 24–9 (source: G.O.R.I.L.L.A Web Site)

Laing, R. D. (1969) *The Divided Self*. London: Pelican

Lefébure, M. (1996) Who will count as a counsellor? Gleanings and tea-leaves. In R. Bayne, I. Horton and J. Bimrose (eds), *New Directions in Counselling* (pp. 5–15). London: Routledge

Masson, J. (1993) *Against Therapy*. London: Harper Collins

Mowbray, R. (1995a) *The Case Against Psychotherapy Registration: A Conservation Issue for the Human Potential Movement*. London: Trans Marginal Press.

Mowbray, R. (1995b) Organic growth. *Counselling News* 19 (September): 8–9 (source: Internet http://lpiper.demon.co.uk/)

O'Hara, M. (1997) Emancipatory therapeutic practice in a turbulent transmodern era: a work of retrieval. *Journal of Humanistic Psychology* 37 (3): 7–33

Pilgrim, D. (1997) *Psychotherapy and Society*. London: Sage

Postle, D. (1998) The alchemist's nightmare: Gold into lead — the annexation of psychotherapy in the UK. *International Journal of Psychotherapy* 3 (1): 53–83 (source: Internet http://lpiper.demon.co.uk/)

Postle, D. and Anderson, J. (1990) Stealing the flame. *Self and Society* 18 (1): 13–15 (source: G.O.R.I.L.L.A Web Site)

Rogers, C. R. (1967) *On Becoming a Person*. London: Constable

Sivyer, J. (1995) The common counsellor. *Counselling* 6 (4): 276–7

Szasz, T. (1972) *The Myth of Mental Illness* London: Paladin

Szasz, T. (1995) The healing word: its past, present and future. Address at the Milton Erikson Evolution of Psychotherapy Conference, Las Vegas, Nevada, 13–17th December (source: Internet http://lpiper.demon.co.uk/)

Thorne, B. (1997) Counselling and psychotherapy: the sickness and the prognosis. In S. Palmer and V. Varma (eds), *The Future of Counselling and Psychotherapy* (pp. 153–66). London: Sage

Thorne, B. (1999) The move towards brief therapy: its dangers and its challenges. *Counselling* 10 (1): 7–11

Wasdell, D. (1992) In the shadow of accreditation. *Self and Society* 20 (1): 3–14 (source: G.O.R.I.L.L.A Web Site)

Wilson, G. (1999) Letter to the editor. *Counselling* 10 (1): 3

11

THE BABY AND THE BATHWATER: 'PROFESSIONALISATION' IN PSYCHOTHERAPY AND COUNSELLING

NICK TOTTON[†]

> I have slowly come to the conclusion that if we did away with 'the expert', 'the certified professional', 'the licensed psychologist', we might open our profession to a breeze of fresh air, a surge of creativity, such as has not been known for years. In every area — medicine, nursing, teaching, bricklaying, or carpentry — certification has tended to freeze and narrow the profession, has tied it to the past, has discouraged innovation. ... The question I am humbly raising, in the face of what I am sure will be great shock and antagonism, is simply this: Can psychology find a new and better way?
>
> (Rogers 1973: 246–7)

I THE RUSH TO PROFESSIONALISATION

> Good morning, lemmings.
> (Railway graffiti near Paddington Station, London)

The unfortunate truth is that the primary response to Carl Rogers' question, in 1973 and now, is not so much 'shock and antagonism' as a deafening silence. Rogers (who developed the term 'counselling' because he was himself unable to get certified as a psychotherapist) is by no means the first significant figure in the field to oppose aspects of professionalisation: for example, Freud vehemently objected to the medical model of psychoanalysis (Freud 1926) which was intimately tied to professionalisation (Jacoby 1986: 145), while Jung said of psychotherapy that 'holding lectures, giving instruction, pumping in knowledge, all these ... procedures are of no use here' (Adler 1976: 534).

Many eminent and well-respected contemporary figures have also expressed reactions ranging from horror to despair at what is happening to counselling and psychotherapy, both in the UK and in the USA (e.g. Heron 1990; Lomas 1996; O'Hara 1997; Thorne 1997). The opponents of headlong professionalisation have largely dominated the argument; but its proponents' strategy of what in German is called *Totschweigen* (deathly silence), combined with remorseless organisational advance, meets with continued success.

---

† This chapter first appeared in the *British Journal of Guidance and Counselling*, 27(3), 1999: 313–24, and is reprinted here by kind permission of the author and the *BJGC*.

What is 'headlong professionalisation'? This question can readily be answered by scanning the pages of just about any recent issue of a trade journal in the field. For example, the August 1998 issue of *Counselling*, the journal of the British Association for Counselling (BAC), includes a letter from David Buckingham which says:

> Counsellor training is still expanding. There are ten times as many diploma courses as there were a few years ago. The cart appears to be before the horse. Courses are offered, places are filled, and there is a hope that there will be enough available clients to provide the practice the students require. ... [H]ow long will it be before placements and clients realise that they are onto a good thing, and begin to charge *us* for the privilege of counselling them?
>
> (Buckingham 1998: 175)

There are also several letters both for and against the then new BAC accreditation requirement of 40 hours of personal therapy or counselling. Those in favour mainly focus on what Richards, Hargaden and Beazley Richards (1998: 173) call 'the need for practitioners to be engaged in a constant process of self examination, especially in the way they relate to others'. The arguments against are mainly either that research has not demonstrated the value of personal therapy in training effective practitioners; or simply that personal therapy is too hard, too unpredictable and too expensive!

Two other pieces from the same issue stand out as relevant. In the *Point of View* section, Sally Saunders argues that

> If counselling trainings are financially directed, they will be consumer led. The consumers ... may understandably choose a course that does not have the demand for personal therapy because it is cheaper to train. ... If counselling training was seen more as an apprenticeship allowing students to develop at their own pace, it might stop the rush for hasty qualification and the pressure to know it all now. ... It is surely time to re-evaluate what counselling is and who should be doing it.
>
> (Saunders 1998: 179–80)

And in an interview entitled 'Counselling and the abuse of power' (Spinelli 1998), Ernesto Spinelli, Academic Dean of the School of Psychotherapy and Counselling at Regent's College, London, questions the introduction of new standards of professionalisation through endless working parties, committees and guidelines:

> [A]ll of these things give an illusion of professional bodies. We say: 'Look, if we go to all of these meetings, if we have all these standards, if we have these codes of ethics, we must be professionals.' And we can hide our questions, about what we are professionals *of*, or *in*, or *about*, by having all these bodies to protect us.
>
> (ibid.: 182)

I am quoting these various viewpoints not in order to make a particular case, but so as to establish the ferment of confusion, doubt and disagreement which currently pervades the field — and through which the professionalisers continue to carve their determined single track.

To speak bluntly, counselling and psychotherapy training in the UK is close to being a bubble: a pyramid selling scheme, in which individuals or organisations near the top of the food chain skim off large profits, and those near the bottom starve or eat each other. Far more practitioners are being trained than there are clients available for them; and a series of emergency measures are being used to stave off the collapse of the system by lengthening the food chain further, inserting more roles and jobs — as well as client and therapist, we now have trainer, supervisor, trainer's supervisor, supervisor's trainer, supervisor's trainer's supervisor: as Spinelli 'sometimes jokingly says' to students and trainees, 'we'll eventually reach a point where we'll no longer need clients, because we can just close the circle, we can counsel each other, supervise each other, and train each other ... *ad infinitum*' (ibid.: 183).

If only this were the case! But unfortunately a supply of clients must be generated, at approximately 15 or 20 times the rate at which practitioners are being turned out (assuming that a full practice has 15 or 20 slots). The best hope for achieving this is to colonise the public sphere of free-to-the-client therapy. But as with pyramid schemes, collapse is inevitable — far sooner, usually, than the participants anticipate. Perhaps we should go back to Sally Saunders' questions quoted above: what are counselling and psychotherapy, and who should be doing them?

II DEEP BACKGROUND

Slowly but surely psychoanalysis was cleansed of all Freud's achievements. Bringing psychoanalysis into line with the world, which shortly before had threatened to annihilate it, took place inconspicuously at first. ... Form eclipsed content; the organisation became more important than its task.

(Reich 1973 [1942]: 125)

All this has happened before. In his 1954 paper 'Therapeutic problems in the analysis of the "normal" candidate', the American psychoanalyst Maxwell Gitelson reports that some analysts 'have begun to despair of the suitability of "normal" candidates for a career in psycho-analysis' (Gitelson 1954: 413). He quotes Hans Eissler, who, after working with someone who wanted therapy 'only for professional reasons', decided that he 'would never again try the analysis of a "normal" person' (ibid.: 414). Gitelson also quotes the then President of the American Psychoanalytic Association, Robert Knight, on how 'the great increase in numbers of trainees ... and ... the more structured training of institutes' had changed the sort of people coming for training. In the 1920s and early 1930s, Knight says,

many gifted individuals with definite neuroses or character disorders were trained. They were primarily introspective individuals, inclined to be studious and thoughtful, and tended to be highly individualistic. ... read prodigiously and knew the psycho-analytic literature thoroughly.

In contrast, perhaps the majority of students of the past decade or so have been 'normal' characters, or perhaps one should say had 'normal character disorders'. They are not introspective, are inclined to read only the literature that is assigned in institute courses, and wish to get through with the training requirements as rapidly as possible. ... Their motivation for being analysed is more to get through this requirement of training rather than to ... explore introspectively and with curiosity their own inner selves. ... The partial capitulation of some institutes arising from numbers of students, from their ambitious haste, and from their tendency to be satisfied with a more superficial grasp of theory, has created some of the training problems we now face.

(Knight 1953, quoted in Gitelson 1954: 414)

There is an uncanny parallel with some of the passages from *Counselling* magazine. The same complaint is being made that people are training for the wrong reasons, coming from the wrong place internally, that they are concerned with the job rather than the work, and with looking into others rather than into themselves; and for the same underlying reasons — like American psychoanalysis in the 1950s, the occupation of psychotherapy and counselling has shifted to a more central and acceptable cultural position.

The rise of the 'normal' practitioner dovetails very neatly with the re-medicalisation of therapy. People have struggled for decades to establish that psychotherapy is, as Freud said of psychoanalysis, 'not a specialised branch of medicine' (Freud 1926); that those wanting therapy are not *sick*, since unhappiness or a desire to change are not illnesses. The drive to professionalisation, the enormous expansion of training, demands a huge increase in clients. The only way to get enough therapy and counselling paid for, it appears, is to get the state and other institutions to pay for it. For this to happen, psychotherapy and counselling must present themselves as somehow *medical*.

In the United States, the dominant issue has been getting therapy paid for by medical insurance. Reasonably enough from their point of view, the insurers have required that the treatment they are paying for is medical treatment: in other words, that the client is defined as ill. A whole profession of 'managed care' has arisen to administer this process; demanding that each client is assigned a 'DSM number' — a psychiatric definition, based on the *Diagnostic and Statistical Manual of the American Psychiatric Association, Fourth Edition*, of the supposed disease entity from which they are suffering. (The diagnostic categories of *DSM IV* are a masterpiece of circularity and vacuity; for example '312.9: Disruptive Behavior Disorder'.) Each DSM number is allotted a fixed number of authorisable sessions, irrespective of the individual client's needs.

Internet users will be familiar with expressions of outrage from American practitioners over the distortions of therapeutic relationship and process entailed. (For a print account see, for example, O'Hara 1997: 24–8; also Totton 1997a: 113–4.) We in the UK may congratulate ourselves on having escaped. But we have our own mild-mannered version of managed care: the presence of counselling and psychotherapy in the National *Health* Service, which, although it lets therapy reach large numbers of people who would not otherwise get it (although they may not always want it or be suitable for it), also means that the concept of audited, cost-effective, time-limited therapy and counselling becomes central (House 1996; Totton 1997a). And, of course, the NHS benefits in turn from the training bubble by being able frequently to pay GP practice counsellors a pittance — it is a buyer's market.

III EXPERT SYSTEMS/LOCAL KNOWLEDGES

> I have felt for some years now like a man who is in danger because he has become imprisoned in the profession of therapy.
>
> (Thorne 1997: 141)

The sociology of professions emphasises two defining features of a profession: the possession of 'expert knowledge' (Giddens 1991; Stehr 1994), and the use of *political strategies* to establish a small elite group in control of its own boundaries. These strategies include 'social closure' (Parkin 1974), 'occupational imperialism' (Larkin 1983), state support and market control (Larson 1977). The medical profession can serve as a template of such processes, and a number of authors have described its use of such strategies to establish a uniquely powerful role for itself (e.g. Cant and Sharma 1996; Griggs 1982; Larkin 1983; Stacey, 1992).

Psychotherapy and counselling — or rather, powerful groups within these occupations — are trying in many ways to repeat the success of medicine. This is partly in resistance to medicine's 'occupational imperialism': one of the powerful forces in the development of the Rugby Conference, which ultimately became the UK Council for Psychotherapy (UKCP), was the fear that psychiatry would attempt to 'own' the activity of psychotherapy, as it does in many European countries (Heron 1990; Wasdell 1992).

Psychotherapy and counselling have responded to the political need for a body of 'expert knowledge' by generating one — radically lengthening and widening trainings, 'technicalising' every aspect of the work, inserting new levels and meta-levels of expertise and qualification. All this in a field where research shows repeatedly that *technique and outcome cannot be shown to be connected*, that '[t]here are ... hundreds of different versions of psychotherapy, and many of them seem to work equally well' (Mair 1992: 146)

This verdict (backed up by, for instance, Orlinsky and Howard [1986] and Frank [1973]) seems to, but doesn't, support the notion of *generic* therapy, which is vital to any notion of expert knowledge: the idea that everyone is in some sense doing the same thing. There are hundreds of different forms of marriage, many of which seem to work equally well; but they are not all the same thing. And what do we mean, anyway, by 'work', in the context of a complex relationship like marriage or therapy? The UKCP, especially, finds itself in the position of gathering together under one roof people whose activities have virtually no point of similarity with one another. (Stacey [1994: 110] sees a parallel situation in medicine.) The rationale is the creation of a generic profession; but it appears that any non-empty definition of what that profession *does* leaves out half of its supposed practitioners.

Many people have expressed unease on every level at this process, but it has often been difficult to produce a clear critique of the notion of expertise. A helpful concept here is that of *local knowledge* (Geertz 1983): a term developed in anthropology and the new field of science studies to describe the opposite pole from generalised expertise which is

> formulated on a global level, that is, within the abstract 'synthetic nature' constructed by science. And the terms it is built on are to be highly standardized, quantifiable and not subject to subjective interpretations. It is through such a model, its language and its terms that the necessary control,

manipulation and supervision ... is established.

(van der Ploeg 1993: 219)

Van der Ploeg's seminal paper 'Potatoes and knowledge' (1993) studies the interplay between agrarian science and local farmers in the Andes. It describes how, from the scientists' point of view, it is 'only logical' to model the needs and procedures of agriculture in a standardised way, with so much nitrogen required equalling such and such a dose of chemical fertiliser, and so on. The practical reality of farming, for someone who knows the intricacies of their environment and works by what van der Ploeg calls *'art de la localité'*, is very different:

> However, the outcome of such methods cannot be exactly predicted. Nor can the necessary methods ... be prescribed in detail. ... Local knowledge ... is, under these conditions, rapidly becoming not just a marginal, but more than anything, a superfluous or even a counter-productive element.
>
> (ibid.: 219–20)

A closely similar struggle between expert systems and local knowledge is being played out within the field of psychotherapy and counselling. Wynne (1995) characterises local knowledges — which are always necessarily plural — as

> interwoven with *practices* ... highly dynamic systems of knowledge involving continuous negotiation between 'mental' and 'manual' [for our purposes, practical] labour, and continual interpretation of production experiences. ... However because it is so multidimensional and adaptive, experience is rarely expressed in a univocal, clear form. This is frequently mistaken for lack of theoretical content ... [But] there is indeed systematic theory, even though this is in a syntax linked to the local labour process and does not presuppose a universal and impersonal world.
>
> (ibid.: 67, my emphasis)

Is this not an excellent description of the 'knowledge system' of psychotherapy and counselling — 'multidimensional and adaptive', 'interwoven with practices'? The concept of local knowledge helps to clarify and support the repeated protests of figures like Peter Lomas (e.g. 1987, 1994) that psychotherapy is a matter of experience, intuition and human sensitivity — wisdom, in fact — rather than of technique and expertise; or Jung's statement that 'any organisation that proposes collective methods seems to me unsuitable, because it would be sawing off the branch on which the psychotherapist sits' (Adler 1976: 534). It underlines the crucial role of self-knowledge (the self being a large part of the *localité* for this particular art), and the real appropriateness of the apprenticeship model.

We can now clarify the quite straightforward socio-politico-economic reasons why counselling and psychotherapy appear to be turning their backs on their own hard-won local knowledges. *A profession must have its expertise* — which must articulate with the hegemonic expertise of its society. This expertise

> would have key characteristics: it would be taught in an organised way, most usually in a university (or at least in an institution that collects, transmits and eventually reproduces knowledge); and it would be standardized and accredited and often have scientific anchorage. ... Expert

knowledge gives some the privilege to speak, to act as arbiters.
(Cant and Sharma 1996: 6)

It is no accident that the expert systems/local knowledges dichotomy is explicitly linked with themes of colonialism and imperialism. Generic psychotherapy and counselling have used a specious version of expert knowledge to colonise and weld into an empire many diverse local craft knowledges — hence distorting them, much as medical chemistry isolates a supposed 'active ingredient' from a medicinal plant (Griggs 1982). The political impetus is so strong that it has managed to ignore how 'scientific research' itself — the system's own borrowed expertise — finds repeatedly that, although therapy and counselling seem generally beneficial, *neither technique nor training significantly affect the benefits reported* (House [1997], Mair [1992] and Mowbray [1995] all offer surveys of relevant research; for a particularly interesting example, see Seligman 1995). What *does* make therapy effective is precisely 'local knowledge' — the 'therapeutic bond' and all the imponderables on which it depends.

Another closely related metaphor has been used by Postle (1997, 1998), drawing on Shiva's (1993) concept of 'monocultures of the mind'. Like the multinational companies, generic psychotherapy and counselling extinguish local ecosystems in the interest of economies of uniformity, 'weeding out' the unique and nonconformist. As Postle points out, 'a register [of acceptable practitioners] *creates* weeds. Indeed for it to make sense, it *has* to create weeds, to justify the high cost of the education of cultivars' (1997: 154, his emphases).

The close parallel between what is happening in psychotherapy and counselling, and the historical, global effect of Western science and capitalism on local knowledge systems, is made eloquently clear in Maureen O'Hara's account of the current American situation:

> Managed care spokespeople openly describe their revolution as the industrialization of health care and, with unconcealed enthusiasm and frequently contempt, declare that the days of 'therapy as a cottage industry' are over. What is happening to therapists in the 1990s is equated with what happened to butchers, bakers and candlestick-makers in the 1800s.
>
> (O'Hara 1997: 24)

IV THE GOOD OF THE CLIENT

> The opinion of the United Kingdom Council for Psychotherapy seems to be that a recognised training is required in order for psychotherapists to be effective. There does not appear to be much evidence to support this opinion.
>
> (Mair 1992: 150)

Professionalisation has its own self-motivating dynamic: once a group decides to carve out a niche as a profession, it inevitably seeks to make boundaries around itself and to control admission. Perhaps the only way to achieve this is by laying claim to a body of expert knowledge. The fundamental motivation involved is quite simply one of self-interest. However, like many social phenomena (Lévi-Strauss 1967), the drive to professionalisation is not conscious of its own dynamic: it holds false beliefs about its own motivations. The primary conscious belief is that professionalisation is *for the good of the client*: that it will protect the public from being preyed upon by dangerous, incompetent and unscrupulous quacks.

Unfortunately there is practically no evidence in support of this belief, and a good deal against it. Richard Mowbray (1995) has extensively documented the practical, philosophical and technical reasons for doubting that registration or licensing protects the client; he draws on a wide range of sources, including Hogan's magisterial four volume work (1979). We can conclude the same thing from the everyday evidence of abusive behaviour in the long-regulated medical and legal professions (Stacey 1992, 1994). What is more, every experienced practitioner knows that practitioner abuse occurs in the most respectable and senior areas of the field, not just on the wild fringes. One well documented example is the past president of the American Psychiatric Association and the American Psychoanalytic Association, and honorary life president of the World Association for Social Psychiatry, who was found to have raped patients whom he injected with amytal (Noel and Watterson 1992).

At least as bad as the false reassurance of expertise, wisdom and unimpeach-ability is the standardised 'complaints procedure' based upon an adversarial, quasi-legal structure quite inappropriate to the sorts of situations which arise in psychotherapy and counselling (Totton 1997b). Grinding on for month after month, fitting the client to the structure rather than the structure to the client, and finally producing at best a largely irrelevant verdict of 'guilty' or 'not guilty', complaints procedures are often disastrous for all involved. Most differences between practitioner and client are far better suited to a conflict-resolution model than to a legal one. What unhappy clients often want more than anything is an apology, an acknowledgement of hurt; and, of course, this is the one thing that the professionalised complaints procedure prevents them from having. In what Brian Thorne has called 'this death-dealing culture of accountability and appraisal where the basic assumption is that nobody is really trustworthy' (Thorne 1997: 147), few practitioners will dare acknowledge error, for fear of being hung, drawn and quartered *pour encourager les autres*.

The most striking aspect of all this is the extraordinary way in which practitioners have amputated their own understanding of human psychological processes. We know about the projection of shadow figures; yet we go on talking about all these dangerous abusive therapists 'out there', and setting up ways to hound and expel scapegoats — as if this will somehow resolve our own feelings of resentment and even hatred towards our clients, for stirring us up in so many painful ways (Winnicott 1947). And accompanying this hatred, there is perhaps a profound *fear* of our clients and how they may treat us.

The professionalisation process can be understood as one of *expulsion*. Something is being got rid of; for overdetermined motivations, including the formation of boundaries towards 'social closure', and the inculcation of public anxiety about who is a 'safe' therapist. But the motivations also include, it seems, a fantasy that we can get rid of all the messy, dirty, chaotic aspects of therapy and counselling — 'cut back' the weeds, the 'sprawling plants' that 'obscure each other's light and deprive each other of nutrients' (van Deurzen 1996; see Postle 1998). This powerful and alarming metaphor, in an address by a former chair of the UKCP, raises Kleinian spectres of infantile envy and hatred, closely parallel to the suggestion that we may be throwing out the baby with the dirty bathwater which we would so much like to deny. But the dirtiness is intrinsic to the baby; and the baby is what we will, as therapists and counsellors, always be left holding.

V 'THERE IS NO ALTERNATIVE'

> Where, I ask, is the soul in all this? Could it be that all the energy I have
> devoted over the years to schemes for accreditation and recognition, all the
> many hours spent in committees and in working parties ... instead of
> improving the quality of therapy and enhancing the well-being of both
> therapists and clients has led instead to the creation of an exclusive
> professionalism and added anxiety, competitiveness and the fear of
> judgement to the lives of those who were previously lovingly and
> conscientiously responding to the needs of their clients?
>
> (Thorne 1997: 147)

The proponents of professionalisation have so far lost the argument — partly
because they have chosen not to join it. Unfortunately, though, arguments are
not everything; tremendously powerful forces are involved. At bottom,
psychotherapy and counselling are reflecting the values of capitalist society at
the end of the twentieth century: standardisation, form over content, 'give the
customer what they want (and never tell them about other possibilities)'. The
one argument to which professionalisers return again and again is a sad but
effective one: it's bound to happen. There is no alternative.

This is not wholly the case. Certainly there is and will continue to be
'professionalised' psychotherapy and counselling: hierarchical, consumer-driven
and shored up by an easy scientistic posture of expertise. It seems likely, though,
that other forms of practice and organisation will in fact survive, and even
flourish. As Foucault tells us, power and resistance are inseparable: every form
of control and centralisation immediately creates an uncontrollable margin. Many
practitioners from all schools have revolted against professionalisation, because
it so directly flouts all their 'local knowledge' — what they have learnt *in practice*
about the interactions which are central to their craft; and because it means
organising collectively in a way which actively contradicts their skilled
understanding of human nature and human groups. Some are already grouping
together to do something else: at least one organisation, the British Independent
Practitioners Network, is striving to create forms of accreditation and validation
which emerge from, rather than flout, therapeutic practice — in this case, based
on a network of peer groups (Totton 1998).

It is inappropriate to take some sort of Luddite stance, mourning the loss of
the Good Old Days: they were never that good, in our field or any other. Local
knowledges have traditionally been hamstrung by lack of meta-perspective, of
the understanding that they are in fact *local* knowledges; without this awareness
they become dogmas and rituals, preventing the development of new and better
ways. The professionalisation debate has, not always intentionally, cast a great
deal of light on hitherto 'unconscious' aspects of our work — including aspects,
like lack of accountability, that urgently need changing. We cannot go back to
the past. The issue is about the future: and the future of psychotherapy and
counselling, just like the future of our society in general, is still in contest.

REFERENCES

Adler, G. (ed.) (1976) *C. G Jung: Letters, Vol II, 1951–61*. London: Routledge and KeganPaul

Buckingham, D. (1998) Letter to the editor. *Counselling* 9 (3): 175

Cant, S. and Sharma, U. (1996) *Complementary and Alternative Medicines: Knowledge in Practice*. London: Free Association Books

Frank, J. D. (1973) *Persuasion and Healing*. Baltimore: Johns Hopkins University Press

Freud, S. (1926). The question of lay analysis. In S. Freud, *Two Short Accounts of Psycho-analysis*. Harmondsworth: Penguin (1962)

Geertz, C. (1983) *Local Knowledge: Further Essays in Interpretive Anthropology*. New York: Basic Books

Giddens, A. (1991) *Modernity and Self Identity*. Oxford: Polity Press

Gitelson, M. (1954) Theoretical problems in the analysis of normal candidates. In R. F. Lax (ed.), *Essential Papers on Character Neurosis and Treatment* (pp. 409–27). New York: New York University Press (1989)

Griggs, B. (1982) *Green Pharmacy: A History of Herbal Medicine*. London: Jill Norman and Hobhouse

Heron, J. (1990) The politics of transference. *Self and Society* 18(1): 17–23; reprinted in R. House and N. Totton (eds), *Implausible Professions: Arguments for Pluralism and Autonomy in Psychotherapy and Counselling* (pp. 11–18). Ross-on-Wye: PCCS Books, 1997

Hogan, D. B. (1979) *The Regulation of Psychotherapists*, 4 vols. Cambridge, MA: Ballinger

House, R. (1996) 'Audit-mindedness' in counselling: some underlying dynamics. *British Journal of Guidance and Counselling* 24 (2): 277–83; reprinted in R. House and N. Totton (eds), *Implausible Professions* (pp. 63–70). Ross-on-Wye: PCCS Books, 1997

House, R. (1997) Training: a guarantee of competence? In R. House and N. Totton (eds), *Implausible Professions* (pp. 99–108). Ross-on-Wye: PCCS Books

Jacoby, R. (1986) *The Repression of Psychoanalysis: Otto Fenichel and the Political Freudians*. Chicago: University of Chicago Press

Knight, R. (1953) The present status of organised psychoanalysis in the United States. *Journal of the American Psychoanalytic Association* 2

Larkin, G. (1983) *Occupational Monopoly and Modern Medicine*. London: Tavistock

Larson, M. (1977) *The Rise of Professionalism*. California: University of California Press

Lévi-Strauss, C. (1967) *Structural Anthropology*. New York: Anchor Books

Lomas, P. (1987) *The Limits of Interpretation: What's Wrong with Psychoanalysis?* Harmondsworth: Penguin

Lomas, P. (1994) *Cultivating Intuition: An Introduction to Psychotherapy*. Harmondsworth: Penguin

Lomas, P. (1997) The teaching of psychotherapy. In his *Personal Disorder and the Family*. Transaction Press; reprinted in R. House and N. Totton (eds), *Implausible Professions* (pp. 215–24). Ross-on-Wye: PCCS Books, 1997

Mair, K. (1992) The myth of therapist expertise. In W. Dryden and C. Feltham (eds), *Psychotherapy and Its Discontents* (pp. 135–60). Buckingham: Open University Press; reprinted in abridged form in R. House and N. Totton (eds), *Implausible Professions* (pp. 87–98). Ross-on-Wye: PCCS Books, 1997

Mowbray, R. (1995) *The Case Against Psychotherapy Registration: A Conservation Issue for the Human Potential Movement*. London: Trans Marginal Press

Noel, B. and Watterson, K. (1992) *You Must Be Dreaming*. New York: Poseidon Press

O'Hara, M. (1997) Emancipatory therapeutic practice in a turbulent transmodern era: a work of retrieval. *Journal of Humanistic Psychology* 37 (3): 7–33

Orlinsky, D. E. and Howard, K. I. (1986) Process and outcome in psychotherapy. In

S. L. Garfield and A. E. Bergin (eds), *Handbook of Psychotherapy and Behavior Change*. New York: Wiley

Parkin, F. (1974) Strategies of social closure in class formation. In F. Parkin (ed.), *The Social Analysis of Class Structure*. London: Tavistock

Postle, D. (1997) Counselling in the UK: jungle, garden or monoculture? In R. House and N. Totton (eds), *Implausible Professions* (pp. 151-8). Ross-on-Wye: PCCS Books

Postle, D. (1998) The alchemist's nightmare: gold into lead — the annexation of psychotherapy in the UK. *International Journal of Psychotherapy* 3 (1): 53-83

Reich, W. (1973) *The Function of the Orgasm*. London: Souvenir Press (orig. 1942)

Richards, S., Hargaden, H. and Beazley Richards, J. (1998) Letter to the editor. *Counselling* 9 (3): 173.

Rogers, C. (1980) Some new challenges to the helping professions. In his *A Way of Being* (pp. 235-59). Boston: Houghton Mifflin (orig. 1973)

Saunders, S. (1998) Envy, elitism and egoism: whose interests are counsellors meeting? *Counselling* 9 (3): 179-80

Seligman, M. E. P. (1995) The effectiveness of psychotherapy: the Consumer Reports Study. *American Psychologist* 50 (12): 965-74

Shiva, V. (1993) *Monocultures of the Mind: Perspectives on Biodiversity and Biotechnology*. London: Zed Books

Spinelli, E. (1998) Interview: Counselling and the abuse of power. *Counselling* 9 (3): 181-4

Stacey, M. (1992) *Regulating Medicine: The General Medical Council*. London: Wiley

Stacey, M. (1994) Collective therapeutic responsibility: lessons from the GMC. In S. Budd and U. Sharma (eds), *The Healing Bond: The Patient-Practitioner Relationship and Therapeutic Responsibility* (pp. 107-33). London: Routledge

Stehr, N. (1994) *Knowledge Societies*. London: Sage

Thorne, B. (1997) The accountable therapist: standards, experts and poisoning the well. In R. House and N. Totton (eds), *Implausible Professions* (pp. 141-50). Ross-on-Wye: PCCS Books; reprinted from *Self and Society*, 23 (4), 1995

Totton, N. (1997a) Inputs and outcomes: the medical model and professionalisation. In R. House and N. Totton (eds), *Implausible Professions* (pp 109-16). Ross-on-Wye: PCCS Books

Totton, N. (1997b) Learning by mistake: client-practitioner conflicts in a self-regulated network. In R. House and N. Totton (eds), *Implausible Professions* (pp. 315-20). Ross-on-Wye: PCCS Books

Totton, N. (1998) The Independent Practitioners Network: a new model of accountability. *Dialogue* 1 (1): 30-3

van der Ploeg, J.D. (1993) Potatoes and knowledge. In M. Hobart (ed.), *An Anthropological Critique of Development: The Growth of Ignorance* (pp. 209-27). London: Routledge

Van Deurzen, E. (1996) Registration: what it will mean to you as a counsellor. 5th St George's Counselling in Primary Care Conference, Keynote Address. Quoted in Postle 1998: 73

Wasdell, D. (1992) In the shadow of accreditation. *Self and Society* 20 (1): 3-14; reprinted in R. House and N. Totton (eds), *Implausible Professions* (pp. 19-32). Ross-on-Wye: PCCS Books, 1997

Winnicott, D. W. (1947) Hate in the countertransference. In his *Through Paediatrics to Psychoanalysis*. London: Hogarth Press, 1987

Wynne, B. (1995) May the sheep safely graze? A reflexive view of the expert-lay knowledge divide. In S. Lash, B. Szerzynski and B. Wynne (eds), *Risk, Environment and Modernity: Towards a New Ecology* (pp. 44-83). London: Sage

12

REGISTERING PSYCHOTHERAPY AS AN INSTITUTIONAL NEUROSIS: OR, COMPOUNDING THE ESTRANGEMENT BETWEEN SOUL AND WORLD

MICHAEL WHAN†

the fully enlightened earth radiates disaster triumphant. The program of the Enlightenment was the disenchantment of the world; the dissolution of myths.

(Theodor Adorno and Max Horkheimer)

For all the while that psychotherapy has succeeded in raising the consciousness of human subjectivity, the world in which all subjectivities are set has fallen apart. Breakdown is in a new place.

(James Hillman)

In this critique, I am raising the following question: *Is not the institutionalisation of psychotherapy by organisations which seek to limit the practice of psychology and psychotherapy by legal means to accredited practitioners and 'officially' prescribed forms of theory and practice maintaining and reinforcing, through that self-same law, an internally split and splitting (psycho-) 'logic' — namely, the rupture between the soul and the world?* This question reflects what I perceive as happening to psychotherapy with regard to 'registration' across Europe, and, in particular, in the United Kingdom. Registration is usually championed in the name of 'protecting the public' against abusive and exploitative practitioners, against 'wild' psychotherapists, to borrow from Freud's notorious phrase. The argument goes that entry into the 'profession' of psychotherapy should be via accredited training organisations, which have themselves been scrutinised by larger 'umbrella' bodies. The latter set the training 'requirements' and 'standards' in terms of what is conceived as 'good practice': this covers 'theory', 'practice' (often understood as 'application', 'technique') and 'ethics'. The focus of this question of registration mostly concerns the practitioners and would-be practitioners, not psychology or psychotherapy itself. Although there may be some criticism of certain 'ideas' and 'practices', by and large psychology and psychotherapy *as such* do not get *fundamentally* questioned. Further, the push for registration, as implied in my question, goes beyond a 'voluntary' register; it seeks the force of the law.

† Extracted from *European Journal of Psychotherapy, Counselling and Health*, 2(3), 1999: 309–323, and appears here by kind permission of the author and *EJPCH*.

In my experience, the wider *cultural*, social, as well as psychological, meanings of registration are largely undiscussed in the public forum. Indeed, apart from seeing the obvious 'protectionism', the 'territorial imperative', in such a legal institutionalisation (that is, ensuring control over the psychotherapy 'market', its economy), apart from a few dissident voices around issues such as 'autonomy' and 'pluralism' — themselves *very* worthy counter-arguments — there appears little deeper critical reflection or debate. So in raising this question publicly, I am concerned with what is happening *culturally*. I am not interested in a politics of personality: that is, I am not attacking individuals, questioning personal motives, but trying to grasp the nettle of ideas, of social and cultural trends.

The notion of psychotherapy from which I offer this critique is probably not one that conforms to the usual conception. Most psychotherapies, as I understand them, are predicated on one or other idea of subjectivity and a drive to 'self-mastery'. In this sense, the 'proper' domain of psychotherapeutic endeavour is directed towards the subjective, towards a subjectivised concept of interiority, and to the notional assertion of subjectivity. Such modalities of psychotherapy are thus predicated upon a metaphysics of subjectivism. As to the idea of psychotherapy from which I speak, I hope this will reveal itself over the course of the next few pages. Essentially, though, I am questioning the notion of subjectivity as the 'proper' or sole domain of psychotherapy. Rather, I would differentiate the psyche from the human subject. By this I mean the psyche or soul as an *autonomous factor* which, though certainly experienced subjectively, is not exclusively of it.

Though I voice my critique largely from within the tradition of Jungian and archetypal psychology, the position I'm taking finds resonances in the 'new paradigm' thinking, as with, say, the physicist David Bohm. At the end of his book *Wholeness and the Implicate Order,* he states '[our] overall approach has thus brought together questions of the nature of the cosmos, of matter in general, of life, and of consciousness'. These, Bohm suggests, are to be considered as 'projections of a common ground' (Bohm 1998: 212). Likewise, I am raising the problematical idea of soulfulness as part of the non-human world as well as the human one, as underlying both; perhaps a position ec-centric in relation to the predominant (centralising) ethos of modern psychotherapy and psychology.

In articulating my argument against statutory registration, I want to set two notions side by side. On the one hand, I shall 'return to Greece', to one of the Presocratics, in order to think psychologically by 'thinking Greek'. Alongside this, I shall refer to Max Weber's thesis concerning the dominant cultural form of the modern world — namely, its 'disenchantment'. Between these two notions, I perceive a *polemos*, a polemical relationship, between the 'ancient' and the 'modern': the modern as seeking to overcome and truly free itself from the ancient and its archaic legacies. At stake in this is the conception of the psyche as subjective only, or whether we open psychology and psychotherapy up to what used to be called the idea of the World Soul, the *Anima Mundi*. I realise this is an immensely difficult claim, but for all its problematical nature, I would stand by the worth of struggling with it; and further, that this struggle is *at the heart* of what psychotherapy is about. Out of this comes the question as to how we conceive psycho-logy, the *logos* of the psyche. And following on from this, how we conceive psycho-therapy; that is, in its original meaning as 'attending' or 'waiting upon' (*therapeia*) the 'soul' (*psyche*).

Put another way, my question is about whether the form that psychology and psychotherapy take — 'form' in the sense of their 'form of consciousness' (Giegerich 1998: 141; Berry 1982: 187

98) — more fully *express* the soul's movement and life. Or do the institutionalised modes of psychology and psychotherapy that 'voluntary' or 'legal' registration necessitate confine the psyche in an untenable way? Specifically, I would contend, they hold psychology and psychotherapy to one or other form of rationalistic, positivistic, secular and humanistic epistemology; to a mode of subjectivism which stands over and against the world as an 'object', as soulless.

To demonstrate this, I will draw from some of the writings of Freud and Jung, not because the notional rupture between the soul (psyche) and world is confined only to their psychologies, but because they well exemplify the problematical nature of depth psychology in relation to this question. Jung, in particular (being the psychological tradition with which I am most familiar), recognises and gives voice to these difficulties in his writings. This question implicates the relationship and relatedness *(eros)* of psychology and psychotherapy to the world. It demands a reflection on the very *logic* of psychology and psychotherapy. To ignore the necessity for such reflection and its cultural implications is to compound a cultural resistance to *ecological awareness and grief* — thus adding to the ecological problems of the world — which otherwise could be more fully reaching the hearts and minds of us all. Hence, we could practise and think a psychology and psychotherapy more sensitive and attentive to the world, to the afflicted realm of nature both within and around ourselves. But what registration effectively does is to place a boundary of legalised control and definition around the notion of the psyche and those permitted to work with it. This works against a more ecologically sensitive psychology and psychotherapy.

Further, from the perspective of the Jungian archetypal psychological tradition, this is contrary to its fundamental psycho-logic. For the psyche is essentially *the unknown* as it enters into the intimacy of our lives. As Jung himself puts it in *Memories, Dreams, Reflections:* 'We know that something unknown, alien, does come our way' (1963: 336). And elsewhere he wrote of the unconscious as 'not this thing or that; it is the Unknown as it immediately affects us' (1977a: 68). If this notion of the psyche as the unbeknown is truly related to and its psychological implications understood, how can an exclusionary boundary be placed around the psyche?

There is an even older precedent for this vision of the psyche. Probably the earliest 'psychological' statement in the West issues from Heraclitus, who voiced the experience of the soul: 'You would not find out the boundaries of the soul, even by travelling along every path; so deep a measure does it have' (Kirk and Raven 1977: 205). How, then, can one meaningfully practise an ecologically minded therapy of the soul, if it has already been legally, institutionally, appropriated by a psychotherapy 'profession'? What notion of the psyche and psychological work is supposedly being professed?

Essentially, the answer to this is a notion confining the psyche to the 'consulting room', one in which *psychological* attention is conflated with the 'clinical gaze'. In his *Twilight of the Idols*, Nietzsche points out the meaning behind this tactic of reducing the psyche to the known: '*Psychological explanation*. To trace something unknown back to something known is alleviating, soothing, gratifying and gives moreover a feeling of power. Danger, disquiet, anxiety attend the unknown — the first instinct is to *eliminate* these distressing states' (1978: 51). What Nietzsche is speaking of here is a psychology under the sway of the spirit of positivism, its aim precisely the disavowal of the experience of the psyche, which presences essentially as a disquieting enigma. What we deal with in psychology and psychotherapy are the images and symbols which mediate the experience of psychic reality: the phenomenal, through how it *appears*, its imaginal forms. Consequentially, these are not to be taken literally, but metaphorically. What they refer to remains in itself ultimately unknown, though it can be sensed, felt, dreamt, lived, experienced. To admit to the psyche's enigmatic nature exposes a theoretical embarrassment, a problem of grounds. For Jungian psychology and the practice of psychotherapy that derives from it, then, the psyche is a deeply problematical notion; like Bottom's dream in A *Midsummer-Night's Dream*, it is *bottomless!* Hence, to follow this positivistic line is to establish a *representation* of the psyche at the heart of which lies a fundamental repression: namely, a repression of its unknownness.

There are further consequences. Since the psyche is both the 'subject' and 'object' of psychology, the psyche itself in-forms the very fundaments of psychological theorising. Indeed, 'theorising' is just another expression of the psyche: 'in any psychological discussion we are not saying anything *about* the psyche ... the psyche is always speaking about *itself*' (Jung 1969: 269). Thus, the psyche cannot be wholly objectified in representational speech and thought. Understood in these terms, there is a *crisis of representation* in psychotherapy which cannot be avoided, a chronic crisis which belongs to its very logic. The soul as the unknown in our lives cuts right into, negates, any self-certain theoretical claims. For the nature of the psychological subject is unlike the 'subject-matter' of the natural sciences, since psychology and psychotherapy cannot rid themselves of either the subjective or the psychic. They are intrinsic to their very constitution. Every psychological approach is essentially a 'subjectively conditioned confession' (Jung 1977a: 160).

What William James called the 'personal equation' is to be found in all psychological thought and practice. The institutionalising process of registration therefore basically reifies, ratifies and legitimates a 'theory' and 'practice' — in other words, as 'objective' — what is 'subjective' by the very nature of *being psychological*. This is the logical predicament which remains hidden beneath the legitimising functions of professionalisation and registration. Psychotherapy thereby conceals its very essence, creating through the law a spurious cohesion, seeming 'rational' grounding and apparent coherence. This is skin-deep only, a 'public persona', and hides from the public the problematical nature of psychology and psychotherapy.

Further, in concealing the *mystery of the psyche* at the heart of psychotherapy, the imaginal basis of psychotherapy is obfuscated and overlaid with literalistic discourses which are drawn upon to claim a privileged authority. Ultimately, the recourse to law is the recourse to coercion, to state power. Registration is the logical and historical culmination of this substitution and reflects the loss of psychotherapy's inner authority, derived from the voice of the soul itself. Authority now has to come from some other source, namely, from the law, which offers it in a *non-psychological* form: registration. The only valid claim the psychotherapist has in his or her work concerns whether or not he or she *speaks and listens psychologically*, nothing else, no other source, and that *speaking and listening* has to *risk the vicissitudes of dialogue with the patient and* the world at large. It cannot justifiably bolster itself legalistically. This would inherently distort the dialogue and dialectic between psychotherapist and patient. It re-introduces a Hegelian 'master-slave' relation, in which the psychotherapist's speech and thought alone carry the statutory *power* or self- and other-recognition.

What is happening, then, to this notion of the soul's mystery? Basically, we have subjectivised it. Instead of experiencing it in the sense of the mystery of life, of being — as an *ontological* mystery — we have turned it into either an empirical or logical mystery: what today we speak of as 'the unconscious'. By *empirical* mystery, I mean one that is, in principle, knowable, that can be intuitively or methodologically uncovered, as, for instance, through the scientific experiment or, as in psychoanalysis, through interpretation. Here we would perhaps talk, rather, of demystification. The notion of a *logical* mystery expresses itself, for instance, in the idea of a 'transcendental subject' — that is, the subject to which all things have to be 're-presented', the 'representational subject', but which, *a priori*, transcends a full self-knowledge. It cannot, as it were, get round to the back of itself in order to see itself seeing. It remains the condition of knowledge, but it cannot be completely transparent to itself.

Hence, registration and its attendant organisational structures and processes are a contemporary form of what Friedrich Schiller and, after him, Max Weber called the 'disenchantment of the world'. Fundamentally, this comprises the increasing *rationalisation* and *bureaucratisation* of everything. It is the programme of the Enlightenment, whereby rationalism comes to dominate all spheres of human and natural life. Thus, in establishing psychotherapy as a 'profession', in subjecting and subjugating 'theory' and 'practice' to standardising measures, to socially and intellectually approved forms, the idea of the soul and the ways of attending to it *(maieutics)* are being increasingly rationalised, and, in terms of the necessary organisational structures and processes of registration, bureaucratised. Only in this way can regulation function. Hence the many have to be subordinated to the one. To claim any grounds for registration, notions of the psyche, psychology and psychotherapy have to be formulated in modes of thought and language that are rationally and bureaucratically 'accountable'. That is, they have to be *explainable* in a way that can be attested legally, have to be *said* in terms that affirm the languages of law, government, administration and the prevailing socio-economic culture. (Witness the effects of the private insurance industry on the practice of psychotherapy!) Can you imagine, for example, the following definition of the task of psychology being inscribed in the constitution of a public psychotherapy regulatory body? It is from Jung and states how he understands the psychological vocation as being 'fundamentally nothing but attempts, ever renewed, to give an answer to the question of the interplay between the "here" and "hereafter"' (1963: 299). Intellectually, such a definition makes a profound sense in terms of the traditions of thought and of the experiences that influenced Jung.

Of course, anyone has the intellectual right to argue against such a definition of psychotherapy, and many, no doubt, would certainly not subscribe to it. Whatever, there is the freedom to accept or reject it. No one has inscribed a definition in law. Dialogue, debate, dialectics, are all possible when intellectual liberty is maintained. Given one or other definition, even if such a definition can be arrived at, the force of law would kill this fundamental freedom in one stroke. It would kill off dialogue, and hence would be a form of suicide; for psychotherapy is nothing if it is not a dialogue, a dialectic. An attempt to define psychotherapy in terms that would accommodate legal, governmental and administrative means would probably have to speak in a 'clinical', 'positivistic' and 'humanistic' form; in other words, one that can give an account of itself in terms of calculative, instrumental reason. Such a definition aims precisely to eliminate the notion of the psyche's mystery and to substitute for it a rationalised concept. The problem with this, however, is that, if the experience of the psyche, the soul, moves us into a place of the unknown, but *imaginally* perceived mystery, how can we fully *know what psychology and psychotherapy are?* But we do make just this assumption when we encapsulate it in rationalistic formulations, for such a knowing is implied by it. If, on the other hand, we accept the mystery of the soul, then the psychological project(tion) cannot be completely accounted for; its cultural direction (teleology) becomes an open question, a dialogue, as it were, with an *as-yet-unknown future.*

The process of disenchantment happens, though, not from the 'outside' alone; *it is inherent within modern psychology and psychotherapy themselves.* Indeed, psychology has been one of the major cultural products of the Enlightenment programme of rationalisation. As will be evident when, shortly, I focus on Jung's thought, he was very aware of this consequence as an outcome of psychology. What statutory registration *further* does, then, is to intensify this tendency within psychology and psychotherapy, to reinforce and ossify them in the 'status quo', in its rationalised concepts of both. Fundamental to this disenchanting logic is the divorce between the notion of the soul and the world. The *inward turn of* psychology and psychotherapy is accomplished by a *turning away* from *the* world, and this turning away becomes compounded by professional and legal structures. Psychology and psychotherapy become *petrified!* Underlying the question of registration are many anxieties that I have rarely heard psychologists and psychotherapists address in public — indeed, just as rarely in private. What about economic anxieties?

To explore this notion of a split between the psyche and the world in more detail, I want to turn now to some of Freud's statements. First, this from *The Future of an Illusion*, in which he writes:

> For the principal task of civilisation, its *raison d'être*, is to defend us against nature ... There are the elements, which seem to mock at all human control; the earth which quakes and is torn apart and buries all human life and its works; water, which deluges and drowns everything in a turmoil; storms, which blow everything before them; there are diseases, which we have only recently recognised as attacks by other organisms; and finally there is the painful riddle of death, against which no medicine has yet been found, nor probably will be. With these forces nature rises up against us, majestic, cruel, and inexorable; she brings to our mind once more our weakness and helplessness, which we thought to escape through the work of civilisation.
> (Freud 1961a: 15–16)

In the following passage, Freud speaks directly of turning away from the world, implying that psychoanalysis is a scientific technique in the human self-defence against, and attack on, nature:

> Against the dreaded external world one can only defend oneself by some kind of turning away from it, if one is to solve the task by oneself. There is,

indeed, another and better path: that of becoming a member of the human community and with the help of a technique guided by science, going over to the attack against nature and subjecting her to the human will. Then one is working with all for the good of all. But the most interesting methods of averting suffering are those that seek to influence our own organism.

(Freud 1961b: 26)

In Freud's writings, the inward turn of psychoanalysis is predicated on a polarisation between 'civilisation' and 'nature'. The relationship to nature is conceived as a struggle in which psychoanalysis, as the application of a psychological scientific rationalism, helps humankind to preserve itself against nature's overwhelming might. At its very inception, psychoanalysis, therefore, takes its stand over and against nature as an 'inexorable' force of destruction. The work of psychotherapy and psychology, in this attitude, at the level of civilisation and culture, is to protect the psyche against the natural world. The psyche and nature are understood through an oppositional fantasy, and the very logics of psychology and psychotherapy, at least in the analytic tradition, are born out of this opposition.

Registration, then, furthers this internal logic of splitting in the way that it, through the medium of the law, literalises and acts out the actual segregation of psychotherapy and psychology in an exclusive enclosure of 'professionalism'. In the way in which this kind of thinking and so-called 'scientific technique' are upheld as 'models' of analytic propriety, as exemplars, then any attempt to think through and practise a psychology and psychotherapy which begins to take more account of the world, indeed conceive of the notion of the soul in a more worldly way, would be dismissed (Hillman 1992). For it would transgress the boundaries that the law has established around psychology and psychotherapy — which is to keep them as much apart from things as possible. It is not enough to think of nature, the world, as a *content* in one's theory, even to talk about them in one's practice — though this is of value as a way of opening up thought, imagination and feeling; it is the form of psychological awareness and practice that would be changed if we took such a thinking to heart and allowed it to *re-inform* us in the work.

The connection between the inward turn and turning away from the world is one deeply rooted in the history of the West. For Jung its basic roots lay in the metaphysics of Christianity. Of this, he wrote:

The gulf that Christianity opened out between nature and spirit enabled the human mind to think not only beyond nature but in opposition to it, thus demonstrating its divine freedom, so to speak. This flight from the darkness of nature's depth culminates in trinitarian thinking, which moves in a Platonic, 'supracelestial' realm.

(Jung 1977b: 176)

This gap between spirit and nature manifests in the languages and practices of Christian spirituality which, in the main, literalise inwardness, conflating the notion of soul with that of human subjectivity. *Interiority* comes to mean human subjectivity. In his *Confessions*, St Augustine describes this opposition between Christian spiritual inwardness and the world:

And men go forth to admire the high mountains and the great waves of the
sea and the broad torrent of the rivers and the vast expanse of the ocean
and the orbits of the stars, and to turn away from themselves.

(1943: X, VIII)

Here, Augustine is speaking against the pagan awe and worship of nature as a
deflection from Christian interiority, the soul and truth. He exhorts elsewhere:
'Do not go outward; return within yourself. In the inward man dwells the truth'
(De Vera Religione XXXIX: 72). This inward turn, the shaping power of Christian
interiorisation, led to 'a new and independent relation to nature whereby the
foundation was laid for natural science and technique ... the world has not only
lost its God ... but also to some extent has lost its soul as well' (Jung 1991: 74).
Jung understands the notion of the psyche as a subjective interiority which
developed through an historical process of interiorisation, culminating in the
emergence of depth psychology and the psychological attitude: 'the psyche has
attained its present complexity by a series of acts of introjection. Its complexity
has increased in proportion to the *despiritualisation of nature*' (1969: 25, my
emphasis). Thus, psychological awareness, psychology, is bought at the price of
nature's loss of soul.

The turn towards the soul is accompanied by the 'disenchantment of the
world'. It is a turn that gathers force in Christian spirituality, but which continues
in the work of psychology and psychotherapy. Psychology carries onward the
legacy of Christian inwardness literally in its conception of interiority as human
subjectivity, binding the notion of the soul to that of the human over and against
a soulless nature. Further, declares Jung, it is the task of a psychology of
consciousness to 'de-psychize nature', to 'take back all archaic projections' (1964:
67). The two key psychological concepts which both reflect and reinforce
psychology's splitting logic, the rupture between the psyche and world, which
continue the process of the despiritualisation of nature — as can be discerned in
these various quoted writings of Jung, and evident with even less self-questioning
in the psychoanalytic tradition — are those of 'interiority' and 'projection'. The
logic of both of these ideas arises from the notion of the psyche's separation
from nature, separation from the world. They are based upon a conception of
being in terms of the 'subjective' as distinct from the 'objective', of 'subject' from
'object', of the psyche as a 'container': the Cartesian mode of consciousness.
This is the spirit in which much contemporary psychology and psychotherapy
both understand themselves and therefore see their task, and in which the
concepts of the 'inner world' and of 'projection' play such a legislative role.

But if, as I am arguing, psychology and psychotherapy are undergoing a
'breaking down' of the notion of the psyche as confined to a clinical conception,
to the consulting room, then their task is to reflect *freely* upon themselves, their
thought and practices. Indeed, I would say that this 'deconstruction', this
'negation', is happening whether we go with it or not. The task is to examine
how the prevailing 'logic' of psychology and psychotherapy confines the
movement of the soul in its relation to the world. We need to be psychologically
aware of our psychology, and to be able to practise a therapy upon our
psychotherapy. This task cannot be confined to a prescribed group since,
culturally, attention to the soul in terms of the world belongs to all those who
concern themselves with this predicament of psycho-logy, with the *logos* of the

psyche. The name '*therapeutae*' refers to, honours, all who attend the soul, who undertake soul-work, whosoever and wherever they are.

I shall look at two examples which open up the question of a psychology of nature. The context of the first one is that of the 'mad God' of Europe. In the following passage, Jung connects the loss of nature's soul with a 'madness' in the Western psyche:

> For the first time since the dawn of history we have succeeded in swallowing the whole of primitive animism into ourselves, and with it the spirit that animated nature. Not only were the gods dragged down from their planetary spheres and transformed into chthonic demons, but, under the influence of scientific enlightenment, even this band of demons, which at the time of Paracelsus still frolicked happily in the mountains and woods, in rivers and human dwelling-places, was reduced to a miserable remnant and finally vanished altogether. From time immemorial, nature was always filled with spirit. Now, for the first, we are living in a lifeless nature bereft of gods. ... Just when people were congratulating themselves on having abolished all spooks, it turned out that instead of haunting the attic or old ruins the spooks were flitting about in the heads of apparently normal Europeans.
>
> (Jung 1964: 211)

This transformation of our concept of nature was the work of 'the scientific enlightenment'. Animated nature has been replaced by the concept of nature of the natural sciences. Physics now gives us our psychology of nature, not 'Paganism' (Giegerich 1997: 9). But does psychology, in its turn, have something to say to the natural sciences such as physics?

Psychology and psychotherapy have to enter into the predicament, and this means into the domain of science — in actuality, they already are in it, though perhaps psychologists and psychotherapists have not yet caught up with what is happening. In this way, they enter into the question of the psycho-logy of nature, of soul and the world. But, Jung asserts, psychology itself has to undergo a transformation, in order for its work of deepening our awareness of what psychology is:

> Psychology actualises the unconscious urge to consciousness. It is, in fact, the coming to consciousness of the psychic process, but it is not, in the deeper sense, an explanation of this process, for no explanation of the psychic can be anything other than the living process of the psyche itself. Psychology is doomed to cancel ['*aufheben*'] itself out as a science and therein precisely it reaches its scientific goal. Every other science has so to speak an outside; not so psychology, whose object is the inside subject of all science.
>
> (Jung 1977a: 223)

Jung's remarks do two things. First, they annul the character of psychological theory as 'explanation'. As pointed out earlier, all psychological statements are themselves the psyche speaking of itself. By what *exclusive* authority, legitimisation, then, can the language of psychology and psychotherapy be legally restricted to a few practitioners? — as if no-one else had the *authority of soul* worth listening to on psychological or psychotherapeutic matters. Secondly, they point to the work of psychology upon itself, if it is to engage with physics on the question of the psychology of nature. Its work has to do with 'the inside subject' of all the sciences. That is to say, with both the movement of interiorisation and interiority, but deliteralised from a conception in terms of human subjectivity.

This work of awareness, as already said, requires the freedom of dialogue as an expression of the movement of the soul. Prescription and proscription resist this dialogical movement. Again, the cultural, social and political conditions, in which this work happens, are blocked by the advent of registration, the essential restriction of dialogue and authority to an 'accredited' few and the prescinding of all the 'other' voices which have something to say on these matters. All of this keeps the notion of soul literalised as human subjectivity and, through the logic and organisation of registration, preserves the split between soul and the world.

Let me end with the second example, a brief 'case study' taken from Jung's *Memories, Dreams, Reflections*. In it, Jung speaks of his father as:

> a sufferer stricken with an Amfortas wound, a 'fisher king' whose wound would not heal — that Christian suffering for which the alchemists sought the panacea. I as a 'dumb' Parsifal was the witness of this sickness during the years of my boyhood ... he had literally lived right up to his death the suffering prefigured and promised by Christ, without ever becoming aware that this was a consequence of the *imitatio Christi*. He regarded his suffering as a personal affliction ... he did not see it as the suffering of the Christian in general.
>
> (Jung 1963: 215)

As Jung points out in this passage, though his father's pain was personally suffered, individually experienced, it was essentially impersonal, collective. In this sense, then, the suffering has already transcended the boundaries of the consulting room. It can be shared there, but it is fundamentally the whole Christian realm and the *logos* of its *pathos* (pathology) that enters through the suffering patient.

The imagery of the wounded 'fisher king' further illuminates the character of this suffering in a way especially relevant in this time of ecological catastrophe. It also indicates the roots of this crisis in the relationship to nature — namely, the turn away from the world in Christian spirituality and in its modern, secular legacy. The development of Christian spirituality and the enormous mental accomplishments it inaugurated, the freeing of consciousness it fostered, led simultaneously to an estrangement from nature, the world of chthonic instinctuality. The alienation from nature underlying Christian spirituality represents a stage in the dialectic of its disenchanting logic. The suffering 'fisher king' and the surrounding 'wasteland' of his kingdom can be understood, then, as the suffering of nature experienced individually, as an *ecological grief*. If we interpret this grief only as personal suffering, looking for causes in a 'clinical history', we completely deny its connection to the affliction of nature. If, however, we acknowledge the suffering as related to what is happening in the natural world, namely, as having an ecological dimension, *that* is the concern of us all. Then a therapy of the soul becomes a *cultural* task and one that cannot be confined to a cultural elite: for today,

The activation of an active, conscious soul life in the face of the present world is necessary and unavoidable. We see grieving all around us, for this condition is us. Our Earth, this source of love, is dying ... As long as this is denied, what belongs to the world will continue to be interpreted as only personal psychological suffering, when in fact it is at the same time a world suffering.

(Sardello 1996: 92–3)

Such an acknowledgement takes us beyond the machinations of legal registration and professionalism, which would reinforce the 'inward turn'. For this only increases the solipsism of consulting-room psychology, intensifies the narcissism of the psychotherapy 'profession', and keeps soul-work in a kind of 'virtual reality', a simulation or parody of itself. No matter how perfect it makes its 'codes of practice and ethics', its 'theory' and 'practice', psychotherapy will be swallowed by its own power-driven shadow. Instead, as therapists we need to *turn outward* — or rather, follow the turn of the soul's images and logic into the world — not holding psychology and psychotherapy cognitively captive in the literal and literalising interiority of the consulting room; the notion of the soul *legally* confined to the clinical, personalistic and positivistic idea of human subjectivity, one in which the soul is given over into the hands of an exclusive supervising band of 'experts', themselves over-supervised and regulated in their efforts to police the psyche and its attendants. Where the latter prevails, so would everyone be further, both personally and culturally, alienated from the experience of soul. Its interpretation would become the legal right only of the sect of 'psychotherapists', and the problem of its worldliness forsaken beneath the welter of 'professional' politics and misappropriation.

REFERENCES

Augustine, Saint (1943) *The Confessions of Saint Augustine,* trans. F. J. Sheed, London; quoted in C. G. Jung (1954) *The Practice of Psychotherapy: Essays on the Psychology of the Transference and Other Subjects, Collected Works* 16
Augustine, Saint *De Vera Religione;* quoted in C. Taylor (1992) *Sources of Self: The Making of the Modern Identity.* Cambridge: Cambridge University Press
Berry, P. (1982) The training of shadow and the shadow of training. In *Echo's Subtle Body: Contributions to an Archetypal Psychology.* Dallas: Spring Publications
Bohm, D. (1998) *Wholeness and the Implicate Order.* London: Routledge (orig. 1980)
Freud, S. (1961a) *The Future of an Illusion.* New York: Norton; quoted in R. Sardello (1996) *Love and the Soul: Creating a Future for Earth.* New York: HarperCollins
Freud, S. (1961b) *Civilization and Its Discontents.* New York: Norton; quoted in R. Sardello (1996) *Love and the Soul: Creating a Future for Earth.* New York: HarperCollins
Giegerich, W. (1997) *The Opposition of 'Individual' and 'Collective' — Psychology's Basic Fault.* The Guild of Pastoral Psychology, Guild Lecture No. 259
Giegerich, W. (1998) *The Soul's Logical Life: Towards a Rigorous Notion of Psychology.* Frankfurt am Main: Peter Lang; see also his: On the neurosis of psychology or the third of the two. *Spring: An Annual of Archetypal Psychology and Jungian Thought* (pp. 153–74). Zurich: Spring Publications, 1977
Hillman, J. (1992) *The Thought of the Heart and the Soul of the World.* Dallas: Spring Publications

Jung, C. G. (1963) *Memories, Dreams, Reflections*. New York: Random House

Jung, C. G. (1964) *Civilization in Transition, Collected Works*, 10

Jung, C. G. (1969) *The Archetypes and the Collective Unconscious, Collected Works*, 9i

Jung, C. G. (1977a) *The Structure and Dynamics of the Psyche. Collected Works*, 8

Jung, C. G. (1977b) *Psychology and Religion: West and East. Collected Works*, 11

Jung, C. G. (1991) *Psychology of the Unconscious*, trans. B. M. Hinkle. London: Routledge (orig. 1916)

Kirk, G. S. and Raven, J. E. (1977) *The Presocratic Philosophers*. Cambridge: Cambridge University Press

Nietzsche, E. (1978) *The Twilight of the Idols*, trans. R. J. Hollingdale, Harmondsworth: Penguin

Sardello, R. (1996) *Love and the Soul: Creating a Future for the Earth*. New York: HarperCollins

13

THE STATUTORY REGULATION OF PSYCHOTHERAPY: STILL TIME TO THINK AGAIN

RICHARD HOUSE[†]

You cannot make men moral by Act of Parliament.

(Charles Waterman)

I was delighted to be asked to contribute a piece on registration to *The Psychotherapist* — and impressed that, notwithstanding its pro-statutory registration position, the house journal of the UK Council for Psychotherapy (UKCP) is prepared to offer space to a writer who takes a robustly different view on regulation. This coheres with *The Psychotherapist*'s pluralistic editorial policy of including 'from time to time … articles of a controversial nature' (no. 15, 2000: 2). I imagine that what follows will be seen as falling into the 'controversial' category!

An incisive article in the journal by Kidd (2000: 36) pointed out that the Alderdice consultation process 'focused on concerns broadly of the accrediting and training institutions rather than the likely effect of the Bill on the profession' — a theme that recurs throughout this chapter. Kidd illuminates a vital issue which has erstwhile been essentially ignored — viz. the effects of regulation on part-time, non-career practitioners. In 1999 I wrote to the UK Department for Education and Employment, the Department of Health and the Inland Revenue, seeking to discover how many active therapy practitioners there are in Britain. The replies conclusively indicated that no one remotely knows the answer to this crucial question. For all anyone knows, the category of 'part-time' practitioner might easily constitute *the majority* of practitioners in the field — yet as Kidd points out, a significant number of them are unlikely to be able to afford the likely cost of registration (ibid.: 37). Under statutory registration, then, 'To Them Who Hath …' will tend to become the norm — a 'Robin-Hood-in-reverse' redistribution of income from poorer to richer, with at least some smaller practices being forced out of business; or in short, a kind of creeping *embourgeoisisement* of the therapy field.

With part-timers, women and low-fee chargers tending to be 'forced out' in such a quasi-Thatcherite 'market rationalisation' process, there is a real danger of the field losing practitioners who offer a *freshness of energy* in the work that full-time therapists cannot naturally offer. Indeed, I believe there are compelling

---

† This chapter first appeared in *The Psychotherapist*, 17, 2002: 12-17, and is reprinted with kind permission of the author and *The Psychotherapist*.

reasons why part-time, non-career practitioners might well, all other things being equal, be more effective therapists than full-time 'career' ones — not least because of the greater freshness of energy they bring to their client work and the greater likelihood of their having a healthily 'grounding' life outside of the therapy world. If there is any substance to this argument, then a statutorily regulated field which effectively disenfranchises at least some of its most effective practitioners *cannot but* do significant harm to the client interest as a whole — not least because 'sources of low cost psychotherapy available to the public may shrink rapidly' (Kidd 2000: 38). It is surely clear that, at a minimum, substantial research should be conducted into these questions before statutory registration is imposed upon the field.

In a recent paper (House 2001), I posed three key questions which, I believe, any coherent case in favour of statutory regulation must explicitly address:

- Should psychotherapy in principle be regulated? (cf. Postle 1998).
- If the answer to the latter question is 'yes', then is the conventional model of 'the professions' remotely the appropriate one for the peculiarly unique practice of psychotherapy?
- If statutory regulation is pursued, will any benefits yielded by regulation for 'the public interest' (if indeed the latter can be operationally defined) outweigh the deleterious effects of regulation (e.g. curtailed innovation; higher fees and training costs, and restricted entry to the field; profession-centred bias and the triumph of institutional vested interests, etc.), so comprehensively detailed by Hogan (1979) and Mowbray (1995)?

I contend that if the answer to *any one* of these three questions is 'no', then the case for statutory regulation unambiguously falls.

Some years ago, I attempted a 'nut-shell' summary of the case against statutory regulation. Quoting from that paper (House 1997a: 32–3):

> The public interest argument in favour of registration simply doesn't stand up to scrutiny.... First, can didactic accreditation and registration procedures be shown to create and guarantee practitioners who are more competent and less likely to harm clients than in a non-registration environment? And secondly, if such a guarantee of competence can't be demonstrated or sustained, then the only remaining rationale favouring registration is that of weeding out and disqualifying abusive or incompetent practitioners.

Yet a wide range of evidence points to the conclusion that, quoting Roberta Russell, 'therapists who have undergone traditional training are no more effective than those who have not' (for an authoritative review of relevant literature, see Bohart and Tallman 1996 — reproduced as Chapter 27, this volume); and (quoting Alex Howard), it would appear that 'highly trained counsellors succumb at least as much as less skilled colleagues [to abusing their clients]' (both quoted in House 1997a).

Nor should these findings be surprising, as less-trained practitioners will tend to be more tentative and nervous with clients, whereas those with greater 'status' and longevity may well be *more* susceptible to the 'expert' counter-therapeutic wielding of power — the level of complaints against (regulated) psychiatrists being a case in point. Just as one cannot 'make [people] moral by Act of Parliament', so 'you cannot legislate against one of the greatest dangers in therapy — that power can "go to the head" of the practitioner, cut him or her off from an intuitive sense of what is right, and encourage arrogance' ('Anna Sands', personal communication). In short, the oft-repeated overriding rationale for statutory registration, that of 'providing the greatest possible protection... for the public' (Casement 2001: 7), may be at best shaky, and at worst completely erroneous.

It has been routine for many therapists to dismiss such conclusions out of hand — after all, it's surely *just plain common sense* that trained practitioners will be more effective and less abusive than their lesser trained counterparts. To the contrary, I believe there are strong theoretical and empirical reasons to support the counter-intuitive view that, overall, *inexperienced and comparatively lightly trained practitioners can commonly be at least as effective as, and no more abusive than, long-standing, experienced ones.* Practitioner therapeutic effectiveness is surely a highly complex, empirically unmeasurable and ultimately mysterious process, with a multitude of variables, many or most of them of the 'intangible' variety (as Karl Menninger convincingly showed). On this view, the positivist 'wild goose chase' of trying reductionistically to isolate therapy's 'active ingredients' is firmly stuck in the 'old paradigm' scientistic world-view of modernity (cf. House, 2003). I am increasingly of the (impressionistic, ultimately unverifiable) view that it is the practitioner's *freshness of energy, enthusiasm and associated interest-in-the-other* that may well be a far more important, and even the decisive 'ingredient' in therapist effectiveness than has heretofore been recognised.

If there is any substance to this intuition, then it would follow that the longer therapists work in this field, the more likely that these qualities will be progressively diminished in their work — with, all other things again being equal, therapists' effectiveness declining as a result. *And such a decline might well more than counteract any increase in effectiveness resulting from greater training and experience.* Certainly, such an analysis would account for the empirical finding that relatively inexperienced practitioners commonly obtain outcome results which are at least the equal of more experienced therapists. At the empirical level, for example, and to add to the plethora of previous confirming studies (Bohart and Tallman 1996), a recent study of effectiveness in a voluntary counselling agency found no difference in client outcome between qualified and trainee counsellors (Archer and Forbes 2000).

I contend, then, that far from statutory registration being of benefit to the client interest, its net effect may well be *profoundly against the client interest.* If the foregoing analysis has any validity, then the institutionalising of therapeutic help might well be harmful to the extent that it ossifies in place a large body of full-time 'career' practitioners whose registered professional identity, and all that goes with it, will be antithetical to the unhampered *freshness* and 'enabling naivity' that those practitioners unencumbered by therapy's 'regime of professional(ised) truth' enjoy (cf. my Chapter 9, this volume).

Elsewhere I have proposed the term 'Professionalised Therapy Form' to denote the constraining 'regime of truth' into which 'clients' (and 'therapists') are discursively inserted when they enter a therapy relationship (for detailed elaborations, see House 1999; Chapter 9, this volume) (a discourse, incidentally, which also emphasises and institutionalises therapist/client *difference* rather than our shared common humanity). In her important recent book *Falling for Therapy,* 'Anna Sands' (2000) has elaborated at length on the way in which therapy's 'discourse' can strongly influence clients' subjective experience, and on the innate precariousness of the therapeutic endeavour. Therapy can, I suggest, routinely become a 'material-generating' activity, constructing a 'regime of truth' which self-fulfillingly creates a framework that serves to guarantee its own legitimacy, and outside the confines of which it is often exceedingly difficult for clients *or* therapists to think. More generally, the quasi-legalistic form taken by the institutionalisation of therapeutic help cannot but cement therapy's 'professionalised form' in place, and will do little if anything to encourage greater practitioner openness and non-defensiveness ('Anna Sands', personal communication), which are, arguably, absolutely central enabling qualities for any therapist to possess.

Moreover, seen in this light, the routine advocacy of 'the greatest possible... education of the public' about psychotherapy (Casement 2001: 7) might ultimately be far less beneficent than it at first appears. Elsewhere, for example, we find therapy's 'regime of truth' alive and well, with ex-UKCP Chair, Emmy van Deurzen's extraordinary characterisation of therapy as 'the professional-isation of motherhood', and her grandiose assertion that psychotherapy should 'move to a position where our new knowledge is applied to an increasingly necessary *reorganisation of the world*' (1996: 17, 19, my emphasis)! Such a brazenly profession-centred blueprint is a very different animal from the aforementioned innocent-sounding 'educational' agenda.

In order to avoid the procedural imposition of a straightjacket of therapeutic orthodoxy, I maintain that therapy, at its best, should be *ongoingly and processually deconstructive* of its professional ideologies (not least, its medical-model associations), clinical practices, and *especially* its organisational arrangements, if the kinds of dangers so ably highlighted by 'Anna Sands', David Smail and others are to be avoided. Moreover, the momentum towards institutional professionalisation is surely significantly out of step with leading-edge developments in postmodern epistemology, participatory and consensual 'organisational' ethics (of which the Independent Practitioners Network is a notable example – Totton 1997; House 1997b), and 'New Paradigm' thinking more generally (cf. John Heron's Foreword to this volume).

In sum, if an ongoingly deconstructive approach to therapy as 'profession', clinical practice and cultural phenomenon is the most healthy future path for the field (House 1999), then one sure way to limit this is to cement in place 'old-paradigm', legally sanctioned organisational structures that freeze rather than facilitate innovation and creativity. As Carl Rogers so poignantly wrote, 'In every sphere... certification has tended to freeze and narrow the profession [in question], has tied it to the past, has discouraged innovation... Can psychology find a new and better way?' (quoted in House and Totton 1997: 4). One need only glance at the appalling malaise that has overtaken our 'hyper-modernised' education system to witness the stultifying, deadening effect that an obsessively regulating, low-trust mentality has on the erstwhile creative art of teaching (House 2000). Are these pernicious cultural forces (termed 'the death throes' of the master-discourse of modernity by Barratt 1993: xii) *really* ones with which we wish to collude?

There are other crucial questions which I have had no space to address in this chapter – for example:

- the unintended consequences (which 'control freakery' routinely ignores) of introducing statutory registration for the field *as a whole*;

- the unspoken-about (and unmentionable?) 'medical-modelisation' of the therapy field through its being associated with a regulatory process imposed through the new UK Health Professions Council;
- that, through the latter process, registrants seem to be getting a regulatory 'mess of pottage', compared with the earlier promised banquet of a high-status, independent profession... (Has anyone even *noticed*? — and have registrants been frankly informed about this?);
- the arguably less-than-reputable 'turf war' aspect of the Alderdice Bill process, with its initial sidelining of the then British Association for Counselling (BAC) and its 'army' of 15,000-odd 'counsellors' (McDevitt 2000);
- the inappropriate and therapeutically incongruent 'academicisation' of the therapy training world (House 2001; Parker 2001), and the exclusionary effects of ever-escalating training costs;
- the incongruent inauthenticity of embracing a top-down, 'power-over' regulatory model for a field which routinely claims to privilege a very different model of empowerment for its clientele — or the inappropriateness of embracing an 'old-paradigm' model of institutional control in a rapidly approaching era of post- or 'trans-modernity'; and finally,
- statutory regulation's unacknowledged propagation of, and collusion with, 'institutional transference', and the *abuse of the transference* that may, as a result, be unconsciously reproduced in our work with an unwitting clientele (Heron 1990).

The great spiritual teacher Jiddu Krishnamurti once said, 'we are addicted to institutions... [they] will never stop what is happening in the world... Organisation in the psychological world is destructive'. All my experience of human organisations, and *especially* therapy ones, leads me to agree with him. Certainly, the important work of Jeffrey Masson and Bob Young points to a very similar conclusion about the 'dysfunctional dynamics' of psychotherapy organisations (e.g. Whan, 1999, reproduced as Chapter 12, this volume).

I will end with a deliberately provocative question: *Can existing or aspiring registrants, in the privacy of their own conscience, with their hand on their heart and beyond all reasonable doubt, sincerely aver that statutory regulation is on balance a beneficent process — rather than one driven by commercial competition and profession-centred self-interest, culturally fashionable, anxiety-driven 'control-freakery', and the 'dysfunctional' institutional dynamics to which all organisations — and especially psychotherapy ones — seem subject?* I would first invite readers to look at whether they are open even to *the possibility* of their answer being 'no'. And if your answer *is* 'no', then, surely, personal authenticity demands that you either make your view known vociferously to your relevant institutional officers, or else withdraw, as a matter of principle, from any organisation that is pursuing the statutory regulation of our field.

REFERENCES

Archer, R. and Forbes, Y. (2000) An investigation of the effectiveness of a voluntary sector psychodynamic counselling service. *British Journal of Medical Psychology* 73: 401–12

Barratt, B. B. (1993). *Psychoanalysis and the Postmodern Impulse*. Baltimore: Johns Hopkins University Press

Bohart, A. C. and Tallman, K. (1996) The active client: therapy as self-help. *Journal of Humanistic Psychology* 36 (3): 7–30; reprinted as Chapter 27, this volume

Casement, A. (2001) Letter to all registrants. *The Psychotherapist* 16 (Spring): 4–7

Heron, J. (1990) The politics of transference. *Self and Society* 18 (1): 17–23; reprinted in House and Totton (eds), *Implausible Professions* (pp. 11–18), 1997

Hogan, D. (1979) *The Regulation of Psychotherapists*, 4 vols. Cambridge, MA: Ballinger

House, R. (1997a) From professionalisation towards a post-therapy era. *Self and Society* 25 (2): 31–5

House, R. (1997b) Participatory ethics in a self-generating practitioner community. In R. House and N. Totton (eds), *Implausible Professions* (pp. 321–34). Ross-on-Wye: PCCS Books

House, R. (1999) Limits to therapy and counselling: deconstructing a professional ideology. *British Journal of Guidance and Counselling*, 27 (3): 377–92; reprinted as Chapter 9, this volume

House, R. (2000) Stress, surveillance and modernity: the 'modernising' assault on our education system. *Education Now* 30 (Feature Supplement); reprinted in his *The Trouble with Education*, Education Now Books, Nottingham, in preparation

House, R. (2001) Psychotherapy professionalization: the post-graduate dimension and the legitimacy of statutory regulation. *British Journal of Psychotherapy* 17 (3): 382–90

House, R. (2003) *Therapy Beyond Modernity: Deconstructing and Transcending Profession-Centred Therapy*. London: Karnac Books

House, R. and Totton, N. (eds) (1997) *Implausible Professions: Arguments for Pluralism and Autonomy in Psychotherapy and Counselling*. Ross-on-Wye: PCCS Books

Kidd, V. (2000) The Psychotherapy Bill: issues for practising psychotherapists. *The Psychotherapist* 15 (Autumn): 36–8

McDevitt, C. (2000) The Psychotherapy Bill — a BAC statement. *Counselling* 11 (4): 209

Mowbray, R. (1995) *The Case Against Psychotherapy Registration: A Conservation Issue for the Human Potential Movement*. London: Trans Marginal Press

Parker, I. (2001) What is wrong with the discourse of the university in psychotherapy training? *European Journal of Psychotherapy, Counselling and Health* 4 (1): 27–43

Postle, D. (1998) The alchemist's nightmare: gold into lead — the annexation of psychotherapy in the UK. *International Journal of Psychotherapy* 3: 53–83

Sands, A. (2000) *Falling for Therapy: Psychotherapy from a Client's Point of View*. Basingstoke and London: Macmillan

Totton, N. (1997) The Independent Practitioners Network: a new model of accountability. In R. House and N. Totton (eds), *Implausible Professions*, pp. 287–93. Ross-on-Wye: PCCS Books

van Deurzen-Smith, E. (1996) The future of psychotherapy in Europe. *International Journal of Psychotherapy* 1 (1): 121–40

Whan, M. (1999) Registering psychotherapy as an institutional neurosis: or, compounding the estrangement between soul and world. *European Journal of Psychotherapy, Counselling and Health* 2 (3): 309–23; reprinted as Chapter 12, this volume

Note

My sincere thanks to a number of colleagues who offered valuable feedback on the first draft of this article, which led to significant improvements.

14
REGULATION:
A TREACHEROUS PATH?

BRIAN THORNE†

Nobody can accuse me of being unconcerned about the development of counsellors and psychotherapists and the quality of the service they offer to their clients. Indeed, it was I who, as early as 1981, steered into being the accreditation process of the then Association for Student Counselling (UK) so that those counsellors working in further or higher education could have something to aim at and feel encouraged in their desire to improve their effectiveness in what was, and remains, a highly demanding and taxing activity. Many years later I served on the British Association for Counselling and Psychotherapy's (BACP) 'Recognition of Counselling Courses Working Group', which led to the establishment of the process by which training courses can obtain what has become the Association's coveted Certificate of Accreditation. And then, in the last decade, I have devoted considerable energy to the work of the United Kingdom Register of Counsellors and have sought to make the gateway to the register as welcoming as possible. All this often arduous work over a period of more than 30 years has been motivated and inspired by the belief that our clients deserve the best we can offer, and that we, the practitioners, deserve every opportunity to deepen our understanding and to enhance our ability in order to engage more confidently and with greater humility in the work which most of us recognise not as a job, but as a vocation of immense significance.

A DARKER SIDE

Today, as I reflect on those 30 years of endeavour, my feelings are mixed. I have no doubt whatever that much has been accomplished which has led to the great benefit of clients and practitioners alike. Counselling and psychotherapy now command a place in our society and culture whereby much human suffering is alleviated and many practitioners have been enabled to give the very best of themselves in their response to those who seek their help. I'm proud of that accomplishment and whatever small share I may have had in it. But there is a darker side. Accreditation of training schemes which began as a source of encouragement and stimulus for practitioners has become an almost

---

† This chapter first appeared in *CPJ: Counselling and Psychotherapy Journal*, 12(2), 2002, and is reprinted with kind permission of the author and the British Association for Counselling and Psychotherapy.

institutionalised part of the therapeutic scene. Accreditation and an 'approved' training are now all but obligatory for the intending counsellor or psychotherapist. There is part of me, of course, which is glad about this — but I'm not at all sure that I like that part of me. I smell the allure of the 'closed shop' and the not easily disguised smugness of the 'expert' who can claim the power to exclude. What is more, when I glance around at the other 'experts', I often ask myself how I have come to be in membership of the same club. I even wonder if my understanding of counselling and psychotherapy, let alone my practice of it, bears much resemblance to that of someone in another room of the same club-house, even though we have managed to create membership rules which allow us both to enter the same building.

We remain nonetheless, for the moment, a voluntary establishment, and however much we may sometimes want it, we do not possess the power to stop others doing in their way what they wish to do as counsellors and psychotherapists, even though they do not carry membership cards.

The threat — or promise — of statutory regulation wonderfully concentrates the mind and, for me, separates the wood from the trees. I know that I oppose it and do so with some considerable passion. It would ensure, I believe, that the darker side prevails. Regulation in the hands of government or the law would inevitably mean a stifling of creativity and the proliferation of therapists who can no longer offer the best of themselves for fear of making mistakes or earning adverse judgement in an increasingly litigious society. What is more, the time would quickly arrive when psychotherapy and counselling were defined in ways which the present pre-paradigmatic state of the activity could not possibly justify. Our knowledge of the evidence base for the theory and practice of counselling and psychotherapy is still growing; we are not yet at a place where it is logical or wise to implement the sort of uniformity that statutory regulation can require.

In contrast, rigorous voluntary self-regulation, when practised in a professional association that is guided by democratic membership, can be responsive to emerging differences and developments. The capacity of BACP to make radical strides in the development of the new *Ethical Framework* is a clear example of this. Without this flexibility, I see the spectres of the medical or scientific model attempting to take centre stage, as if counsellors and psychotherapists were scientists and not artists, and their clients patients and not self-determining persons. I'm also singularly unimpressed by the arguments of those who favour statutory regulation which seem, when they are analysed, to revolve around:

- it is inevitable anyway, so let's make sure we play our cards most advantageously to suit our own ends;
- it is necessary to protect the public and would-be clientele;
- it will guarantee effective practitioners and force out the charlatans.

I believe all three of these arguments to be false. My fairly careful study of the research evidence did not convince me that a 'licensed professional' protects clients from abuse. There is even some evidence to suggest that it does the reverse, as it attracts precisely the person who succumbs to the allurement of power, and who is therefore more likely to abuse it. There is no evidence that long and complex training programmes produce better therapists than shorter trainings or even, in exceptional cases, no training at all. I wrote earlier of the desirable quality of humility in therapists. Behind much of the thinking and activity directed towards statutory registration I detect not humility but scarcely veiled arrogance and power seeking — and, what is more, I recognise all of these attributes in my own heart and mind, and they frighten me.

CALL FOR CONSULTATION

The notion of the inevitability of statutory regulation warrants a final comment. It is clearly not the case that government has always wanted this. On the contrary, previous administrations have made it evident that they did not want it and had no intention of pursuing it. The present government seems keen on the idea, but they, too, make it clear that they could not impose it upon a resistant majority of practitioners. My impression is that BACP has assumed, for whatever reason, that the majority of its members do indeed favour statutory regulation. The time is now overdue for this assumption to be put rigorously to the test. I believe it is the responsibility of the Association to carry out a truly consultative process into this all-important question before we are finally swept into something which we may subsequently bitterly regret. And I write as one who cares deeply about the soul work in which we are all involved — which, incidentally, is for me somewhere approaching an acceptable definition of counselling.

15

PSYCHOLOGISTS, LICENSING BOARDS, ETHICS COMMITTEES AND DEHUMANISING ATTITUDES: WITH SPECIAL REFERENCE TO DUAL RELATIONSHIPS

ARNOLD A. LAZARUS[†]

He looked down at us from the podium, adjusted the microphone (again) and stated flatly, 'Any time you cross a professional boundary you place your entire career in jeopardy'. He waited for that to sink in. I looked around me. Everyone in the audience seemed to be paying very close attention. This was one of those risk-management seminars in which carefully chosen speakers told us how to hang on to our licences. I have attended two of those seminars and found them extremely scary. On both occasions, when 4.30 or 5.00 p.m. rolled round and we disbanded, I felt anxious and paranoid. I was not alone. As I learned later, most of the seminar attendees felt similarly. It was drilled into us that seeing clients was hazardous. Make one false move and our careers could be plundered. Uncompromising licensing boards and ethics committees would condemn us and strip us of our licences and livelihoods. The next day (and for two or three days thereafter) I viewed my clients as dangerous adversaries, as potential litigants, and I was on guard. Fortunately, this soon wore off, and I once again reverted to being the flexible and humane clinician I see myself as.

In both the seminars I attended, we learned the myriad ways in which one can fall foul of a licensing board, and considerable time was spent discussing the perils of dual (or multiple) relationships. One of the lecturers was adamant that any time a therapist entered into a dual relationship, the treatment was likely to be undermined. Unless there was an explicit therapeutic reason to spend time with a client outside the office (as when doing *in vivo* desensitisation, for instance), a therapist was well advised to have no dealings with a client in any other setting. Somewhat facetiously, I raised my hand and inquired if it was permissible for a therapist to send out for sandwiches and share them with his or her client in the office. The answer was an emphatic 'NO' — unless there happened to be a clear-cut and defensible treatment rationale (such as promoting eating behaviours in an anorexic client). The thinking behind this totalitarian

---

† This chapter originally appeared as Chapter 15 of Lazarus, A.A. and Zur, O. (eds) (2002) *Dual Relationships and Psychotherapy. New York: Springer Publishing Co.*, and is reprinted with kind permission of the author and the publishers.

line of reasoning seems to be that seemingly innocent acts can all too readily lead to unethical behaviours. Some 'experts' contend that even the most well-intentioned therapist may discover that boundary crossings are likely to foster sexual liaisons. The utter absurdity of this view as a widespread and general probability has been addressed in several places throughout my co-edited book *Dual Relationships and Psychotherapy* (Lazarus and Zur 2002), so I will not rebut it here.

The defenceless psychologist

The foregoing is not intended to minimise the ubiquitous dangers that mental health practitioners face from their ethics committees and licensing boards. Just how vulnerable are psychologists in front of a State licensing board? In four words — they are *extremely* vulnerable. Bryant Welch, an attorney and psychologist, explains exactly why in the first 2001 edition of the document *Insight: Safeguarding Psychologists Against Liability Risks,* published by American Professional Agency, Inc., of the Chubb Group of Insurance Companies (Welch 2001). He points out that in our judicial system, the five decision-making functions — investigator, prosecutor, juror, judge and appellate hearing — are kept separate. Why? So that no single entity can establish domination. This dispersal of authority allows each one to check on the rulings and authority of the others. But as Welch explains, in most states the law permits licensing boards to serve as investigator, prosecutor, judge, jury and appeals court. 'In many cases', he writes, 'the board also serves as the complainant, filing charges against psychologists themselves' (ibid.: 2). He adds, 'The biggest problem is that nothing protects a psychologist from an arbitrary or irrational decision by the licensing board' (ibid.).

Welch also stated that 'the cost of a defence before a licensing board is potentially staggering' (ibid.: 5), and he added that some clients had paid $60,000 in attorney fees having 'hardly begun their defence' (ibid.). But there is more. In many instances, if you are a professional clinical psychologist or licensed psychotherapist, and are summoned to appear before a licensing board or ethics committee, it may be formidable if not impossible to prove your innocence.

Totalitarianism

Under our system of jurisprudence, if you are accused of committing a crime, you are entitled to a fair trial. You are presumed innocent until proven guilty. But unlike civil and criminal court proceedings, many licensing boards provide no right of discovery. Williams (2000b) makes clear that you may be summoned to a board hearing without having any idea of what the testimony against you will be. In most US states, a psychologist cannot take depositions of opposing witnesses to prepare his or her defence. In fact, the defendant may not be permitted to discover who the witnesses will be. Moreover, with many licensing boards there is no statute of limitations. Thus, you may be faced with the impossible task of preparing a defence based on events that occurred years ago and for which exculpatory records and witnesses may be unavailable.

It cannot be overstated that psychologists have lost their licences without fair hearings, due process of law or clear standards. A psychologist may pay many thousands of dollars for attorneys and expert witnesses, appear before an administrative law judge, win the case, and be allowed to remain in practice, only to receive a letter from the board revoking his or her licence. Yet as Martin H. Williams (2000a: 81) has underscored, 'We must realize that sometimes a defendant who is charged with loathsome ethical violations has, in fact, done nothing wrong'. His article 'Victimized by "Victims"' incisively explains the antecedents, dynamics and consequences of groundless and false complaints against psychotherapists. The biggest myth of all is that only those who have done something wrong are accused and only those who deserve sanctions get sanctions.

Peterson (2001: 339) documents how blameless psychologists lost 'their livelihood, savings, and health because of the practices of their licensing boards'. Williams (2001) provides examples of the unfair manner in which state licensing board practices bypass due-process protection. Saunders (2001), in a powerful message against oppression, refers to 'a disguised form of professional fascism, embedded in part in the professional regulatory atmosphere of APA, and in particular in the disciplinary process for psychologists operated by State licensing boards' (ibid.: 15).

Consequently, many psychotherapists who are cognisant of the persecutory climate tend to embrace prohibitions and construct rigid boundaries that often undermine their clinical effectiveness, and ironically, render them more susceptible to litigation (C. N. Lazarus 2001). Terrified providers are apt to permit risk-management principles to take precedence over humane interventions. This is not to gainsay the desirability of constructing a sensitive, intelligent and pragmatic code of ethics — prescriptions and proscriptions to guide inter-collegial conduct, as well as patient and therapist rights and obligations. In my own chapter in *Dual Relationships and Psychotherapy*, I stress that something must be done about the totalitarian mentality of many ethics committees and licensing boards (see A. A. Lazarus 2002); the enforcement of ethical regulations should follow democratic, not autocratic principles.

DUAL RELATIONSHIPS

It is my view that dual relationships may have been so strongly prohibited because many of the people who compiled the ethical rules were psychodynamic thinkers. Psychoanalysis with its clinical-transferential rationale prohibits all forms of dual relationships (despite the fact that Freud and many of his contemporaries and successors crossed boundaries and entered into significant dual relationships). What is viewed as a dual relationship or another boundary crossing in psychoanalytic therapy may be an integral part of behaviour therapy. Williams (1997) points out that what cognitive-behaviour therapists, existentialists or humanists may view as salubrious interventions, psychoanalysts would regard as 'transference abuse'. Must all approaches to therapy work within the confines imposed on us by one theoretical orientation?

Gary Schoener, the executive director of the Walk-In Counseling Centre in Minneapolis, Minnesota, sent me an e-mail on 4th April 2000 in which he discussed 'overlapping relationships'. He wrote,

> You run into clients in a church parking lot — that's an 'encounter'. They turn out to go to your church — that's an overlapping relationship. You

and they attend a Sunday school class that predominantly involves listening to lectures. That's overlapping with some potential to become dual. The pastor offers a parent support group in which people are to spill their guts about their child-rearing problems. To participate in that group with a current client is riskier and may be a dual relationship with a potential conflict of interest.

Personally, I would avoid this degree of overlap or duality.

I receive a similar response from many quarters when mentioning that with some clients, a sense of camaraderie develops when one steps outside the bounds of a sanctioned healer, and that this tends to enhance treatment outcomes. 'I'm sure this is so', many colleagues have said, 'but we trust your judgement in these matters and fully believe that you know when and when not to extend a boundary.' They then go on to say that when it comes to many of the other people in practice, their level-headedness and sagacity may be extremely faulty. Thus, they contend that it is in the best interests of their clients, our profession and society at large to forbid them to stray beyond strictly prescribed boundaries. My counter-argument is that instead of imposing a universal ban, it is better to educate health providers to assess risks and contraindications and for boards and committees to hear complaints and make individualistic case determinations. But the Code of Ethics adopted by the American Psychological Association (1992), the National Association of Social Workers (1999) and the various boards of certified counsellors (i.e. American Counseling Association 1996), and marriage and family therapists (i.e. American Association for Marriage and Family Therapists 2001; California Association of Marriage and Family Therapists 1997) are all wary of dual relationships. They all warn against treating friends or family members.

I argued against this prohibition during a talk I gave to the Division of Clinical Psychology at the 1997 American Psychological Association Convention (Lazarus 1998). I emphasised that my own formative experiences belie the putative dangers that supposedly lurk behind those who provide clinical services to family members, friends or associates. I mentioned that I have helped many a friend and family member with issues ranging from marital spats to intense phobias. It made no difference if a caring aunt or a total stranger was being treated for claustrophobia via systematic desensitisation and *in vivo* exposure. However, I studiously avoided treating any relative who was unstable or deeply troubled. For example, when one of my relatives requested therapy from me, I referred him to a colleague because, given his bizarre perceptions, had I become professionally involved, the most likely outcome would have been alienation from that wing of the family. This matter goes to the heart of my argument. Let us modify the edict 'Never treat family members or friends' to '*It is advisable to be cautious about treating close associates, and it is inadvisable to treat family or friends who suffer from severe personality disorders or other major psychopathology*'.

Ethics committees have expelled psychologists from membership, and State licensing boards have revoked their licenses for having engaged in dual relationships. Ebert (1997: 145) alluded to 'unfair and inconsistent decisions ... used by state licensing authorities' often with catastrophic results. He also stressed that 'dual-relationship rules must not impede a psychologist's ability to perform optimum work', and he stressed that 'some policies surrounding dual relationships could be considered as gender discrimination' (ibid.: 143). In

Chapter 29 of *Dual Relationships and Psychotherapy*, Miriam Greenspan incisively underscores that whereas an ethic of non-abuse for professional relationships is clearly necessary, she is doubtful whether the language of boundaries and the admonition to eschew all dual relationships achieves this objective. In fact she argues that it conceals the political dimension of violence against women. She deplores what she terms 'the distance model' and offers, instead, 'a connection model of therapy', arguing that the 'rigidification' of boundaries may produce more, not less power abuse in therapy. Similarly, Zur (2000) has shown that the prohibition of non-sexual dual relationships can prove deleterious to the treatment process.

POST-TREATMENT FRIENDSHIPS AND INTIMACIES

Let's segue into a discussion of post-treatment sexual relationships. Though there are some who contend that sex between client and therapist may be salubrious in some instances, I am squarely in the camp that denounces sex with a client. It is fraught with far too many potentially powerful and unpredictable emotions — it is apt to corrode trust, undermine objectivity and introduce the elements of unfair advantage taking and exploitation (to mention only a few hazards and objections). But what about post-treatment relations? Is friendship or sex permissible when therapy is over and the formal doctor-patient relationship no longer pertains? Two-year and five-year mandatory waiting periods are on the books in some quarters, whereas others forbid sex with former clients in perpetuity. Blanket rules of this sort strike me as absurd. Surely it is person- and situation-specific?

For example, say a young, single, heterosexual female client consults a young, unmarried, heterosexual male therapist. She is basically stable and well functioning but is having difficulties at work with an unsympathetic employer. After two role-playing and assertiveness training sessions, she is able to bring matters to a head, and at her third and final session she reports that she quit her job and found another that augurs well for the future. The therapist recommends a couple of books on assertive behaviour to reinforce her new found skills. Several months later they meet at a party where they have a long and interesting chat and would like to start dating each other. 'You have to wait for an additional 16 to 18 months', would be the edict of some, whereas others would decree, 'Impermissible! Once a patient, always a patient'. The same rules would apply had the client been in therapy for 5 years of intensive treatment for sexual identity problems coupled with a personality disorder, bipolar proclivities and obsessive-compulsive tendencies. A therapist who worked in a locale that upheld the two-year post-treatment ban would presumably be permitted to engage in sexual relations with this former client. I submit that in matters of this kind, the 'forbidden in perpetuity' rule should pertain. Thus, I am arguing for a case-by-case determination of such matters.

As an extremely wise and perspicacious colleague pointed out to me, the APA Code of Ethics (1992) is a litigator's dream, exposing any psychologist practitioner to being blindsided even though he or she is doing the right thing for the client. Part of the intent behind the book *Dual Relationships and Psychotherapy* is to disseminate information that may enable matters to be placed on a far more equitable plane.

ACTING DISRESPECTFULLY TOWARDS CLIENTS

I have noticed that psychotherapists who are strongly opposed to boundary extensions and adhere to a 'strict professionalism' often have what strikes me as an offensive way of relating to their clients. Here is a typical example. I was at a meeting (rather pretentiously called a 'Ward Round') where several psychiatric residents took turns presenting cases to about two dozen mental health professionals. A young woman was being interviewed by one of the psychiatric residents. The dialogue continued more or less as follows:

Patient: May I ask how old you are?
Resident: Why is that important?
Patient: It's no big deal. I was just curious.
Resident: Why would you be curious about my age?
Patient: Well, you look around 30 and I was just wondering if I am correct.
Resident: What impact would it have if you were not correct?
Patient: None that I can think of. It was just idle curiosity.
Resident: *Just* idle curiosity?

As I watched these exchanges, I grew uncomfortable. It seemed to me that the patient wished she had never raised the issue in the first place and that she was feeling more and more uneasy. It did not seem that the dialogue was fostering warmth, trust or rapport. On the contrary, it resembled a cross-examination in a courtroom and appeared adversarial.

In psychoanalysis it is deemed important for the analyst to remain neutral and non-disclosing so the patient can project his or her needs, wishes and fantasies on to this 'blank screen'. It makes no sense for this to become a rule for all therapists to follow. It has always struck me as ill-mannered and discourteous to treat people in this way.

I recommend the following type of exchange in place of the aforementioned example:

Patient: How old are you?
Resident: I just turned 29. Why do you ask?
Patient: I was just curious. It's no big deal.
Resident: Might you be more comfortable with or have greater confidence in someone older?
Patient: No, not at all.

At this juncture, I would suggest that the topic be dropped. Notice the recommended format: first, answer the question and then proceed with an inquiry if necessary. In this way, the patient is validated and not demeaned. Why am I dwelling on such a seemingly trivial issue? Because it is not a minor or frivolous point, and I have observed this type of interaction far too often — usually to the detriment of the therapeutic process. I see it as part and parcel of a dehumanising penchant among the many rigid thinkers in our field, those who legislate against all dual relationships and deplore all boundary extensions. These are the members of our profession (and they are not a minority) who regard themselves as superior to patients and tend to infantilise and demean them in the process. It is significant that younger and more recently trained psychotherapists endorse more conservative views on ethics and boundaries than those who are older and less recently trained (see Lamb and Catanzaro 1998).

Regrettably, far too many therapists embrace the widespread belief in the 'power differential', which holds that the patient is in a one-down position and is unable to refuse requests and directives from the therapist. It seems to me that some practitioners need to see themselves as omnipotent, thereby rendering all patients readily susceptible to coercion. Thus, their clients are bizarrely overprotected, which, like exploitation, is not beneficial for them and tends to undermine the therapy. It is particularly unfortunate to regard patients as 'untouchables' instead of simply treating them as fellow human beings.

REFERENCES

American Association for Marriage and Family Therapists (2001) *AAMFT Code of Ethics*. Washington, D.C.: Author. Retrieved 8th July 2001, from http://www.aamft.org/about/revisedcodeethics.html

American Counselling Association (1996) *Code of Ethics and Standards of Practice*. Alexandria, VA: American Counseling Association

American Psychological Association (1992) *Ethical Principles of Psychologists and Code of Conduct*. Washington, D.C.: Author

California Association of Marriage and Family Therapists (1997) *Ethical Standards for Marriage and Family Therapists*. San Diego, CA: Author

Ebert, B. W. (1997) Dual-relationship prohibitions: a concept whose time never should have come. *Applied and Preventive Psychology* 6: 137–56

Lamb, D. H. and Catanzaro, S. J. (1998) Sexual and nonsexual boundary violations involving psychologists, clients, supervisees, and students: implications for professional practice. *Professional Psychology: Research and Practice* 29: 498–503

Lazarus, A. A. (1998). How do you like these boundaries? *The Clinical Psychologist* 51: 22–5

Lazarus, A. A. (2002) Something must be done about the totalitarian mentality of many ethics committees and licensing boards. In J. Zeig (ed.), *The Evolution of Psychotherapy: The Fourth Conference*. Phoenix, AZ: Zeig, Tucker

Lazarus, A. A. and Zur, O. (eds) (2002) *Dual Relationships and Psychotherapy*. New York: Springer

Lazarus, C. N. (2001) Foundations of pharmacopsychology. In S. Cullari (ed.), *Counseling and Psychotherapy: A Practical Guide Book for Trainees and New Professionals* (pp. 246–88). Boston: Allyn and Bacon

National Association of Social Workers (1999) *Code of Ethics*. Retrieved 27th July 2001, from http://www.naswdc.org/Code/ethics.htm

Peterson, M. B. (2001) Recognising concerns about how some licensing boards are treating psychologists. *Professional Psychology: Research and Practice* 32: 339–40

Saunders, T. T. (2001) After all, this is Baltimore — Distinguished Psychologist of the Year address. *The Independent Practitioner* Winter: 15–18

Welch, B. (2001) *Insight: Safeguarding Psychologists against Liability Risks* (1st edn). *Caution: State Licensing Board Ahead*. Amityville, NY. American Professional Agency, Inc., Chubb Group of Insurance Companies

Williams, M. H. (1997) Boundary violations: do some contended standards of care fail to encompass commonplace procedures of humanistic, behavioural and eclectic psychotherapies? *Psychotherapy* 34: 239–49

Williams, M. H. (2000a) Victimized by 'victims': a taxonomy of antecedents of false complaints against psychotherapists. *Professional Psychology: Research and Practice* 31: 75–81

Williams, M. H. (2000b, Winter) APA ethics committee considered prohibiting solo practice. *The Independent Practitioner* 20 (1): 46–9

Williams, M. H. (2001). The question of psychologists' maltreatment by state licensing boards: overcoming denial and seeking remedies. *Professional Psychology: Research and Practice* 32: 341–4

Zur, 0. (2000). In celebration of dual relationships: how prohibition of nonsexual dual relationships increases the chance of exploitation and harm. *The Independent Practitioner* 20: 97–100

PART II:
ENABLING INNOVATION AND DIVERSITY

IIA: ENABLING ACCOUNTABILITY AND CO-OPERATION

EDITORIAL INTRODUCTION AND COMMENTARY

One of the counter-arguments of the pro-professionalisation movement has been that there are no better alternatives than those currently being aggressively pursued. Whilst many of the sceptics believe that no regulation remains the least damaging alternative, others have developed exciting and innovative models which demonstrate that there are, indeed, many possible viable alternatives available. Some such solutions are put forward in this section, along with models for therapeutic communities which embody a spirit of co-operation, communication and tolerance.

First, DAN HOGAN presents a number of recommendations based upon his seminal 1979 4-volume work *The Regulation of Psychotherapists*, and around a central tenet that what should be regulated is output (the work that is produced by the therapist), rather than input (the qualifications, supervision etc. that the therapist undertakes). The latter has not been shown to influence therapeutic success, whereas the former is in itself a marker of that success. In Chapter 17, DENIS POSTLE models a possible alternative form of registration based upon one of Hogan's recommendations — full disclosure. This entails empowering clients to make more informed choices about therapists by requiring the latter to make available to the former full information about how they work, and through increased education for clients so that they can better interpret that information.

In Chapter 18, GARI TOMKINS also calls upon the trade associations to abandon protectionism and look to a more facilitative and pluralistic future. YVONNE BATES then argues that it is bodies such as the BACP, rather than the Government, who seem to be pushing for regulation and compulsory registration, creating a homogeneous, academically trained in-group and a poly-diverse, disempowered out-group. Bates calls for the creation of new, non-hierarchical occupational communities to counteract this process.

Finally in this section NATALIE SIMPSON describes an existing alternative form of community. The *therapy-abuse.net* web site hosts a virtual community where clients and therapists can work together to study the problems and abuses of therapy and to develop creative solutions. Though not without its problems *therapy-abuse.net* nonetheless is a groundbreaking and leading-edge approach to mature, non-mystifying communication and co-operation in the therapy world.

16

PROFESSIONAL REGULATION AS FACILITATION, NOT CONTROL: IMPLICATIONS FOR AN OPEN SYSTEM OF REGISTRATION VERSUS RESTRICTIVE LICENSURE

DANIEL B. HOGAN[†][*]

OVERVIEW

For more than a quarter of a century the mental health professions have brought to bear a panoply of weapons in waging a fierce battle to control the field of psychotherapy. However, their efforts, made in the name of protecting the public from harm, have probably caused more harm than good. What we should have at this date in history is plentiful services delivered to all populations at a reasonable cost and with minimal risk. Instead, what we have are fewer services at higher costs and with many populations totally unserved. And it is not at all clear that the public has been protected. Sadly, this need not be the case.

Further, lost in the morass of competing claims for professional hegemony is a host of crucial issues for professionals in the field of counselling and psychotherapy. Ever clearer is the need to go back to the basics. For example, we need to determine the extent and type of harm of which practitioners are capable, because this is, after all, the whole basis for licensing. Then we need to determine what kinds of regulation are most likely to prevent such harm. Of course, any such system will have its own costs and impacts, and these need to be determined, including unintended negative side-effects. Part of that equation includes an analysis of what a particular set of regulations will do to the profession as a whole. In the case of psychotherapy and counselling, these issues are particularly salient, because the profession is new and emerging.

Finally, at a more fundamental level I shall argue that we need to reconceptualise the entire process of regulation. Instead of an almost exclusive emphasis on control and discipline, we need to see how regulation can facilitate the development of the profession. We need to move away from restrictive licensing laws to a system of simple registration. Instead of focusing on restricting

---

† Chapter appears with kind permission of the author, who holds copyright.
* Portions of this article have been excerpted and adapted from *The Regulation of Psychotherapists: A study in the philosophy and practice of professional regulation*. Cambridge, MA: Ballinger, 1979.

practitioners from entering the field, we need to embrace the entire range of therapists focusing on a sound disciplinary system and good education of the public. This will ultimately prove more effective; it will have less negative costs; and it will result in a more positive impact. In fact, such a system would probably serve a host of other professions equally well.

I made this argument in detail 20 years ago with the publication of a four-volume series *The Regulation of Psychotherapists: A Study in the Philosophy and Practice of Professional Regulation*. Now, as I write in 1999 as the millennium approaches, my conclusions and recommendations have not changed. The intervening time has only reinforced my opinion of their validity. And we now have some examples suggesting that alternative approaches can actually work.

BACKGROUND

Until recently psychotherapy has been a lucrative field that many professions have wanted to control. Today as many as six or seven professions, including psychiatry, psychology, social work and nursing, lay claim to the therapy field, making it a true minefield for the unlicensed to navigate at their peril. The primary weapon for professional control has been licensure — the ability of a government to limit the practice of a profession to those who are qualified. A critical piece of ammunition provided by licensure to the professions has been the use of governmental laws to establish entry requirements that must be met before a person can practise. In the United States, this control is exercised at the individual State level. Licensing primarily takes two forms: the most restrictive prohibits the practice of a profession without a licence, which is only granted if one meets certain stringent requirements; less restrictive, but still highly impactful, are title protection acts that forbid the use of certain titles unless one is licensed and meets certain qualifications.

The number of licensing laws regulating counselling and psychotherapy has increased astronomically over the last 50 years. In the United States, all States now license psychologists and physicians, while many States license social workers, marriage and family therapists, and a host of other counselling groups. Each of these groups has created a description of what it means to practise that particular profession. This definition either explicitly or implicitly includes 'psychotherapy' and 'counselling' within its purview. The proliferation of licensing laws parallels a similar trend in many other occupations and professions. In the United States, at least one quarter of all employed labour in some States has been composed of licensed professionals. As knowledge and information replace capital as the key item of value in our society, the professional classes will continue their ascendancy. As long ago as 1968, the eminent sociologist Talcott Parsons wrote that:

> The professional complex ... has already become the most important single component in the structure of modern societies. ... The massive emergence of the professional complex, not the special status of capitalistic or socialistic modes of organization, is the crucial structural development in twentieth-century society.

> (ibid.: 545)

Whenever professional associations have gone to individual State legislatures to argue the case for licensing, it has been in the name of protecting the public. It is plain, however, that self-protection and the desire for economic well-being are also at work. Most licensing laws have been proposed and drawn up by the very professionals being regulated. In addition, they are usually exclusively administered by those same professionals. Many licensing boards have no public members whatsoever. Some US State laws actually require the governor to choose board members from a list drawn up by the local professional association. The professionals who run the board are generally granted wide discretionary powers, including the right to determine what academic institutions will have their credentials honoured and what type of written examination will be required.

These mental health professions have sought to dominate the field by requiring entrants to possess certain advanced academic credentials, to pass rigorous exams, to possess significant supervised experience as well as specified other characteristics. And they do so by laying claim to a broad field that would seem to have no boundary. Witness, for example, what has been the State of Louisiana's definition of psychology: 'Psychology is hereby defined as the study and application of the principles of behaviour.'[1] If the practice of psychology so defined is illegal without a licence, one wonders what is left for the rest of us to do without violating the law.

THE ISSUES

The question, of course, is how well licensing has served the general public. Good reason exists to believe that most licensing laws are counterproductive. Several factors contribute to this result. First, a boundary issue exists. It turns out to be difficult, if not impossible, to define the field clearly enough for licensing purposes. I have argued elsewhere that this rises to a constitutional issue based on the 'void-for-vagueness' doctrine. The result is that government agencies attempting to enforce licensing laws will constantly be meddling in the bailiwick of other professions, including education and religion.

Second, while licensing is meant to ensure that only (minimally) competent professionals are admitted to practise, little evidence exists that current entrance requirements have any bearing on necessary skills or any relationship to performance. Even if it were, it seems clear that the requirements are way above what is minimally necessary to be competent. Despite this lack of evidence, professional associations continue to maintain that practitioners must possess doctoral degrees, must have years of supervised experience, and must successfully complete passage of a difficult written exam to enter the field.

Through the use of meta-analytic research techniques, we are now able to summarise across research studies and determine fairly definitively whether certain hypotheses are true or false. As a result, research findings have led to a conclusive determination that psychotherapy as a whole is effective. We also know that certain therapeutic techniques are more effective than others, at least for certain quite specific conditions. But we do not yet know whether one therapist is likely to be better than another therapist. We do not know whether people with credentials perform at a higher level than those without. In fact,

---

1. La. Rev. Stat. Ann §37:2352(5), 1974.

what evidence exists suggests that certain human qualities in the therapist are probably more critical to positive outcomes than advance degrees. Reviews of the impact of strict licensing laws on the quality of service delivered have been neutral at best, and negative at worst.

Third, evidence on disciplinary enforcement, one of the cornerstones of the licensing process, reveals a woefully inadequate system. Licensing boards rarely take action against those who are licensed, but practising unethically or incompetently, no matter how egregious their offence. When action is taken, it is frequently to protect the name of the profession, not the public. The fact that disciplinary boards lack adequate funds and technical skills virtually ensures that this will not change, even if the above problems were resolved.

Another function of licensing laws is the prevention of unlicensed practice. This tends to be sporadically enforced, despite the fact that it is in the economic interest of the professions to do so. When enforcement does occur, it is frequently aimed at curbing competition, not dangerous practices, as when lawyers attempt to prevent real-estate brokers from writing contracts for the sale of land.

In addition to not protecting the public, licensing tends to have negative side-effects. First, higher than necessary and irrelevant entry requirements restrict the number of persons able to enter the professions, exacerbating shortages in the supply of personnel. Second, through making it unnecessarily difficult for professionals licensed in one State to be licensed in another, licensing aggravates problems in the geographical distribution of practitioners. Third, broad definitions of practice, overly restrictive regulation of paraprofessionals and the absence of alternative routes to licensure have unnecessarily decreased the overall supply of services. These three problems produce a fourth, which is a significant increase in the cost of professional services. Fifth, licensing inhibits important innovations in professional practice, training, education and the organisation of services. It does so through disciplinary provisions and ethical standards that create difficulties in advertising services and restricting how services may be delivered, through reliance on accreditation agencies whose criteria are not based on whether schools or programmes produce competent practitioners, and through defining quality in terms of what is currently acceptable by the majority of practitioners, not empirical evidence of effectiveness. Finally, reliance on academic degrees and other irrelevant or unnecessary entrance requirements results in serious discrimination against minorities, women, the aged and the poor.

In fact, according to some political scientists, the pervasiveness of licensing is an indication that the United States is returning to a guild society reminiscent of the Middle Ages. Like the guilds, licensed professionals have established and enforced compulsory membership, creating a monopoly. Like the guilds, licensing standards have become higher and the cost of licensure has increased. Like the guilds, periods of apprenticeships have been lengthened, the number of apprentices has been restricted, and the possibility of licensure through apprenticeship or work experience has generally been eliminated.

Thus, since psychotherapy is such an ill-defined field, since reliable and valid standards do not exist to determine whether practitioners are competent, since not enough is known about how to train practitioners effectively, and since methods of measuring competence and selecting practitioners have not been agreed upon, restrictive licensing laws are inadvisable.

A reconceptualisation of the regulatory process

What are some basic principles to which all proposals for regulation should conform? First, the purpose of regulation needs to be reconceptualised. The prevailing view defines law and regulation as a form of social control that comes into being through an exercise of authority. Regulatory laws are seen as a means of implementing restrictions that are enforced by sanctions. This focus on control is a logical outgrowth of the positivistic philosophy of law advocated by Austin, Kelsen and H. L. A. Hart. The field of professional regulation has adopted this legal philosophy lock, stock and barrel. The result has been an emphasis on control, discipline, the elimination of quackery and charlatans, and the protection of the public from incompetent and unethical practice.

Another broader conception of the regulatory process is advisable, however. Lon Fuller of the Harvard Law School has argued that the basic purpose of laws is to provide a framework for, and method of, facilitating human interaction. Thus, regulations are designed not only to protect the public, but they should be framed in such a way that they meet the needs of that public. When the purpose of professional regulation is conceived of in this fashion, issues arise that are normally ignored. The overarching purpose of regulation becomes not only protecting the public from harm but also ensuring that the quality, quantity and cost of mental health services are improved.

Licensing laws, then, should be viewed as a method of facilitating the interaction of the professions and the public, in addition to being a method of controlling professional activity. This view serves to focus on whether licensing is having deleterious side-effects, and whether the hidden costs of licensing laws are worth their supposed benefits. It also brings to the fore the potential value of licensing as a vehicle for educating the public about the professions. Licensing laws should serve to demystify the professions. Regulations should promote client autonomy and responsibility. Perhaps most important, viewing licensing laws through this lens makes evident that traditional laws may have an extremely calcifying effect on the emerging profession of psychotherapy. This is especially so if rigid, arbitrary and unproven criteria are used to judge whether practitioners should be granted a licence and whether academic and other training programmes should be accredited for licensing purposes. One of the emphases of regulation becomes how best to encourage the constructive development of the psychotherapy profession.

It is absolutely essential to recognise that licensing laws are not meant to ensure a high level of professional competence, only that a practitioner is not likely to harm the public. This means that licensing laws should adopt minimum requirements for entrance into a profession, and these requirements should be clearly related to minimally competent practice. In this regard, licensing laws should emphasise the regulation of output, not input. Hence, they should be concerned with a person's actual skills, not how those skills were obtained. Since so little is known about the effective training and selection of professionals, a further purpose of licensing should be to promote a pluralistic system for the delivery of professional services.

RECOMMENDATIONS

The following recommendations would do much to move us down this path:

Regulation of output, versus input and process:
Regulation through licensure constitutes control of input, since it establishes standards and criteria governing entrance into a profession. Because current requirements have not been shown to be related to effective performance, alternatives should be considered. Competency-based measures represent a sounder attempt at regulation, since they attempt to correlate particular skills with effective performance. Regulations that are based on output measures or correlated with them are strongly to be preferred. Registration laws (see below) represent an output-based system, since they allow all practitioners in, and then regulate their practice through the disciplinary arm of the registration board.

Registration, not licensing or certification:
Regulation through registration, in which practitioners are required to register with a government agency or board, but are not required to meet any academic or other prerequisites, is the most desirable form of regulation. Where licensing laws have entrance requirements, only the unlicensed use of specific titles should be restricted, not the right to practise. Registration allows all people to practise so long as they provide certain information to the State. Practitioners can, however, be removed from the roles if they engage in incompetent, harmful or unethical activity. Registration has the advantage of bringing all people into the fold, ending the turf wars that currently exist.

Minimal use of restrictive licensing laws:
Licensing laws that restrict practice to those who possess academic credentials should be avoided. Even if licensing laws do not restrict the right to practise, but prohibit only the unlicensed use of certain titles, they are inadvisable. (They may, however, represent a necessary evil, since insurance reimbursement is so frequently tied to the existence of at least a certification law.) Restrictive licensing should not be employed unless the following conditions are met:

- The profession being regulated is mature and well-established.
- The profession has a clearly defined field of practice.
- The profession has a significant public impact.
- The net benefits of licensing outweigh any negative side-effects by a substantial amount.
- Less restrictive alternatives are unavailable.
- The potential for harm from incompetent or unethical practitioners is significant, pervasive and well documented.
- Reliable and valid measures exist to determine whether practitioners are qualified to practise.
- Adequate financial and human resources will be provided for the operation of the regulatory board or agency.

Full disclosure requirements:

All licensing laws should require practitioners to disclose relevant information to clients and the public, including the name, address and methods of contacting the government disciplinary agency, fee structure and status of confidentiality. Clients should be given a copy of the rules and regulations of the board and what constitutes unethical or incompetent practice. Practitioner education, experience, supervision status, methods used and techniques in which certification by an outside organisation has been achieved, are among the types of disclosure that would be valuable.

Increased education of the public:

Although little used until now as a method of professional regulation, education of the public has the potential to be a powerful tool in protecting the public from harm. To be effective, however, considerable effort, money, time and commitment must be devoted to developing a sound programme for public education and the dissemination of information. State agencies should undertake programmes to help educate potential clients of therapists as to what to look for in a therapist, what questions to ask, and what to do if dissatisfied with therapeutic services. State agencies should act as a conduit for information supplied by various professional groups to inform the public as to the state of the art in psychotherapy.

Encouragement of a proliferation of professional associations and accrediting organisations:

Professional associations and accrediting organisations will and should continue to play a strong role in the regulation of psychotherapists. Because of the lack of consensus on standards of practice, methods of training and methods of selection, however, it will be crucial to create a situation in which many such associations and organisations coexist, each advocating different methods and theories for the training and certification of therapists. The goal should be a pluralistic system in which the public can choose any of a variety of therapists. By carefully monitoring the effectiveness of therapists certified by different associations, long-term research might begin to establish which methods of training and selection produced the most competent or least dangerous therapists. In the United States a national certifying agency has been put into place to certify accreditation organisations in the health field.

Exploration of the value of client evaluations:

Because at least some aspects of a professional's practice are subject to direct evaluation by a client, such as client satisfaction and what the therapist actually said and did, the use of such evaluations should be explored by licensing bodies. The idea would be to have these evaluations available to the board and perhaps to the public.

Special laws for specific problems and the use of existing criminal law:

Where special dangers are identified in the psychotherapeutic process, and where traditional avenues of dealing with them are ineffective, special laws should be enacted. Existing fraud and sexual harassment laws should be strengthened and used to prevent some of the abuses that currently occur in professional practice. This alone would obviate much of the need for licensing.

Balanced representation of interests, not professional control:
The basic policies of the regulatory board or agency should not be set by a board composed solely of professionals, but should have a balanced representation of appropriate constituencies, including the public, clients and government officials. Licensing boards or agencies should be administered by personnel skilled at their task. Thus, discipline should be carried out by trained investigatory staff. The board or agency should have adequate financing and should not rely on registration fees for its continued operation.

Specific ideas:
- *Narrow definitions of practice:* Definitions of practice should be carefully and narrowly drawn. The more a regulation restricts practice to a limited few, the more rigidly this guideline needs to be applied.
- *Competency-based standards and criteria:* Licensing requirements should be competency-based and related to actual performance. Academic credentials should only be used if they have a demonstrable relationship to performance.
- *Focus on definitions of minimal competence:* Licensing requirements should be aimed at a minimal level of competence, not high quality.
- *Legitimacy of alternatives paths to licensing:* Whether academic credentials are used or not, licensing laws should allow persons to be licensed on the basis of proficiency examinations, educational equivalency measures, apprenticeships, or certification by an appropriate professional association.
- *Maximum delegation of functions to para-professionals:* Restrictive licensing laws should allow licensed persons to delegate any and all functions to paraprofessionals, unless demonstrated danger would result. Delegation provisions should only require direct, over-the-shoulder supervision where absolutely necessary.
- *Accreditation:* Where academic credentials are a requirement of licensing laws, the further requirement that the degree must be from an accredited institution or programme should only exist if accreditation is determined by truly competency-based measures. Otherwise, the encouragement of multiple accrediting agencies should take place, with accompanying research on their impact and effectiveness.
- *Avoidance of standardised national examinations:* The use of standardised national examinations by licensing boards should be avoided unless evidence exists that these examinations have a demonstrable relationship to competent practice. In other words, they must have predictive validity, not simply content validity. Further, even with demonstrable validity, it still may be worthwhile to avoid standardisation to allow the possibility of even better measures or alternative examinations that are equally predictive.
- *Use of a wide variety of selection methods:* Since little agreement exists about what selection methods are best for determining professional competence, licensing boards should experiment with the use of supervisor evaluation, evaluations of role-playing and taped samples of actual performance, acceptance of certification by appropriate professional associations, and other selection procedures.

- *Performance-based re-licensure and continuing competence:* Although demonstration of continuing competence should be an essential feature of all licensing laws, no evidence exists that continuing education requirements are a good measure of that competence. Instead, licensing boards should require a demonstration of continuing competence based on a proficiency examination or direct evidence of competent performance. A quick perusal of the offerings of organisations that supply continuing education programmes will quickly show how absurd most such requirements are. Most courses have marginal relationship to protecting the public, and one will find few courses that focus on ethics or the dangers of the therapeutic process.
- *Generous use of exemptions:* All licensing laws should contain specific exemptions for professionals certified by recognised professional associations in the psychotherapy/counselling field. The criteria for determining whether a professional association is recognised should be based on whether the association has a membership of reasonable size, standards and criteria for admission that are based on competent practice, a method for disciplining incompetent or unethical members, and methods for periodically reviewing members' continuing competence.
- *Generous grandparent clauses:* When a new licensing law is enacted, adequate provision must be made to protect the rights of those who do not meet the education (or other) requirements of the law, but who have been practising prior to the law's enactment.

While my basic position is against restrictive licensing, I recognise that it may be politically necessary in some instances to protect the rights of non-traditionally-trained practitioners or those without a high enough academic credential. For instance, where the rights of counsellors to practise with master's degrees in education are potentially infringed by a psychology licensing law requiring a doctorate, a counsellor licensure law may be the only method of protection (of and for counsellors, not the public) available. But such laws should not then restrict others from practising who do not meet the provisions of the law regulating counsellors.

THE FUTURE: DOES AN ALTERNATIVE SYSTEM HOLD HOPE?

Is there any hope that we might see the dawning of a new regulatory environment in which the above-described recommendations might flourish? I am not sure. Over the past 20 years, professional associations have made stronger and stronger attempts to totally control the marketplace. State societies have lobbied for restrictive practice acts to replace simple title protection laws. They have removed exemptions and called for very limited grandparent clauses. They have placed broad definitions of practice on the plates of legislatures to extend the scope of their influence.

At the same time, several individual States in the United States have enacted registration laws and have attempted to implement a variety of the above recommendations, including Maine, Vermont and Colorado. As far as I can determine they have been a success. Vermont, for example, adopted a registration law in the form of a 'Roster of Psychotherapists' whose purpose is:

- To ensure that consumers of psychotherapy services are provided with the information relating to the training and qualification of non-licensed and noncertified providers of psychotherapy necessary to enable them to make informed decisions concerning their choice of providers.

• That psychotherapists who are non-licensed and non-certified are entered on a roster and practise according to established standards of professional conduct and be subject to disciplinary procedures if they fail to adhere to those standards.

• That the term psychotherapy as used in this chapter be narrowly interpreted to ensure that only those persons who provide services that clearly fall within the definition of psychotherapy are subject to the provisions of this chapter.[2]

This law has been in effect since 1994 and appears to have worked effectively, according to Board member Lauren Berrizbeitia (personal communication, 22nd February 1999). She states that the number and type of complaints that they receive are similar to other professional groups, such as psychologists. They have more practitioners listed on their roster than other major professions such as psychology and social work. The original law was passed with some trepidation. When it came up for 'sunset review,' the State legislature did not even bother with the review process since it concluded that the law was obviously effective and valuable.

The State of Colorado has passed a statute establishing a Grievance Board for all psychotherapists who are not licensed by another profession, such as psychology or social work. This requires registration of all such practitioners and provides a vehicle for disciplining those who are errant or wayward. The legislature conducted a multi-year study of the effectiveness of restrictive licensing and concluded that no demonstrable protection of the public could be found. According to Goodrich (cited in Grohol 1998), in a recent year psychiatrists were subject to a larger number of, and more serious, offences than the registered group of therapists, despite the fact that the registered group outnumbered the psychiatrists by 4:1. This suggests that whatever the dangers posed by psychotherapeutic practice, protection is not being provided by traditional forms of licensing with its reliance on academic credentials. An active disciplinary board with a broad-based register seems a far better solution.

The future of counselling and psychotherapy in the United Kingdom would appear to be at a critical juncture today. If restrictive licensing is adopted, then I fear that the field will be crippled for years to come. If, however, professional associations are able to put aside their ill-founded beliefs in why they should be the only ones to rule the roost, and if they can adopt an inquiring and research-orientated stance, then perhaps a path can be laid to allow a system of registration that would allow the profession to flourish and develop in a sound, positive fashion.

REFERENCES AND FURTHER READING

Austin, J. (1954) *The Province of Jurisprudence Determined.* London: Weidenfeld and Nicolson (orig. 1832)

2. Vt. Stat. Ann. Title 26, Chapter 26, §4081.

Blanck, G. (1963) Development of psychotherapy as a profession: a study of the process of professionalization. Unpublished Ph.D. dissertation, New York University; abstracted in *Dissertation Abstracts* 24 (7), 1963, p. 2974

Freund, P. A. (1965) The legal profession. In K. S. Lynn and the Editors of *Daedalus* (eds), *The Professions in America* (pp. 35–46). Boston: Houghton Mifflin

Fuller, L. L. (1969) Human interaction and the law. *American Journal of Jurisprudence* 14: 1–36

Grant, J. A. C. (1942) The gild returns to America. *Journal of Politics* 4: 303–36, 458–77

Grohol, J. M. (1998) Why don't current psychotherapy licensing regulations work? A review and suggestions for change. (Online). Mental Health Net. Available at http://www.cmhc.com/archives/editor29.htm (1st March 1998)

Hart, H. L. A. (1961) *The Concept of Law*. Oxford: Clarendon Press

Hogan, D. B. (1974) Encounter groups and human relations training: the case against applying traditional forms of statutory regulation. *Harvard Journal on Legislation* 11: 659–701

Hogan, D. B. (1976a) The experiential group and the psychotherapeutic enterprise revisited: a response to Strupp. *International Journal of Group Psychotherapy* 26: 321–33

Hogan, D. B. (1976b) The advantages of accreditation through the International Association of Applied Social Scientists. *Group and Organization Studies: The International Journal for Group Facilitators* 1: 394–7

Hogan, D. B. (1977) Competence as a facilitator of personal growth groups. *Journal of Humanistic Psychology* 17(2): 33–54

Hogan, D. B. (1978) State licensing, academic credentials and accreditation: implications and recommendations for postsecondary educational institutions. Washington, D.C.: Occasional Paper #1, National Centre for the Study of Professions; reprinted in *Drug Program Review* 6(2), 1978: 19–28

Hogan, D. B. (1979a) *The Regulation of Psychotherapists* (4 vols). Cambridge, MA: Ballinger
> I. *A Study in the Philosophy and Practice of Professional Regulation.*
> II. *A Handbook of State Licensure Laws.*
> III. *A Review of Malpractice Suits in the United States.*
> IV. *A Resource Bibliography.*

Hogan, D. B. (1979b) Is licensing public protection or professional protectionism? In P. Pottinger and J. Goldsmith (eds), *Defining and Measuring Competence* (pp. 13–24). San Francisco: Jossey-Bass

Hogan, D. B. (1980) The impact of professional certification on counseling psychology. *Counseling Psychologist* 9(1): 39–43

Hogan, D. B. (1981) Defining what a competent psychotherapist does: problems and prospects. *Resources in Education* October (*ERIC Reports* Document #ED201929, September 1980)

Hogan, D. B. (1982) When little is known, what are we to do?: the implications of social science research for regulatory policy. *Professional Practice of Psychology* 3 (1): 19–25

Hogan, D. B. (1983a) *Professional Regulation* (special double-issue guest editor.) *Law and Human Behavior* 7 (2–3): 99–305

Hogan, D. B. (1983b) The effectiveness of licensing: history, evidence, and recommendations. *Law and Human Behavior* 7(2–3): 117–38; earlier version in *Resources in Education* July 1981 (*ERIC Reports* Document #ED198439, Arlington, VA, November, 1980)

Hogan, D. B. (1983c) Professional regulation: an introduction to the issue. *Law and*

Human Behavior 7(2–3): 99–101

Kelsen, H. (1945) *General Theory of Law and State* (translated by A. Wedberg). Cambridge, MA: Harvard University Press

Parsons, T. (1968) Professions. In D. L. Sills (ed.), *International Encyclopedia of the Social Sciences*, Vol. 12 (pp. 536–47). New York: Macmillan Publishing Co.

17

PSYCHOPRACTICE ACCOUNTABILITY: A PRACTITIONER 'FULL-DISCLOSURE LIST'

DENIS POSTLE

What does a prospective psychotherapy/counselling client need and deserve from a process of practitioner accountability? Revising my last book, *The Mind Gymnasium* (Postle 1988, 2003) for re-publication has repeatedly put me in the position of adopting a client perspective — what do people seeking help with the human condition need to know when hiring a psychopractitioner? They need to know a lot more than they are likely to at the moment.

Many practitioners and employers and, consequently we might expect, most clients/service users still see accountability through the narrow, professionalised lens of hoop-jumping — 'qualification' and 'training'. Two other lenses are likely to be more relevant — *effectiveness;* and how we maintain our *capability* as practitioners.

First, then, effectiveness. Psychotherapy and counselling don't generally subscribe to the practice, commonplace in management and technical training, consultancy and language interpretation, of eliciting client feedback after events. Asking for feedback on our presumed effectiveness and paying attention to what we hear makes it more likely that clients will benefit from their time with us. This is not to argue that psychopractice is free of feedback on effectiveness, only to note that it is usually informal. For example I, and I imagine other practitioners, invite clients to take time at the end of the year or end of the quarter to review progress or development.

Recent inquiries based on more formal approaches — that in effect asked 'Did it work?', 'Did I get the help I needed?' (Duncan and Sparks 2002; Lambert et al. 2001) — point to a handful of effectiveness factors that challenge the sacred cows of professionalised psychotherapy. For example, the value of academic and technical competence — credentialling — in terms of 'qualifications', training and Continuing Professional Development (CPD) is seen as contributing as little as 15 per cent to client outcomes. Placebo effects — hope and expectations — are held to be at least as important. The quality of the rapport between the partners in the therapeutic or, as I prefer, educational alliance count for as much as these two together; and furthermore, what the client brings in the way of support, resourcefulness, education, and lived experience of survival and problem-solving account for approaching half the outcome.

So if the *resourcefulness of the client* makes a very high contribution to therapy outcomes, how can this be facilitated or enhanced? Apart from underlining the importance of a facilitative/client-centred approach, *client education* seems one obvious answer — an option that is almost entirely neglected by the bodies such as the UK Council for Psychotherapy (UKCP), the British Association for

Counselling and Psychotherapy (BACP), the British Psychological Society (BPS) and the British Confederation of Psychotherapists (BCP) that seek to dominate accountability in the UK.

When they seek a practitioner, the vast spread of self-help books, magazine articles, radio programmes and web sites that refer to psychological matters are likely to mean that clients may be well informed, if haphazardly, about the *territories* of counselling and psychotherapy. They are not likely to be knowledgeable about what to expect, how to choose someone fitted to their needs or what is involved in hiring a practitioner. Personal recommendation aside, clients finding a practitioner through medical referral, the Yellow Pages, or checking out one of the psychotherapy organisation directories in the public library, are likely to know little or nothing about the person with whom they are starting to work. A recipe for a poor match between what the client needs and what the practitioner offers. After all, the psychotherapy/counselling relationship may affect how the whole of the rest of their life plays out. As I see it, the issue from a client's perspective is not getting it absolutely right or eliminating risk, but *increasing the chances* of a fruitful match.

Alongside effectiveness there is the question of how to sustain practitioner competence. How can practitioners be helped to navigate life's swamps and precipices and still be present for the clients that bring their lives to us? I borrow from industrial quality assurance the notion of *capability*: if we become, through a mix of education and experience, capable of delivering effective psychopractice, how do we stay capable? Supervision, the ongoing discussion of current concerns and declaration of potential risks; plus some form of CPD certainly helps us stay capable. However I want to argue that both CPD and supervision are limited in their support of capability because disclosure of where a practitioner is *as a person* tends to be optional or absent.

To summarise, present forms of psychotherapy/counselling accountability rely too much on input 'qualifications', and training, and on CPD events plus supervision to support and sustain practitioner capability, while neglecting client education and information. How could they be replaced by, or become transformed into, a new kind of accountability structure, one more congruent with what is now known about outcomes and client/practitioner power relations, and consequently more attuned to clients' interests?

I am convinced that the missing element in present approaches to accountability is *disclosure*. Full disclosure to peers of information about where the practitioner is in their life as well as how their practice is going; and disclosure of relevant information to clients about available practitioners.

The British Independent Practitioners Network (IPN) (*ipnosis* 1999-) has pioneered Continuing Self and Peer-Assessment and Scrutiny (*CSPA and S*) (House and Totton 1997) as an ongoing process of quality assurance that in my experience wonderfully supports and maintains practitioner capability. *CSPA and S* requires continuing (eye-) contact with practitioners, not only as people who deploy models, skills and experience — but also with the practitioner as a person with a life — so that contingencies that might skew, distort or undermine the quality of alliances with clients can be surfaced, supported or confronted. *CSPA and S* itself depends on practitioners getting to know each other very well in a safe enough and confidential enough forum for *non-disclosure* or *resistance to disclosure* to become a focus for attention. For example, a practitioner who, not for the first time, casually says they are so tired they could scream, might be disclosing something about their current life that is likely to affect the quality of their work with clients and that merits confrontation by peers.

Secondly, and the main but related focus of this chapter, how can disclosure of information about practitioners be extended and deepened so as better to support consumer choice? I propose that this requires development and installation of an innovative accountability process through which practitioners publish, in some detail, who they are, how they got to be practitioners, what their life experience and working orientation is, and doing this on a scale sufficient that a *client* can make some kind of informed guess that this is someone with whom *they* could work.

On the following pages I outline a proposal for such a psychotherapy/ counselling accountability process. It requires, I believe, a switch of gestalt from the present secretiveness/reticence of professionalised psychopractice to what has been called a 'full disclosure' model. Mowbray lists Will Schutz, Dan Hogan, Roberta Russell and S. J. Gross as advocating full disclosure as a basis for accountability (Mowbray 1995: 205–9). Since such shifts of paradigm are often hard to grasp in the abstract, I will describe my proposal for a full disclosure accountability structure as if it existed. By the time this text is in print I hope there will be a web site that demonstrates the potential of the scheme.

A practitioner 'full disclosure' list [PFD*list*]

What would be the key elements of disclosure?
Participation in the PFD*list* requires a statement in each of the following categories. (*NB: Practitioners may choose to make minimal or detailed statements.*)

- Life experience: work, jobs, roles, responsibilities; relationships — single, married, divorced, separated, partnered; children, grandchildren, adopted children, step-children; sexual orientation. A recent photograph.
- Practitioner development: education, training, relevant life experience/skills transfer, competency process (qualification, accreditation, Self and Peer Assessment etc.).
- Practitioner style: approaches/orientation(s) statement; ethical statement; terms and conditions including charges; weekly client load, specialties and preferences, who they wouldn't work with, confidentiality, note-keeping, supervision.
- Practitioner competence: supervision, continuing practitioner development, client feedback.
- Practitioner 'referees' statements: documents from three peers who:
  1 attest to the accuracy and integrity of the claims to competence of the practitioner in the statements made in the disclosure.
  2 provide a brief account of the process through which they keep this information up-to-date.
- Practitioner confidentiality: note-keeping, supervision.
- Practitioner/client disputes: details of practitioner's conflict resolution process and details of whom to contact.
- Practitioner trade activities: publications, journal contributions, research, books, interviews, trade association roles.

What form should this information take? What would be mandatory?

The *categories* of disclosure should be mandatory but practitioners need to be free to say as much as they like (but not nothing) in response to each of the categories. Similarly, the style of presentation is also a matter entirely for the practitioner. Styles seem likely to range from the purely factual to more discursive, or narrative. The openness to, and ease of change of, entries by practitioners (see below) is intended to encourage a 'disclosure culture' that is both self-sustaining and self-correcting through its appeal to clients and service purchasers.

How would the PFDlist be implemented as an institution?

The PFD*list* information would be held in a *government-funded computer database* accessible through any standard web browser. Access to this database would be free to users and, because the task of preparing and updating an entry is considerable, to practitioners also.

Since the PFD*list* entries would be in the public domain, local initiatives to publish *paper directories* for the IT-challenged would be likely and desirable.

A sector of the PFD*list* would make available a moderated *user forum* where users and practitioners could exchange information and experiences.

The PFD*list* would by managed by a small secretariat charged with the maintenance of the List and its functions. They would *not* be responsible for conflict resolution but would maintain a mediation/advocacy resource (see below), which might from time to time be drawn on for disputes that could not be locally resolved.

How could we ensure that clients experience it as user-friendly?

The user-friendliness of the whole system would be a commonplace IT design task. The 'friendliness' or otherwise of the entries would be entirely a matter of practitioner capacity and choice. Easily accessible, though password-protected access to the PFD*list* would mean that practitioners could edit, add to and develop their entry as the need or occasion demanded. Non-IT practitioners would be able to mail additions or amendments to the PFD*list* manager.

How would it be administered/financed?

The PFD*list* is a service enhancement for psychopractice users that needs to be free at the point of access. To enable this, government funding would be essential. However, this should be taken to imply government participation/support/ facilitation rather than control. The database function is a commonplace IT function for which tenders could be invited. The layer of necessary management could be sub-contracted to an existing contractor responsible or adjacent to the Department of Health. The *list* manager and staff would be charged with maintaining the database, promoting it and taking action on abuses or deficiencies in List entries (see below)

Does PFDL amount to statutory regulation by another name?

The PFD*list* applies to the task of accountability what we know about the uses and abuses of power both interpersonal and institutional, while at the same time respecting the lack of agreement on what constitutes competent or effective psychopractice. Out of that, it seeks to make available the widest range of psychopractice offerings while at the same time giving users adequate information about who/what, may or may not, meet their needs, and how to complain and seek redress if they experience an abuse of power and trust. Government supported, but not government controlled.

Which practitioners would be included/excluded from the PFDlist?
Any person offering services in the psychopractice area would be entitled to an entry on the PFD*list*. Non-registration should be tolerated but not encouraged.

How would practitioner statements be verified?
Practitioner statements have to be verified by the referees who are named and posted with the entry. If the accuracy of the statements is significantly challenged, the PFD*list* manager in the first instance would invite the referees to check out the challenge/objection. Their response may lead to the PFD*list* manager requiring that the entry be edited or withdrawn. However, the intention of the PFD*list* is to display carefully framed statements by practitioners that have been peer-assessed sufficiently well for accuracy before posting as to generally eliminate significant challenges. Indeed, such a challenge would indicate a failure of the refereeing process.

What sanctions might there be for inaccurate or misleading statements?
The aim of the PFD*list* is not to eliminate risk but to honour users needs for personal safety and value for money, without eliminating the 'wildness' and unpredictability implicit in effective psychopractice. If disputes arise the PFD*list* will seek to enable all parties to reach some resolution through mediation and advocacy rather than adjudication of guilt and blame, i.e. 'sadder and wiser' being more important than 'right/wrong'.

The PFD*list* management *would not be responsible for resolving disputes* but they would develop and maintain access to legal and advocacy/mediation resources to enable clients and practitioners to progress disputes. The costs of such facilities could be contained through an insurance charge on PFD*list* participants.

Disputes about misleading or inaccurate statements, or allegations of fraud or abusive practice, should be explored and resolved by the practitioner's designated dispute process and his/her referees. If they are unresolved, then they should be referred to the PFD*list* manager's layer of advocacy and mediation services. Persisting with misleading, fraudulent or inaccurate statements should lead to removal from the PFD*list*.

The List management would maintain pages on the PFD*list* web domain for posting apologies, explanations, notices of agreement, settlement or failure to agree.

What sanctions might there be for abusive behaviour?
Complaints or allegations of abusive or other behaviour by a practitioner in contravention of her/his stated practice description should in the first instance be pursued via the practitioner's stated dispute process. If redress or satisfaction is not reached through these means, then the management can be asked to invoke mediation/advocacy services. If the dispute/complaint is resolved as an instance of abuse, i.e. behaviour that the practitioner's referees cannot support, this would result in removal of the practitioner from the PFD*list*.

Re-instatement on to the list would require the re-establishment of the initial criteria, including the support of the same referees.

What would be the PFDlist's relations to other 'lists' such as those maintained by the IPN, BPS, UKCP, BPS and the BACP's UK Register of Counsellors?
Multiple lists of practitioner offerings appear to be in clients' interests since they maximise choice. A single government-sponsored listing that is inclusive of the wide range and variety of psychopractice offerings would go a long way towards securing a free market in these services.

The PFD*list* is intentionally inclusive: for instance, practitioners would be free to specify dispute procedures that lead to existing accountability bodies such as the IPN, BPS, UKCP, BPS and BACP. The PFD*list* is intended to promote benign co-existence between these and the dozens, possibly hundreds of other institutions whose members might be participants.

How would the PFDlist resolve the range and divergence between the styles of psychopractice that are currently available?
Client education would be an essential feature of the PFD*list*. The list would publish and maintain user-orientated information about how to hire a practitioner, what to expect, and guidance on how to negotiate with them. Several divergent, even contradictory guides might be expected to co-exist side-by side in reflection of the comprehensive disagreement in the field about routes to competency and the kinds of contracting that psychopractice entails. In addition, organisations and individuals would be free to take web space to present the claimed virtues of their particular way of working with clients. The intention of this would be informative/educational, and a role of PFD*list* management would be limited to discouraging, and if need be removing, organisational statements that amounted to advertising or promotion, while encouraging the display of articles, research, personal experiences etc.

Drafts of the proposal that I have outlined in this chapter have produced mixed reactions. Some people missed the point of the integration of practitioner accountability and client choice and saw the PFD*list* as a form of advertising; others warned that psychodynamically inclined practitioners wouldn't want to disclose anything at all because it 'would distort the transference', as though a client's ignorance of what they were getting into didn't also distort (or generate) transference; two people were concerned that this amount of disclosure 'would provide clients with ammunition'; there were understandable anxieties that any government involvement would amount to a takeover and that the internet format would exclude too many clients. An objection that I feel has validity, but which is also a reminder of the purist reaches of psychotherapy, is that in helping clients find someone who was a good match for their needs, the PFD*list* would promote collusion through eliminating or reducing the chances that clients benignly meet a practitioner whom they *wouldn't* consciously choose. The trouble with the present randomness is that it too often seems to lead to unhelpful mismatching, ineffectiveness and clients struggling to adapt to the practitioner's style.

My aims in devising the PFD*list* have sought to satisfy two criteria. First, to further confront the creative inadequacy of the Department of Health and the UK trade associations, the UKCP, BCP, BPS and BACP. Their notions of hierarchically structured accountability, based on archaic and discredited input forms of quality assurance, without ongoing face-to-face contact, mimic existing, deeply flawed, medical-style accountability (cf. Totton's Chapter 11, this volume). Like the GMC and the medical Royal Colleges, the psychotherapy trade associations are intrinsically exclusive and imperious in their relation to both registered practitioners and clients. Contrary to their assertions about client safety, through their claims of privileged, superior knowledge, they harm clients' interest by undermining the credibility of the very broad reach of personal and professional development work of which they are only a small part. As outcomes research seems to show and as others have argued (Mowbray 1995), this supposed virtue and its false promise of client safety is an 'emperor's new clothes' assertion.

Secondly, after more than a decade of resistance to, and confrontation of, the professionalisation of psychopractice, I have sought to answer a personal question: Might there be government-sponsored form of accountability for counselling and psychotherapy and their relatives in the field of personal development that I could sign up to? And if so, what form would it take? I feel that the PFD*list* would be good enough.

REFERENCES

Duncan, B. and Sparks, J. (2002) Heroic clients heroic agencies: partner for change. Nova Southeastern University. Full Disclosure List demo: http://www.mind-gymnasium.com/

Gross, S. J. (1977) Professional disclosure: alternative to licensing. *Personal Guidance Journal* 55: 586–8

Hogan, D. B. (1979) *The Regulation of Psychotherapists*, 4 vols. Cambridge, MA: Ballinger

House, R. and Totton, N. (eds) (1997) *Implausible Professions: Arguments for Pluralism and Autonomy in Psychotherapy and Counselling*. Ross-on-Wye: PCCS Books

Independent Practitioners Network (1999) Principles and Procedures, *ipnosis: a journal for the Independent Practitioners Network* — http://ipnosis.postle.net

Lambert, M. J. (n.d.) The effectiveness of psychotherapy: what has a century of research taught us about the effects of treatment? http://www.cwru.edu/affil/div29/lambert.htm

Lambert, M. J., Whipple, J. L., Smart, D. W., Vermeersch, D. S., Nielsen, S. L. and Hawkins, E. J. (2001) *Handbook of Psychotherapy and Behavior Change*, 5th edn. New York: Wiley

Mowbray, R. (1995) *The Case Against Psychotherapy Registration: A Conservation Issue for the Human Potential Movement*. London: Trans Marginal Press

Postle, D. (1988) *The Mind Gymnasium*. London: Macmillan

Postle, D. (2003) *The Mind Gymnasium*: CD-ROM edition. London: WLR

Russell, R. (1981) *Report on Effective Psychotherapy: Legislative Testimony*. New York: Hilgarth Press

Shutz, W. (1979) *Profound Simplicity*. USA: Joy Press

18

THE FALLACY OF ACCREDITATION: RE-ENSOULING PSYCHOTHERAPY AS AN ALTERNATIVE TO ACCREDITATION

GARI TOMKINS[†]

The attempt by Government and psychotherapeutic trade organisations to regulate and 'professionalise' psychotherapy is ignorantly betraying psychotherapy's nature and essence. I suspect that the people behind such moves do not understand what it is they are trying to regulate. By appropriating the word to their own ends, they are effectively marginalising psychotherapy, pushing true psychotherapy into the shadows. As W. H. Auden said, 'When words lose their meaning I am sure physical violence takes over'. The drive to accreditation and registration is symptomatic of how far mainstream psychotherapy has strayed from its essence. The fact that psychotherapy effectively needs re-ensouling demonstrates how far this process has gone. To reverse this tide of well intended ignorance, positive steps are required to place soul back in its rightful place, at the centre of the work — ironic, really, given the actual meaning of the word 'psychotherapy': to attend to the soul.

I strongly advocate that the Government and the various trade organisations cease this drive towards regulation and accreditation. I believe this drive is based on a fear of human nature and the fantasy that everything can be made safe (and perhaps the desire to make psychotherapy a middle-class activity). If fear and mistrust in human nature are enshrined in the work, then what chance does any process as subtle as soul-making stand? I am for the removal of structures that inhibit the manifestation of soul. These structures shrink-wrap soul, suffocating the very life force out of the work. Psychotherapists practising in an environment where uncomfortable feelings are outlawed by rules supposedly designed to protect the client, but that in actuality serve to keep the therapist safe, are hardly going to be of much use to their clients. Removing the structures that do not serve soul will mean a radical venture into trusting human nature, rather than fearing it.

Care needs to be taken when re-ensouling psychotherapy that any structures that are set up create more space for the client's soul, not less. We need to stop disempowering and nannying clients by encumbering their therapists to the point of incapability with ever-increasing regulation. To get round the conundrum of how to protect clients whilst not banishing soul from the work, it seems to me that

† This chapter is an edited extract from a much larger paper which can be viewed in its entirety at www.individualpsychotherapy.com. It first appeared in *ipnosis*, issue 5, Spring 2002, and appears here courtesy of the author.

there is only one way ahead — the re-empowerment of the client.

I offer the following suggestions in the hope that they will help this process and consequently develop better psychotherapeutic practice. I am aware that as a psychotherapist I run the risk of entering into the same power-over, know-better dynamic. In the absence of any focalised client voice you will have to judge for yourself the value of these suggestions that also come from my own experience as a client.

GOVERNMENT

Central Government could initiate a public information campaign to educate the public as to the nature of psychotherapy, its benefits and limits, how to choose a therapist, how to recognise malpractice and what to do to gain redress and compensation if they experience it (cf. Postle's Chapter 17, this volume). Furthermore, in the absence of any focalised client forum, perhaps with the exception of POPAN, the Government could provide resources to set up some kind of client representative organisation that could help with a true re-ensouling of psychotherapy.

By promoting psychotherapy the Government could encourage its citizens to take more responsibility for their own mental, emotional and spiritual well-being and live less stressed and more healthy, soulful lives.

In outlining the limits of psychotherapy the Government would help people to have realistic expectations of the work and what is expected of them in the work. This would help people to know what kinds of issues could be helped by psychotherapy and whether they have sufficient resources of time, money and energy in order to be able to commit to the work.

Educating the public about psychotherapy would make them better informed as to the type of therapist they might need and the kind of questions they could ask of a prospective therapist. If the public knew that they should trust how they feel about a prospective therapist and not just rely on what the therapist says, or what the certificates on the wall supposedly say about them, they would be more likely to choose a suitable therapist. The public could also do with knowing that they are perfectly within their rights to decline a particular therapist without a particular reason, even when they go through a referral service.

Demystifying psychotherapy in these ways (as far as it can be demystified) would make clients more able to recognise abusive situations or malpractice, something that regulation or accreditation will never prevent. Putting this information in the hands of the client helps to empower and protect them from exploitation in an activity where the therapist is often seen as 'the one who knows'.

The Government could also educate the public as to their rights if they want to make a complaint against their therapist. As things stand, it might be best for the Government to provide legal aid and/or litigation specialists to pursue such complaints through the courts. The present situation where clients complain to trade organisations is inevitably weighted towards the protection of their members. There are few, if any, mechanisms in place for any kind of compensation to the client. Their most commonly applied sanction is to stipulate that the offending member undergo further training or supervision, a punishment that amounts to little more than a slap on the wrist for the therapist and, in terms of any kind of compensation, a slap in the face for the client. Such complaints often result in the re-traumatising of the client as they are re-exposed to the alleged abuser and the initial trauma… all this occurring under the auspices of people who are supposedly skilled in handling emotionally charged situations.

The courts are the most likely place where the client stands a chance of receiving a fair hearing and any kind of recompense. My advice to anyone seeking redress with a recalcitrant practitioner is to go directly to court. There are many laws covering human rights that cover the kind of malpractice of which one might accuse a practitioner. A simple change in existing law would empower the court to include in its penalty the possibility of prohibiting the offending practitioner from using the title of 'Psychotherapist' to describe themselves or their work. In the future the Government could establish a specialised court, tribunal or ombudsman for dealing with such situations, which would combine the legal power of the law with a more comprehensive understanding of psychotherapy. A specialised court or ombudsman could be responsible for holding a record of therapists who have had claims brought against them and the outcome of such actions. This record could be made available to the public, bringing the kind of transparency Government is apparently seeking to bring to complaints procedures.

TRADE ASSOCIATIONS

Trade associations will need to make a fundamental shift in their attitude if they wish to be part of re-ensouling psychotherapy. They seem to have ring-fenced for themselves an area of the psychotherapeutic plain, by setting criteria and charging fees to those therapists who want to be within their auspices. Therapists in effect pay not only to maintain their stake in something that was already theirs but also to increase their stake because 'their' organisation shuts out/disenfranchises those who do not pay. The organisation publicises and promotes its supposed legitimacy, puffing itself up into some kind of trustworthy body to which the less informed public naïvely ascribes authority. This sounds very similar to the bullying way in which the trade associations in the early stages of the industrial revolution set themselves up, using their size to capture the market and supplant the long-standing tradition of master and apprentice. The motives of these organisations seem to be self-serving, trading on people's fears of exclusion, of not being able to attract clients and the consequent loss of income and livelihood.

The British Independent Practitioner's Network, with its peer accreditation system, has gone some way to reversing this top-down, power-over structure that the trade associations display. Their peer accreditation system, however, stops short of a client-centred model as it simply replaces the requirement for the client to give up their sovereignty to some distant anonymous rubber-stamping authority with the requirement that they give it up to their therapist's peers and colleagues. The same problem as with other trade organisations remains — at the outset the client is encouraged not to trust their own experience. How a therapy underpinned by such legitimisation can ever hope to succeed is beyond me. Likewise, how any complaints under such a system can claim to be free of the vested interests of the accused therapist's colleagues continues to confound me.

What the trade associations could do is use their size and organisational structures to promote psychotherapy and counselling to the public, and inform them how to access it.

They could work to increase the profile of psychotherapy within the field of medicine by educating doctors, psychologists, psychiatrists and related practitioners as to its efficacy when used to treat various disorders. The trade organisations are also best placed to set up research projects to investigate these claims. Personally, I would particularly like to see them actively challenge the short-term perspective taken by modern drug therapy that seems to lead to long-term dependence, lower quality of life and a tendency for patients to be using services through a revolving door. Statistics in the British National Health Service take a short-term view, using short-term symptom relief as their yardstick rather than ongoing health. We have a National *Ill* Service, not a National Health Service, where cure is the removal of a patient's symptom and not the long-term well-being of their soul.

The trade associations could, in partnership with training organisations, as I mentioned earlier, lobby the Government and business for funds to help train and re-train therapists in a more client-led psychotherapeutic approach. The trade associations could use modern communication technology, i.e. the Internet, to go beyond their rather one-way, top-down, power-existing form of printed journals with selected articles and edited letters. They could give up their 'know better' patronising attitude and recognise the wealth of resources they have in their members and encourage them to develop networks of communication and information distribution amongst themselves.

TRAINING ORGANISATIONS

In order to align themselves with a more client-led psychotherapy, most, but not all, training organisations will need to reorientate themselves to a more individual approach. When friends ask me about how to become a psychotherapist I suggest they find themselves an experienced therapist and enter therapy for some time, maybe a year or two, whilst dropping any aspirations to becoming a therapist. At present, being in personal therapy is increasingly becoming a requirement of most trainings. Whilst wanting to be a therapist is certainly reason enough for entering personal therapy, I think it is important to distinguish between the experience of going to therapy voluntarily as part of training, and that of a client who is generally driven to it reluctantly. If, after some time and having come to terms with their personal psychodynamics, the prospective therapist still feels sure about wanting to be a psychotherapist, they could ask their therapist to help prepare them for this. Their therapist could then highlight areas of learning or experience they might need to focus on, and in due course support them when they start to work with clients.

Attending a basic counselling course to learn basic communication and listening skills would probably be advisable for all prospective therapists. I do not see it necessary for prospective therapists to attend three years of training to learn how to listen. Such trainings tend to fill the trainee therapist's beginner's mind with various models, theories and techniques that do little more than inhibit their ability to listen and respect the individual uniqueness of the client in front of them.

Applying what I would advise a friend to do to training schools would mean the training schools allowing trainees to be more self-directing in their learning. People wanting to become psychotherapists will come with a variety of skills and abilities as well as aspirations. In order to honour this, and their trainees' individual uniqueness, an individual approach is needed. For this reason, there is a need to return to the old style of training analysis, much akin to the master and apprentice relationship. This particular kind of relationship allows for the individual attention and intimacy necessary for an individual and soulful relationship to develop: one to one is, after all, the form which the work they do will eventually take, not the high-intensity morass of emotions generated by modern trainings conducted in groups.

Training organisations would have to relinquish the authority they assume over trainees. By making the trainee the centre of the work it ensures a strong demonstration as to the sovereignty/authority of the client in the therapeutic relationship. This would remove the unnatural objective pass/fail criteria that have been transferred from Academia into today's training courses where trainees are expected to meet both objective and subjective criteria set by trainers in the role of assessors. This sets up all kinds of performance anxieties and distorted behaviour in trainees as they try to show enough vulnerability and stability to make them effective therapists… ironically referred to by a colleague as 'crying enough but not too much'. The removal of the pressure to perform would lead to a far more honest, open and trusting environment for learning. Group supervision under an assessing supervisor as happens in present-day courses trains the therapist in how to conceal their biggest blunders and potential learning experiences, thereby depriving them of the effective supervision they need and the client of an effective therapy.

Under such a scheme, training schools would need to be more open and flexible to the flow of trainees from one training school to another as the trainees seek to learn what they believe they need. Training organisations could provide basic counselling-skills training as well as comprehensive lecture series to cover psychotherapy theory as well as more specialist or esoteric lectures. All these lectures could be open to trainees and experienced practitioners alike, who would be able to choose what meets their needs in an à-la-carte fashion rather than having to swallow the whole of a rather narrow menu. Unfortunately it seems that Gestalt South-West, who had been operating such a system, are having to move to a more directive authoritarian system in the face of accreditation requirements from trade associations.

The whole outcome of these changes that honour the trainee's own authority and autonomy would be the transmission of a profound lesson as to the sovereignty of their client's own process/psyche/soul. This recognition of the client's sovereignty must be the fundamental underpinning of any ensouled training course.

PSYCHOTHERAPISTS

So, finally, what could therapists do to re-ensoul psychotherapy?

Individual supervision is essential to good practice. Individual supervision as opposed to group supervision allows for the kind of intimacy in which the therapist can bare their most vulnerable selves, and in which client confidentiality is best protected. Group supervision can be useful in addition to individual supervision. In group supervision particular issues or themes can be looked at, as can any difficulties that arise for a supervisee in their individual supervision. However skilled, experienced or aware a therapist is, to assume one is free from unconscious influences is an act of extreme hubris and shows a gross ignorance as to the workings of the psyche. To believe that one has sorted out one's own unconscious material to the point where one is not likely to get caught in the unconscious dynamics of the therapeutic relationship means taking a position of certitude and closes the therapist off to the individualness of their client. In fact, some of the most profound work in psychotherapy comes from the effective use of the unconscious dynamics generated by the client towards the therapist and the therapist towards the client, known technically as transference and counter-transference respectively. I believe there is a widespread misunder-standing as to the use of counter-transference, where therapists are deluding themselves into believing that they can spot their own unconscious dynamics in relation to the client. The reality is however that this awareness only comes to light later. Effective supervision can hasten this process and will minimise, but never eradicate, the potential risk of harm that may come to the client.

Another step towards re-ensouling the practice of psychotherapy from within is a change of attitude by therapists. The kind of shift required is that of seeing themselves not as a profession but as service workers, as being poly-employed, not self-employed. Their clients, who have the right to hire and fire them, are in fact the therapist's employers. The word 'profession' has its roots in the claim of being skilled in a certain occupation and therefore tends to lead the public into believing that they can hand over responsibility to the therapist. Therapists can never do the work for clients, and to encourage such an abnegation of responsibility goes against the very core of effective work. Psychotherapy is not like mainstream medicine: it is not a miracle pill to be swallowed that magically cures the client, but something the client has actively to engage in. The therapist cannot do the work for the client, just as they cannot live the client's life for them. Psychotherapists can only work with the client, assisting and supporting them as they change themselves and their lives. Clients are the ones with the power to hire and fire, and it is the therapist's duty not to divest their clients of their sovereignty and autonomy. Therapists are there to empower, not disempower their clients, especially by not assuming, 'professing' or insisting they are a better authority for the client than they are for themselves.

As the therapist's employer, a client has the right to interview the therapist, who should respect this right, being honest and open about their training, experience and realistic about the chance of the client achieving the successful outcome to the work they are seeking. The client surely has a right to know a few basic things about the stranger to whom they are about to bare their soul. Therapists who avoid such questions, and imply that it is the client's insecurity that makes them ask, only demonstrate their own lack of empathic ability and an insensitivity to the vulnerability of the client. If a client did not have these feelings of insecurity and vulnerability, they would probably not be suitable for psychotherapy!

The removal of the threat of registration and accreditation, the weapons of fear employed by Government and trade associations, will improve the work of those who experience fear in the face of them. Those who invest their authority in governing bodies are likely to benefit from the challenge of owning their authority and bringing it into the practice room where their clients might then be able to avail themselves of the services of a whole human being.

Therapists need to take up the challenge of being more responsible for their own work and development. This may well not involve additional formal training, more supervision and so on, but by them living a more soulful life themselves. If the therapist is living a soulful life, a life full of soul, then the client coming into the psychic orbit of such an individual is bound to be affected for the better. This is, and must be, the ultimate challenge for a therapist, to improve their practice by living their life more soulfully. No legislation, no codes of conduct or list of ethics can prescribe how they should do this. The challenge is an entirely individual one, requiring the therapist to live, embody and demonstrate what they are trying to effect in their clients. It is not just about how they conduct themselves in their work but in all areas of their life. A decent therapist is not someone who has written many books on psychotherapy, headed professional organisations or trained on the most exclusive courses... A decent therapist is someone who lives a soulful life and can help others to live their life in accord with their own soul.

19

AKHENATEN'S FOLLY:
IMPOSED BELIEFS IN COUNSELLING AND
PSYCHOTHERAPY COMMUNITIES

YVONNE BATES

In the context of our present pervasive madness that we call normality, sanity, freedom, all our frames of reference are ambiguous and equivocal.
(R. D. Laing 1969)

IMPOSED BELIEFS IN ANCIENT EGYPT

The dynastic period of Ancient Egypt lasted three millennia, and throughout that time only one ruler attempted to impose a monotheistic culture. Born Amenhotep IV, this pharaoh declared the Sun Disk or 'Aten' to be the only god, changed his name to Akhenaten, closed down the temples of all the other gods and built a fabulous new capital city, Armana, on a barren site in the desert where the sun rose from a gap in the mountainside. The previous capital of Egypt, Thebes, had been a pantheistic city. Armana, on the other hand, was entirely constructed around a central temple to the Sun Disk, and all religion and doctrine was deemed to emanate from that central source.

Historians can only speculate about his reasons for doing this; some argue that it was a conscious attempt to curtail the power of the leaders of the different cults (and hence, to increase his own). Others argue that it was, at least at a conscious level, a genuine epiphany. He certainly seemed to be in no doubt as to the rectitude of his position and of his absolute right to insist that his people join him.

Akhenaten may have died believing that his attempt to impose his beliefs on his people had been reasonably successful. The fear the pharaoh commanded over his citizens shielded him from open dissent or rebellion. But whilst there may have been an illusion of conversion, this was superficial. The old gods continued to be worshipped in secret, and Akhenaten was despised.

Within 40 years of his death, people felt able openly to reject his reforms, and Akhenaten's name was obliterated. Armana was abandoned to return to the desert, all references to Akhenaten were removed from temple walls, stelae and obelisks, and all the former gods were reinstated. The definitive log of all pharaohs throughout time, built by Seti I, contained the cartouche of every single pharaoh in history bar four; Akhenaten and his immediate 'Armana' successors, Neferneferuaten, Tutankhamun and Ay.

Whether it is the quest for power or a genuine belief in the righteousness of one's position, the temptation to impose one's views on others, as Akhenaten did, is a seductive one. And when some person or group actually has the power to do so, history shows us time and again that oppression, misery, war and destruction usually ensue.

IMPOSED BELIEFS IN COUNSELLING AND PSYCHOTHERAPY

From the perspective of a counsellor/psychotherapist, one can see the Akhenaten principle — the imposition of beliefs on others — in operation at various levels. For example, it can be seen in Western culture, where we are told that we must believe that terrorists and paedophiles are subhuman and/or evil, and that countries which do not practise democracy according to our leaders' beliefs should not be allowed to develop the same weapons that we ourselves possess.

At an occupational level, one can observe what House (2003: 14) calls therapy's 'regime of truth' in operation: '... therapy, in its modern profession-centred form, increasingly functions as a "regime of truth" ... whose accompanying practices self-fulfillingly construct an ideological framework which then reinforces and guarantees the conditions of its own existence'.

Then, at a national occupational level, the Akhenaten principle can be seen in the attempts to impose a set of beliefs known as 'statutory regulation' on therapy practitioners (whether one believes the larger occupational bodies or the Government to be assuming the role of Akhenaten in this case). This book contains numerous arguments against this ideology (e.g. my Chapter 10 and the chapters in Part IB) which I will not repeat again here.

One may also, perhaps, be cognisant of the Akhenaten within oneself, which manifests itself whenever one does any of the following: judge a colleague's theories or practices as 'unethical'; attempt to create rules which one feels one's colleagues must follow; fail to question one's assumptions about what is right and wrong; actively or passively collude with the usurping of power; claim any greater right to exist in the community than another person or group; fail to acknowledge that clients' opinions about psychotherapy are just as valid as those of the practitioner, or that clients are *at least* an equal stakeholder in the occupation; use ridicule, slating criticism or academic jiggery-pokery to suppress or silence innovation and the free expression of ideas.

IMPOSED BELIEFS IN OCCUPATIONAL COMMUNITIES

Between the national level and the level of the individual, one finds the occupation's associations, networks and organisations, and it is this level that provides the focus for the rest of this chapter. These bodies impose sets of beliefs on us by making compulsory the adherence to rules, principles, procedures, codes of ethics, accountability paradigms and, often, certification requirements, with the following justifications:

- *It's what the body was set up to do.* The word 'impose' is used above advisedly; powerful people in such organisations typically argue 'we're not imposing anything; if you don't like it, you can simply go and join another organisation, or start your own'. Even if this were desirable, it is becoming less of an option as entry on to compulsory national registers soon may only be possible via the gateways provided by these bodies. Moreover, the 'like it or lump it' approach is an abdication of responsibility for basic human caring and co-operation, tolerance, compassion and respect. It is also ultimately self-defeating as it expels difference, innovation and diversity, thus rendering the body stagnant and developmentally inept. It is also grounded in old-paradigm, patriarchal, modernist notions of hierarchy and universal truths. (My personal experience is that this reluctance to evolve is often the case in organisations where the founding members and/or their 'disciples' are still very much involved.)

- *It is democratic or consensus-based.* Even those with little or no power in an organisation may, through cultural indoctrination, believe that since everyone has a single vote, everyone has equal status, and that they therefore have the power themselves to effect change. This is adherence to an ideology which has been vigorously contested:

   No, Democracy is not identical with majority rule. Democracy is a State which recognises the subjection of the minority to the majority, that is, an organisation for the systematic use of force by one class against the other, by one part of the population against another.

   (Lenin 1919);

and…

   Democracy means government by discussion, but it is only effective if you can stop people talking.

   (Atlee 1957)

   People hold power in different forms, even where positional power does not apply — for instance, the power to reward, the power to punish, referent power (achieved through identification), expert power (achieved through the assumption of greater knowledge) and informational power (having information in accord with others' beliefs or values) (French and Raven 1959, cited in Cardwell et al. 2000). Power is thus wielded in practitioner communities in many ways, even where a formal hierarchy does not exist, and thus often makes a mockery of the democratic process.

- *Without hierarchy, rules, principles and procedures, the occupational community would be worthless.* This argument claims that some hierarchy is not only necessary, but desirable, as it creates social cohesion and is the *use*, not *abuse*, of power. This is a flagrantly patriarchal view and flies in the face of basic feminist sociological principles (e.g. Hartmann 1993). Chaplin (1988: 3–4) relates this principle to counselling:

   Feminist counselling rejects the prevailing hierarchical model of thinking … It recognises the interconnection between different, even opposite, sides of life and of ourselves. This is a totally different approach from the one on which most of our modern thinking is based … This emphasis on the interconnections between things and people is related to ecology and alternative holistic medicine, to new age spirituality and humanistic psychology. It is also related to other 'progressive' movements in the world that are struggling towards greater justice and equality. It is about respecting differences such as female/male, black/white, as opposed to the present view of difference that is concerned with superiority and inferiority, winning or losing, or flat denial of difference altogether.

If we were able to run our occupational community in a non-hierarchical way, without rules, principles and procedures, we would be fostering this spirit of interconnectedness, equality and co-operation, rather than perpetuating the Animal Farm-like situation we have at present — that is, that *'All animals are equal but some animals are more equal than others'* (Orwell 1945). Moreover, a space for practitioners *and* clients (who would not just be welcomed, but who would have equal status within the community) to interact with other practitioners and clients would be immensely valuable in terms of their learning from each other and sharing and supporting one another. This undoubtedly would be conducive to responsible and accountable practice.

- *Its principles and procedures are in the best interests of the client.* This book amongst many others offers convincing arguments that ethical codes *per se* may not be ethical (cf. Pattison's Chapter 5, this volume). Moreover, the assumption of the role of 'protector of the client' as well as 'supporter of the practitioner' by an occupational body creates a multi-layered conflict of interests. This renders the body dysfunctional and means that people in higher positions within the hierarchy have too much influence — in particular, those deciding the professional fate of a practitioner in light of a complaint made against her. '[The ethics board] combines the roles in criminal law played by the prosecutor, police, judge, jury, and (professional) executioner ... wherever there is great power [such as this], of course, there is great potential for abuse' (Saunders 2002: 216). (In the sense that the occupational body supposedly represents the practitioner, and the people who handle complaints are part of the hierarchy of that same community, one should also add 'defence lawyer' to Saunders' list.)

    The claim by occupational bodies that compulsory qualifications or certification are safeguards for the client has been substantially and consistently refuted over the past 30 years. Rogers (1973: 365–7) was amongst the first to challenge the logic of this assumption:

    The first and greatest effect is to freeze the profession in a past image ... there are as many certified charlatans and exploiters of people as there are uncertified ... the urge toward professionalism builds up a rigid bureaucracy ... We must face the fact that in dealing with human beings a certificate does not give much assurance of real qualification. If we were less arrogant, we might also learn much from the 'uncertified' individual, who is sometimes unusually adept in the area of human relationships ... So, though I know it must sound horrendous, I would like to see all the energy we put into certification rules, qualifications, licensure legislation, and written and oral examinations rechaneled into assisting clinical psychologists [etc.] to become so effective, so devoted to human welfare, that they would be chosen over those who are *actually* unqualified, whether or not they possess paper credentials.

In short, there is apparently not one shred of evidence to show that codes of ethics or certification criteria protect clients in any way from abusive practices.

THE POSTMODERN COMMUNITY

Is it possible to organise an occupational body in a way that encourages diversity and accommodates potentially infinite ways of working and of being accountable on its members? What would be the make-up of a non-hierarchical, pluralistic occupational body grounded in postmodern, new-paradigm principles?

Perhaps a starting-point would be for such a community not to define itself as a body at all, but rather as a *space*. Objects (or ideas, or people) can move around freely within a space, whereas in a body they are, by and large, fixed and restricted. Many humanistic practitioners describe counselling or psychotherapy as a 'safe space' for clients. It could be argued, therefore, that establishing an occupational space would be a good model of the therapeutic principle. In person-centred counselling, the counsellor creates and maintains a boundaried space, into which the client comes and develops/does whatever feels appropriate for him. The client can flourish because for once he has freedom to be himself within that space, rather than battling against one force or another trying to mould him to fit into their structures. Such a principle could also underpin the infrastructure within which counsellors operate (and in which clients also *de facto* participate.)

Rules, regulations, principles, procedures and entry requirements are concepts which apply to bodies rather than spaces, and so the presence or absence of such effects would be a good indication of how clear the space is. The absence of such declarations is a vital component of diversity, since the exclusion of people, principles and practices means that true pluralism is lost.

The longevity of the space would depend on people's ability to argue persuasively for the continued avoidance of rules and structure. But ultimately this could not be enforced, since this would introduce a self-defeating 'power-over' condition. The most realistic stance might therefore be to accept that the community might wither and eventually perish as a result of such attentions. One might argue, rather philosophically, that an embracing of finitude is in keeping with existential principles and thus may be a healthy ethos to adopt.

It should also be acknowledged that the originator(s) of the concept and founders of the space might have power because of their significance to it in a historical sense. This may be unavoidable, and the temptation to use this power to define, proceduralise or regulate what happens in the space would need to be resisted.

Such a space would be open to all practitioners, clients — and indeed the public. Enterprises could develop within the community, for example training centres, news groups, workshops, encounter groups, consultancy services (e.g. supervision) and so on. Like-minded practitioners and clients would naturally be drawn to one another and may decide to agree to a common way of working or accountability model, and thus create a body within the space.

A community such as this would not impinge upon the needs of some of its participants to pursue 'accreditation' and registration. Indeed, there could be a body or bodies within the space which offer accreditation procedures and routes on to national registers. Likewise, as stated above, there could be bodies offering arguments against registration. The ability to hold such divergent positions within one culture would be a great strength, and the potential for learning through communication would be profound.

One might ask how this proposed community or space differs from what we have now, or, more precisely, what we had until the Akhenaten principle started to take effect in the corridors of power. To some extent, it *is* a question of returning to the state we enjoyed in the middle part of the twentieth century, in the sense of there being much less imposed hierarchy and assumed ethical and procedural rectitude. But it is also about fostering a new sense of co-operation and cross-fertilisation. Opting-in would be required, whereby community members would be actively choosing to embrace the postmodern philosophy underpinning the community.

LIFE BEYOND AKHENATEN

Sadly, it seems unlikely that an occupational community such as this will be realised in the foreseeable future. Resistance to new-paradigm, postmodern and feminist proposals such as this can be intense, and comes in three basic forms: pragmatic, philosophical and emotional.

The pragmatic argument, it seems, rests on the assumptions that (1) it is impossible to avoid power-over relations, and that no community could function without someone's needs or wishes being overlooked or overruled at some point; and (2) the paradoxical nature of postmodernism renders it incapable of underpinning a community. Howard (2000: 358) expresses this paradox thus:

> If there are only opinions and appearances then nothing is real, nothing is true and nothing is important. Moreover no one then has any basis to say there are only opinions. Such a statement is not 'true'; it is merely another opinion. Postmodernism thereby castrates itself before it is in a position seriously to break into, and break down, the activities and interests of anyone else.

Arguments such as these cannot be refuted, but the unattainableness of a goal is not an adequate reason to dismiss its pursuit. An occupational community which aspires to true equality and pluralism, and towards the avoidance of grand truths and power-over relations, could be good enough, in the same way that someone who aspires to Christian goals, unattainable in the absolute, is a good-enough Christian, and in the same way that a person-centred practitioner who aspires to the core conditions, unattainable in the absolute, is a good-enough therapist.

Resistance based on a fundamental disagreement with the philosophy can be inferred from the following feedback received on an earlier draft of this chapter, where Postle (2002, personal communication) claimed that a community such as that described above would create:

> a structure-free entity ... a denial of the immense value of human social creativity ... devising structures ... organisations ... some of which are

abusive and some of which are good enough ... I don't think it is either feasible or desirable to rid ourselves of hierarchy, and I feel it is unhelpful to demonise it ... The notion you describe resembles a nation-wide encounter group in which anyone is in principle 'free' to do anything but where in practice ... with the likely absence of emotional competence ... the most distressed people will tend to set the agenda.

This statement indicates a single philosophical viewpoint, that is, that there is a measurable continuum of 'emotional competence' and that hierarchy is required so that the more 'emotionally competent' can lead and/or protect the less competent. Herein lies one of the aforementioned paradoxes. By asserting that Postle is wrong, and that occupational communities would be better if they were non-hierarchical, we are claiming that our reality is superior to Postle's, which would not be in keeping with the very philosophy of pluralism we are attempting to introduce! The new-paradigm community could therefore only ever be populated by people who chose to be a part of it and who were convinced of its worth. Thus, the extant old-paradigm communities could not be converted unless each and every one of their participants wanted them to be. Personal experience to date suggests this is most unlikely. For instance, a recent proposal that a new-paradigm community could be wrapped around an existing organisation, leaving it intrinsically untouched, met with open hostility. This also provides an example of the third form of opposition, *emotional resistance*. Attempts even to discuss a paradigm shift in extant occupational communities seems to provoke great fear, specifically, ironically, of loss of control, that postmodernism will be imposed! There seems to be a concomitant irrational and equally ironic fear that it would be socially fragmenting and will lead to 'rampant individualism'. That a philosophy of non-hierarchical pluralism and inclusivity is feared for its oppressive and anti-social properties speaks unpalatable volumes about how deeply our society is entrenched in modernist, patriarchal dogma.

Whilst we continue to discuss and debate these issues, the Akhenaten principle continues to intensify. Counsellors and psychotherapists, like the citizens of ancient Egypt, are becoming disillusioned, turned off and dispirited. One can perhaps take heart in the fact that those Egyptians were able to hold on to their beliefs until the time came when they could safely voice them again. If we can do the same, then even if our worst fears for the future of counselling and psychotherapy are realised in the short term, the rich and varied spiritual dimension of counselling and psychotherapy will live within us until a future emerges where it can once again be expressed.

REFERENCES

Atlee, C. (1957) Speech at Oxford, 14th June 1957. *The Times*, 15th June.
Cardwell, M., Clark, L., Meldrum, C. (2000) *Psychology for A-Level*. London: Collins
Chaplin, J. (1988) *Feminist Counselling in Action*. London: Sage
Hartmann, H. (1993) The unhappy marriage of Marxism and feminism. In S. Jackson (ed.), *Women's Studies: A Reader* (pp. 13–16). Hemel Hempstead: Harvester Wheatsheaf

House, R. (2003) *Therapy Beyond Modernity: Deconstructing and Transcending Profession-Centred Therapy*. London: Karnac Books

Howard, A. (2000) *Philosophy for Counselling and Psychotherapy: Pythagoras to Postmodernism*. Basingstoke: Macmillan

Laing, R. D. (1969) *The Divided Self*. London: Pelican

Lenin, V. I. (1919) *State and Revolution*. London: Pelican

Orwell, G. (1945) *Animal Farm*. London: Penguin

Postle, D. (2002) Personal communication

Rogers, C. R. (1973) Some new challenges to the helping professions. *American Psychologist* 28 (5): 379–87

Saunders, T. R. (2002) Can boards of examiners constitute the ultimate, harmful multiple relationship? In A. A. Lazarus and O. Zur (eds), *Dual Relationships and Psychotherapy* (pp. 212–23). New York: Springer Publishing Co.

Note

My thanks to the colleagues who gave their support and offered invaluable opinion on earlier drafts of this chapter.

20

VERBAL AND EMOTIONAL ABUSE IN THERAPY:
ENCOUNTERS BETWEEN THERAPY CLIENTS ON THERAPY-ABUSE.NET

'NATALIE SIMPSON'

INTRODUCTION

For many people, abuse of clients by therapists means sexual abuse. Other kinds of abuse are often omitted entirely in discussions of the subject, or else are seen as significant only in that they can be predictors of sexual abuse. One of the reasons for this is that while sexual abuse can be defined with reasonable clarity, it is much harder to detect and recognise other types of abuse that may be occurring within the therapy relationship.

My interest in abuse in therapy arises from a six-month period of hypnotherapy and psychoanalysis. No physical sexual contact occurred between my therapist and I; indeed, he hardly ever touched me, although he did make suggestive sexual comments to me. When he terminated the therapy I felt as if I would never recover from the desolation. It also seemed to me that my reaction to the therapy was greatly out of proportion to what had actually happened. I wanted to understand why this was, but I also felt ashamed that I had let the therapy affect me so much. Although I thought that discussing my experience with other people would help me, I felt that I could not describe fully what it meant to me, and I was also afraid that people would think I was dangerously mentally ill, or that I was a weak and self-obsessed person.

However, there was a new and rapidly evolving means of help available to me: the Internet. I was already registered with an Internet Service Provider (ISP) and an e-mail address linked to my own name, but I registered with a second ISP and created a new e-mail address under a different name. I knew that my anonymity was not watertight, but I reasoned that the chances of coming into contact with someone who would have both the desire and the knowledge to uncover my true identity was small.

The next step was to find out if there were, somewhere among the millions of Internet users, any other people, clients or therapists, who would find some resonance with my experience. Within the Internet, there are four main ways of establishing contact with other people: web pages, discussion groups or boards, newsgroups and chat rooms. Web pages can be created by anyone who has access to the Internet, and most ISPs in the UK provide a small amount of space free of charge, so there was a possibility that someone like me had already set up a web page describing their experience. Other people have set up discussion groups, where people exchange e-mails with other people in the group. Newsgroups are another means of carrying out a discussion. Finally, chat rooms allow a discussion with shorter messages but with almost immediate responses. All these resources can be found on the Internet by entering appropriate keywords into databases, or 'search engines', that have been set up for this purpose.

I did not make much use of chat rooms because of the need to have a telephone connection to the Internet during the whole discussion, which at that time was quite expensive. I did, however, find newsgroups to be very useful. In the *alt.hypnosis* group I made contact with a sensitive and helpful hypnotherapist who gave me useful advice and support. In the *sci.psychology.psychotherapy.moderated* group, I posted a message asking about transference, and received a reply from 'Rosie Alexander' (see her Chapter 30, this volume), who sent me a copy of 'Dangerous liaison', an article she wrote for *The Times* newspaper. I read it with a sense of wonder. Here was someone whose experience had similarities in quality to mine, but yet was more extreme in intensity. This was a significant encounter for me because it meant that I could at last be sure that I was not alone.

It was Rosie Alexander who pointed me towards a new website which had been set up by Marion, an Australian psychoanalyst who had at that time been running a successful practice for 14 years. This is often the way in which useful resources can be found on the Internet: rather than conducting a systematic search, word of mouth can lead to success much more quickly. Marion had set up a discussion list which was open to everyone, and Rosie and I both joined. Marion stated on the site that the purpose of the list was 'to raise consciousness [of verbal and emotional abuse] in the interests of better practice'.

When Rosie and I joined the Therapy-Abuse list (see *www.therapy-abuse.net*), there had been only five messages posted and no discussion had been established. Rosie posted a message inviting people to discuss their experiences of transference, but I had doubts about posting a message about something that was very personal and important to me, when I knew nothing about the other members of the group, and did not even know how big the group was. My way of dealing with this was to 'put a toe in the water' by posting general messages first and then starting to reveal more about my personal experience as other people responded.

The list was moderated message-by-message. This means that every message that is posted to the list is first sent to the moderator, who decides whether it should appear on the list. This arrangement is rare on the Internet because of the amount of work that is required of the moderator, but Marion believed it was necessary to safeguard contributors from attacks or insensitive replies. At first, Marion was the sole moderator of the list, but she later shared the task with other people.

It is now more than four years since the first message to the list was posted, and it is rare for a day to go by without at least one message being posted. This is an unusually long time for a list to be running, especially for a topic that has received so little attention in the past. Over that period of time, many list members have said that they have found it to be of great help to them, but the list has also encountered some serious problems. In this chapter I shall explore both the benefits and the drawbacks of the list, and then consider how discussions may develop in the future.

THE BENEFITS

Many participants have made comments at the time of joining the discussion list that suggest that the list has helped them simply by the fact of its existence. The website and the discussion list are evidence that they are not imagining what happened to them and that they did not simply overreact to insignificant events in their therapy. Although other sites on abuse in therapy do exist, they tend to concentrate on sexual abuse. Even talking to trained people can be difficult. 'I had to ring up the Samaritans one night to try to talk about my counselling experiences. The woman I spoke to was baffled. Why did I need the Samaritans when I already had a counsellor?' (Magdalena).

List members have also said that it is difficult to find people to talk to about their experience, partly because they think people will not understand, and partly because they feel so foolish and ashamed of what happened. Through the list, some of these people have found a sympathetic, knowledgeable and helpful audience.

> I can't begin to tell how much it means to find someone with a similar experience. I feel so all alone. I'm not really at liberty to talk about this to people I know ... and when I do people don't have a clue and blame me a lot.
>
> (Vanessa)

Talking to other people about abuse in therapy provides more than comfort and validation; it can also provide a new perspective. For example, clients in the UK often have therapy that is free at the point of use. This limits the client's options, as the client often does not have the choice of going to another therapist. The client may feel that it would be very ungrateful to complain about the therapy, since (s)he is not paying for it.

> Flash forward 18 months [after leaving therapy with an abusive therapist]. I'm sitting talking to a member of my local council about the problems I'm having with the centre [where the abusive therapist worked]. 'So what do you want to do?' 'I want to stop this problem from happening to someone else [...] I wouldn't want to harm the centre, because I like what they are doing, offering free therapy to poor people.' 'Who told you it was free?' 'They did.' 'They get a massive grant from the local council, and from other organisations too numerous to mention. Your therapy cost the local council — thousands of pounds!!!'
>
> (Ray)

However, if the client realises that the therapist *is* getting paid, although not by the client, then this can change the perception of the power imbalance and open up more choices to the client. These discussions can therefore be very helpful to clients who feel that they are in situations where they have no options and nowhere to go.

The list has provided practical support to some members. One client sent a triumphant message to the group when she finally left her therapist. Another member asked her therapist for her money back — and received it, together with an apology. Afterwards she described her feelings of grief and sadness, 'the deep regret that if only a few sessions had gone differently, our misunderstandings could have been averted, a feeling that none of this had to happen'.

It can take a surprisingly long time for clients who have been abused in therapy to get over the abuse. It seems as if trust has been broken at a very fundamental level, and clients have reported experiencing varying degrees of emotional disintegration, obsession and self-loathing. Again, discussion on the list has helped people realise that it is normal to take a significant time to recover, thus sometimes relieving the guilt they feel at not yet having put the experience behind them.

> Once [abusive therapists] start digging around, most of them are using bulldozers, instead of hand shovels or toothbrushes to carefully sift through the information. The next problem is that if they can't find what they are looking for, you have to put all the stuff back, on your own, which is very painful. This is why I get a bit angry when people talk about moving on.
>
> (Ray)

> But for me it has only been one year, and I have been beating myself up about the fact that it's been a whole year and I am still obsessed with it all. I often catch myself wondering when it's going to go away ... from the sound of many of you, it sounds like it may take much longer than I had hoped.
>
> (Zoe)

Many survivors of therapist abuse go back into therapy to help them get over the abuse. Although there are obvious problems to overcome, the second course of therapy is often successful, but by no means always. Thus, there have been angry messages about therapy in general, but also messages about the benefits of therapy when it is done well.

PROBLEMS ON THE LIST

Looking back over the four years of the list's existence, it is interesting to recall that, initially, the main problem was getting people to post messages. One action that helped to get the list moving was for the moderator to post questions or suggestions for discussion. Also, when more members joined, the discussion list seemed to reach a critical size, and discussion thereafter usually consisted of several messages a day. However, as is usual on Internet lists, the majority of members have never posted a single message (they are known as 'lurkers').

The first serious controversy on the list was triggered by a member posting a message to the list that she intended to send privately to the moderator. This type of error is very common in Internet discussions and can lead to embarrassment, or even 'flame wars', where conflict and misunderstandings escalate as people send angrier and angrier messages. The member talked about her relationship with a teacher of psychology students, and suggested that it might be a good idea to invite the students to join the list, so that 'they can learn first-hand, through this virtual medium, about the pain that clients deal with when therapy goes wrong, or is mismanaged'. As the list was open to anyone with an interest in the discussion topic, she understood that there was no need for her to seek the moderator's permission, but she had decided to discuss it with the moderator first out of courtesy because a sudden expansion in the list might increase the moderator's workload.

The message triggered an unusually large number of replies. Some list members were optimistic, believing that this was potentially a valuable way of raising awareness of abuse to the new cohort of trainee therapists. It was suggested that new members would be helpful to the discussion, opening it out, developing new perspectives and increasing depth of understanding.

> I don't think it helps to discuss abuse over and over again without a firm desire for healing and moving forward. I don't think we should be so arrogant as to think we are the experts on therapist abuse. We don't know it all. If we claim to, then we are just like the therapists who say they know what's best for us.

> (Diane)

Others were worried that the presence of psychology students would change the nature or 'flavour' of the list and would destroy the trust that had been built up by members. One member suggested that psychology students would use list members to practise their newly learned techniques, and thus risk harming them.

A member suggested that the psychology students should be allowed to join the list, but a framework of rules should be set up to govern the form and content of interactions between them and the existing members. 'My first rule would be that any psych student or professional should identify themselves as such when addressing the list or individuals on it.'

This desire for a division between psychology students and abused clients reminded another member of her childhood experiences of racial hatred and segregated schools. The moderator agreed with the analogy, asking why psychology students and ex-clients were considered to be non-overlapping groups. She mentioned that she herself was studying psychology in the hope that this would be reassuring, since she was already trusted by the group. Unfortunately, the remark seemed to have the opposite effect, increasing anxiety and suspicion.

Finally, a list member attacked the moderator, accusing her of lack of compassion and empathy, and of running the list out of self-interest. The moderator then resigned, and another moderator took over the moderation of the list.

Discussions about what had happened and why it had happened took place outside the list. More than one person suggested that the moderator had been seen by list members as a therapist, and that they were transferring their emotions that they felt for their abusive therapists on to her. The new moderator took this view, and with the aim of preventing similar problems in the future, wrote in her introductory message that although she was a practising therapist, she was taking the role of group moderator here, not group therapist.

Trouble soon erupted again. Messages were posted which could be interpreted as containing personal attacks on other members. Originally, the list had not been set up as a support list: it was intended to be a means of serious discussion, and members were specifically asked to keep their descriptions of personal experiences to a minimum. However, it very soon became clear that some list members had such an urgent and desperate need for support that it would be less than compassionate to deny them the chance to share their stories. However, there were also list members who wanted to probe more deeply into issues such as how much responsibility the client should take for abuse, and whether regulation of therapists would protect clients. The two agendas always had an uneasy co-existence; now it seemed that they were incompatible.

The moderator tried to reduce the number of unacceptable messages by posting a message saying that members were not allowed to discuss 'perceived or real abuse between list members' and that any such messages would be deleted. However, this measure did not work, partly because it is not always easy to distinguish between messages which make strong arguments and those which are abusive. Some members wrote to the moderator complaining that their messages had been rejected, while messages that attacked them had been approved. Some of these messages were abusive.

At this stage the list was nearly shut down. Instead, a decision was made to close the list to new members. The discussion continues, and eventually the individual moderation of messages will cease. New members can still join the list, but they can do so by invitation only. The 'Verbal and Emotional Abuse in Psychotherapy' website, at *www.therapy-abuse.net*, continues to attract visitors. The site contains a number of articles drawn from different sources, and there are also some extracts from discussions that have taken place on the list.

Maintaining the site and the discussion list has taken a considerable amount of work. Moderating each message requires a moderator to log in and check the messages at least once every 24 hours. There are e-mails to deal with, both from list members and from new visitors to the site. The site itself needs maintenance work to keep it up to date. It is difficult to find people who have enough interest in the subject to put in the time and effort required, but who are able to remain detached enough to do these jobs fairly and without being adversely affected by them.

THE FUTURE

Traditionally there has been a separation between the voices of therapists and those of clients, with the former dominating the literature. In the discussion list, I always hoped that a true dialogue would open between therapists and clients, but this rarely happened, and only for brief periods of time. There is evidence from the first crisis on the list that some clients felt threatened by the possibility of therapists being present; it would not be surprising if therapists on the list also sometimes felt threatened, since some messages expressed anger at therapists in general, not just those who had abused clients.

However, I am hopeful that in the future there will be more opportunities for clients and therapists to discuss all aspects of therapy, including the problem of abuse, without the clients seeing the therapists as supreme beings or evil sadists, and without the therapists seeing the clients as inferior, sick or incompetent.

In September 2002 I attended a conference organised by POPAN (see www.POPAN.org.uk), a UK organisation which campaigns against abuse by professionals. At the conference, ex-clients of therapy, therapists, and therapists who had been abused as clients all met together to discuss the problems as equals. To me the occasion was important not because of the information conveyed but because the event took place at all. It was pointed out that in order for the dialogue to work, clients and therapists have to be willing to take on each other's perspectives. Some therapists are able to do this, particularly those who have found their own therapy during training to be unsatisfactory. For clients, the ability to change perspective may come from being able to talk to therapists, sharing information as equals and being willing to listen to different interpretations of the same situation.

Exciting developments are also taking place in the quarterly independent magazine for therapists, *ipnosis* [see *www.ipnosis.com*]. For the past year, at the editors' invitation, I have produced or commissioned articles written by clients to be published alongside the work of therapists. The magazine is now promoting better communication between therapists and clients by hosting an e-mail discussion on a set subject, with the highlights of the discussion printed in the subsequent issue of the magazine for all subscribers to read.

The movement towards better and more open communication between therapists and clients is encouraging, but there is still a long way to go. I would like to see more situations where clients and therapists can communicate without feeling threatened by each other. I would like both clients and therapists to be more aware of how subtle abuse can be, and to be able to recognise it more easily. Many therapists have a network of peers and supervisors with whom they can discuss cases to get another perspective and thus perhaps spot warning signs before much damage can be done. In contrast, clients are often unable to discuss their therapy with anyone. It is usually assumed that the only support a client needs is his or her therapist; clients' experiences in therapy have shown that this is a dangerous assumption to make.

IIB: ENABLING PRACTICE

EDITORIAL INTRODUCTION AND COMMENTARY

Having established some alternative models for accountability and for occupational communities in Part IIA, this section proposes alternative models for practice itself – alternatives which are of a distinctly postmodern flavour.

We are delighted that the author of the path-breaking book *Conversation, Language, and Possibilities: A Postmodern Approach to Therapy*, HARLENE ANDERSON, is represented in this anthology. Anderson's chapter sets out the fundamentals of her 'postmodern collaborative' approach to therapy, drawing as it does upon postmodernist thinking to illustrate how client/professional relationships can be far more collaborative than the traditional modernist model of hierarchical expertise could ever envisage — with clients becoming ever more able and willing to take full participative responsibility within the professional relationships into which they enter (cf. Bohart and Tallman's Chapter 27, this volume, and also the client contributions of Rosie Alexander and Anna Sands, Chapters 2 and 30 respectively). JOHN FREESTONE then offers us an approach to therapy which describes *a way of being* in the therapeutic relationship which he terms 'the Aquarian Paradigm'. With close affinities to Zen, Eastern and postmodern thinking, and to 'perennial wisdom' more generally, Freestone describes the kind of therapist sensibilities which are most likely to enable therapeutic growth and change in what is becoming an increasingly postmodern world. The kind of awareness and being-qualities that he describes could not be further removed from the outmoded cognitive control-fixations of modernist therapy that were exposed to relentless deconstruction in Part IA.

NICKY HART then explores the ways in which language is inevitably infused with issues of power in therapy relationships. Far from the modernist view of language which sees it as a neutrally 'objective', representational conveyor of meaning, Hart maintains that the dynamics of power which are necessarily exercised through language are critical to the therapeutic process — and that as a result, therapy discourse can all too easily exercise a hidden normalising function. It follows from this analysis that in order to minimise the constraints upon free exchange which these processes create, 'we must have the courage and the patience to challenge ourselves and our work continually' (cf. House's Chapter 9). JOHN KAYE's chapter embraces many of the insights previously outlined to present an approach to therapy practice which he terms 'non-iatrogenic psychotherapy', or 'non-regulative praxis'. For Kaye, conventional modernist therapy is demonstrably 'multiply iatrogenic'; and his response is to propose and develop a non-pathologising narrative therapy for family therapy in which he argues, *inter alia*, that 'we *can* get outside particular disciplinary discourses in order to question their (and our) practices of power', and that we should embrace 'an ongoing critique of [our] own power-knowledge'.

In the penultimate chapter, GAEL ROWAN echoes the concerns of Michael Whan (Chapter 13, this volume), Jungian maverick James Hillman and spiritual psychologist Robert Sardello in making a passionate plea for the reassertion of *the primacy of soul* in psychotherapy. For Rowan, 'the capacity of the therapist to experience soul in relationship is fundamental and constitutes a core condition for the healing of a client's deepest wounds'. Again, such an approach to therapy takes us way beyond any modernist conception of therapy, with the latter being quite unable to encompass 'soul' as the experience of something which is intrinsically ineffable. Finally in this section, RICHARD HOUSE attempts the highly ambitious (some might say 'foolhardy'!) task of outlining just what a transmodern, 'post-professional' therapy might look like, in the process encompassing many if not most of the critical concerns displayed in this volume.

We passionately maintain that if therapy is to continue to evolve through and beyond Late Modernity, rather than becoming a monument to the limitations of objective, deterministic science, then bold, visionary indications for therapy practice like the ones outlined in this section are, and will continue to be, essential. And we believe, further, that there is sufficient inspiration and insight in these diverse contributions to at least suggest what a viable and enabling postmodern therapy practice might look like.

21

A Postmodern Collaborative Approach to Therapy: Broadening the possibilities of clients and therapists[†]

Harlene Anderson

What has influenced my ideas and work?

Over the years my work has been influenced by therapy conversations and conversations about therapy that I have taken part in with clients, colleagues and students. In particular, I have had a sustained interest in clients' experiences of therapy: What are their descriptions of successful and unsuccessful therapy, and what do they identify as the characteristics of successful and unsuccessful client-therapist relationships? This question is always in the background: 'How can therapists create the kinds of conversations and relationships with their clients that allow all participants to access their creativities and develop possibilities where none seemed to exist before?'

The primary contexts of my practices include the Houston Galveston Institute and the clinical and training programmes that I consult with abroad. The Institute is a non-profit clinical, teaching, consultation and research centre where we work mostly with public agency clients who are often mandated to therapy, and our students include master level, doctoral level and postdoctoral interns.

The world around us is fast changing — shrinking, becoming enormously more complex and uncertain — and our societies and cultures are becoming more intertwined. Many familiar explanatory concepts seem no longer helpful in accounting for and addressing the complexities of these changes and the impact they have on human beings and our everyday lives. What I have learned from clients has led me to question some familiar concepts such as: universal truths, knowledge and knower as independent, language as representative, and the meaning is in the word. Such concepts risk placing human behaviour into frameworks of understanding that seduce therapists into hierarchical expert-nonexpert structures, into discourses of pathology and dysfunction, and into a world of the known and certainty.

---

† This paper was originally written as a talk and did not include references. The reference list includes authors who have influenced my conceptualisation and practices as well as some of my own writings. Please refer to www.harlene.org for a more extensive list of writings.

The postmodern challenge

A search for new ways to describe and understand clients' successful experiences of therapy and therapists led me down a meandering path and to the place where I have now paused: *a postmodern collaborative approach* to therapy, education, research and organisational consultation. Postmodernism (referring to the philosophical movement rather than the artistic movement) offers a broad challenge to the culture, traditions and practices of the helping professions. It invites us to examine and re-imagine our traditions and the practices that flow from them, including: how problems are conceptualised, client-therapist relationships, the process of therapy and therapists' expertise.

Broadly speaking, 'postmodern' refers to a family of concepts that critically challenge the relevance of universal or meta-narratives, including a self-critique of postmodernism itself. The central challenge, according to psychologist Kenneth Gergen (2001), focuses on the assumptions of the centrality of individual knowledge, an objective knowable world and language as the carrier of truth. Although the postmodern family has many diverse branches, there is a common consistent trait that I find appealing: the concept that *knowledge and language are relational and generative.*

Knowledge (what we think we know or might know) is linguistically constructed, its development and transformation is a communal process, and the knower and knowledge are interdependent. Knowledge, therefore, is not static or 'out there' waiting to be discovered; rather, it is fluid and created. Authoritative discourses from this perspective give way to knowledge constructed on the local level that has practical relevance for the participants involved.

From a hermeneutic philosophical perspective, understanding is an interpretative process that is influenced by language, history and pre-understanding. We are always in the process of trying to understand and searching for meaning — the search itself creates meaning. Language in this perspective is the vehicle through which we try to understand and create knowledge about our world and ourselves.

Language (spoken and unspoken communication or expression) is the primary vehicle through which we construct and make sense of our world. As philosopher Richard Rorty (e.g. 1979) suggests, language does not mirror what is; for instance, it is not an outward description of an internal process and does not describe 'accurately' what actually happened. Rather, language allows a description of what happened and an attribution of meaning to what happened. It gains its meaning and its value through its use: the meaning of a word is in its use. Language thus limits and shapes our thoughts and our expressions.

What is created in and through language (realities such as knowledge, truth and meaning) is multi-authored among a community of persons. That is, the reality that we attribute to the events, experiences and people in our lives does not exist in the thing itself; rather, it is a socially constructed attribution that is created within a particular culture and is shaped and reshaped in language. What is created, therefore, is only one of multiple perspectives — realities such as narratives or possibilities. Language, therefore, is fluid and creative.

Like Gergen, I do not suggest that nothing exists outside linguistic constructions; whatever exists simply exists, irrespective of linguistic practices

(Gergen 2001). Rather, I focus on the meanings of these existences and the actions they inform, once we begin to describe, explain and interpret them.

Transformation (e.g. new knowledge, expertise, identities and futures), therefore, is inherent in the inventive and creative aspects of language. This transformative nature of language invites a view of human beings as resilient; it invites an appreciation of each person's contributions and potentials. This invitation is similar to psychologist Mikhail Csikszentmihalyi's (Seligman and Csikszentmihalyi, 2000) emphasis on positive psychology as more promising than deficit-based psychology.

HUMAN SYSTEMS AS LINGUISTIC SYSTEMS

Combined, the above perspectives have influenced my notion of human beings as systems in language or language systems. They are meaning-making systems. Therapy becomes one kind of language or meaning-making system.

PHILOSOPHICAL STANCE: A WAY OF BEING

I think of my approach to therapy as a philosophy of therapy rather than a theory or model. Philosophy focuses on questions about ordinary life: self-identity, relationships, mind and knowledge. It involves ongoing analysis, inquiry and reflection.

The postmodern conceptualisations of knowledge and language inform what I call a *philosophical stance*. This refers to a way of being: a way of thinking about, experiencing, being in relationship with, talking with, acting with and responding with the people we meet in therapy. Consistent with this view, the philosophical stance becomes a *philosophy of life* — a world-view that does not separate professional and personal.

Characteristics of the philosophical stance
The philosophical stance has several interrelated characteristics. The stance represents a belief — an attitude, a posture, a tone — that communicates to the other that they are a unique human being, not a category of people, and that they are recognised and have something to say worthy of hearing. If a therapist holds this belief, it becomes an authentic and natural way of connecting, collaborating and constructing with others, not a technique. Combined, these characteristics invite the opportunity for a therapy that is more participatory and collaborative and less hierarchical and dualistic. And importantly, though the stance may have common identifiable expressions, it is unique to each therapist and human system, the circumstances, and what is required.

CONVERSATIONAL PARTNERS

The collaborative therapist and client become *conversational partners* as they engage in *dialogical conversations* and *collaborative relationships*. Dialogical conversation and collaborative relationship refer to a two-way process: a back-

and-forth, give-and-take, in-there together activity and connection where people talk *with* each other rather than *to* each other. Inviting this kind of partnership requires that the client's story take centre stage. It requires that the therapist constantly learn — listening and trying to understand the client from their perspective and in the client's language.

In my experience, this *therapist learning position acts to spontaneously engage the client as a co-learner, or what I refer to as a mutual or shared inquiry* as they co-explore the familiar and co-develop the new. In this inquiry, the client's story is told in a way that clarifies, expands and shifts it. The newness is created, co-constructed from within the conversation in contrast to the newness being imported from outside of it. In this kind of conversation and relationship all members have a *sense of belonging*; and in my experience, this sense of belonging invites participation and shared responsibility. Dialogical conversations and collaborative relationships go hand in hand. Think about it: the kinds of relationships we have form and inform — enhance and limit — the kinds of conversations we have and vice versa.

CLIENT AS EXPERT

The collaborative therapist considers the client as the expert on his or her life and as the therapist's teacher. The therapist respects and honours the client's story and takes seriously what the client has to say and how they choose to say it. This includes the many ways in which the client may express their knowledge. For instance, the therapist does not have expectations that a story should unfold in chronological order or at a certain pace. The therapist does not expect certain answers, and does not judge whether an answer is direct or indirect, or right or wrong. Inherent in this approach is an appreciative belief in the good and the positive — which most human beings value and want in striving towards healthy successful relationships and qualities of life.

Often a therapist is working with more than one person, whether that person is a member of the client's personal or professional system. The therapist appreciates, respects and values all of the voices and their realities. Multiple voices and their multiple realities become the *richness of differences* with infinite *possibilities* inherent in them.

NOT-KNOWING

The collaborative therapist is a not-knowing therapist. Not-knowing refers to the way in which the therapist thinks about their knowledge and expertise. The therapist does not believe they have superior knowledge or a monopoly on the truth. They bring and offer what they know or think they might, but always hold it and present it in a tentative manner. That is, the therapist offers his or her voice, including previous knowledge, questions, comments, opinions and suggestions as simply food for thought and dialogue. The therapist remains willing and able to have their knowledge (including professional and personal values and biases) ignored, questioned and changed.

Not-knowing can be misunderstood as a therapist knowing nothing, pretending ignorance or forgetting what they have learned. No. It simply refers to how a therapist positions oneself with their knowledge, including the timing and the intent with which that knowledge is introduced.

Being public

Therapists often learn to operate from invisible private thoughts — professionally or personally and theoretically or experientially informed — such as diagnoses, judgements or hypotheses about the client that influence how they listen and hear and guide their questions. From a collaborative stance, the therapist is open and makes their invisible thoughts visible. For instance, if a therapist has an idea or an opinion it is shared with the client, offered for food for thought and dialogue. It is not a matter of whether a therapist can or cannot say or ask about anything, but rather the manner, attitude and timing in which they do so. Keeping therapists' thoughts public minimises the risk of therapist and therapist-client monologue — being occupied by one idea about a person or situation. Monologue can subsequently lead to a therapist's participating in, creating or maintaining what are often thought of as internal characteristics of clients such as 'resistance' and 'denial'.

Mutual transformation

The therapist is not considered an expert agent of change; that is, a therapist does not change another person. Rather, the therapist's expertise is in creating a space and facilitating a process for dialogical conversations and collaborative relationships. When involved in this kind of process, both client and therapist are shaped and reshaped — transformed — as they work together.

Uncertainty

Being a collaborative therapist invites and entails uncertainty. When a therapist accompanies a client on a journey and walks alongside them, the newness (e.g. solutions, resolutions and outcomes) develops from within the local conversation, is mutually created and is uniquely tailored to the person or persons involved. How transformation occurs and what it looks like will vary from client to client, from therapist to therapist, and from situation to situation. Put simply, there is no way to know for sure the direction in which the story will unfold or the outcome when involved in a dialogical conversation and collaborative relationship.

Everyday ordinary life

Therapy from a postmodern collaborative perspective becomes less hierarchical and less dualistic. It resembles more the everyday ordinary conversations and relationships that most people prefer. This does not mean chit-chat, without agenda, or a friendship. Therapy conversations and relationships occur within a particular context and have an agenda: a client wants help and a therapist wants to help. Clients and problems are not categorised as challenging or difficult. Each client is simply thought to present with a dilemma of everyday ordinary life.

CHALLENGES AND IMPLICATIONS

If a therapist assumes such a philosophical stance, they will naturally and spontaneously act and talk in ways that create a space for, and invite, conversations and relationships where clients and therapists *connect, collaborate* and *construct* with each other. Because the philosophical stance becomes a natural and spontaneous way of being as a therapist, theory is not put into practice and there are no therapist techniques and skills, as commonly exist with most therapies. Instead, *the characteristics are the 'guidelines'.*

A postmodern collaborative approach contrasts with therapy approaches in which professional knowledge externally defines problems, solutions and preferred outcomes — creating expert-nonexpert dichotomies. The strength of the approach is in the relationships and conversations that are created between the client and the therapist and in the possibilities inherent in these. Therapy inherently becomes less hierarchical and dualistic, less technical and instrumental, and more an insider rather than an outsider endeavour.

Clients report a sense of ownership, belonging and shared responsibility. Therapists report a new-found sense of appreciation for their clients, a renewed sense of enthusiasm and an increased sense of competency and hopefulness for their work. They also report a reduction in burnout.

RECENT PROJECTS AND AREAS OF INQUIRY

I translate my postmodern collaborative biases to all of my practices, and I have found that *possibilities are broadened for both client and therapist*. My long-time interest in the client's voice and what we can learn from them continues in my present areas of inquiry which include:

Handmaidens to power: I interviewed women who are executive/administrative assistants to corporate leaders, to learn about their professional and personal histories, their roles and responsibilities in the organisation, and how they think they contribute to their executives' and their organisation's success. I invited them to identity their knowledge and skills, how these are used or underutilised. I was also interested in how they described their relationships with their bosses and what they identified as the characteristics of successful relationships.

The voices of homeless women with a history of substance abuse: I wanted to learn from the women about their unique experiences regarding their problems and prior treatment, what they identified as the characteristics of successful treatment, and what they identified as their competencies. I wanted to invite their voices and expertises to help provide personalised, individually tailored counselling. I created, along with colleagues Judy Elmquist, Debbie Feinsilver and Eileen Murphy, a collaborative clinical research project in which we facilitated women accessing their own voices, interviewing and talking with each other, and producing their collective 'advice to therapists'.

Maximising the effectiveness of therapists and clients in the juvenile justice system: seeking the potential: I was puzzled as I met two kinds of therapists who worked with the juvenile justice population: burnt-out therapists who talked pejoratively about their work and their clients, and therapists who talked positively and with energy about their clients and their work. Along with colleagues, I created a research forum in which we could learn about what contributes to therapist competence and effective outcomes in this challenging population, from an agency therapy staff and their administrators, community colleagues, and clients.

REFERENCES AND FURTHER READING

Anderson, H. (1997a) *Conversation, Language and Possibilities: A Postmodern Approach to Therapy.* New York: Basic Books

Anderson, H. (1997b) What we can learn when we listen to and hear clients' stories. *Voices: The Art and Science of Psychotherapy* 33 (1):4–8

Anderson, H. (2000a) Becoming a postmodern collaborative therapist: A clinical and theoretical journey, Part I. *Journal of the Texas Association for Marriage and Family Therapy* 5 (1): 5–12

Anderson, H. (2000b) Supervision as a collaborative learning community. *Supervision Bulletin.* Fall 2000. Washington, D.C.: American Association for Marriage and Family Therapy

Anderson, H. (2001a) Postmodern collaborative and person-centered therapies: What would Carl Rogers say? *Journal of Family Therapy* 23: 339–60

Anderson, H. (2001b) Becoming a postmodern collaborative therapist: a clinical and theoretical journey, Part II. *Journal of the Texas Association for Marriage and Family Therapy* 6 (1): 4–22

Anderson, H. (in press) Social construction therapies. In G. Weeks, T. L. Sexton and M. Robbins (eds), *Handbook of Family Therapy.* New York: Brunner-Routledge

Anderson, H. and Goolishian, H. A. (1988) Human systems as linguistic systems: evolving ideas about the implications for theory and practice. *Family Process* 27: 371–93

Boyd, G. (1996) *The Art of Agape Listening.* Sugarland, TX: The Agape Press

Gergen, K. G. (1999) *An Invitation to Social Construction.* Newbury Park, CA: Sage Publications

Gergen, K. G. (2001) Psychological science in a postmodern context. *American Psychologist* 56: 803–13

Rorty, R. (1979) *Philosophy and the Mirror of Nature.* Princeton, NJ: Princeton University Press

Seligman, M. and Csikszentmihalyi, M. (2000) Positive psychology: an introduction. *American Psychologist* 21: 5–14

Shotter, J. (1993) *Conversational Realities: Constructing Life through Language.* Newbury, CA: Sage Publications

22

UNKNOWING:
THE AQUARIAN PARADIGM AND
THERAPY

JOHN FREESTONE

There are different kinds of knowing,
What is written, what is growing,
Whence the wind and whither path,
The strewn, the mown, the after-math.
There are different ways of seeing,
Through the eyes and through the being,
Why the contours of the globe
Seem folded in occipital lobe.

INTRODUCTION

In this chapter I explore ideas that have always interested me but which became
more insistent as I trained, qualified and worked as a counsellor. I am increasingly
convinced of their relevance to therapy as I discuss them with my peers and
witness the consequences of their widespread neglect or misunderstanding. I
have come to think of them as 'the Aquarian paradigm', not to refer strictly to
the astrological sign, but to pay homage to Marilyn Ferguson's inspiring and
extensively referenced book, *The Aquarian Conspiracy* (Ferguson 1981). I use the
word 'paradigm' to denote a personal or cultural belief system.

Writing this chapter has been challenging because of the paradoxical nature
of the ideas, or, to put it more correctly, the paradox that arises when trying to
express them without denying them, since they centre around a single idea of
unknowing. I am in accord with Socrates when he observed, 'I know nothing
except the fact of my ignorance', a position which might seem to leave nothing
else of consequence to add. Believing that there is more of consequence to add
has required a lot of faith and support.

The Aquarian paradigm is not a systematic dogma, but a *refutation of dogma*.
This means that defining it is problematic, if not impossible, because definitions
are essentially dogmatic; but unless I attach some words to an idea, I cannot say
anything about it. I offer the following, therefore, as descriptive elaboration,
reflections on this central theme of unknowing, rather than formal definition.

The Aquarian paradigm is *the concept that all conceptual knowledge is uncertain,
possibly unverifiable and relative to the knower*. It may be necessary to emphasise
that these qualities are ascribed only to *conceptual*, i.e. *categorical* or *theoretical*

knowledge, and that there may be other kinds of knowing that are more trustworthy. Elaborating further, conceptual knowledge is...

uncertain — While the Aquarian paradigm does not rule out the pragmatic value of any particular theory, it retains a critical level of doubt about all theory, including itself. In this sense it is perhaps *the* philosophical attitude, since it clings to nothing known in preference to what may emerge. It does not decide that a statement is true or false on a balance of evidence, or on the basis of the number of people who believe it, or on the force or authority with which it is asserted;

possibly unverifiable — The Aquarian paradigm considers 'objective reality' as possibly unknowable by the human mind — or perhaps altogether fanciful, a creation *of* the mind. The currently dominant paradigm operates on the assumption that, while we may not know the truth yet, it is assuredly 'out there' to be discovered, and can be adequately conceptualised; and

relative to the knower — This means that each of us is essentially isolated in our conceptualisation, and that coincidence of expression does not indicate conformity of understanding. We may say we agree, but we cannot verify that we understand each other completely.

I will reflect on current practice and education of therapists from this perspective, but would first like to explore its basis, how it reveals itself, and some of the things that get in its way.

MAKING MEANING: PARADIGM THEORY

These ideas are in accord with developments in the physical sciences, which have been undergoing a paradigm shift for a century (cf. Clarkson's Chapter 7, this volume). By a pleasing synchronicity, some of the words used to describe the new scientific paradigm also have non-scientific, plain-English meanings, most notably 'Relativity' and 'Uncertainty'. These scientific principles and their colloquial interpretation suggest that our observations depend on our viewpoint and are not absolutely verifiable. They allow for multiple, partial and subjective truths, but inhibit our natural compulsion to find an origin, a fixed place from which everything can be measured correctly.

Information theory and neuroscience suggest that the human mind acquires conceptual knowledge by comparing patterns of experience and building cognitive models, which are to some extent malleable and self-organising. In this way, it seems, we make meaning. Biological survival requires that these models are largely unconscious and have predictive capability, otherwise the meaning of every experience would have to be construed from scratch, demanding valuable processing time in the brain.

However, there is a price to pay for this automation. The unconscious nature of the models and their relative reliability cause us to trust our ideas about the objects and systems around us: what a human being looks like, how to cross a road or what a therapeutic relationship involves, for example. Daniel Goleman (1988) describes how our internal model of reality dims our awareness of present experience and colours it according to what the model predicts, giving rise to perceptual errors: we hold a shop door open for a manikin; we assume a car will stop because the driver has seen us crossing; we find we have misunderstood a client by making assumptions.

Goleman explains this by describing a trade-off between anxiety and attention. Experience that might disrupt our current understanding is accompanied by feelings of threat, and tends to be censored, creating blind-spots in attention. He relates this effect to uncertainty, and also to the inhibition of innovation: 'The central characteristic of the information that signals stress is uncertainty ... The new, by definition, is unknown; novelty is the essence of uncertainty, which in turn is the harbinger of possible threat.' (1988: 41)

This matches closely much of Ferguson's research into paradigms, and from a synthesis of the two I postulate several processes in the evolution of knowledge:

- *Consolidation* is the process whereby a particular paradigm gains cognitive weight and takes on the appearance of reality. During this, new observations are assimilated into the current paradigm, because they do not threaten the validity of it. This repeated confirmation, or at least lack of contradiction, brings a sense of security. As Goleman and Ferguson suggest, new or apparently contradictory data cause anxiety.
- *Denial* is the blind-spot phenomenon, the filtering and repression of experience as the result of anxiety. Ferguson writes, '...the brain chooses between conflicting views. It represses information that does not fit with its dominant beliefs ... We are caught between two evolutionary mechanisms, denial and transformation' (1982: 75–8); and Goleman reminds us that we often not only forget, but forget that we have forgotten as part of the defence.
- *Entrenchment* is the habituation of current thinking patterns by a combination of consolidation (positive reinforcement) and denial (filtered contradiction). Imagine that the mind-map is a forest, and our thoughts journeys through it. To navigate the forest efficiently and arrive at our destinations predictably, we make paths between the trees. Over time, since we tend to stay on the paths, we erode them deeper and deeper in the landscape. The earth on either side now creates a barrier against exploring new areas and making new paths, and eventually stops us seeing beyond them. This habituation process has a physical expression in the way synaptic pathways are fixed in the brain: repeated connections are strengthened while unused ones diminish and terminate.
- *Paradigm shift*, which Ferguson also calls 'transformation', happens with a significant accumulation of experience that appears to contradict our present understanding. At first this experience is discounted or denied, but eventually it demands recognition. Ferguson (1982: 27–8) writes,

    A new paradigm involves a principle that was present all along but unknown to us. It includes the old as a partial truth, one aspect of How Things Work, while allowing for things to work in other ways as well. By its larger perspective, it transforms traditional knowledge and the stubborn new observations, reconciling their apparent contradictions.

- *Expansion* denotes open-mindedness, in contrast to entrenchment. It is facilitated by cumulative paradigm shifts, because repeated changes of viewpoint give rise to doubt about the validity of the current one.

The Aquarian paradigm is in effect a *paradigm of paradigms*. It takes an overview and recognises the meta-pattern, the evolution of our knowledge as repeated transcendence of old paradigms. It is a paradigm shift itself, and may be subject to the same denial. While it is still a matter of opinion, it accepts the relativity of previous *and current* opinions. It extrapolates doubt *ad infinitum*.

At first we see only the trees. Then, climbing to the top of one, we see the wood, and so form a new paradigm. If we could continue rising, our view of the land would widen, we would see the shape of the Earth, then the Solar System and other galaxies. Briefly, modernism suggests that we can stand outside the Universe (metaphysically) and observe it. Postmodernism suggests that we cannot (cf. Burr and Butt's Chapter 8, this volume). We do not know that another paradigm shift will not occur.

COLLECTIVE FORESTS: THE THERAPEUTIC LANDSCAPE

Just as the individual tends to habituate and formalise knowledge, so does the group. Almost every waking moment we negotiate life with reference to cultural norms of which we are fully, partially or not at all aware. At the group level of meaning-making we can see the opposing forces of entrenchment and expansion, the tension between our needs for security and innovation. However, at this level there is an added impetus towards entrenchment: the powerful dynamics of group identity. The intense satisfactions and anxieties of belonging produce a collective tunnel-vision, favouring conformity at the expense of innovation, diversity and individuality.

Systems of therapeutic organisation, from education to legislation, are engaged almost exclusively with the business of consolidating a range of specific paradigms. They elaborate and attenuate their current systems of knowledge, fail to question their reality, repress contrary experience, remain unaware of their entrenchment and consequently are rarely transformed. The systematisation of therapy is portrayed as regulating its practice in accordance with 'established facts'. The authoritative claims of these appeal to two main categories of thinking.

The first is a kind of organic growth of material around the insights of theorists such as Freud or Berne, which relies to a large extent on the charisma of the founder and the anecdotal evidence of his or her followers. Often it seems that a 'good idea', such as the importance of libidinal impulses or the appearance of ego states, mushrooms into a massive and complex edifice. Its constructs are repeated and developed with increasing confidence until the sense that they are *only* constructs can be lost. The arguments between disciples of different models is testimony to the seriousness with which they view them.

The second type of authority is sought through some form of scientific investigation. The validity of *absolute* scientific proof seems no longer tenable from a postmodern vantage point, even in the 'hard' sciences. I grant that scientific knowledge is generally accepted on the basis of statistical significance rather than absolute proof, but this mathematical test is also questionable, since it is just a human invention, a pragmatic measure. It depends on a comparison of the measured frequency of an effect with what chance would predict. However, *by how much they must differ* for the effect to be deemed 'significant' is not given in nature, it is established by tradition. Similarly, people are divided up into arbitrary categories by how they match our assessment criteria, and their care plans are defined (or treatment refused) accordingly.

As dogma is criticised there is a movement towards 'evidence-based practice'. While I admit that *experience* should inform practice, there are dangers associated with the application of standard interventions, based on scientifically trusted *evidence*, as an occupational methodology. The so-called-facts that influence service provision are generally arrived at by studies of large populations, which arguably furnish poor criteria on which to base decisions in the therapy room. Conversely, the experience happening at the time *within* the therapy room is undermined. If research suggests that a particular approach or intervention is preferable, therapists who trust such evidence are in any particular case more likely to overlook subtle counter-indications. Many of a therapist's intuitive hunches are unconscious, and it might be years before their existence comes to light and their investigation influences the scientific model. Even then, this will only be through the same process with its inherent generalisation. This cannot be discounted in therapy, where the usefulness of an intervention may be eliminated immediately by minor changes in the complex, multi-dimensional matrix of a relationship. In addition, people generally resent, and may even be damaged by, being treated as representative of statistical groups rather than unique individuals. Evidence-based practice, trusted too much, can impoverish relationships with individual clients.

The difficulty of systematising therapeutic knowledge is apparent when we consider the most nebulous aspects of experience, such as religious and spiritual experience, consciousness and altered states, the 'paranormal', placebo and so on. These, whilst arguably being highly relevant to the human condition and therefore highly significant considerations in therapy, are the most impervious to scientific analysis. They seem more approachable through sensitive, open-minded conversation.

Science is a language describing concepts, and conceptual knowledge should be treated with caution. From medical diagnoses to the names of physical objects, we use words and the concepts they represent to chop experience into bits to squeeze into abstract boxes. Words can only be defined in a circular way. Conceptual knowledge has no first principle, no fundamental particle from which to construct reality.

Psychologists have struggled for decades to apply the methods of 'hard' science to their 'soft' subject; meanwhile, physical scientists have learned that their own science is not 'hard' at all, but full of fuzzy logic and indeterminacy. This is not a mere academic irony to be noticed and forgotten: soft science is put into hard practice in the world.

The current paradigm has always approved of decisions founded on theoretical conjecture and anecdote. It increasingly supports the dubious statistical significance of abstract hypotheses, extrapolated from data gathered some time ago from large groups of other people, with a nonchalant disregard for the most weighty immeasurable influences. Yet it mistrusts and incapacitates the current existential experience and insight of both therapist and client. This is a much greater threat to clients' health than the publicly projected one of insufficiently policed practice, and it is ignored by policy-makers. Our trust in orthodoxy is beginning to be questioned, but the infallibility of science is an idea so ingrained in our culture that we often fail to notice it or pursue our objections. We habitually acquiesce like rocked infants to the false authority of scientific rationalism, which increasingly sidelines ordinary care within helping relationships.

The Aquarian perspective does not discount any form of evidence, but warns us to consider each critically and take all with a pinch of salt. Science and anecdote can provide information, just as the senses of the therapist can. The danger arises if we trust certain types of information too much.

There is another illegitimate authority, however, that seems to claim almost infallible moral rectitude. It appears mainly in the corridors of power, where we might expect humility to risk the greatest loss. For example, the British Association for Counselling and Psychotherapy's (BACP) recently updated *Ethical Framework for Good Practice in Counselling and Psychotherapy* is claimed to be 'the most exacting work' by 'the UK's experts in ethical practice', in consultation with 'experts in professional ethics' from other fields. In this way BACP chisels deeper into the professional psyche its stony-faced dogma concerning both ethics and good practice.

What is ethical expertise? Is ethical behaviour not a subjective matter, relative to the individual and their culture, and should not this understanding be arrived at during a mature inquiry into ethics? By suggesting that it has already dealt with ethics, a professional body inhibits its members from pursuing ethical questions personally to any depth (cf. Pattison's Chapter 5, this volume). Many therapists accept the ethical codes of their professional body too readily, and see no conflict between this and encouraging the autonomy of clients.

TRAINING OR EDUCATION?

The postmodern paradigm has undoubtedly influenced therapy (see, for example, Anderson's Chapter 21, this volume), but in the majority of training programmes it is paid lip-service. During my certificate course, for instance, there was a lot of talk about 'student-centred learning'. We, the students, were encouraged to think about our learning needs and ask for topics and activities to be included, but not a single suggestion was ever taken up. Each was rejected by embarrassed tutors blaming the pressure of the curriculum. This ostensibly empowering, but actually didactic training style can encourage therapists to patronise their clients with a similar disguised authority.

Models of therapy are generally presented as formal systems of nested information, giving the impression that all we know about helping can be organised in a tree-structure, like the files on our computers, and that all we have to do is learn it. Analysis and labelling of therapeutic knowledge readies us for analysing and labelling clients. It does not encourage the fluid, sensitive insights into human processes and relationships that travelling or studying art and philosophy can. It also hinders student-centred learning, since the student's digestion of these bite-size chunks tends to become the purpose of the training.

Setting out to understand and be able to teach genuine care, we have only succeeded in *describing some of the behaviour associated with it*, a consequence of the modernist paradigm, which deals only in measurable quantities. It emphasises *training* as opposed to *education* of practitioners, suggesting that the way to approach therapy is by the application of knowledge and the perfection of skills, rather than the development of congruent values and personality strengths. Knowledge and skills can be gained through training, but education involves the discovery and encouragement of innate qualities.

The current paradigm persists even when the training is concerned with these qualities, and sets out to enable a humble, emancipating style of practice, creating a mismatch between practical aims and training style. In the training of person-centred practitioners, for instance, the attainment of the 'core conditions' is usually judged on the basis of behavioural demonstration.

The difference between genuine attainment and behavioural demonstration is ignored from the moment we take our first taster course in counselling skills and learn how to sit in a manner that *indicates* we are listening. Rarely are students encouraged to engage with the existential nuances of their own listening process as a method of improving it. Current training serves to refine and consolidate the professional role-playing thereafter, as if the aim were to make clients feel that they are relating to real people; rarely does training address what it means to be a real person with another. Accreditation and statutory regulation increase the incentive to play the behavioural game, to jump through hoops for personal gain at the expense of integrity. We can be trained to fake anything, including those qualities our overseers deem necessary for safe practice (and we can easily forget that we are faking), but we can't be trained to be genuine or caring or compassionate. These are qualities we must find (and be helped to find) within ourselves.

THE AQUARIAN SPIRIT

The passages above address a few of the processes that I feel are at odds with the principles of relativity and uncertainty, and may suggest better choices. I would have liked to have developed the implications of the Aquarian paradigm here more concretely, but to do so risks misrepresenting it. It follows naturally from the principles that none of the processes I have criticised above can legitimately be judged right or wrong in any objective sense. Practising behaving compassionately *can* develop compassion, for instance. The Aquarian paradigm opens up the field of possibilities — *infinitely* wide — and choices within this must be based on preferences and pragmatic concerns.

Engaging with this paradigm seems to be accompanied by an almost irresistible urge to return to the refuge of certainty and build rigid structures on that foundation; but to be certain denies the principle, and to build too rigidly denies its scope. I have seen this urge in myself and others. I have seen groups of people build structures based on pluralistic values and then reject them again to protect what they have built. Also, those who have seen the danger of authoritarianism sometimes adopt the position of the revolutionary, advocating sweeping it away and installing pluralism, clearly a contradiction in terms. Attacking established structures tends to create more fear within them and increase their defence. Evolution may be a better approach than revolution. Building new structures alongside the old is congruent with diversity, and clients and practitioners will vote with their feet

The value of the Aquarian paradigm is that it frees us from boxes, the illusion of true prose. Do we question whether a poem is true or false? It reminds us that all statements are poetic — not true or false, but relatively true and false at the same time. It reminds us to be humble in the fragility of our truth, and to honour another's truth. Seeing the fragility of theirs, it invites us to voice our own sensitively, yet resist being silenced, brain-washed or coerced.

It can be dizzying to recognise that what we thought of as solid ground is more like restless ocean; but repeatedly failing to find a foothold eventually persuades us to let go and learn to swim in this mysterious realm. Our resistance seems to be generated only by fear, and what we expect to be loss becomes emancipation.

Renouncing absolute faith in conceptual knowledge seems to coincide with apprehension of other kinds of knowledge. If we clear our heads a bit, we may find we have trustworthy hearts. Therapy as we have known it mumbles apologetically about things like love, compassion, intuition and spirituality. About intuition, Radhakrishnan writes, 'There is a knowledge which is different from the conceptual, a knowledge by which we see things as they are, as unique individuals and not as members of a class or units in a crowd' (1937: 108). He could have been writing about therapy, or the 'new' paradigm, but was recounting experience as old as humanity — experience which we still fail to appreciate.

REFERENCES

British Association for Counselling and Psychotherapy (2002) *Ethical Framework for Good Practice in Counselling and Psychotherapy*. Rugby: BACP

Ferguson, M. (1982) *The Aquarian Conspiracy: Personal and Social Transformation in the 1980s*. London: Paladin (orig. 1981)

Goleman, D. (1988) *Vital Lies, Simple Truths: The Psychology of Self-Deception*. London: Bloomsbury

Radhakrishnan, J. (1937) *An Idealist View of Life*. London: Unwin

23

THE POWER OF LANGUAGE IN THERAPEUTIC RELATIONSHIPS

NICKY HART

> The irreducible elements of psychotherapy are a therapist, a patient and a regular and reliable time and place. But given these, it is not so easy for two people to meet.
>
> (R. D. Laing)

The issue of power within therapy is a complex one and is rarely addressed within the therapeutic literature. The mechanisms by which power is exercised through relationship and through language are explored in other disciplines such as sociology, philosophy, psychology, linguistics and so on but, as yet, there is little evidence that therapists see the relevance of this literature to psychotherapy. It is argued here that the dynamics of power exercised through language within relationship are critical to the therapeutic process, just as they are to any other relationship.

A contradiction often seems to exist between the emphasis within therapeutic practice on self-reflection, on the one hand, and on the other, the resistance of therapists to reflect on their own use of power and influence as agents of change at both the individual and social level. Much has been written in the last decade on the increasingly powerful position of psychotherapy as a cultural institution (Gergen 1991; Parker 1997; Rose 1989). The focus of Western culture on the individual and the desire for self-knowledge has elevated psychologists and psychotherapists to positions of power as a result of the perception that they are experts in the field of understanding the self. Rose explains the attraction of psychotherapy thus: 'It promises to make it possible for us all to make a project of our biography, create a style for our lives, shape our everyday existence in terms of an ethic of autonomy' (Rose 1990: 254).

However, I want to argue that the notion of freedom to explore the inner worlds of the psyche is illusory: the normalising function of therapeutic discourse is now very carefully hidden within the ideology and language of humanism. By suggesting that therapy is client-centred, the power, in theory — but also the responsibility — is placed firmly with the client: '... psychotherapy can easily become, and indeed frequently does become, a kind of disguised moral campaign which places colossal and entirely unreasonable demands on the individual' (Smail 1996: 44). The 'conditions of possibility' (Foucault 1977) are determined, and the trend towards self-surveillance continues, creating a much more effective means of social control than any overt system of disciplinary power.

Although this political analysis of psychotherapy is valuable and relevant, the specific manner in which this power is exercised within the therapeutic relationship has rarely been explored. In psychotherapy, power is rarely wielded by a powerful therapist over a submissive client but rather exists, and is employed in, much more subtle ways. This is not to say that abusive therapists do not exist; and as Masson (1988) has documented, there do appear to be, at least, occasional instances of this phenomenon. However, such behaviour, unfortunately, characterises a wide variety of relationships, and is relatively easy to understand even if not condone. What is more interesting, in my view, is the exploration of the dynamic of power within relationships of perceived equality. To some extent, the practice of psychotherapy draws upon a medical discourse whereby the therapist is positioned in a more powerful position than the client by virtue of her role within the institution. Both therapist and client implicitly conform to their roles, and the relationship exists and develops within that framework. It often bears a strong resemblance to a doctor/patient relationship, especially if conducted within a health-service setting.

However, particular models of therapeutic practice, such as the person-centred approach of Carl Rogers, emphasise the mutuality of the therapeutic relationship. The essence of the therapeutic process in this approach lies in a notion of empowerment of the client; of facilitating the client's journey out of his distress into a more fulfilling and autonomous way of being. My scepticism revolves around the possibility that a therapist and client can meet each other as two individuals on an equal footing; and my contention here is that although, as therapists, we may believe in the value of that goal and may collude in the belief that our relationship with our clients is mutual and non-exploitative, this is a naïve understanding of the nature and dynamic of relationships. The way in which power operates in relationships where its existence is not explicitly acknowledged is a fascinating area of exploration and, in my view, opens up an area of research which will allow us to understand better the nature of the therapeutic relationship in more depth.

A discussion of what is understood by the word 'power' would (and has) filled the pages of many eminent tomes and cannot be undertaken here, but it is important to realise that simplistic and judgmental assumptions are often made about the notion of power. Power carries with it negative connotations; and although the work of Foucault is often invoked when discussing notions of power in therapy to support this conception of power as a 'bad' influence, Foucault actually evades the issue of agency by using terms that fail to identify who wields power or how they do it. Megill (1985) suggests that to understand Foucault's notion of power in his later work, we have to look again at Nietzsche's concept of the 'will to power' implying that power is creative.

In *Madness and Civilisation* (1967),[1] Foucault presented a negative conception of power, as a force which excludes and represses, but in the 1970s work he asserts that power is positive and productive, 'Power produces, it produces reality; it produces domains of objects and rituals of truth' (Megill 1985: 241, quoting from *Discipline and Punish*, 1977: 196). The value of Foucault's writings on power lies in the notion of power as a force in relationship. It is not possessed but practised, not an attribute but an exercise (Kendall and Wickham 1999). It is this interpretation of Foucault's conception of power that provides us with a framework within which to explore the impact of power within a therapeutic relationship.

1. First published in America in 1965 and in England, 1967 this was a shortened version of Foucault's original 1961 publication entitled 'Folie et deraison: Histoire de la folie à l'age classique'.

The complexity of power in relationship is developed in Lupton's (1997) notion of complicity within doctor-patient relationships. Lupton, following Foucault, offers an explanation in the form of a critique of the medicalisation critique, pointing out that the medical profession, in addition to receiving power by virtue of their privileged position in society, is also given power through the complicity of their patients: 'Rather than being a struggle for power between the dominant party (doctors) and the less powerful party (patients) there is a collusion between the two to reproduce medical dominance' (ibid.: 98). In other words, the dynamic of power within relationship is a much more subtle process than the use of violence or coercion. It is a form of persuasion, through the use of rhetoric, that certain ways of behaving and thinking and feeling are more appropriate and healthy than others:

> Power is not a possession of particular social groups, but is relational, a strategy that is invested in and transmitted through all social groups. This more complex view of power goes some way to recognising the collusive nature of power relations in relation to medicine.
>
> (ibid.: 99)

So, to return to psychotherapy, if we now think about power not as something to be minimised within a therapeutic relationship, but something that is an inevitable part of that relationship, and which may, in fact, be a creative force, we can begin to explore the dynamics of power in more detail. The therapeutic relationship is dialogic, facilitative, reciprocal, co-operative, collusive, combative, abusive and antagonistic, and mainly relies on the medium of talk.

By employing research methodologies more commonly used to analyse conversational text, it is possible to explore the process which occurs within a therapy session and to see the therapist and client as protagonists within a dialogical battle for control over the agenda and the relationship. This is achieved by constructing the framing concept of *levels of communication* occurring within the dialogue. Such a notion is consistent with therapeutic paradigms, including that of Carl Rogers. For Rogers the individual can operate from the level of the experiential self or from the deeper level of the organismic self. This Rogerian framework, however, is value laden in that the aim of therapy is to promote the preferred mode of functioning (i.e. from the organismic self). Within the operation of the therapeutic encounter, the person-centred rhetoric promotes the notion that underneath the client's words lies a deeper level of meaning which can be sensed by an empathic and motivated therapist. It could be argued not that different levels and meanings do not exist in discourse but that there is no value in a notion of a 'true' or 'real' meaning which can be revealed through the skills of a genuine, empathic and congruent therapist. If it is understood that talk is not referential or representational, then the *content* of speech is not the important criterion for understanding. The functional units of talk are not statements or utterances made by the speaker, but rather the parts of speech that are accepted by speaker and listener as relevant.

Thus, it is an interactional unit, not a conversational unit which is basic to talk (Goffman 1974). The sequence of changes in the frames for events, or what Goffman refers to as 'footing', is crucial to the construction of meaning. An interaction involves a relationship moving along a number of dimensions managed by devices such as challenges, defences and retreats, not requests and assertions (Labov and Fanshell 1997). When a conversation is structured according to the rules of therapeutic discourse, there are constraints on what can be said and what can be heard. This is partly to do with role alignment and the acceptable conversational formats associated with the roles of therapist and client. It is also because therapy operates within a number of discursive frameworks such as therapy models, psychological theories, medical diagnostic classifications, professional relationships and codes of practice which all impose constraints on the relationship and the shape of the interaction (Fish 1999).

Parker, following Foucault, sees the therapeutic discourse as offering only certain conditions of possibility to the client. In Western culture this discourse is based on psychological models of the self which position psychological distress within the intra-psychic domain to the exclusion of the social and political context (a theme that recurs throughout this volume), and thereby making the client responsible for resolving his own problems through the confessional technique (Foucault 1981; Parker 1998). Thus, if a client presents with a story of distress which does not comply with this psychological model of distress, they will either be deemed unsuitable for therapeutic intervention or their story may be shaped in such a way that it eventually does fit with this model.

Therapy is typically based on traditional, modernist views of language involving transmission of facts — the client's story to the therapist and the therapist's response to the client. The alternative dialogic view would be that the client is *actively constructed* through the listening process. In other words, it is through the telling of the story, the therapist's understanding and interpretation of the meaning of the story and the discussion of the story between the therapist and the client that gradually creates a meaning which is shared by both therapist and client. In order for this to happen, there must be a context which exemplifies shared values. The world of the speaker and the receiver must overlap enough for them to inhabit a space together for long enough to construct a shared meaning. The nature of this context is determined by the therapist, who provides the receiving context because it is she who possesses the skill and the resources to make this happen. The type of receptive environment provided determines what is said as well as how it is received:

> Thus, the utterance does not entirely belong to the speaker, it belongs to at least two people. It also does not belong entirely to the present but also to the future. Like bridges, utterances have to have both ends to exist — they are two-sided acts, the products of reciprocal relationships between speakers and listeners of present and future.
>
> (Riikonen and Smith 1997: 55)

However, the implicit assumption here is that both therapist and client are motivated to behave reciprocally and are able to overcome the constraints of their own positions, experiences and prejudices in order to inhabit this shared space. The argument presented here is that this is not always the case, and in fact therapists and clients, rather than striving for mutuality, exert their power through language by managing the conversation in order to meet their own ends, or the needs of the organisation for which they work. These skills are a normal part of everyday conversation, but when combined with the skills of persuasive rhetoric used by a therapist, the discourse of the therapist can become dominant and the client will only be heard when his story fits within this dominant discourse.

Lakoff argues that what makes therapeutic discourse particularly interesting is that it inhabits an intermediary position between everyday discourse and persuasive discourse. It contains characteristics of both:

> there is the appearance of an egalitarian, reciprocal conversation, but in terms of deeper intention, the reciprocity turns out to be only superficial. The therapist can ask questions which the client soon learns not to ask; and if the latter should attempt to ask such a question, the therapist, rather than give an answer, will usually treat the question as a tacit invitation to ask another question, or make an interpretation.
>
> (Lakoff 1982: 27, 28)

The anomaly in therapeutic discourse is that although the client typically holds the floor for the majority of the time, which is usually a sign of power in conversation, the therapist maintains power through other means. For instance, it is the therapist who determines beginnings and endings, and decides on the meaning of the contributions made by the client. Therapeutic discourse is a complex example because it is both non-reciprocal and bilateral. Both participants make true contributions to the conversation and, in fact, take turns (usually an indication of reciprocity); but the contributions vary in their surface forms and are open to different interpretations. Ordinary conversation is expected to be spontaneous and include hesitations and gaps rather than be smooth flowing, as is often the case with persuasive discourse. Therapeutic discourse, on the surface, takes the form of ordinary conversation, and does include a spontaneous element, certainly within the clients' narrative; but when unpacking the therapist discourse there is often evidence of a more prepared script. However, it is a script which must be flexible and responsive to the client utterances and therefore is not equivalent to persuasive discourse in the form of a lecture for instance.

Ordinary conversation is full of rituals and well-worn phrases. It has surprisingly little novelty. Persuasive discourse, however, always strives for novelty. It is the novel element that makes it persuasive, and this may be apparent at the level of content or in the structural format through use of words and phrases that are unfamiliar to the listener. In therapeutic talk, the client is often exposed to a vocabulary and style of social intercourse which is unfamiliar. This puts the client at a disadvantage, it could be argued, but also contains that element, novelty, which makes the discourse persuasive. Thus, if a therapeutic conversation is analysed using techniques more commonly used to analyse conversations, it is possible to identify the dynamics of the conversation and the way that linguistic skills and devices are used to manage that conversation. It is through their use of persuasive rhetoric that therapists may influence clients and work towards constructing the client and their problem within a therapeutic discourse. This then enables therapy to take place. Clients will often comply with this process as a result of their complicity with the therapist and their need to hand power over to someone they have identified as the expert. As Rennie writes, 'clients often arrive with their own ideas of what is wrong with them and what they need. Of course they may eventually see things otherwise as a result of their interaction with the counsellor' (Rennie 1998: 113).

Some empirical evidence based on process analyses of therapeutic encounters offers some support for this view. For example, a study by Kathy Davies (1986) demonstrated how the therapeutic agenda is often redefined by the therapist in line with the therapeutic model. In her analysis of a therapy session Davies argues that the client's initial presentation of her problems can be understood as a 'goodness of fit' between the client's situation and her expectations of the situation. However, the issues presented in this way do not open up possibilities for therapy work as they relate more to the position of women in society and social and cultural expectations regarding gender. So the client's story is transformed by the therapist into a 'problem for further therapy work' by focusing on intra-personal issues which the client herself had not raised and continues for some time to resist, before finally complying with the therapeutic agenda. This type of 're-formulation' of clients' stories through persuasive discourse and therapeutic rhetoric is the predominant way in which power is exercised over clients in therapy.

In my own analysis of a therapy session, the client's story revolved around existential issues of meaning and morality (Hart 2002). His anger and hurt were located within a social and political arena that rendered him a victim of racism and as an individual with a strong moral sense and a continuing struggle with a life-threatening illness. He wished to create some meaning for himself that would explain the relationships which he had experienced and the way in which he had been treated. His agenda was an interpersonal one. In fact he sums up his own assessment of his situation in a statement towards the middle of the session:

> Y'know it has something to do with being a man, it has something to do with, with the race thing, y'know. It has something to do with the relationship, maybe the failure of a relationship a, a lot of things, y'know — a father not being in the home with his children. I really feel like being a victim.

The client is drawing on social and cultural discourses that enable him to see himself as having been positioned, by the nature of his race, gender and relationship experiences, within a victim role. His view of himself is predominantly that of a black man who has suffered as a result of the context in which he lives: not an unusual discourse for 1970s America.

However, as in Davis's example, the presenting problem defined in this way does not offer much scope for therapeutic work and the therapist must reformulate it in a way that does. In this case the therapist carefully reiterates the points made by the client about gender, race and role, but adds the important ingredient of emotion. The problem has now been redefined as the inability of the client to own and express his hurt.

> It goes back to some of those things you were mentioning — a man doesn't admit he's hurt, a black man especially doesn't admit that he's been hurt by anything. A father doesn't admit that he's been hurt by being away from his children. Just too many things that say no, no, no, no — don't let it out.
> But inside there's the hurt. A phrase came to me a minute ago, that if you could let that out I don't know if this will ring true with you or not, if you could let that out it would be the voice of the victim.

Using a person-centred discourse the therapist reformulates the client's story as an intra-psychic conflict based on the client's alienation from his true self. His problem is that he is unable to express his emotions. The client's attempts to define his problem within his own agenda are thwarted by the therapist in this manner throughout the session.

In this session the client and therapist never really meet or create a shared understanding. My argument here is that the reason for this is that the therapist and client arrive at the therapy room as products of their position, experience, education, race, class, personality and so on: they are constrained by the discourses they bring with them as well as by the therapeutic discourse itself. Often they each have their own agenda and their own manner of asserting this agenda through the way in which they use language to present themselves and to control the interaction. For each to enter the world of the other, I would argue, is difficult, if not impossible, within the traditional conceptions of relationship; but to establish a temporary relationship where the 'space between' may be used therapeutically for each to gain a better understanding of the other and of themselves may be possible.

Some would argue that through the powers of *empathy* it is possible to transcend difference and to find a place where we can meet with clients at the level of 'humanness' where we can share the same understanding and vision. I am not suggesting that this is not a desirable and worthy aim, but I am concerned that we often underestimate the difficulties involved in realising this goal and may overlook, or at best minimise, the social, political and cultural constraints that surround therapeutic work, and the fact that we are agents of social change. We may underestimate the power that we exert, perhaps below the level of awareness, on clients, and also the power that our society exerts over others through us. Through an analysis of therapeutic process focused on how relationship is managed through conversational interaction, we may gain deeper insights into the subtle ways in which we influence and persuade our clients through the rhetoric of therapeutic discourse.

As reflective practitioners it is important that we constantly question our practice, not just in terms of our therapeutic skill but also in terms of the political and cultural discourses that influence our work. These are ethical issues which are just as relevant as traditional concerns such as competence to practise. The influences of our culture may be subtle, and it is easy to forget that although we are individuals we are also products of our socialisation, our education, class, gender and so on. We work within organisations imbued with philosophies and beliefs which determine the kind of work that we can do, the approach we adopt with our clients and the types of relationships that we are able to form.

The relationship between social control and therapy has become prominent recently as, in Britain, we have been presented, as I write, with the draft of the new Mental Health Bill. The proposed changes to the understanding of diagnostic categories for mental illness and the resultant implications remind us yet again of the way in which language can determine the treatment of individuals and ultimately determine limits to freedom.

Conclusion

Power and influence are at their most potent within the framework of a caring, non-judgemental and altruistic relationship. My clinical experience leads me to believe that the power of love will always be stronger than the power of hate, and a therapeutic relationship founded on the characteristics of love commands an extremely powerful position as a healing force. Take this relationship and place it within a social context where the ethos of individualism and self-awareness have become paramount, where the expectation of happiness and fulfilment are inherent and the political has become the personal, and the therapist occupies a position of unparalleled power. This is not to say that the therapeutic element in therapy resides in the power and responsibility of the therapist — in fact this may well be the case; but to fail to address the way in which power operates in therapeutic relationships, or to deny its presence, or even to advocate for its elimination prevents an exploration of therapeutic process which may be illuminating. Most of us see ourselves as ethical, professional and reflective practitioners. We sign up to the belief that therapy is a powerful healing force. We must also have the courage and the patience to resist complacency and to challenge ourselves and our work continually in a bid to reach a deeper understanding of the nature of the work that we do.

REFERENCES

Davies, K. (1986) The process of problem re-formulation in psychotherapy. *Sociology of Health and Illness* 8 (1): 44–74

Fish, V. (1999) Clementis's hat: Foucault and the politics of psychotherapy. In I. Parker (ed.), *Deconstructing Psychotherapy* (pp. 54–70). London: Sage

Foucault, M. (1977) *Discipline and Punish: The Birth of the Prison*. London: Allen Lane

Foucault, M. (1981) *The History of Sexuality, Vol. 1*. Harmondsworth: Penguin

Gergen, K. J. (1991) *The Saturated Self*. New York: Basic Books

Goffman, E. (1974) *Frame Analysis*. New York: Harper Colophone Books

Hart, N. M. T. (2002) Power, relationships and ethics in psychotherapy. Unpublished doctoral dissertation, Department of Psychology, City University

Kendall, G. and Wickham, G. (1999) *Using Foucault's Methods*. London: Sage

Labov, W. and Fanshell, D. (1997) *Therapeutic Discourse: Psychotherapy as Conversation*. New York: Academic Press

Lakoff, R. T. (1982) Persuasive discourse and ordinary conversation, with examples from advertising. In D. Tannen (ed.), *Analysing Discourse: Text and Talk*. Washington: Georgetown University Press.

Lupton, D. (1997) Foucault and the medicalisation critique. In A. Peterson and R. Bunton (eds), *Foucault, Health and Medicine*. London: Routledge

Masson, J. (1988) *Against Therapy*. London: Fontana

Megill, A. (1985) *Prophets of Extremity*. Berkeley: University of California Press

Parker, I. (1997) *Psychoanalytic Culture: Psychoanalytic Discourse in Western Society*. London: Sage

Parker, I. (1998) Constructing and deconstructing psychotherapeutic discourse. *European Journal of Psychotherapy, Counselling and Health* 1 (1): 65–78

Rennie, D. (1998) *Person-Centred Counselling: An Experiential Approach*. London: Sage

Riikonen, E. and Smith, G. M. (1997) *Re-Imagining Therapy: Living Conversations and Relational Knowing*. London: Sage

Rose, N. (1989) *Governing the Soul: Therapeutic Technologies of Human Subjectivity*. London: Routledge

Rose, N. (1990) Psychology as a 'social science'. In I. Parker and J. Shotter (eds), *Deconstructing Social Psychology*. London: Routledge

Smail, D. (1996) *How to Survive without Psychotherapy*. London: Constable

24

PSY NO MORE:
TOWARDS A NON-IATROGENIC
PSYCHOTHERAPY

JOHN KAYE[†]

> Can anyone do effective therapy without becoming an instrument of social
> control, without participating and contributing, often unknowingly, to the
> construction or the maintenance of a dominant discourse of oppression?
>
> (Gianfranco Cecchin 1993: ix)

Since its inception, psychotherapy has undergone seemingly dramatic changes
in orientation, as have the models derived from these orientations. The most
recent of these has occurred over the last decade, largely influenced by the notion
that our realities are socially constructed and language-constituted. With
language seen as being active and constitutive rather than simply representative,
the therapeutic encounter has come to be thought of as a milieu for the creative
generation of meaning and therapy itself as a process of semiosis — the forging
of new meaning in the context of collaborative discourse (Gergen and Kaye 1992).
Whether this development is a discontinuous one — representing a revolutionary
break from the essentialist notions of diagnosing and solving identifiable
intrapsychic or intrasystemic problems — is open to question.

A related and equally important issue concerns whether this constructionist
development has the potential to contribute to social well-being or whether
psychotherapy remains implicitly immured in maintaining the social order, with
all its inherent structural inequities. As one of what Nikolas Rose terms the
psysciences, psychotherapy may be viewed as acting to adjust people to their
society, thus participating in a regulative practice and, by extension, in the
maintenance of the social order with its commodifying and unjust consequences.
This is particularly pertinent given Hillman and Ventura's (1992: 3) impassioned
contention that 'We've had a hundred years of analysis and people are getting
more and more sensitive and the world is getting worse and worse'. While many
problems reside in personal hurts or conflicts and others in dysfunctional
relationship patterns, and while all are individually experienced, Hillman and
Ventura's words point to the twin dangers of individualising the problems people
experience whilst ignoring their possible socio-cultural base (cf. Smail's Chapter
3, this volume).

† This chapter first appeared as Chapter 2 of Parker, I. (ed.) (1999) *Deconstructing
Psychotherapy*, London: Sage, and appears here by kind permission of the author and
publishers Sage Publications Ltd.

This consideration must lead us to question whether the enterprise of psychotherapy is largely trapped in a limiting paradigm by virtue of its focus on the intrapsychic causation of problems to the relative exclusion of a concern with the loss of certainty wrought by a changing world or by structurally ingrained inequities — of class, race, gender, economic deprivation and unfavourable living conditions. While it would be somewhat utopian to expect psychotherapy to attempt to find solutions to the injustices of the world, it is surely not too much to ask that therapists engage with issues of social context, together with the role of social inequities in the causation of psychological distress. It would also be remiss for therapists not to take these issues into account in their work, for as Judith Cross (1994) points out, if we ignore the role played by social inequity, we may inadvertently be acting to ask our troubled consultees to adjust to the unjust.

Further, in focusing on the amelioration of individual pain, we run the risk of implying that the sufferer is in some sense either deficient or responsible for the problem — a form of victim-blaming. At the same time, I question whether the language of psychotherapy is necessarily permeated by concepts of deficit as asserted by critics of modernist practices such as Drewery and Winslade (1997) and Gergen (1994). Similarly, I also question the tendency on the part of some critical theorists and those of a constructionist or narrative persuasion to portray those psychotherapies which locate the source of problems within the person as sinister organs of state control, clandestinely hegemonic, colonising and reproductive of inequitable power relations.

PSYCHOTHERAPY AS A NORMALISING PRACTICE

Most psychotherapeutic practices both treat the individual as the locus of pathology (thereby diverting attention from the role played by socio-cultural factors in the genesis of psychological distress) and are informed by assumptions of:

1. an underlying cause or basis of pathology;
2. the location of this cause within the individual and their relationships;
3. the diagnosability of the problem;
4. treatability via a specifically designed set of techniques.

Implicit in these suppositions are the concepts of normality and abnormality, the normatively good or bad and the presumption of a true root cause which can be objectively established, known and remediated. Within this frame, psychotherapy can be seen as an instrumental practice consisting of the treatment of what is judged to be mental disorder and abnormal or dysfunctional behaviour. Therapists working within these parameters seek to bring about a restructuring or reprogramming of behaviour in both individuals and families against some criterion of the normal, the deviant, the well-adjusted, the problematic and non-problematic. From this perspective, therapy is concerned with altering established behaviour patterns and belief systems and with the establishment of alternative, more functional or more socially acceptable patterns.

This model of practice has been questioned on both theoretical and politico-ethical grounds. First, models based on notions of normality or abnormality are potentially pathologising. As Gergen (1991) has pointed out, the assumption of a problem residing in the individual together with a language of deficit or deficiency can be iatrogenic, leading to what he calls 'a spiral of infirmity'. The act of helping too is problematic. Most psychotherapies incorporate a theory of function and dysfunction as well as an associated set of activities whereby it is assumed that change can be induced in another by the specially trained and accredited. In this frame, therapeutic activity:

1. involves the exploration and examination of the consultee's story within the terms of the therapist's frame of reference; and
2. attempts to engage the other actively in the process of reinterpreting their narrative within the therapist's frame, developing new behaviours in accord with it.

As I have written elsewhere (Kaye 1996), this conceptualisation perpetuates the concept of the therapist as having privileged knowledge, a socially accredited expert who can both provide an authoritative true version of a problem and act according to a set of prescribed activities to correct it. In practice this gives rise to a top-down and instrumental therapist-centred activity — one in which the therapist acts instrumentally via dialogue on the 'client's' narrative and behaviour in order to change it, rather than working collaboratively together with the 'client' towards new solutions which the 'client' finds fitting.

The issues discussed to date raise valid questions about the relative innocence or socio-cultural neutrality of therapy. For the issue of what constitutes the normal or the deviant, the functional or dysfunctional is as much a socio-cultural variable as a medico-psychological constant. To understand this, one need only trace the changes in DSM categories over the years as these follow changes in socially-constructed attitudes and mores. More theoretically, as Ian John (1998: 26) has cogently argued,

> psychological knowledge of any description, whether scientifically authorised or not, is itself in the world, or a part of the world. Like the psychological enterprise that revolves around it, it is shaped and constrained by social forces. It bears the marks of the culture from which it has arisen and is at the same time a constituent element of that culture. Neither the knowledge, nor the enterprise, are part of a natural order that stands outside of society, and it cannot be assumed that they are necessarily benign, beneficent or emancipatory.

Psychotherapy is not informed only by a technico-rational repertoire; it embodies both a moral-ethical discursive formation, prescribing what is socially normative, and a liberal humanist discourse, which instantiates the notion of people as rational autonomous individuals possessing a fixed identity, an essential self vested with agency and a consciousness which is the cause of their beliefs and actions. And just as psychological and psychiatric discourse treat the individual as the locus of pathology, so the moral-ethical and humanistic discursive repertoires make the individual the locus of responsibility. This then *does* justify queries regarding the role of psychotherapy as a normalising, socially regulative discipline implicitly caught up in maintaining a given social order, as well as queries regarding the consequences for those who seek psychological help.

FRAMES OF PSYCHOTHERAPY

Whatever the differences between the various models of therapy, all operate within two primary frames. One, a receptive helper frame, privileges the consultee's narrative and seeks to engage him or her in a process of self-discovery in partnership with an empathic listener who establishes a climate of trust and understanding. The other, a re-visioning frame, seeks to ensure participation in the therapeutic process by drawing on the authority vested in the therapist. This approach casts and directs the search for problem solution within the terms of the expert therapist's conceptual and linguistic frame — establishing a hierarchical relationship which privileges the therapist's perspective. These two alternate frames represent differences in emphasis — they are not incompatible opposites.

The receptive helper frame

When we experience a problem, most of us, I think, hope that gaining some understanding of the problem or its cause will help resolve it. Under these circumstances, too, we might turn to another, hoping to be listened to with understanding, and expecting that the other's perspective might prove helpful in providing us with insight or an explanation that would lead to a solution. Equally importantly, we also experience a need to be heard, understood and treated with understanding, to have our experience of events believed rather than rejected, to have our authorship of experience confirmed rather than disconfirmed.

The provision of a context in which one connects with the experiential world of another and in which that other feels their world of experience to be accepted and acknowledged as meaningful is a central element of the helping interview. Crucial to the provision of an accepting climate is what I have previously called the receptive stance (Kaye 1993). The receptive stance is characterised by an openness to the other's experience, a readiness to learn about their world, a canvassing of multiple possible perspectives. It calls for an endeavour to immerse oneself in the other's story, to understand their point of view, to convey an understanding of how the gloss they put on experience makes sense to the person in the light of the premises themselves. It implies a form of interested inquiry which holds the premises open for exploration. In this way neither participant in the therapeutic dialogue is bound by the consultee's dominant story or its governing assumptions and presuppositions. Viewed in this manner, the active attempt to understand another's experience can involve its exploration as well as prompting alternative constructions to emerge.

Many therapists who work within this frame in seeking to understand and explore the problem as presented by their 'clients' adopt their frame of reference, thereby limiting the range of possible exploration. While it is vital to gain an understanding of the other's world, change is likely to be limited to the extent that therapists limit their attention solely to the consultee's frame of reference. A focus on helping people to explore the presenting problem as they see it, on clarifying by means of empathic communication, or even on confronting them with contradictions in their communication, will not necessarily disrupt the behaviour patterns and belief systems which constitute their difficulty, let alone create new horizons of possibility. This is because, by adopting the other's framework as their point of reference, therapists are in danger of being bounded or governed by the other's view of reality and thereby unwittingly ratifying it.

Again, while it is necessary to understand the other's perspective, an exclusive focus on understanding the content of their communication encourages a transactional dynamic whereby there is no mutual search for transformative understanding but, rather, the other determines the nature of the transaction, implicitly defining what is to be discussed, explored or avoided. People seek confirmation of their beliefs; they try to elicit particular behaviour from others; they tend to avoid exploration of painful or threatening material. If this occurs in therapy, change or growth of understanding is less likely to occur — they are simply continuing to dwell within the belief system or mode of transaction which comprises their problem.

Unfortunately, many counsellors unknowingly collude in this, thereby limiting their potential effectiveness. By endeavouring to be understanding, to reflect understanding and to facilitate exploration of the 'client's' chosen themes, they restrict themselves to their frame of reference, rather than responding to it from a superordinate framework. As a result, they are prevented from establishing a situation which would enable the other to examine their behaviour from a new perspective, to draw new distinctions which might trigger the evolution of new meanings. Rather, the 'client's' narrative, together with the discursive formations in which it is embedded, remain unchallenged, and a solution is sought within the story's terms — thereby circumscribing the teller's options.

Paradoxically, the activity of helping and launching the other on a journey of self-discovery may itself serve to reinforce the problem experienced by the consultee. The placement of a person in the subject position of patient or client implicitly locates the problem within the person, thereby potentially attributing ownership of the problem to him or her. This can encourage interiorisation of the problem, thereby confirming the presupposition of the self as constituting the problem and the individual as responsible for it (or its amelioration). This individualising focus set within a discourse of individual responsibility may render both therapist and consultee oblivious to the socio-cultural constitution of the difficulty or its location in adverse social conditions. Further, the very practices prescribed by traditional therapies (self-evaluation, self-scrutiny) precisely parallel the practices whereby people are ushered into limiting subject positions.

The re-visioning frame and meta-communication

In the previous section, I suggested that therapeutic change is likely to be limited if the therapist remains immured within the consultee's frame of reference. What is required is a superordinate frame, one in terms of which the therapist responds to the other's narrative, in which the narrative is recontextualised, thereby triggering the development of new meaning and opening up visions of the possible. Specifically, problem dissolution and the evolution of new meanings is most likely to occur in a context which is both receptive and provides responses which:

1. bring the other to attend *to* rather than *from* their beliefs and presuppositions;
2. have them explore their assumptive world from a new perspective;
3. prompt the emergence of new ways of construing experience and changed interpersonal attributions; and

4. promote a questioning of the restraints imposed by beliefs which have been taken for granted as true.

For this to occur, three superordinate skills seem necessary:

1. the ability to construct a transactional context which involves the participant(s) in the activity of being different;
2. the ability to focus beyond the 'client's' here-and-now communication and behaviour by systematically relating it to a higher order framework, thereby reframing it and transforming its meaning; and
3. the ability not only to communicate empathic understanding but to communicate about the consultee's communication, or comment on its connotations.

In this way, the therapist can maintain a receptive stance while also offering statements, questions and frames which might generate new distinctions and meanings — a form of meta-communication.

On the therapeutic importance of meta-communication
Any communication can be treated as something to be understood in its own right. It can also be responded to as a member of some other category of behaviour. A person's request for a hug, for example, may be responded to as such, or classified as an instance of dependency. Similarly, in therapy the helpee's communication may be responded to with understanding, or the therapist may adopt a meta-perspective — for example, by citing the communication as evidence of another category of behaviour — an instance, perhaps, of a transactional style which might cause conflict with others or of a misperception which contributes to the person's distress.

As I have already indicated, tacitly to accept by responding understandingly to what another says serves to ratify it along with its attendant governing constructs. To examine the communication (however understandingly) and to communicate about it does not have this effect. To respond to a communication by treating it as an instance of a super-ordinate class of behaviour places that communication in a new context, thus tending to disrupt automatic patterns of interpretation, attribution or transaction. While Haley (1963) discusses this as the imposition of a therapeutic paradox, it can more simply be seen as changing the contextual embedding of a behaviour or of an interpretive attribution, and thus its meaning.

The ability to 'meta-communicate' and to adopt a 'second-order' perspective (Watzlawick et al. 1967) is therefore of particular importance in therapy. It enables the therapist to avoid becoming entrapped in the other's world and triggers a shift in the way the person organises their world. Instead of their being allowed to attend *from* their constructs, thereby having these same constructs confirmed, by means of therapeutic meta-communication people can be enabled to attend to their constructions from an alternate perspective, thereby bringing their world-model and behaviour into question. The shift of perspective necessitated by meta-communication serves to highlight previously unnoticed connections between behavioural events, beliefs and feelings as well as to disrupt previously automatic behavioural sequences.

Establishing a framework in terms of which the therapist communicates about the clients' communication would thus appear to be of central importance to the change process.

On therapeutic frames and their implications

The ability to metacommunicate, or as Efran and Clarfield (1992) would have it, to respond orthogonally, requires that the therapist work within some framework of understanding or theoretical frame. One cannot, indeed, not have a theory. All therapists act within the bounds of some theory of human nature, of human problem formation, its genesis and cure, and within the parameters of some theory of therapeutic procedure. Gergen (1994: 239) talks of how transaction within this frame necessarily involves a process of hegemonic narrative replacement in which the process must inevitably result in the slow but inevitable replacement of the client's story with that of the therapist. The client's story does not remain a free-standing reflection of truth, but rather, as questions are asked and answered, descriptions and explanations reframed, and affirmation and doubt disseminated by the therapist, the client's narrative is either destroyed or incorporated — but in any event replaced — by the professional account.

I find this an unconvincing overgeneralisation, one which is based on an over-literal translation of the narrative concept, and a confusion between theories of problem formation on the one hand and therapeutic practice on the other. It overlooks the complexity of meaning-generation via conversational interchange, confounds the inevitability of working within a frame with the imposition of a solution, and flies in the face of Maturana's concept of the impossibility of instructive interaction (the impossibility of any direct uninterpreted transference of meaning from one person to another). It is, overall, a strangely modernist statement for a constructionist to make, suggesting as it does a lineal conveyor-belt notion of information transfer.

No school of therapy has an invariant narrative which it seeks to impose on the client in a process akin to ideological conversion. Certainly, we are inevitably involved in influencing the production of meaning in our consultee's life, and undoubtedly, therapeutic interpretation is heavily laden with the presuppositions of the therapist, as Gergen avers (1992: 3). As one engages with another, their experience is ineluctably reinterpreted within the frame of our interpersonal repertoire, utilising words which emerge from, or are sourced within, the constituent concepts of that repertoire. We cannot but shape that of which we speak. However, the articulation of a response within this frame hardly constitutes an imposition or the take-over of another's narrative — even if that other comes to use some of the same concepts. And while therapeutic interpretations may be heavily laden with the presuppositions of the therapist, this hardly constitutes narrative replacement.

All therapies provide a conceptual frame which will hopefully enable people to view their experience from a novel perspective, thus opening up opportunities for new ways of construing the events of their lives. Gergen's point confounds this with the imposition of a solution, an imperialistic colonisation. The crucial issue is the nature of the frame (some being more prescriptive, subordinating and limiting than others) rather than the fact of there being a frame. The implied notion that one should be somehow neutral and not allow one's viewpoint into one's engagement with the other, aside from its impossibility, smacks of the very hegemonic superiority that post-colonial critics are seeking to undermine.

A note on colonialism and psychotherapy as regulatory praxis

My critique of the notion of narrative replacement is not to deny that a process of colonisation can occur in therapy. It is beguilingly easy for therapists to create, via their questioning, the version they think they perceive. At their best, if treated as possible hypotheses, where these versions fit for the client, they allow for the drawing of new distinctions or punctuations or experience which enable them to generate new, less problematic possibilities for themselves. At their worst, they represent a circular activity in which the therapist finds the patterns they hypothesise to be there and attempts to impose these — a form of intellectual colonialism (Amundson and Stewart 1993; Hoffman 1993; McCarthy and Byrne 1988). This can lead to a fixity or stereotypy of both thinking and discourse which can potentially limit the consultee's opportunity to forge alternative meanings, solutions and narratives for themselves. As Amundson and Stewart (1993: 113) would have it, 'If under the temptation of certainty, specified knowledge and expertise is held fast, the selection process becomes restricted'.

The problem of colonising interaction is, however, yet more subtle. Psychotherapy is inescapably a product of the ethos prevailing at a given historical period and the theoretical conventions of the times. It is a culturally constructed technology inscribed with the canonical assumptions of the culture, its paradigmatic beliefs and disciplinary practices. To paraphrase Jerome Bruner (1990), given that psychotherapy is immersed in culture, it must be organised around those meaning-making and meaning-using processes that connect the person to culture. As he writes,

> because it is a reflection of culture, it partakes in the culture's way of valuing as well as its way of knowing. In fact it *must* do so, for the culture's normatively oriented institutions — its laws, its educational institutions, its family structures — serve to enforce folk psychology.
>
> (ibid.: 4)

The word 'enforce' leads to a notion of psychotherapy as a normalising discipline implicitly caught up in maintaining a given social order, as Foucault (1979) would suggest, and therefore implicated in the regulation of people. As Michael White (1991), drawing on Foucauldian concepts, has argued, modern psychotherapies are infused with ideologically saturated regimes of truth specifying particular power relations between consultant and consultee and which also govern the nature of the interaction (cf. House's Chapter 9 and Hart's Chapter 23, this volume) — that is, what may be discussed *and* the mode of interaction. Not only is the consultee initially placed in a subordinate position, but the process can entail particular techniques of discursive regulation or practices of power which, in turn, produce and reproduce those rules and practices implicated in the maintenance of specific technologies of the self. Further, the very practices prescribed by psychotherapy (self-evaluation, self-scrutiny, self-regulation) precisely parallel the practices whereby people are recruited into limiting subject positions.

In this light, psychotherapy may be regarded as, at the very least, potentially if not necessarily regulative. That is, it may position individuals to become complicit in their own subordination by implicitly inducing them to conform to specifications of personhood derived from dominant assumptions of normality, limiting role prescriptions or moral codes governing exemplary ways of being

— discursive formations which problematised their experience in the first place. As Nikolas Rose (1990) asserts, therapy may well recruit people into engaging in practices or technologies of self in which they attempt to discipline, govern or change themselves in relation to socially mandated specifications of personhood while attention is drawn away from both the social location of difficulties and oppressive discursive practices.

If, as a socially sanctioned disciplinary technology, modern psychotherapeutic practice does unreflectively reproduce dominant discourses and mechanisms of control while masking inegalitarian regimes of truth, if the practice implicates the subjects of the discipline in their own subjection (Foucault 1979, 1988), it thereby exercises limiting, subjugating and iatrogenic effects. Its very instantiation of self-scrutiny draws attention to the personal and encourages self-doubt while excluding attention to discursive positioning. In this way (and even taking into account the relational focus of family therapy), it embodies an individualising ethic, simultaneously privileging liberal-humanistic notions of self, agency and autonomy on the one hand and a democratic, socially normative and conforming ethic on the other.

Within the above frame, psychotherapy may thus be plausibly construed as an ideologically driven practice which supports and is supported by the institutions of our society, may serve as an instrument of social control preserving the dominant culture, maintains inequitable, disempowering or subordinating social conditions, practices and arrangements constitutive of the problems people experience (Cushman 1990; White 1991). In this view, psychotherapy may act to perpetuate the causes of the problems it seeks to treat by confirming and normalising oppressive or problematising social beliefs, norms and mores.

FROM NARRATIVE TO DISCURSIVE THERAPY

The remainder of this chapter will discuss the move to narrative therapies before moving on to explore the idea of *discursive* therapy — one that privileges an exploration of the discursive regimes by which people are positioned rather than being reproductive of self-interrogative practices. The critique of modern psychotherapeutic practice has prompted the development of collaborative rather than top-down or interventionist approaches to therapeutic practice. These are deconstructive in spirit, and they avoid objectivist assumptions, as illustrated by a number of the contributors to this volume. Drawing on a range of postmodern and post-structuralist ideas, they are distinguished by a corresponding shift away from models:

1. which attribute privileged knowledge to the therapist; and
2. in which the therapist as objective expert acts on the other to produce change.

The stance towards therapy which informs the above quotation entails what I have called a receptive stance, and what Anderson and Goolishian (1992) thought of as working from a position of 'not knowing'. It implies a wanting to understand, a receptiveness towards and curiosity about the other's construction of experience, together with an active searching for (and openness to) the not-yet-said, the yet-to-unfold, rather than a reductive reframing of the other's communication in accordance with some predetermined theoretical frame. The development of therapies consonant with this stance has been influenced by

1. the language turn in the social sciences with its emphasis on the language-constituted nature of 'reality'; and
2. the parallel thesis that human action is situated in a socially constructed world, and that language provides the matrix for human understanding and experiencing.

The concurrent understanding on the part of therapists of a post-foundational persuasion is that they cannot directly know the 'cause' of a problem, and their role in producing a reading or version of that problem has prompted their realisation that they are ineluctably working in the world of meaning — its siting in discourse, its construction and its interpretation. This has been accompanied by a focus on how people construe their lives and relationships, as well as in seeking an understanding of this via the accounts they give of experience — their self-narratives.

Accordingly, therapists drawing on narrative and social constructionist concepts construe people as living out narratives negotiated in the social arena, actively constructed in discourse with others, drawing on culturally provided constructs and utilising the genres, canons and rules of the culture for the negotiation of meaning. These psychotherapists have accordingly evolved therapeutic frames derived from hermeneutics, constructionism, and literary and narrative theory. Within this framework, one prominent approach is to liken people's stories to texts, the meanings of which can be 'read' or interpreted in dialogue, and which are amenable to deconstruction and re-storying. In this way, the metaphor of the therapist as co-author of a new, less problematic narrative has been born (Schafer 1981; Spence 1982; White and Epston 1989).

From this perspective, therapy is viewed as a form of narrative construction with change inhering in the emergence of new personal realities and narratives. As Goolishian (1990: 4) put it:

Change in therapy as the dialogical creation of new narrative rests in the capacity to re-relate the events of our lives in the context of new and different meaning. We live in and through the narrative identities that we develop in conversation with each other. The skill of the therapist is the expertise to participate in this process.

On narrative prescriptiveness

The narrative commitment to viewing the therapeutic encounter as a milieu for the creative generation of meaning represents a major break from modern approaches based on diagnosing and treating identifiable problems residing within the person. The shift is from a preoccupation with veridicality to verisimilitude, from truth to narrative meaning and its effect on lives. Ironically however, the re-storying metaphor employed in much narrative therapy retains the individualist cast in that the focus remains on the 'inside story' — an internal model of function or 'narrative' located within the mind of the individual person. The commitment to narrative can reinforce an ethic of individualism to the exclusion of the socio-cultural. It also implies a narrative essentialism vested in a reification of self, its reconstruction and reformation, or the discovery of a new true self or core identity via self-exploration and self-understanding.

To the extent, too, that the narrative construct is itself singular, it is potentially prone to a form of narrative rigidity. That is, it may promote the fashioning of a unitary, integrated identity or self-story within the bounds of conventional narrative roles which limit rather than expand choices or the capacity to operate flexibly across different contexts. Thus, Ken Gergen and I have argued for a version of therapy which privileges narrative multiplicity over narrative singularity:

> Each narrative of the self may function well in certain circumstances but lead to miserable outcomes in others. To have only a single means to make self intelligible, then, is to limit the range of relationships or situations in which one can function satisfactorily.
>
> (Gergen and Kaye 1992: 179)

The disavowal of expertise

Associated with the 'not-knowing' stance advocated by Harry Goolishian (1990) is a rather simplistic disavowal of expertise arising from a crass misinterpretation of his profound, hermeneutically derived dialogic position on the part of many professing narrative therapists. Given the impossibility of gaining direct unmediated knowledge of any phenomenon, it is clear that we cannot 'know' another's experience and therefore we are in this sense not experts. Yet the very ability to formulate or understand this concept represents a form of specialist knowledge — or expertise. As 'constructionist' or narrative therapists, this presumably enables us to construct a dialogic frame in which new meanings can emerge. The skilled therapist *is* an expert in this sense. To disown this, to disown knowledge (which is in any case socially constructed) or to disown that one works within the bounds of a given orientation is simply fraudulent.

The proposition that we cannot gain access to an objective reality does not require the abandonment of knowledge or expertise, or of having an informed theory of helping. Further, as Efran and Clarfield (1992: 207–8) point out,

> To act as if all views are equal and that we-as-therapists have not favourites among them undercuts the very sort of frank exchange we want and expect to have with our clients. It patronises them, compromises our own integrity, and treats open dialogue as if it was an endangered species needing 'hothouse' protection.

The contribution of the therapist's point of view is hardly in itself colonising, nor does it deny either mutuality or respect for the consultee's world of reality. The withholding of one's viewpoint, on the other hand, is not merely a prescription for therapeutic impotence but itself constitutes a response — one cannot *not* respond. It can further be seen as disrespectful and condescending. What is required, rather, is the further expertise to develop a reflexive position towards our own stance, its implications and consequences.

The above points act as a counterpoint to the totalising concerns raised by particular interpretations of post-structuralism and feminist critical theory that working with people from a base of 'expert knowledge' might be intrinsically oppressive, and indeed that therapy may be reproductive of oppressive practices of power.

Perhaps an end to the overgeneralised ideological debates around therapy as a practice of power might occur if therapy were to be construed — and conducted — not as a top-down activity enshrining inequity but as a collaborative endeavour that relies on the interweaving of the particular 'expertise' and awarenesses of each participant, in a frame designed to promote the generation of new meanings. While hierarchy is unlikely to be eliminated in therapy, this frame allows one to view the therapeutic transaction as a process in which there is a shift from hierarchic skew to mutuality. It also displaces the notion of acting instrumentally on the other to change them in favour of the collaborative attempt to open up new possibilities and choices.

What is required, however, is the further expertise to develop a reflexive position towards our own stance, its implications and consequences.

Discursive therapy
Implicit in the narrative metaphor employed by Goolishian (1990) is also a dialogic position which emphasises meaning as being created via conversational interchange. According to Anderson and Goolishian (1988: 372), therapy is

> a linguistic event that takes place in what we call a therapeutic conversation. The therapeutic conversation is a mutual search and exploration through dialogue, a two way exchange, a criss-crossing of ideas in which new meanings are continually evolving toward the dissolving of problems ... Change is the evolution of new meaning through dialogue.

To employ the evocative phrase coined by Louis Sass (1994), therapeutic change does not merely rely on the malleability of reality but involves an active creation of meaning. In this sense, therapy may be construed as a generative and constructive (rather than simply remedial) process of meaning creation which seeks to forge new understandings via the juxtaposition of multiple perspectives in conversational interchange. It is a process which involves the reinterpretation or resymbolisation of discourse in a novel context — one which

1. differs from that which conventionally governs discourse in the area; and
2. creates novel distinctions and thereby generates new meanings.

In this way, generative inquiry can point to a possible world — 'something disclosed in front of the text rather than hidden behind it', as Ricouer (1971) would have it; or in Goolishian`s (1990) words, 'the not-yet-said'. This process could not occur without the exchange of linguistically and culturally available constructs. In the process of therapeutic interchange, we perforce use what Bruner (1990: 11) calls 'symbolic systems' already in place, already 'there', deeply entrenched in culture and language. They constitute a very special kind of communal toolkit whose tools, once used, make the user a reflection of the community. In this light, a further set of concepts needs to be considered in delineating a discursive therapy, the cultural specifications inscribed in the socially constructed and historically situated networks of ideas, meanings and beliefs acquired by virtue of membership of our culture(s).

These networks of ideas and associated practices — discourses — make us subject to normative cultural prescriptions, thereby positioning us to think or act in given ways, and are in this way important determinants of behaviour.

That is, as Zimmerman and Dickerson (1994: 235) remind us, 'cultural stories, far from being neutral, lead to constructions of a normative view, generally reflecting the dominant culture's specification, from which people know themselves and against which people compare themselves'. Indeed, as Bruner (1990: 58) avers, 'the very structure of our lexicon, while it may not force us to code human events in a particular way, certainly predisposes us to be culturally canonical'.

Given this gloss, narrative- and language-based approaches to therapy, with their implication that there is nothing outside the text, are both limited and limiting — for they de-politicise the broader social context by which people are positioned, with a consequent lack of attention to inequitable social arrangements, people's material conditions and, indeed, power imbalances within a range of social groupings.

Thus, Fish (1993) points out that changing a destructive narrative to a more positive narrative within the same cultural discourse is not identical to getting free of that cultural discourse. Criticising the tendency of some narrative therapies to isolate the therapist-family system from any social, historical economic or institutional context, he writes:

> Splitting off a separate world of language divorced from any notion of a relevant social and material realm, they enforce a conceptual blackout which begins at the edges of the family's story or conversation. There is nothing for the therapist who operates solely within these models to mentally see, hear or touch but the content and arrangement of the words the family uses while in the therapist's office.
>
> (Fish 1993: 228)

This argues for a greater socio-political awareness on the part of therapists, one which enables people to challenge the truth regimes to which they are subject and in terms of which they govern themselves. For example, to the extent that self-surveillance is implicated in the maintenance of problem-saturated subject positions, a therapeutic orientation embodying the above principle would shift the focus of interaction from an exploration of individual experience to examine its discursive location. From this perspective, while it may be useful to have people reclaim aspects of experience previously marginalised in the interests of conformity to a dominant narrative, it is equally important to set a context in which people are at the same time enabled to examine the effects of dominant socially constructed value constellations and behaviour specifications on their lives.

While showing no disbelief in the consultee's troubled story or its experiential veracity, this orientation would:

1. seek to enable the consultee to examine the aspects of experience or action possibilities marginalised or excluded by the dominant story;
2. put in question the practices of self associated with problem-saturated, limiting or impoverished subject positions;
3. work towards exploring the dominant socio-cultural discursive formations and associated practices by which the person is positioned rather than merely changing meanings within the dominant cultural frame; and
4. create the conditions which would enable consultees to question and take a position towards these discourses.

Overall, it offers a temporal narrative experience in which the author's positioning rather than the author is the centre of attention. This occurs in the context of an emancipatory therapeutic climate in which the therapist:

1. is curious, receptive and ready to learn from the other;
2. maintains awareness of the political, socially reproductive consequences of their practices; and
3. avoids imposition of limiting role prescriptions, rigid theoretical frames or practices in which are inscribed privileged versions of what constitutes the normal.

TOWARDS A SOCIALLY CRITICAL POSITION

The word 'psychotherapy' unavoidably carries overtones on acting instrumentally on another in order to remedy some psychological defect or deficiency. In this chapter, however, I have tried to advance some ideas informed by a post-structuralist and constructionist awareness which provide a break from regulatory normalising and socio-culturally reproductive modernist practices. While this goal is partly realised in narrative and collaborative approaches to therapy, I have argued for a discursive therapy. The difference between this deconstructive socially critical position and the narrative position is that the narrative still largely locates problems within an individual meaning-structure, whereas a critical discursive approach seeks to examine the socio-culturally constructed discursive complexes and practices by which people are positioned, or the social conditions in which they find themselves.

My position clearly overlaps with that of theorists whose concern is with the political processes of social control, and who consider it an imperative explicitly to redress discrimination, oppression or marginalisation in their therapeutic endeavours. This can run the danger of the top-down prescriptiveness criticised in modernist practices. The discursive approach creates a context in which the other, by examining their discursive positionings, may become alerted to their regulatory implications, thus opening up new meanings, perceptions and action options. However, removing the problem from the person and placing it in their discursive position may not be sufficient. It still leaves responsibility with the individual to change, and locates the problem *with* the person if not within. And this may position us as agents of stasis. In social justice terms, might we not, as Dulwich Centre does and the Family Centre Group at Lower Hutt, New Zealand do, work to create a context in which the marginalised gain voice in a culturally congruent fashion? And strive to create a context in which minorities are heard, become visible and able to make a difference, at least in their local communities, rather than remaining submerged in the dominant culture?

There will always be a cohort of therapists solely interested in working with individuals and their personal problems. In this way, psychotherapy will be limited by its governing paradigm. However, many have over the years worked with larger systems. While it would be grandiose to think we should 'change the world' and its political structures, thus righting all wrongs and ridding ourselves of all inequities, there is a place for us to be involved in social change — for some of us, perhaps, by alerting our colleagues or the public via our writings; for others, working for change in socio-political structures.

Bearing in mind Sawicki's (1991) caution that no discourse is inherently liberating or oppressive, it behoves all of us as practitioners not blindly to follow (or merely seek to refine) practice prescriptions, but rather to scrutinise the institutional and disciplinary knowledges by which we are positioned. While we may never be able to establish a position outside the discursive field from which accurately to view our practice, we *can* get outside particular disciplinary discourses in order to question their (and our) practices of power. The readiness to adopt a stance or metaperspective towards the discursive prescriptions which regulate our practice might serve, at least partially, to mediate against unreflective and unwittingly iatrogenic practice.

In turn, an ongoing critique of its own power-knowledge may help prevent postmodern and post-structuralist deconstructive practice from forging a new hegemony with its own regime of political correctness and certitude — a new superordinate and subordinating order of surveillance. Perhaps, too, the paradigm shift mooted at the beginning of this chapter will emerge from a second-order questioning and re-cognising of therapy and its role as a socio-culturally constructed enterprise rather than from a mere sharpening of its practices.

REFERENCES

Amundson, J. and Stewart, K. (1993) Temptations of power and certainty. *Journal of Marital and Family Therapy* 19 (2): 111–23

Anderson, H. (1997) *Conversation, Language, and Possibilities: A Postmodern Approach to Therapy*. New York: Basic Books

Anderson, H. and Goolishian, H. (1988) Human systems as linguistic systems: preliminary and evolving ideas about the implications for clinical theory. *Family Process* 27 (4): 371–93

Anderson, H. and Goolishian, H. (1992) The client is the expert: a not-knowing approach to therapy. In S. McNamee and K. J. Gergen (eds), *Therapy as Social Construction* (pp. 25–39). London: Sage

Berg, I. and de Shazer, S. (1993) Making numbers talk: language in therapy. In S. Friedman (ed.), *The New Language of Change*. New York: Guilford Press

Bruner, J. (1990) *Acts of Meaning*. Cambridge, MA: Harvard University Press

Cecchin, B. (1993) Foreword. In L. Hoffman, *Exchanging Voices: A Collaborative Approach to Family Therapy*. London: Karnac Books

Cross, J. (1994) Politics and family therapy. *Dulwich Centre Newsletter* 1: 7–10

Cushman, P. (1990) Why the self is empty. *American Psychologist* 45: 599–611

Drewery, W. and Winslade, J. (1997) The theoretical story of narrative therapy. In G. Monk, J. Winslade, K. Crocket and D. Epston (eds), *Narrative Therapy in Practice: The Archaeology of Hope*. San Francisco: Jossey-Bass

Efran, J. S. and Clarfield, L. E. (1992) Constructionist therapy: sense and nonsense. In S. McNamee and K. J. Gergen (eds), *Therapy as Social Construction* (pp. 200–17). London: Sage.

Fish, V. (1993) Poststructuralism in family therapy: interrogating the narrative/conversational mode. *Journal of Marital and Family Therapy* 19 (3): 221–32

Foucault, M. (1979) *Discipline and Punish: The Birth of the Prison*. Harmondsworth, Middlesex: Peregrine Books

Foucault, M. (1988) *The Care of the Self: The History of Sexuality Vol. 3*. London: Allen Lane/Penguin Press

Gergen, K. J. (1991) *The Saturated Self: Dilemmas of Identity in Contemporary Life*. New York: Basic Books

Gergen, K. J. (1992) Introduction. In S. McNamee and K. J. Gergen (eds), *Therapy as Social Construction*. London: Sage

Gergen, K. J. (1994) *Realities and Relationships: Soundings in Social Construction*. Cambridge, MA: Harvard University Press

Gergen, K. J. and Kaye, J. D. (1992) Beyond narrative in the negotiation of therapeutic meaning. In S. McNamee and K. J. Gergen (eds), *Therapy as Social Construction*. London: Sage

Goolishian, H. (1990) Therapy as a linguistic system: hermeneutics, narrative and meaning. *The Family Psychologist* 6: 14–45

Haley, J. (1963) *Strategies of Psychotherapy*. New York: Grune and Stratton

Hekman, S. (1990) *Gender and Knowledge: Elements of a Postmodern Feminism*. Cambridge: Polity Press

Hillman, J. and Ventura, M. (1992) *We've had a Hundred Years of Psychotherapy and the World's Getting Worse*. San Francisco: Harper

Hoffman, L. (1993) *Exchanging Voices: A Collaborative Approach to Family Therapy*. London: Karnac Books

Howard, G. (1991) Culture tales: a narrative approach to thinking, cross-cultural psychology and psychotherapy. *American Psychologist* 46 (3): 187–97

John, I. (1998) The scientist-practitioner model: a critical examination. *Australian Psychologist* 33 (1): 24–30

Kaye, J. D. (1990) Toward meaningful research in psychotherapy. *Dulwich Centre Newsletter* (Adelaide) 2: 27–38

Kaye, J. D. (1993) On learning to see through the eyes of another. *The Calgary Participator* 3 (1)

Kaye, J. D. (1996) Towards a discursive psychotherapy. *Changes* 14 (2): 232–7

McCarthy, I. C. and Byrne, N. O'R. (1988) Mis-taken love: conversations on the problem of incest in an Irish context. *Family Process* 27: 181–98

Maturana, H. R. and Varela, F. J. (1988) *The Tree of Knowledge: The Biological Roots of Human Understanding*. Boston, MA: Shambhala Publications

Monk, G. and Drewery, W. (1994) The impact of social constructionist thinking on eclecticism in counsellor education: some personal thoughts. *New Zealand Journal of Counselling* 16 (1): 5–14

Ricouer, P. (1971) The model of the text: meaningful action considered as a text. *Social Research* 38: 529–62

Rose, N. (1990) Psychology as a 'social science'. In I. Parker and J. Shotter (eds), *Deconstructing Social Psychology*. London: Routledge

Russell, R. L. and Van den Broek, P. (1992) Changing narrative schemas in psychotherapy. *Psychotherapy* 29 (3): 344–54

Sass, L. A. (1994) The epic of disbelief: the postmodernist turn in psychoanalysis. *Partisan Review* 61 (1): 96–110

Sawicki, J. (1991) *Disciplining Foucault: Feminism, Power and the Body*. London: Routledge

Schafer, R. (1981) *Narrative Actions in Psychoanalysis*. Worcester, MA: Clark University Press

Schon, D. (1983) *The Reflective Practitioner: How Professionals Think in Action*. London: Maurice Temple Smith

Spence, D. (1982) *Narrative Truth and Historical Truth*. New York: Norton

Tomm, K. and others (1992) Therapeutic distinctions in an on-going therapy. In S. McNamee and K. J. Gergen (eds), *Therapy as Social Construction*. London: Sage

Watzlawick, P., Beavin, J. and Jackson, D. (1967) *Pragmatics of Human Communication*. New York: Norton

White, M. (1991) Deconstruction and therapy. *Dulwich Centre Newsletter* (Adelaide) 3: 21–40

White, M. and Epston, D. (1989) *Literate Means to Therapeutic Ends*. Adelaide: Dulwich Centre Publications

Zimmerman, J. L. and Dickerson, V. C. (1994) Using a narrative metaphor: implications for theory and clinical practice. *Family Process* 33: 233–45

25
SOUL IN PSYCHOTHERAPY: AN INDIVIDUAL ACCOUNT

GAEL ROWAN[†]

In the final analysis, we count for something only because of the essential we embody, and if we do not embody that, life is wasted.

(C. G. Jung)

The following piece is about the 'essential we embody', our uniqueness, our individuality, our soul, and about the ways in which the theory and practice of psychotherapy facilitate or hinder its embodiment. I will argue that the capacity of the therapist to experience soul in relationship is fundamental and constitutes a core condition for the healing of a client's deepest wounds. Soul *is* individuality and, as James Hillman says, expresses itself through pathology. Without the willingness to allow soul into the therapeutic relationship the therapist will inevitably miss the essence of the client, their individuality, soul and deepest wound. The therapist who is not prepared to meet with soul is in danger of retraumatising the wound rather than healing the soul.

Soul is not an idea or a *belief* in something intangible; it is rather an *experience* of something ineffable. Soul is part of the mystery at the centre of human existence and as such is indefinable, though we may be able to point to it; and when we experience soul it is unmistakable. Hillman, in his book *The Soul's Code*, argues passionately that,

> ...we need to make clear that today's paradigm for understanding a human life, the interplay of genetics and environment, omits something essential — the particularity you feel to be you. By accepting the idea that I am the effect of a subtle buffeting between hereditary and societal forces, I reduce myself to a result. The more my life is accounted for by what already occurred in my chromosomes, by what my parents did or didn't do, and by my early years now long past, the more my biography is the story of a victim. I am living a plot written by my genetic code, ancestral heredity, traumatic occasions, parental unconsciousness, societal accidents.
>
> (Hillman 1997: 6)

This paradigm is insidious and pervasive, accepted and adhered to by many psychotherapists, including some who call themselves 'transpersonal'.

For the client there is little therapeutic worth in the therapist's *belief* in soul;

† Chapter first appeared in *ipnosis*, no. 2, Summer 2001, and is reprinted with kind permission of the author.

holding a theoretical framework in which soul exists is not enough. The therapist must be capable of experiencing soul in relationship with the client. It is this possibility of meeting in soul that allows the possibility of the deepest healing. Many people, including psychotherapists, are afraid to meet and be met in this way. It requires a willingness to let go of all masks, roles and preconceptions of who we are. For the therapist it means letting go of theories and ideas about not only who the client is, but who the *therapist* is. Soul meeting means a willingness to be revealed, to stand psychologically naked with another; a willingness to not only facilitate change within the client, but to be changed oneself. This demands a great deal of the therapist, indeed it demands *all* of the therapist. It is perhaps hardly surprising, therefore, that some therapists seem to prefer the safety and comfort of the known, and that even those who profess a belief in soul subject their clients to a subtle reductionism in their understanding and use of the transferential relationship. This tendency is apparent in much of the therapeutic literature and I have experienced it myself with a 'transpersonal' therapist.

Developmental theories are useful and necessary, but they are not the whole truth. Psychotherapists who hold that we are simply the product of our parental inheritance may take their clients to a point of social adjustment and reasonably healthy personal functioning, which may be all that a particular client is interested in. However, those clients who wish to be *individuals*, to individuate, must pay attention to their individuality, to their soul, and must find a therapist who is able to *experience* them as an individual. For these clients a psychotherapist who continually reduces them to being the product of their parents may be not only limiting but damaging.

Relevant here is my own experience with a therapist who continually reduced my experience to pathology arising from my relationship with my father. He claimed he understood me very well, and perhaps in terms of the parental transferential relationship, he did; but I didn't *feel* understood. I felt put into a box that was too small for me and which denied a great deal of my experience. I feel confirmed here by Firman and Gila when they write in their book *The Primal Wound*:

> ...the client who is so sensitive about being misunderstood *is* in fact being misunderstood at some level. It is nonempathic to side-step culpability here, claiming the client is simply projecting the infantile past and is therefore overly sensitive or is misperceiving reality. When this type of interpretation is made, the therapist takes on an authoritarian role *vis-à-vis* the client. The therapist, and the therapist alone, presumes to possess the objective truth about the relationship — clearly a nonempathic stance.
>
> (Firman and Gila 1997: 237–8)

This is exactly what happened with my therapist, who actually said, 'You have to trust in my objectivity. How can I support you if you don't trust in my objectivity?'. To me this shows a profound misunderstanding of the therapeutic process. In taking this stance, rather than relating to me as an individual, which is precisely what was needed, he was attempting to fit me into his world, rather than truly to understand mine. If I had trusted his objectivity over my own reality I would have betrayed my individuating process and betrayed my soul.

What, then, is the relevance of theories of human development and of the transferential relationship within this broader, deeper, soulful context of human being? The connecting factor, it seems to me, is pathology, and in particular the primal wound. The primal wound is a wound to our individuality and arises in infancy for all of us because our parents, no matter how much they love us, cannot completely respect our individuality if they are not completely in contact with their own individuality. A wound to individuality is a wound to the soul, and in contacting soul we contact the wound. The soul is innate: we are born with our own individual uniqueness; the wound is developmental, it arises out of the relationship of our individual soul with our parents and the environment. In this context I see the transference as the vehicle of expression of the unconscious developmental conditions in which the wounding occurred. But the transference is not only an action replay of the relationship with the parents; it also has soulful or archetypal roots. 'Transference always has its archetypal roots ... although transference is essentially archetypal, the archetypes manifest in specific personal circumstances. ... The very phenomenon of transference is archetypal' (Jacoby 1984: 82). So the transference is the playing out, within the therapeutic relationship, of the dynamics of the relationship with the parents, and as such it points to what is *beyond* that relationship; that is, the soul. The transference can be seen as the vehicle, and the relationship with the parents as the material, through which the archetypes express themselves and through which soul is made.

In working with the transference, we as therapists have a choice about where we put the emphasis. Do we, as psychoanalysis does, emphasise the personal experiences of the past? Or do we focus on the deeper purpose, on what the soul might be trying to express, on what it means for the healing process that this particular transference is being manifested by the unconscious in this particular therapeutic relationship? The form the transference takes tells us something about what the soul needs to compensate to bring balance and wholeness through the relationship between therapist and client. In my view, we need to pay attention to both sides based on the particular needs of each particular client. However, there is a danger in ignoring the more soulful, archetypal view, of missing the client's individuality, missing the soul, and reducing them to a mere product of the parents. If we wish to work with the deepest wound then we must be willing to experience soul, to see beyond the specific material of the transference, beyond the parents, beyond the personal, and into the transpersonal. The working through, or suffering of, the transference itself is the manifestation of the inner workings of the soul. I think it is in the capacity to see beyond the transference that a different-enough relational experience is created between therapist and client, facilitating healing of the soul rather than retraumatisation of the wound.

This healing requires immense sensitivity and gentleness as well as subtlety and depth on the part of the therapist. It also requires great courage and trust on the part of the client. Most importantly, it requires that both therapist and client be willing to bare their souls. This baring of souls means that each must be willing to be seen. It is different for each participant in the therapeutic process, as for the client it may mean working with the actual content of her experience whereas for the therapist it is likely to be more subtle, involving less revelation of the details of her life. Whatever form it takes, and it will be different for each individual as it is an individual process, the willingness to stand naked with another is essential. The other side of this, because the way to the soul is through the wound, is that in order to work with clients at this level the therapist also needs to be able bear their own wound. In revealing the soul, the wound is revealed; in feeling the joy of the soul, the pain of the wound is felt. The level of our intimacy with our own pain is *exactly* the level of intimacy we are capable of with another. The depth to which I am able to *bear* my soul is the depth to which I am able to be authentic; the depth to which I am able to *bare* my soul is the depth to which I am able to be empathic. This capacity for authenticity and empathy determines the depth to which the relationship is therapeutic.

In conclusion, I have tried to show that soul is both the source of individuality and intimately related to our deepest wounding, and that psychological theories which do not include soul are in danger of missing the individual and thereby lessening the effectiveness of therapeutic practice. I see the willingness to allow soul into the therapeutic relationship as a core condition of the most effective therapy. This has profound implications for the training of psychotherapists and the role of accreditation. The question of how it is possible to train therapists in the art of soulful meeting is a crucial one if psychotherapy is to meet the deepest needs of the soul to individuate.

REFERENCES

Firman, J and Gila, A (1997) *The Primal Wound*. Albany, NY: SUNY Press
Hillman, J. (1997) *The Soul's Code: In Search of Character and Calling*. London: Bantam
Jacoby, M. (1984) *The Analytic Encounter: Transference and Human Relationship*. Inner City Books

26
REFLECTIONS AND ELABORATIONS ON 'POST-PROFESSIONALISED' THERAPY PRACTICE

RICHARD HOUSE[†]

In my book *Therapy Beyond Modernity* (House 2003), several chapters from which the current chapter is a distillation, I attempt to lay bear some of the self-serving effects of individualised therapy's profession-centred 'regime of truth' (see also my Chapter 13, this volume). I will first summarise some of the main conclusions to emerge from *Therapy Beyond Modernity* (hereafter *TbM*) in its wide-ranging critique of what I call 'profession-centred therapy'. These conclusions will then serve as a back-drop for my subsequent elaboration of some possible characteristics of a viable 'post-professional' therapy world. I maintain that it is only through the principled and enlightened development of *a post-professional ethos* for therapeutic help that the kinds of profession-centred abuses outlined in *TbM* can be transcended.

'PROFESSION-CENTRED' THERAPY UNDER SCRUTINY

The question of professionalisation and 'scientification'
What I have come to call 'didactic' professionalisation refers to an institutional, dominator-hierarchical process which routinely becomes antithetical to the individual empowerment and responsibility-taking of both practitioners and clients (cf., for example, Postle's Chapter 17, this volume). For House and Totton (1997b: 1), the institutional professionalisation of the therapy field 'would be a disaster' — a conclusion which can at first appear to be counterintuitive, and which is by no means reached merely, or even primarily, because of the many reasons so ably articulated by Mowbray (1995) (stifled creativity and innovation, an increasing preponderance of 'defensive' psychotherapy, restricted entry to the field and an associated 'gentrification' of therapy, and so on). (These and other related arguments are fully articulated in both House and Totton 1997a and in the chapters constituting Part IB of this volume.) In *TbM*, I argue that the institutional sedimentation of therapy's professionalised conventions actively creates an increasingly abusive therapeutic environment, thereby rendering therapy far more likely to enmesh clients in its thrall, and curtailing rather than

† This chapter is extracted and adapted from House, R. (2003) *Therapy Beyond Modernity: Deconstructing and Transcending Profession-Centred Therapy*, London: Karnac, and is reprinted by kind permission of the author and Karnac Books.

enhancing client freedom in the process. My concern is that such a professionalisation process, far from being beneficent for clients (as the 'official' rhetoric has it), may well itself be intrinsically abusive, and be doing net harm to the field as whole (cf. Hogan 1979, and his Chapter 16, this volume).

I maintain, further, that there is an important (and heretofore largely ignored) link between didactic professionalisation in the therapy field, on the one hand, and the 'old-paradigm' values and practices of a technocratic, soulless modernity on the other — a theme which recurs from time to time throughout this volume. One notable exception to this 'silence' is Schaef in her much neglected book *Beyond Therapy, Beyond Science*:

> Historically, we have always seen that when an old cultural paradigm is dying and on the verge of collapse, there is a tendency to become more rigid in the old paradigm, *to set up progressively stricter controls*, and to try to kill off new ideas and dissenters through the use of the regulatory and legal arms of the culture ... *As the old paradigm is being challenged professionally, politically, and economically, the arm of regulation and control gets stronger and stronger*.
>
> (Schaef 1992: 226, my emphases)

We should surely be trying to step outside of the conditionings of modernity, and locate our helping/healing practices within an historical, consciousness-evolutionary context, rather than ossifying them into ever tighter 'regimes of institutionalised truth' which can easily become antithetical to human potential development. I maintain that this lethal cocktail — comprising the ideology of modernity, the fear-driven dominator-hierarchical attempt to police the therapy field, and the considerable vested interests (both material and power-related) infusing the whole process — make the ongoing deconstruction of therapy's most hallowed and taken-for-granted assumptions absolutely crucial if we are to avoid creating a self-serving, sometimes abusive, *therapist*-centred practice (cf. my Chapter 9, this volume).

The limitations of theory and the 'core theoretical model'

Technocratic, positivist ways of knowing are, I believe, inherently limited and limiting, and are beginning to give way to far more holistic, participative, tacit-intuitive, and even spiritual-clairvoyant ways of knowing (Hart 1998; Hart et al. 1997). The integration of postmodern thinking with the diverse ideas of, for example, David Bohm, Jacques Derrida, J. W. von Goethe, Martin Heidegger, J. Krishnamurti and Rudolf Steiner (to name but six) offers very considerable possibilities for developing a truly coherent, participative and humane philosophy of living (cf. House 1999) — of which a *post-professional* therapy will be but one aspect.

In recent years, within the therapy field there has been a quite passionate debate about the centrality or otherwise of what is called the 'core theoretical model' (or CTM), particularly in relation to practitioner training (Feltham 1997; Wheeler 1998). There exists a tension, if not a radical incoherence, at the core of most therapy training, for 'the common aim of psychotherapy — autonomy — is belied by the reality of training institutes which demand conformity from trainees, and by psychotherapy which either mystifies clients or subtly converts them to belief in the tenets of the particular approach' (Feltham 1997: 122).

The notion of 'schooling into a regime of truth', or the inculcation of an ideology, is strongly suggested when considering the rationale typically offered in favour of a CTM, described thus by Feltham:

> Failure to embrace one model in depth results in practitioners who are confused, lacking in rigour, and whose knowledge base is thin. Trainees ... must learn and hone the practical and clinical attitudes, skills and techniques associated with a particular approach if they are to become competent practitioners ... They cannot achieve ... maturity without first having had a thorough grounding in a coherent model ... [P]ractitioners should hold strong theoretical positions.
>
> (Feltham 1997: 118)

Within the world-view of modernity, theory is typically clung on to as representing some kind of 'objective truth', promoting methods which are, thereby, assumed to be pretty much infallible. From a critical postmodern stance, perhaps the profession's determination to promulgate CTMs has far more to do with colluding with the anxiety-driven needs for control and certainty than it does a sober and appropriate engagement with the uncomfortable reality of intersubjective relationship and existential uncertainty. Feltham again:

> All therapeutic models are partly fictions ... Many of us cling to an ideological object ... Arguably, all such ideologies act as opiates and *their true function is to infuse us with a reassuring but defensive sense of certainty and direction* in an unpredictable and frightening world.
>
> (ibid.: 120, 123–4 *passim*, my emphasis)

I am certainly not arguing that it is somehow wrong or 'unhealthy' to need comfort in a frightening world; but I *am* arguing that it can hardly lead to very effective or authentic therapeutic practitionership to have what is an emotionally driven security need so successfully camouflaged and obfuscated by a garb of illusory objectivity, and of which not even practitioners themselves seem to be aware. This is one area, then, in which the 'new paradigm' critique of the modernist world-view seems to me to become absolutely crucial (Alcoff 1996; Barratt 1993; Polkinghorne 1990).

Informed consent and the abuses of profession-centred therapy

> The situational difficulty for all clients is that this first encounter is inscrutable ... there is a discrepancy of knowledge between the two parties about what therapy is as a process, ritual or stylised conversation.
>
> (Pilgrim 1997: 117)

In Chapters 3 and 4 of *TbM*, I set out the diverse ways in which I believe the prevailing profession-centred form taken by individualised therapy can become routinely, surreptitiously — and unconsciously — abusive. The question of 'informed consent' is a much neglected yet absolutely core issue in the inherently self-serving and sometimes mesmerising regime of truth that profession-centred therapy can set up. I maintain that it is extremely problematic if not impossible for there to exist anything remotely approaching informed client consent in therapy (see *TbM*, Chapters 2 and 6). And this situation can only be exacerbated in an oversupplied practitioner market in which therapists wishing to make a living compete fiercely for a given client base (Clark 2002), and therefore have a survival-driven vested interest in clients succumbing to the entangling accoutrements of profession-centred therapy with its common tendency to encourage long-term work via the artificially frame-engendered dynamics of attachment and dependency (cf. *TbM*, Chapter 3).

Therapists very rarely inform clients at the start of therapy that the experience can sometimes be harmful, with there never being any guarantee that a given therapy will not be harmful. Moreover, therapists probably hardly ever tell their new clients that it is impossible for either client or therapist to give informed consent to therapy at the beginning, or that the therapy frame may well encourage the triggering of deep attachment dynamics which might make it very difficult for the client to choose to leave the therapy once they are attached to it (cf. *TbM*, Chapter 6). Clients whose personality disposition leaves them particularly prone to will-subverting *addictive* attachment-behaviour may be especially susceptible in this regard — indeed, this is clearly (and revealingly) a chronically under-researched area in a field which is awash with profession-centred literature. In my experience, moreover, these are extremely thorny and quintessentially ethical issues which (unsurprisingly!) receive no attention whatsoever in the therapy institutions' allegedly comprehensive Codes of Ethics. Denis Postle has been at the forefront of attempts to respond to the inscrutable nature of the therapy experience from the client's point of view (see, for example, his Chapter 17, this volume); and the *Ipnosis* journal has been at the forefront of the recent, welcome and long-overdue attempt to give clients a major voice in commenting upon the nature of therapy and its potential abuses (Alexander and Bates 2002; Sands and Bates 2002; see also Chapters 2, 20 and 30, by Sands, Simpson and Alexander respectively, in this volume).

ELABORATING ON THE 'POST-PROFESSIONAL' ERA

Until such time as the need for individualised, professional therapy has been transcended, perhaps the best we can do is to embrace a deconstructive therapeutic practice (see Parker 1999; see also my Chapter 9 and Kaye's Chapter 24, this volume), and hope and trust that the new millennium will bring forth new cultural forms for supporting people with their difficulties of living. Clearly such an approach requires striking a delicate and sensitive balance between fearless critique, on the one hand, and offering constructive suggestions as to the specific nature that a less self-serving and abusive therapy might take, on the other.

I would describe *a processually deconstructive therapy* as having a goodly proportion of the following distinguishing characteristics (some of which do, of course, overlap with each other). (In Chapter 12 of *TbM*, the following section is heavily referenced and more fully articulated, and the reader is referred to the book for that more detailed elaboration.)

- *noughth*, theoretical or classificatory devices like that which follows would be redundant;
- *first*, it would eschew preconceived theoretical frameworks, having an inclusive, pluralistic approach to 'local knowledges' which values diverse

ways of 'knowing' (cf. Totton's Chapter 11, this volume);

- *second*, it would be founded in a postmodernist, deconstructionist epistemology, rather than a positivistic, modernist one (see, for example, Chapters 7–9 inclusive, this volume);
- *third*, it would gravitate towards a new paradigm, spiritual, transpersonal ontology (cf. Clarkson's Chapter 7, this volume), eschewing a one-sided egotistical individualism, recognising that healing practices from *every* culture and epoch are of value, and attempting to locate the therapy phenomenon within the broader evolution of human consciousness;
- *fourth*, it would tend to be essentially hermeneutical, with a phenomen-ological/existential focus;
- *fifth*, it would accommodate critical, post-structuralist perspectives on the so-called 'invention' of contemporary subjectivity and the 'regime' of the (modern) self (cf. Rose's Chapter 4 and Kaye's Chapter 24, this volume);
- *sixth*, it would address the interface and cross-fertilisation between psychology and philosophy;
- *seventh*, it would tend towards a non-institutional, responsibility-embracing, and participative approach to ethical conduct, and a de-professionalised, devolved structure along the lines of John Heron's 'self-generating practitioner community' concept (cf. the chapters in Part IIA, this volume);
- *eighth*, it would tend to sympathise with the project of critical and feminist psychological perspectives;
- *ninth*, it would typically challenge the 'myth of normality', and reject the language of 'abnormality' and so-called 'psychopathology';
- *tenth*, it would problematise the ideology of 'developmentalism' within developmental psychology;
- *eleventh*, it would strive for a radical transparency, openness, and 'power-with' way-of-being with clients (as in the Person-Centred tradition) — minimising the exploitative power dynamics of profession-centred therapy (see, for example, Hart's Chapter 23, this volume);
- *twelfth*, it would be 'ordinary' and quite deliberately non-mystifying, eschewing pretensions to therapist technical-instrumental 'expertise';
- *thirteenth*, its focus would be upon *taking care* (see Smail's Chapter 3, this volume), privileging non-possessive human love over technique or clinical 'treatment' ideologies;
- *fourteenth*, it would embrace 'play' (Winnicott), 'the dance' of relationship, and creativity;
- *fifteenth*, it would likely embrace a (social) constructionist rather than a positivist/objectivist framework, tending towards being conversational, narratival, story-focused, and dialogical (cf. Kaye's Chapter 24, this volume);
- *sixteenth*, it would privilege notions of the indissolubly co-creative intersubjectivity of human relationship, rather than an intra-psychic, subject/object ontology (cf. ibid.);
- *seventeenth*, it would commonly be time-limited or of relatively short duration, minimising the triggering of infantilising dependency dynamics (cf. earlier discussion) — and yet stay true to person-centred values;
- *eighteenth*, it would be flexible rather than obsessively 'boundaried' in nature (cf. Lazarus's Chapter 1, this volume);
- *nineteenth*, it would embrace 'extra-therapeutic' phenomena — the social, the

cultural, and the political — at least as much as it does the intra-psychic (a recurrent theme in this book);
- and *twentieth*, it would be open about the nature of 'change', by no means slavishly following the old-paradigm (and professionally self-serving) view that therapeutic change *necessarily* has to be long-winded and painful.

Clearly, this brief sketch cannot remotely do justice to the form that an explicitly post-professional, deconstructive therapy might take. The articulation of that task was started in Ian Parker's important anthology *Deconstructing Psychotherapy*, and taken forward in *TbM*; and in future it will no doubt be picked up and developed in diverse ways (with this volume being just one example of that important process). However, no matter how assiduously we might strive to create a non-self-serving therapeutic culture that is maturely post-professional, and which responds to the concerns expressed earlier in both this chapter and in my Chapter 9 of this volume, at least some of the inherent contradictions nestling at the very heart of the therapeutic project will surely remain.

TOWARDS A POST-PROFESSIONAL THERAPY WORLD? — AN EXAMPLE

I now consider briefly one possible feature which might obtain in an enabling post-professional therapy world: the question of organisational arrangements.

Post-professional organisational arrangements: the case of the British Independent Practitioners Network

The editors of the anthology *Implausible Professions* (House and Totton 1997a), both active participants in the Network, collected together a number of papers which directly address the future of 'psycho-practice' in a post-professional era. The IPN, in which I have personally been closely involved since its founding conference in November 1994, is a Network which attempts to respond openly and creatively to at least some of the concerns raised in this book. Totton (1997a) succinctly sets out the 'new model of accountability' that the IPN represents (see also his Chapter 11, this volume); and Heron (1997) and House (1997) have set out in detail the form that what Heron calls a 'self-generating practitioner community' might plausibly take in a post-professional world (see also Heron's Foreword to this volume).

The IPN is a response to the mounting disquiet in the therapy field with the soulless and incongruous values characterising the didactic professionalisation process. The Network was founded at an inaugural national conference held at the (appropriately named) Open Centre in London in November 1994, growing out of a proposal made by Em Edmondson and Nick Totton for a radically different approach to therapist accountability, as the registration bandwagon was beginning to gather ominous momentum in the British therapy world. Before long the Network had become a steadily growing alternative to the institutional, dominator-hierarchical model promulgated by the therapy bureaucracies (Kalisch 1996; Postle's Chapter 17, this volume), with several hundred participating therapists of richly diverse orientation in practitioner-groups all over Britain.

The Network has no hierarchical power structure, and no executive making centralised decisions about what qualifications are necessary or acceptable for effective practitionership. Administration is facilitated in an open, participative way at meetings which anyone can attend. Relatedly, no individual can speak for the Network, as there exists no power structure that could confer such authority on any one individual. It can also be seen from this description that the Network has a group, communitarian ideology, rather than the 'privatised', individualising focus that is repeatedly challenged throughout this volume.

To quote directly from the Network's collectively written advertising brochure: the IPN

> makes no distinction between more or less qualified, or 'registered' members, as we recognise that there are many routes to being a good practitioner ... We specifically favour a richly pluralistic and multi-skilled ecology [of therapeutic practice] ... We are committed to defending freedom of practice and creating a culture of openness and challenge. The Network grows out of the belief that no organisation has the right or the ability to decide who should practise therapy, facilitation or equivalent skills.

The Network is therefore a form of 'self-generating practitioner community' in which participatory ethics (Brown 1997; House 1997) (requiring responsibility-taking by all involved) are privileged over didactic, responsibility-eschewing institutional Codes of Ethics (cf. Pattison's Chapter 5, this volume; and my *TbM*: 82–90). The only unit of Network membership is a *practitioner group* of at least five members, all of whom stand by each others' work through regular face-to-face engagement in ongoing peer-group experience via self and peer assessment (SAPA) and accreditation. (The carefully developed SAPA procedure used by the '*Leonard Piper*' IPN Group, in which I have been a participating member for eight years, is set out in detail in Lamont and Spencer 1997.) The 'standing-by' process means that each and every practitioner has a built-in and intrinsic interest in the quality of their colleagues' therapeutic work. And it is of central importance that the Network's organically self-regulating participative system of validation and accountability has been quite explicitly fashioned so as to be consistent with the core values of pluralistic therapeutic practice.

To become a full 'member-group', each practitioner-group must develop and establish organic links with two other groups, such that the two link-groups feel able to 'stand by' their work. There has been a great deal of discussion within the Network as to the precise meaning and procedural implications of 'standing by' — a debate which will no doubt continue to unfold and deepen as the Network matures. The overall Network structure is therefore horizontal rather than vertical or hierarchical — rendering it far more in tune with recent progressive developments in organisation theory than the hierarchical therapy bureaucracies (cf. Heron's Foreword to this volume).

The Network stands for an approach to difficulties or complaints which encourages the willingness to own 'mistakes' in an atmosphere of non-defensive openness (Totton 1997b), and thereby seeks to transcend the regressive 'victimhood', blaming dynamics (Hall 1993) that dominate conventional punitive, shame-inducing and victimhood-reinforcing complaints procedures.

There are regular weekend National Gatherings (two or three a year), open to anyone to attend, together with occasional Regional Gatherings. It is interesting to note that the values underpinning the IPN do seem to have much in common with the Person-Centred and community-building philosophy of Carl Rogers

(Rogers undated), as Gassner (1999) has very clearly articulated. Overall, the IPN is founded in the values of creative pluralism (House and Totton 1997a; Samuels 1997), an unambitious modesty, and the celebration of growth and human potential development, rather than in those of infantilising hoop-jumping, 'power-over' hierarchy, ambition-infused institutional intrigue and a preoccupation with so-called 'psychopathology'.

It would be wrong to imply that the Network's strugglings with the intricate and subtle dialectic between radical individualism and communitarian values has not been variously challenging, frustrating, and even sometimes exhausting (e.g. House, in preparation). Yet these 'birth pangs' are arguably a *necessary* and unavoidable process with which *any* human grouping struggling towards a mature, operational *social community ethic and praxis* must contend. The extraordinary subtlety and complexity of what is at stake in all this is beautifully summed up by the spiritual philosopher Rudolf Steiner in his 'Motto of the Social Ethic', given to Edith Maryon in 1920 (and cited in Lipsker 1990: 60):

> The healthy social life is found when in the mirror of each human soul the whole community finds its reflection, and when in the community the virtue of each one is living.

There are many interesting philosophical and procedural commonalities yet to be explored between the IPN, on the one hand, and on the other, both the Quaker movement and the worldwide Steiner (Waldorf) educational and Camphill Community movements, founded as the latter is in the anthroposophical principles deriving from Rudolf Steiner's work.

CONCLUSION

> [B]y sequestering it in a private room, *therapy removes soul from the world* ... Symptoms ... do not belong to the individual but *to the culture as a whole* ... Psychotherapy is an abstraction, culturally sanctioned in a world of materialist abstractions... [P]sychotherapy ... seems to me a deviation contributing to the destruction of culture ... [These] conclusions... have led me, a practising psychotherapist, to the necessity of relinquishing this practice.
>
> (Sardello 1990: 14–29 *passim*, my emphases)

My concern, then, has been to explore how we might salvage the 'baby' of therapeutic enablement from the bathwater of self-serving profession-centred therapeutic practice; and to this end I have argued for a new, *post-professional ethos* within the therapy field. For those who might be sceptical about the viability or practicality of the post-professional framework I am championing here, I am greatly encouraged by the fact that I personally know a number of therapists who work in principled ways that coincide with many of the 21 'post-professional criteria' outlined earlier, and who in the process do everything they can *not* to collude with and encourage the profession-centred tendencies inscribed within profession-centred therapy. The work of erstwhile therapists like Georg Groddeck, James Hillman, Robert Sardello and Anne Schaef also inspires in me the hope that there are at least some signs of a qualitatively different kind of post-professional, 'new paradigm' therapeutic practice beginning to emerge. Yet I also know practitioners who in my judgement do very little if anything to respond to the potential abusiveness of profession-centred therapy's regime of truth; and my hunch (based admittedly on personal anecdotal experience) is that the latter type of practitioner probably substantially outnumbers the former.

I certainly don't wish to 'psychopathologise' the therapy field as a whole, not least because such a pathologising world-view is, I believe, not only epistemologically unsustainable, but can easily amount to little more than *ad hominem* abuse which obscures far more than it reveals. Yet I do hope that before launching the counter-attack — or heading for the bunkers — therapy practitioners will feel able to consider closely and relatively undefendedly the challenges I have mounted to profession-centred therapy, both here and in *TbM* — challenges whose careful consideration can, in my view, only lead to less self-serving and more enabling post-professional therapeutic practices.

Finally, and following Cushman (1995), perhaps the increasing cultural ascendancy of 'the therapeutic' within modern culture parallels deeper processes in the evolution of individualised consciousness and ego/self-hood, of which the vast majority of us are unaware ... and yet which it may be crucial to identify, and struggle to understand, if we are to fashion a therapy which is facilitative of a healthy human evolution, rather than being just one more ideological trapping of late modernity. This is indeed an urgent task as we increasingly encounter and fashion the 'trans-modern' transition that will take us through and beyond the death throes of a technocratic and soulless modernity.

REFERENCES

Alcoff, L.M. (1996) *Real Knowing: New Versions of the Coherence Theory*. Ithaca, New York: Cornell University Press

Alexander, R. and Bates, Y. (2002) An interview with Rosie Alexander. *Ipnosis* 8 (Winter): 9–12

Barratt, B. B. (1993) *Psychoanalysis and the Postmodern Impulse: Knowing and Being since Freud's Psychology*. Baltimore: Johns Hopkins University Press

Brown, L. S. (1997) Ethics in psychology: *cui bono?*. In D. Fox and I. Prilleltensky (eds), *Critical Psychology: An Introduction* (pp. 51–67). London: Sage

Clark, J. (ed.) (2002) *Freelance Counselling and Psychotherapy: Competition and Collusion*. Hove: Brunner-Routledge

Cushman, P. (1995) *Constructing the Self, Constructing America: A Cultural History of Psychotherapy*. Reading, MA: Addison-Wesley

Feltham, C. (1997a) Challenging the core theoretical model. In R. House and N. Totton (eds), *Implausible Professions* (pp. 117–28). Ross-on-Wye: PCCS Books (reprinted from *Counselling*, 8 (2), 1997: 121–5)

Gassner, J. (1999) The Independent Practitioners Network and the person-centred approach. Seminar held at the Norwich Centre, January (mimeo)

Hall, J. (1993) *The Reluctant Adult: An Exploration of Choice*. Bridport: Prism Press

Hart, T. (1998) A dialectic of knowing: integrating the intuitive and the analytic. *Encounter: Education for Meaning and Social Justice* 11 (3): 5–16

Hart, T., Nelson, P. and Puhakka, K. (eds) (1997) *Spiritual Knowing: Alternative Epistemic Perspectives*. Carrollton, GA: State University of West Georgia, Studies in Social Sciences Vol. 34

Heron, J. (1997) A self-generating practitioner community. In R. House and N. Totton (eds), *Implausible Professions* (pp. 241–54). Ross-on-Wye: PCCS Books

Hogan, D. (1979) *The Regulation of Psychotherapists*, 4 vols. Cambridge, MA: Ballinger

House, R. (1997) Participatory ethics in a self-generating practitioner community. In R. House and N. Totton (eds), *Implausible Professions* (pp. 321–34). Ross-on-Wye: PCCS Books

House, R. (1999) The psychology of self, society and ecological survival (Review Feature of Caroline New's *Agency, Health and Social Survival*). *European Journal of Psychotherapy, Counselling and Health* 2 (1): 103–17

House, R. (2003) *Therapy Beyond Modernity: Deconstructing and Transcending Profession-Centred Therapy*. London: Karnac Books

House, R. (in preparation) The individualism/communitarian dialectic and the IPN. *Ipnosis* (forthcoming)

House, R. and Totton, N. (eds) (1997a) *Implausible Professions: Arguments for Pluralism and Autonomy in Psychotherapy and Counselling*. Ross-on-Wye: PCCS Books

House, R. and Totton, N. (1997b) Introduction. In R. House and N. Totton (eds), *Implausible Professions* (pp. 1–10). Ross-on-Wye: PCCS Books

Ipnosis: An Independent Journal for Practitioners, quarterly (The Alexander Group, P.O. Box 19, Llandysul, Ceredigion, SA44 4YE)

Kalisch, D. (1996) Letter to the Editor. *Self and Society* 24 (2): 38–9

Lamont, J. and Spencer, A. (1997) Self and peer assessment: a personal story. In R. House and N. Totton (eds), *Implausible Professions* (pp. 295–303). Ross-on-Wye: PCCS Books

Lipsker, B. (1990) Three pillars. In C. M. Pietzner (ed.) *A Candle on the Hill: Images of Camphill Life* (pp. 59–60). Edinburgh: Floris Books

Mowbray, R. (1995) *The Case Against Psychotherapy Registration: A Conservation Issue for the Human Potential Movement*. London: Trans Marginal Press

Parker, I. (ed.) (1999) *Deconstructing Psychotherapy*. London: Sage

Pilgrim, D. (1997) *Psychotherapy and Society*. London: Sage

Polkinghorne, D. (1990) Psychology after philosophy. In J. E. Faulconer and R. N. Williams (eds), *Reconsidering Psychology* (pp. 92–115). Pittsburgh, PA: Duquesne University Press

Samuels, A. (1997) Pluralism and psychotherapy: what is good training? In R. House and N. Totton (eds), *Implausible Professions* (pp. 199–214). Ross-on-Wye: PCCS Books

Sands, A. and Bates, Y. (2002) An interview with Anna Sands, parts 1 and 2. *Ipnosis* 6 (Summer): 4–6; 7 (Autumn): 18–19

Sardello, R. (1990) Introduction. In R. Steiner, *Psychoanalysis and Spiritual Psychology: Five Lectures, 1912–21* (pp. 1–29). Hudson, NY: Anthroposophic Press

Schaef, A. W. (1992) *Beyond Therapy, Beyond Science: A New Model for Healing the Whole Person*. New York: HarperSanFrancisco

Totton, N. (1997a) The Independent Practitioners Network. In R. House and N. Totton (eds), *Implausible Professions* (pp. 287–93). Ross-on-Wye: PCCS Books

Totton, N. (1997b) Learning by mistake: client-practitioner conflict in a self-regulated network. In R. House and N. Totton (eds), *Implausible Professions* (pp. 315–20). Ross-on-Wye: PCCS Books

Wheeler, S. (1998) Challenging the core theoretical model: a reply to Colin Feltham. *Counselling* 9 (2): 134–8

PART IIC:
WHITHER THERAPY?

EDITORIAL INTRODUCTION AND COMMENTARY

This concluding section looks at possible alternatives for the future of psychotherapy and counselling. The chapter entitled 'The active client: therapy as self-help' is a remarkable vision by ART BOHART and KAREN TALLMAN of how therapy could be reframed (using an existential-humanistic paradigm, although applicable to all models of therapy) so as to be viewed as a self-help process. This vision places the therapist as consultant, a resource upon which the client can draw along with anything and everything else at her disposal, in addressing her psychological and spiritual needs. This simple, elegant model has an inspiring, intuitive appeal and offers genuine hope for a way forward.

ERNESTO SPINELLI's vision, described in Chapter 28, may be seen as quite complementary to that of Bohart and Tallman. The exemplar of Leslie Farber cited by Spinelli represents the humble, egalitarian and human approach to therapy, where the client is respected as autonomous. Within this exciting chapter there is one brief section which we believe stands strongly against the ethos of this anthology, but which is included (in edited form) in the spirit of diversity and pluralism which we advocate. We are referring to the section in which Spinelli is critical of 'a developing category of therapeutically focused texts written by ex-clients: the "Read-about-how-psychotherapy-fucked-me-up-and-how-awful(-or-evil)-it-is" genre'. This is an opinion which the editors strongly oppose. Rather, we feel that there are pitifully few texts in the vast profession-centred therapy literature written by clients and ex-clients. Moreover, every book and article we have read in this category has been of some, and in most cases, very considerable value, attempting to construct a dialogue between clients and therapists, and not some sort of narcissistic assault on therapy, as Spinelli's analysis might be interpreted as implying. Yet the delicious paradox is that we also wish to honour Ernesto Spinelli's chapter as one of the most innovative and openly honest in the entire anthology.

Following DAVID BRAZIER's thought-provoking sociological portrait of therapy's place within our culture, therefore, the final chapter of *Ethically Challenged Professions* is given over to the author of one of the bravest books ever written about therapy, 'ROSIE ALEXANDER'. In it she calls again for a future of co-operation and collaboration wherein the ills of psychotherapy and counselling can be overcome by clients and practitioners working together — a collaboration which we passionately believe is vital if our occupation is to evolve successfully.

27

THE ACTIVE CLIENT:
THERAPY AS SELF-HELP

ARTHUR C. BOHART AND KAREN TALLMAN[†]

TWO EXAMPLES

Lisa was agitated today. She was very frustrated by her inability to express her anger. She wanted to do something. Her therapist described a 'two-chair' technique as a way she might express her feelings towards her boyfriend. The typically unassertive Lisa said, 'NO! No, I won't be moving from chair to chair. But I will talk to the chair. You keep your eyes downcast.' She completed her modified usage of the technique and then seemed peaceful and content for the first time in a great while.

We stumbled across some curious dialogue in our review of the therapy tapes from our analogue study of experiential versus non-experiential empathy responses (Tallman et al. 1994). The experiment required the therapist to deliver weak unhelpful empathy responses in one condition. As a result, in one case the therapist was awful. The client seemed exasperated at being unable to communicate her perception of her situation. At that point, to our surprise, the client took a new direction and began using the session to do good work in spite of the therapist's hollow unempathic responses. On other occasions we again heard clients do good work in the 'poor response' condition. What could this mean? Is not the therapist the agent of change? Why do some clients improve in spite of variations in therapist quality?

The questions we consider in this chapter are: What is the nature of therapy? Does it consist of an expert professional, playing a role analogous to a medical doctor, who knows how to diagnose what is wrong with clients and then treat their disorders? Or is it the provision of a place, a set of experiences and a relationship, which active clients use to foster their own self-growth? These two views represent fundamentally different perspectives, or meta-models underlying practice.

The first meta-model is the 'medical-like' model, and it is dominant in the field today (Orlinsky 1989). It is growing even more dominant because of its close fit with the philosophy of managed care. The second meta-model is the model we propose. It is philosophically derived from existential-humanistic perspectives, although it is ultimately compatible with doing therapy from a wide range of perspectives.

We first contrast an existential-humanistic philosophical perspective with

† Chapter first appeared in the *Journal of Humanistic Psychology*, 36(3), 1995: 7–30, and is reprinted with kind permission of authors and Sage Publications, Inc.

the medical-like view. We then argue that although the 'medical-like' meta-model dominates the field, the research actually supports an existential-humanistic meta-model. We further argue that all therapy is ultimately self-help and that it is the client who is the therapist. In this we join with others who are increasingly emphasising the importance of the client as the active ingredient in therapy (Duncan and Moynihan 1994; Gold 1994; Miller et al. 1995; Orlinsky et al. 1994).

EXISTENTIAL-HUMANISTIC MODELS OF THERAPY

Many existential-humanistic (EH) approaches share the assumption that it is ultimately clients who change themselves in therapy. Carl Rogers (1957), for instance, believed that clients find their own paths to their own solutions if therapists provide a safe, empathic relationship.

Therapists are not experts on the client, on the client's condition, or on how to treat that condition (cf. Kaye's Chapter 24, this volume). Rather, therapists are experts on their experience, and on perceiving and reacting to the moment-by-moment process between themselves and clients. This includes the ability to help clients focus on and explore their values and experiencing. It also includes attending, prizing and caring.

In some EH models, the therapist's relationship to the client is similar to relationships between members of self-help groups — people help people through sharing their own personal experience with one another. The therapist is a fellow traveller or a fellow struggler (Kopp 1972), and is not telling the client the truth from an expert's perspective. To the contrary, the therapist is sharing his or her personal reactions. How the client uses them is in the client's hands. EH models emphasise client responsibility and choice, so the client is always the active agent.

Therapists may use techniques. However, techniques are neither necessary nor mechanistically applied. For instance, Resnick (1980), writing on Gestalt therapy, has said, 'If every technique that any Gestalt therapist had ever used before we never used again, true Gestalt therapists would barely be affected' (p. x). Techniques are better seen as ways of being with the client rather than as procedures that operate to make things happen *in* the client

In EH models the client is treated as a whole person. Many approaches adopt a part-person model. Psychological problems are seen as arising from malfunctioning internal mechanisms. Object relations theory assumes that malfunctions in the ego create psychological dysfunction. If the whole person exhibits the behaviour called 'splitting', it is because the ego includes split object representations. Cognitive therapy sees dysfunctional schemas as the cause of problems, and behaviour therapy views problems as dysfunctional habits. None of these theories sees problems as arising from the whole person's struggle to make his or her life work.

Existential-humanistic theories, in contrast, view psychological problems as arising from fundamental issues in living. Greening (1992), for instance, has delineated four existential challenges. The individual must confront life and death, meaning and absurdity, freedom and determinism, and community and aloneness. Failure fully to confront and develop balanced responses to each of these fundamental challenges can lead to psychological problems. For client-centred therapy, psychological problems arise when individuals fail to continue to grow and to stay in process (Bohart 1995b). It is therefore actions and choices by the whole person as he or she struggles to live that results in dysfunctional behaviour, not broken internal mechanisms, conditioned habits or dysfunctional cognitions.

From the EH perspective, it is also this same whole person who will ultimately and creatively find personally meaningful resolutions. Therapists facilitate the process but do not make it happen, any more than midwives make birth happen.

THE 'MEDICAL-LIKE' MODEL

In contrast to the EH model, the medical-like model patterns therapy along the lines of medical practice. Psychological problems are not the product of actions or choices taken by whole persons to resolve major life issues, but rather the result of dysfunctional mechanisms or habits in clients. The therapist is like a physician who diagnoses the client's condition and then prescribes and administers treatment. As with medicine, it is assumed that different client conditions require different treatments. It is the treatment or intervention that fixes whatever is malfunctioning in the client. For instance, cognitive interventions operate on dysfunctional schemas to modify them; transference interpretations create insight and strengthen the ego; and assertion training stamps in good habits to replace bad habits.

The therapeutic relationship in such a model is not egalitarian, although it may be collaborative. The therapist is the expert. The relationship is either seen as a precondition to good treatment, analogous to a good 'bedside manner' in medicine, or as an intervention in its own right. As a precondition, it is important to establish a good relationship so that the client will comply with the therapist's treatment. As an intervention, it is assumed that the therapist must modify his or her relationship stance to have the maximum effect on the client (Lazarus 1993).

Interventions or treatments are thought of as analogous to medications, and Stiles and Shapiro (1989) have called this the 'drug metaphor'. An intervention operates on a client in a mechanistic fashion. In this sense, clients ultimately become recipients of potent drug-like change interventions. Even the relationship is analogous to a drug that brings about changes in clients.

This does not mean that the medical-like model does not emphasise client collaboration. As in medicine, client compliance is essential. If clients do not take the medication or collaborate in the treatment, then the interventions will not work. However, it is the interventions that ultimately change the client.

The medical-like model can be compatible with a behavioural perspective. Although behaviourists may reject the medical model of symptomatology, they still believe that it is the therapist whose interventions modify dysfunctional behaviours and habits in the client. There is no concept of *an active client* creatively generating new solutions from within. Behaviourists can emphasise self-help (Marks 1994), but it is a self-help predicated on clients learning therapist-selected self-management skills. Different problems require different interventions selected by the therapist who is the expert on what the client needs. It was a behaviourist, Gordon Paul (1967: 111), who framed the question that represents the thinking of most medical-like therapists: *'What* treatment, by *whom*, is most effective for this individual with *that* specific problem, under *which* set of circumstances?'

The medical-like model leads to a relentless search for new interventions and more and more specificity in matching treatment to condition. Because change is ultimately precipitated by the therapist rather than client-generated, therapists devise treatment plans. Ideally for this perspective, treatment manuals will ultimately dictate therapist choice of appropriate procedures for different disorders (Task Force... 1995).

In sum, in the medical-like model, the therapist is an expert at assessing what kind of condition the client has. The therapist is also an expert on what should be done to the client. As with medicine, differential treatments are prescribed for different client conditions. It is the treatments that are alleged to be the active ingredients. Clients are agents in the change process only in the sense that they must comply with and implement the procedures decided on by the therapist. This model underlies the practice of many current therapists.

REVIEW OF THE RESEARCH

In our view, research supports an EH view of therapy over the medical-like view. First, if the medical-like model were correct, then the kind of professional training in diagnosis and applying treatments which most therapists receive should make them better therapists. However, the evidence is that this is not true. Christensen and Jacobson (1994) noted that a number of research reviews (Berman and Norton, 1985; Durlak 1979; Hattie et al. 1984; Stein and Lambert 1984) have failed to find evidence of significant differences between professionals and para-professionals in terms of effectiveness, although some para-professionals have received some training from professionals. Evidence also does not generally support the idea that more experienced therapists are more effective (Christensen and Jacobson 1994; Lambert and Bergin 1994). Smith et al. (1980) found a correlation of 0.0 between experience and effectiveness. Strupp and Hadley (1979) found that experienced therapists were no more helpful than a group of untrained college professors selected for their relationship skills. Jacobson (1995) found that novice graduate students were more effective at doing couples therapy than trained professionals. Svartberg and Stiles (1991), in a meta-analysis of research on short-term psychodynamic therapy, concluded that inexperienced therapists were more effective than more experienced therapists.

This does not mean that therapists possess no expertise at all. There is evidence that some therapists are more helpful than others (Luborsky et al. 1980). However, it would appear that it is differences in personal qualities that make some therapists more effective, as Carl Rogers (1957) suggested long ago.

A second problem with the medical-like model is that if it were correct, then the use of techniques and interventions should account for more of the variance in helpfulness than does the therapeutic relationship. However, the opposite is the case. The relationship appears to be considerably more important than the use of techniques. For instance, Duncan and Moynihan (1994), based on Lambert (1992), have estimated that the relationship accounts for 30 per cent of the variance, whereas the use of techniques accounts for only 15 per cent. Orlinsky et al. (1994) reported that outcome in therapy is best predicted from the strength of the therapeutic alliance. Svartberg and Stiles (1994) found that the strength of the therapeutic alliance correlated +0.48 with outcome in brief psychodynamic therapy, whereas the therapist's expertise at using brief dynamic therapy procedures correlated -0.55. Castonguay (1993) found that the use of the techniques of cognitive therapy did not correlate with outcome, but the therapeutic alliance did.

A third problem with the medical-like model is that it predicts that different treatments are needed for different client conditions. Lambert and Bergin (1994: 175) noted that 'researchers, influenced by mechanistic models, have placed their bets on technique factors as the more powerful agents in change ...'. However, the research for the most part contradicts this position. Bergin and Garfield (1994: 822) concluded that '[w]ith some exceptions ... there is massive evidence that psychotherapeutic techniques do not have specific effects'. Lambert and Bergin (1994: 181) noted that 'this is not to say that techniques are irrelevant but that their power for change is limited when compared to personal influence'. However, it should be noted that there are some researchers who continue to believe in specific effects of specific treatments (Barlow 1994; Lazarus et al. 1992). Those who believe this have recently begun to argue that specific treatments are needed for more serious disorders (Lazarus 1995), although the evidence on this is sparse.

Compatible with conclusions about the non-specificity of techniques, the 'dodo bird' verdict that all therapies work about equally well continues to be accepted by most researchers (Lambert and Bergin 1994; Stubbs and Bozarth 1994). For instance, Beckham (1990) and Robinson et al. (1990) have concluded that different forms of therapy for depression are equivalent in effectiveness. Research on experiential-humanistic therapies shows them to be as effective as other brands for a wide range of disorders, including depression and anxiety (Greenberg et al. 1994).

If this were medicine, it would be surprising to find that vastly different approaches all worked about the same with a wide range of disorders. These findings indicate, as Lambert and Bergin (1994: 167) noted, that 'common factors loom large as mediators of treatment outcome'. It is factors common to all therapies that are primarily responsible for their effectiveness rather than unique approaches or techniques.

What is the most important common factor? There is increasing evidence that it is not something that is found in the different therapies. Rather, it is the client (Orlinsky and Howard 1986; Orlinsky et al. 1994; Stiles et al. 1986). Duncan and Moynihan (1994), drawing their conclusions from Lambert (1992), estimated that the client accounts for 40 per cent of the variance in successful therapy. Bergin and Garfield (1994: 825–6) noted:

> Another important observation regarding the client variable is that it is the client more than the therapist who implements the change process ... Rather than argue over whether or not 'therapy works', we could address ourselves to the question of whether or not 'the client works!' ... It is important to rethink the terminology that assumes that 'effects' are like Aristotelian impetus causality. As therapists have depended more on the client's resources, more change seems to occur.

Duncan and his colleagues (Duncan and Moynihan 1994; Miller et al. 1995) have based their whole approach on the idea that the client is the primary change agent and that therapists would do well to work within the client's framework. Gold (1994) has presented a number of examples of the active, creative and innovative efforts of clients.

Research on self-help procedures also supports the importance of the active role of the client. Christensen and Jacobson (1994) cited a number of studies showing that both self-help books and computer-administered therapy work as well as therapy administered by therapists. Selmi et al. (1990) found that computer-administered cognitive-behaviour therapy worked as well as therapist-administered therapy for depression. A study at a major Southern California health maintenance organisation found that computer-assisted therapy worked as well as therapist-provided therapy (Jacobs 1995). Scogin et al. (1990) and Gould and Clum (1993) have done meta-analyses of self-help books, finding them equivalent in effectiveness to psychotherapy. For instance, Beutler et al. (1991) found that self-help produced reductions in major depressive disorder equivalent to those found for psychotherapy.

Related to this, Pennebaker (1990) has accumulated evidence showing that expression and self-disclosure appear to be both psychologically and physically beneficial. In one study, college students wrote about traumatic experience for 15 minutes a day for 4 consecutive days. At a 6-month follow-up, it was found that these students, compared to a control group, showed a 50 per cent reduction in visits to the student health centre. In a related finding, Segal and Murray (1994) found that talking into a tape-recorder worked about as well as cognitive therapy in helping individuals resolve feelings about traumatic experiences.

Finally, Jacobs and Goodman (Goodman and Jacobs 1995; Jacobs and Goodman 1989) have argued that self-help groups not only can work as well as psychotherapy, but may substantially replace psychotherapy in the future.

The findings on self-help procedures once again contradict the medical-like model of therapy. Although some of the self-help materials have been designed by experts, the fact that many clients can implement their own self-improvement is incompatible with a model that emphasises the importance of professional intervention. Self-help procedures, of course, are also used in medicine (e.g. back exercises). However, in medicine they are the exception rather than the rule. No one would expect that clients could remove their own appendixes, or prescribe their own antibiotics using a self-help book. Yet there is virtually no psychotherapeutic procedure that has not been used in some form or other as a self-help procedure.

In addition, not all self-help procedures require guidance by experts. Self-disclosure techniques, such as journalling and talking into a tape-recorder, can be used by participants with no expert guidance at all. In a similar manner, many self-help groups do not rely on expert guidance.

In sum, the overall thrust of evidence is incompatible with the medical-like model, but the data *are* generally compatible with EH models of therapy. Change in therapy is ultimately in the hands of the client. Techniques are not procedures with specific effects that operate precisely on clients; techniques, on the whole, play a relatively minor role. The kind of expertise which therapists possess has more to do with their personal abilities than it does with what they have gained through professional training.

THE ACTIVE CLIENT AS THERAPIST

We wish to take the implications of the above conclusions one logical step further and suggest that *all therapy is self-help*. This is consistent with many EH perspectives and, in fact, is derived from our EH backgrounds (primarily client-centred). Basically we suggest, following others like John Rowan (1994), Otto Rank (Raskin and Rogers 1989), and Carl Rogers (Raskin and Rogers 1989), that it is the client who is the therapist. Professional (or, as Rowan calls them, 'designated') therapists are resources that clients use in their self-change processes, as they use a wide range of other resources (self-help books, talk shows, journal workshops, friends, relatives, clergy, meditation, literature, jogging, music, movies, poetry, etc.). It is the active client who takes what he or she gets from the therapist or from other resources, and creatively figures out how to resolve problems and move his or her life forward in more meaningful directions. It is the client, therefore, who uses the experience with the therapist or other resources as material to be therapist for him- or herself.

We take it as a postulate that at an underlying level all clients are being active. Being active is human. What we mean by 'active' is that individuals are trying to find resolutions to the dilemmas that confront them in living. Some ways of trying to find resolutions are productive, and others are not.

In both therapy and life, many individuals are productively active. Being productively active means that they proactively approach and examine the issues related to their problems, do not give up or back off when confronted with challenge, actively engage in thinking and self-exploration, and generate tentative new directions for potential change and then explore further (Tallman 1996).

Other individuals are counterproductively active. For instance, taking action may consist of becoming totally passive, as with the possum. Individuals who feel totally helpless may believe that there is no point in taking other kinds of action. The action they do take is to stop and withdraw. In therapy, some clients may take the action of waiting on the therapist for direction and guidance. Still others may not perceive themselves as needing therapy and take the action of actively resisting it or undermining it.

However, even these individuals are actively trying to forge some liveable way of being in the world. Thus, as we define it, they too are being active. The job of the therapist with these individuals is to help them turn their counterproductive activities in a more productive direction. A basic condition for doing this is that therapists understand and appreciate them as human beings who are being active, albeit unproductively.

Once clients turn their efforts in proactive directions, it is they who solve their own problems, using the resources provided by the therapist.

How does the idea that it is the active client who is the therapist follow from the previously cited research? We have cited research reviews suggesting that clients account for 40 per cent of the variance in therapeutic outcome, whereas the relationship accounts for 30 per cent and techniques for 15 per cent. One could argue that although clients are an important part of the change process, so also are expert therapists. Such an argument, however, fails to take into account the data that many clients do quite well with self-help materials. Further, evidence that non-professional therapists are as helpful as professional ones, and that many individuals benefit from self-help groups, indicates that the professional expertise of the therapist is also not a necessity.

In addition, why is it that experts who practise widely-differing therapeutic approaches all seem to have about the same effects? There are more than 400 different therapies, and more are being produced every year. How is it that a depressed client can get better by challenging dysfunctional cognitions, by practising social skills, by engaging in the Gestalt two-chair procedure, or by simply talking to an empathic listener? How is it that people can get better by sleeping (Morita therapy), by dancing, by engaging in body work, by talking about the past, by going on wilderness camp-outs, by journalling, by exploring their 'inner child', by confronting their families of origin, by exploring their feelings, by practising new behaviours, by accessing deep experiencing potential (Mahrer 1995), by engaging in role-play procedures, by talking to an empathic listener, by being confronted or by meditating?

It seems to us that the most parsimonious explanation for all of the above is that change is primarily a product of the active client, who makes the therapy work, regardless of what therapy he or she is using. Clients come into therapy when they are struggling. Therapy is one resource they may choose. For some people, professional help may not be necessary — self-help materials may be all they need. Or they may do better with a self-help group, or with other forms of personal growth experiences (e.g. Esalen workshops, meditation, etc.). It is similar to exercise: some individuals appear to stick with their exercise regimens if they have a professional trainer. Others do better on their own. Still others do better if they exercise in groups.

There are many individuals for whom therapy is the ideal setting for them to do their work. Therapists can support these people in their efforts to help themselves explore, evaluate, discover, decide, learn and develop. In particular, the presence of a therapist may be just what is needed when clients are feeling very fragile, or are in a crisis state. Even within therapy, client preferences for different approaches will vary. An action-orientated client may appreciate some structured techniques that permit him or her to do something rather than simply discussing the problem. For some clients, the relationship may be very important. Others may wish to use a therapist, but primarily for their ideas or their techniques rather than for the relationship *per se*.

Effective therapists offer three things to clients. First, they offer working space and time. Clients often enter therapy feeling demoralised (Frank 1973). Therapy provides a safe place where clients can be listened to, listen to themselves, think and feel. In such a safe space, clients can begin to regain a sense of themselves as proactive, unravel the threads of their problems, gain perspective and use their intrinsic creative problem-solving abilities. In support of this idea, Zimring (1990) has found that clients in client-centred therapy show increases in their ability to think intelligently. In a similar manner, O'Hara (1986) has suggested that the therapist's function is like a research assistant providing support for the client, who engages in the active search process of therapy.

The common element underlying all effective therapy is, therefore, a structured space within which to explore options, to experience and re-experience aspects of self and problem, and more intelligently to synthesise new ways of being and behaving. With this in mind, it then makes sense that widely different therapies might be equally effective for a wide range of problems. Further, it follows that there are many different ways of providing a facilitative therapeutic relationship. Therapists may be highly active or quite passive, use many techniques or few, as long as they provide useful working space. Because there are many possible ways for therapists to be helpful, it may be more important for the profession to explore what therapists can do wrong to get in clients' way than to try to decide on the right way to be a therapist.

Secondly, therapists can provide techniques. However, techniques do not mechanistically 'do therapy' on clients. Giving a client a technique is like giving the client a tool. The client uses it to make something new. Two clients given the same technique may use it in quite different ways. Techniques are structured opportunities for clients to explore their own experience, gain perspective and work through their problems. So there will not necessarily be a close one-to-one relationship between a technique and its effects.

As two examples, consider Gendlin's (1990) focusing technique and the Gestalt two-chair technique (Greenberg 1994). Both are best thought of as procedures that provide a structured experience within which clients make their own discoveries. They allow client creativity; they do not mechanistically precipitate change.

Techniques are thus *affordances* (Gibson 1979) — processes that afford opportunities for certain kinds of experiences. Because the client who uses the technique is a whole person, the client may be able to approach his or her problems from a multiplicity of productive directions, gaining insight into the unconscious (psychodynamic), exploring feelings and values (humanistic), practising skills (behavioural) or changing cognitions (cognitive). It is the whole person — the active client — who takes these various part-processes and uses them in his or her self-growth.

Thirdly, therapists provide their interactive presence — which is particularly important for existential-humanistic therapists. This functions in two ways. First, EH therapists typically respond as persons to clients. They offer their reactions as fellow creatures rather than from a superior position of professional expertise. As long as this feedback is given in ways that invite thinking, experiencing and exploring (i.e. not in punitive or critical ways), such feedback should facilitate clients working through issues in their lives. Such feedback might stimulate clients to explore what they want out of relationships, how they relate to others, how they relate to themselves, how they make basic choices and set priorities, and what it is like to be living their only life.

The second way an interactive presence functions is that therapy can become a co-constructive experience (Jordan 1997; O'Hara 1997). Therapist and client together can resonate and 'bounce off one another' in developing potential new pathways (Bohart 1995a; Bohart and Tallman 1997). New possibilities for thinking, experiencing and acting develop from the mutual sharing, just as two children can move each other to higher developmental levels on Piagetian tasks through co-constructive dialogue (Perret-Clermont et al. 1991). When therapy functions this way, it is more like what goes on in self-help groups (Goodman and Jacobs 1995) — individuals getting together collaboratively to facilitate growth.

No matter what happens in therapy, however, it is ultimately the active client who makes changes in the way he or she actually lives life. The ideas, new directions or possibilities, or behavioural prescriptions learned in therapy are never specific enough to dictate exactly how an individual will adapt them to his or her circumstances. This is especially true because circumstances are ever-shifting and never quite the same from one time to another, necessitating constant creative application. Thus, *real* therapy happens when individuals use what they have learned or discovered to make concrete changes and decisions as they live on a moment-to-moment basis. Even highly directive therapies provide no more than hints or pointers that must be creatively actualised by the whole person as he or she makes major life decisions. 'It is part of the cure to wish to be cured' (Seneca).

Because it is the active client who is the therapist, clients may sometimes even be able to overcome bad working conditions provided by therapists, just as many resilient children are able to thrive despite highly aversive life experiences (Masten et al. 1990). In the studies previously cited on more effective versus less effective therapists, there was a number of clients who succeeded with the less effective therapists. In a therapy analogue study referenced earlier (Tallman et al. 1994), students were given short therapy sessions during which they received either good or poor empathy responses. Although the students indeed rated the poor empathy responses as less helpful, a number of them nonetheless were able to use the responses therapeutically. One of us as an undergraduate heard a professor say, 'Most children grow up in spite of their parents, not because of them'. Certainly it is better if therapists are facilitative, but the fact that some clients can take even non-facilitative comments and use them to their own advantage supports the idea that it is the client who is, ultimately, the therapist.

IMPLICATIONS

Client as agent

If the power to effect change comes from the client, then why do people need therapists? If therapy is really self-help, why do clients seek the help of therapists? We believe this dilemma can be resolved by changing the way we view the roles of the client and therapist. The client grows by using the provisions offered by the therapist and the therapy setting. The therapist provides the time, place, justification and opportunity for the client to work. The client is supposed to (has the right to) think about, experience and explore him- or herself and the situation for a protected time period. A good therapist adds a sense of hope, safety and support. The client can then explore all of the relevant information, searching for meaning, opening to deeper experiencing, investigating options, developing new choices, brainstorming about new possibilities, examining neglected hypotheses and testing out hunches. Clients might use many sources of data, including their feelings and emotions, bodily reactions, their relationship with the therapist, historical events, recent events, therapist responses, techniques and the therapist's ideas.

This view is fundamentally a health and growth model of therapy. It is a positive view that assumes that people are at some basic level sensible, growing and struggling to improve their lives (Gendlin 1967). Even when clients seem to be resisting, their behaviour can be seen as sensible with a logic behind it to be discovered by therapists and clients together. Clients, and people in general, are resilient, self-righting systems (Masten et al. 1990). They are characterised by their ability to bounce back and to transcend and grow beyond even highly negative circumstances. Therapists need not 'fix' clients, but rather help clients mobilise this capacity.

Believing that it is the client who is the therapist also means that clients may find resources in their natural environments that they can use as therapy. Thus, to give an actual example, a depressed client decided to go into the yard and garden. The client felt productive in helping new life to grow. This mobilised an inner sense of effectivity, and promoted a feeling of giving to the world. These made the client feel better and more like 'opening out' to the world, even helping him to feel more forgiving towards self and others. Gardening became therapy because the client made it so.

Therapist interventions do not function like back exercises do in medicine. Back exercises mechanistically operate to cause changes in the client's back. If the client alters the back exercise, it may not work. In contrast, psychotherapy clients creatively interact with therapist interventions. Clients may creatively alter an intervention and still make it work. The mechanisms, direction and timing of change come from the client. The active client model therefore rests on a fundamentally different model of learning from the dominant model in our culture. As Gendlin (1990) has pointed out, most models assume that whatever is inside the client has come from outside. Clients, for instance, are alleged to change in therapy by internalising their therapists. Or they change by internalising better ways of thinking or behaving taught by the therapist. The idea that learning can be creatively self-generated has not generally found favour in a culture that emphasises the idea that useful knowledge is implanted in people from without. Most models of therapy, indeed, rest on this assumption.

In contrast, the active-client model assumes that all important learning is fundamentally self-generated, even if stimulated by experiences from without (see also Boyd and Fales 1983). This applies equally well in education where we have heard more than one professor of education observe that although teachers may provide the materials, it is students who actually teach themselves. Compatible with our perspective on therapy, some findings have suggested that the way in which students actively interface with the tasks of learning — reshaping them for their own purposes — can enhance productivity, and may be more important than what the teacher does (Csikszentmihalyi 1977; Rohrkemper and Corno 1988).

The positive role of the therapist

If one adopts an active-client point of view, how would this change the role of the therapist? In one sense, very little needs to be altered. The primary difference might be the attitude adopted by the therapist. Methods for supporting clients' development follow from the attitude of respect and faith towards the client and the belief that it is the client who effects change and the therapist who offers help and company. A helpful therapist recognises that clients have vastly greater reserves of data about their history, experiences and life environment, and are therefore the best experts on themselves. Clients could even be process experts, with the ability to choose that process which would best be used at any one point of time, like the client we described at the beginning of this chapter (Tallman 1996).

Also, it might not matter much if therapists adopt relatively more directive and authoritative roles, or less directive, egalitarian roles. Good therapists who are more authoritative may function like mentors. Mentors may know more about a particular domain of knowledge (e.g. Chaucer) than the person they are mentoring. But their job is to guide 'mentees' to think for themselves and to develop their own skills. Mentors do not provide treatment and intervene; rather, good mentors offer suggestions in a way that invites the mentee to think actively and evaluate the suggestion on his or her own, and only to accept it if the mentee comes to see the value in it. Furthermore, in a good mentor-mentee relationship, the mentee can come back with something in response, and the two can engage in a productive dialogue. In any case, it is the mentee who actively takes and uses what the mentor has to offer. A mark of good mentors is that their students often go off in new and creative directions rather than simply carry forward the work of the mentor.

A second model of the therapist is 'therapist as fellow traveller', a model which is more equal and non-directive. It would be more like two graduate students collaborating on a research project, engaging in a co-creative dialogue and solving problems together. Members of self-help groups operate along the lines of this model.

In either the case of therapist as mentor or as fellow traveller, the relationship would be one of genuine dialogue and meeting-of-persons (Friedman 1985). The meeting-of-persons might not be full; the dialogue may be confined to areas relevant to why the client is consulting the therapist. However, the relationship would be a real one, not an intervention to be modified to have certain effects on the client. Compatible with this, one feature of the active-client model is that it would also expect therapists to be their unique selves. Like their clients, therapists are also active, creative people. The most basic requirement of this model is a respectful attitude towards the client and faith in the client's self-righting capacities.

Further, because clients must ultimately manufacture solutions in their own life spaces from their own experience, the materials that a client from one culture might need might be vastly different from the materials needed by a client from another culture. This would mean that therapists would be open to the use of 'folk' methods in the therapy (Comas-Diaz 1992), or to any unique solution that might fit the client's life space.

Despite the idea that it is the client who is the therapist, this does not mitigate or reduce the professional therapist's responsibility to be as helpful as possible and to act ethically. Therapists need to act in ways that facilitate clients' mobilisation of their own self-evolutionary potential, not in ways that impede its use, or in ways that are hurtful or harmful.

Another implication of the active-client view is that the typical language used in talking about psychotherapy is not useful under this model of change. Both the words 'intervention' and 'treatment' make less sense in this context. Providing resources or interactive experience or a good working space do not seem like either treating or intervening. When we compared the therapist to a mentor, we noted that mentors neither treat nor intervene with mentees. It also does not fit to talk about the effects of interventions or the effectiveness of therapy, for both imply a mechanistic relationship between therapeutic intervention and outcome. Rather than talk about the effects of a technique, it is more meaningful to talk about the uses to which the technique can be put. Similarly, instead of talking about whether therapy is effective, it makes more sense to talk about whether therapy is useful to clients.

RESEARCH IMPLICATIONS

If it is the active client who is ultimately the therapist, then research efforts should be directed more to what clients do than to what therapists do. How do clients use what is given them? How do they take their experiences in therapy and actively use them to modify their lives outside of the therapy session? How do clients interpret the activities and messages we give them?

What little we know so far about how clients experience therapy indicates that they do not necessarily experience it as therapists do (Elliott and James 1989). Further, the factors that they generally see as helpful are not usually technique factors (Lambert 1992), but rather more general processes like providing support (Elliott and James 1989; Orlinsky and Howard 1986). But we still do not know how clients use such processes for their own self-improvement.

Secondly, rather than ask: 'Which interventions are effective for treating which client conditions?', we should ask: 'Which approaches will which clients find more useful?'. As we have already mentioned, it may be that different clients will find different approaches useful in their self-help efforts. Several authors have already suggested that matching approach to client may be more useful than matching approach to client condition or problem (Beutler and Clarkin 1990; Prochaska 1995). In a study already mentioned that compared self-help books to therapy for the treatment of depression, it was found that independent clients did better with self-help books, whereas dependent clients did better with a live therapist (Beutler et al. 1991).

There is some evidence that bears on the 'active client as therapist' hypothesis. Elliott and James (1989: 460) concluded on the basis of a small number of studies that

> clients are much more planful, active and conscious in their approach to therapy than has been implied in previous research. Indeed the literature reviewed earlier suggests that clients approach their therapy with tasks and intentions in mind and actively evaluate therapist interventions in relation to these tasks

Wood (1995) cited the results of a study where unemployed engineers who received professional counselling adjusted less well and had less success in getting re-employed than those who met in a self-help group. However, much more research on how clients produce their own therapy is needed.

SUMMARY AND CONCLUSIONS

We have argued in this chapter that the question 'What makes psychotherapy work?' has been answered. The answer is: 'the active client'. We have also argued that the field has overfocused on the importance of therapist interventions. If we want to understand how therapy works, we must shift our attention to how active clients learn and find creative resolutions to their problems. Not only must we learn to use the client's frame of reference more (Duncan and Moynihan 1994), and rely on the client more, but we must truly understand that it is *the whole person of the client who generates the processes and solutions that create change*. The Hebrew word *tsadaka* captures what the therapist does: offer a gift to the client so that he or she can help him- or herself.

The gifts the therapist gives are, first of all, a safe working space in which clients can dialogue and creatively think, experience and explore. Secondly, therapists give procedures that clients can use to create new experiences for themselves and, through such creation, develop new perspectives and new solutions. Thirdly, therapists give their own interactive experience and feedback.

The existential-humanistic perspective on the client's role in therapy, therefore, can provide a basis for all therapeutic practice. Within this framework, therapists may offer clients a wide range of growth-promoting activities and procedures from a wide range of approaches, as long as they are offered as aids to client self-growth rather than applied to clients as mechanistic techniques designed to change them.

References

Barlow, D. M. (1994) Psychological interventions in the era of managed care. *Clinical Psychology: Science and Practice* 1: 109–22

Beckham, E. E. (1990) Psychotherapy of depression. Research at the crossroads: directions for the 1990s. *Clinical Psychology Review* 10: 207–28

Bergin, A. E. and Garfield, S. L. (1994) *Handbook of Psychotherapy and Behavior Change* (4th edn) (pp. 821–30). New York: Wiley

Berman, J. S. and Norton, N. C. (1985) Does professional training make a therapist more effective? *Psychological Bulletin* 98: 401–6

Beutler, L. E. and Clarkin, J. F. (1990) *Systematic Treatment Selection: Toward Targeted Therapeutic Interventions*. New York: Brunner/Mazel

Beutler, L. E., Engle, D., Mohr, D., Daldrup, R. J., Bergan, J., Meredith, K. and Merry, W. (1991) Predictors of differential response to cognitive, experiential, and self-directed psychotherapeutic procedures. *Journal of Consulting and Clinical Psychology* 59: 333–40

Bohart, A. (1995a) The meeting of minds: constructivist implications for psychotherapy. Paper presented as part of a symposium on 'How is constructivism reshaping the clinical methods of psychotherapists?', Alvin Mahrer (Chair). New York: American Psychological Association Convention, August

Bohart, A. (1995b). The person-centered therapies. In A. Gurman and S. Messer (eds), *Essential Psychotherapies*. New York: Guilford

Bohart, A. and Tallman, K. (1997) Empathy, the active client, and experiencing. In A. C. Bohart and L. S. Greenberg (eds), *Empathy Reconsidered: New Directions in Psychotherapy*. Washington, D.C.: American Psychological Association

Boyd, E. M. and Fales, A. W. (1983) Reflective learning: key to learning from experience. *Journal of Humanistic Psychology* 23: 99–117

Castonguay, L. (1993) Understanding psychotherapy for depression: the role of techniques, relationship, and their interaction. Unpublished manuscript, Stanford University (awarded 'Best Paper,' Graduate Student Paper Competition, Division 29 of the American Psychological Association, 1993)

Christensen, A. and Jacobson, N. S. (1994) Who (or what) can do psychotherapy?: the status and challenge of nonprofessional therapies. *Psychological Science* 5: 8–14

Comas-Diaz, L. (1992) The future of psychotherapy with ethnic minorities. *Psychotherapy* 29: 88–94

Csikszentmihalyi, M. (1977) *Beyond Boredom and Anxiety*. San Francisco: Jossey-Bass

Duncan, B. L. and Moynihan, D. W. (1994) Applying outcome research: intentional utilisation of the client's frame of reference. *Psychotherapy* 31: 294–301

Durlak, J. (1979) Comparative effectiveness of paraprofessional and professional helpers. *Psychological Bulletin* 86: 80–92

Elliott, R. and James, E. (1989) Varieties of client experience in psychotherapy: an analysis of the literature. *Clinical Psychology Review* 9: 443–67

Frank, J. D. (1973) *Persuasion and Healing*. Baltimore: Johns Hopkins University Press

Friedman, M. (1985) Healing through meeting and the problematic of mutuality. *Journal of Humanistic Psychology* 25: 7–40

Gendlin, E. T. (1967) Therapeutic procedures in dealing with schizophrenics. In C. R. Rogers, E. T. Gendlin, D. J. Kiesler and C. B. Truac (eds), *The Therapeutic Relationship and its Impact* (pp. 369–400). Madison: University of Wisconsin Press

Gendlin, E. T. (1990) The small steps of the therapy process: how they come and how to help them come. In G. Lietaer, J. Rombauts and R. Van Balen (eds), *Client-Centered and Experiential Psychotherapy in the Nineties* (pp. 205–24). Leuven, Belgium: Leuven University Press

Gibson, J. J. (1979) *The Ecological Approach to Visual Perception*. Boston: Houghton Mifflin

Gold, J. R. (1994) When the patient does the integrating: lessons for theory and practice. *Journal of Psychotherapy Integration* 4: 133–58

Goodman, G. and Jacobs, M. (1995) The self-help, mutual support group. In A. Fuhriman and G. Burlingame (eds), *Handbook of Group Psychotherapy* (pp. 489–526). New York: Wiley

Gould, R. A. and Clum, G. A. (1993) A meta-analysis of self-help treatment approaches. *Clinical Psychology Review* 13: 169–86

Greenberg, L. S., Elliott, R. and Lietaer, G. (1994) Research on experiential psychotherapies. In A. E. Bergin and S. L. Garfield (eds), *Handbook of Psychotherapy and Behavior Change*, 4th edn (pp. 509–42). New York: Wiley

Greening, T. (1992) Existential challenges and responses. *Humanistic Psychologist* 20 (1): 111–15

Hattie, J. A., Sharpley, C. F. and Rogers, H. J. (1984) Comparative effectiveness of professional and paraprofessional helpers. *Psychological Bulletin* 95: 534–41

Jacobs, M. J. (Chair) (1995) *Computer Psychotherapy: The Direction of the Future?* Los Angeles: Symposium presented at the Western Psychological Association, April

Jacobs, M. J. and Goodman, G. (1989) Psychology and self-help groups: predictions on a partnership. *American Psychologist* 44: 536–45

Jacobson, N. (1995) The overselling of therapy. *Family Therapy Networker* 19: 40–51

Jordan, J. (1997) Relational development through mutual empathy. In A. C. Bohart and L. S. Greenberg (eds), *Empathy Reconsidered: New Directions in Psychotherapy*. Washington, D.C.: American Psychological Association

Kopp, S. (1972) *If You Meet the Buddha on the Road, Kill Him!* New York: Bantam Books

Lambert, M. (1992) Psychotherapy outcome research. In J. C. Norcross and M. R. Goldfried (eds), *Handbook of Psychotherapy Integration* (pp. 94–129). New York: Basic Books

Lambert, M. J. and Bergin, A. E. (1994) The effectiveness of psychotherapy. In A. E. Bergin and S. L. Garfield (eds), *Handbook of Psychotherapy and Behavior Change*, 4th edn (pp. 143–89). New York: Wiley

Lazarus, A. A. (1993) Tailoring the therapeutic relationship, or being an authentic chameleon. *Psychotherapy* 30: 404–7

Lazarus, A. A. (1995) Different types of eclecticism and integration: let's be aware of the dangers. *Journal of Psychotherapy Integration* 5: 27–40

Lazarus, A. A., Beutler, L. E. and Norcross, J. C. (1992) The future of technical eclecticism. *Psychotherapy* 29: 11–20

Luborsky, L., McClellan, A. T., Woody, G. E., O'Brien, C. P. and Auerbach, A. (1985) Therapist success and its determinants. *Archives of General Psychiatry* 42: 602–11

Mahrer, A. R. (1995) *The Complete Guide to Experiential Psychotherapy*. New York: Wiley

Marks, I. (1994) Behavior therapy as an aid to self-care. *Current Directions in Psychological Science* 3: 19–22

Masten, A. S., Best, K. M. and Garmazy, N. (1990) Resilience and development: contributions from the study of children who overcome adversity. *Development and Psychopathology* 2: 425–44

Miller, S., Hubble, M. and Duncan, B. (1995) No more bells and whistles. *Family Therapy Networker* 19: 52–63

O'Hara, M. (1986). Heuristic inquiry as psychotherapy: the client-centered approach. *Person-Centered Review* 1: 172–84

O'Hara, M. (1997) Relational empathy: beyond modernist egocentrism to postmodern holistic contextualism. In A. C. Bohart and L. S. Greenberg (eds), *Empathy Reconsidered: New Directions in Psychotherapy*. Washington, D.C.: American Psychological Association

Orlinsky, D. (1989) Researchers' images of psychotherapy: their origins and influence on research. *Clinical Psychology Review* 9: 412–42

Orlinsky, E. E. and Howard, K. I. (1980) Gender and psychotherapeutic outcome. In A. M. Brodsky and R. T. Hare-Mustin (eds), *Women and Psychotherapy* (pp. 3–34). New York: Guilford

Orlinsky, E. E. and Howard, K. I. (1986) The psychological interior of psychotherapy: explorations with the Therapy Session Reports. In L. S. Greenberg and W. M. Pinsof (eds), *The Psychotherapy Process: A Research Handbook* (pp. 477–502). New York: Guilford

Orlinsky, D. E., Grawe, K. and Parks, B. K. (1994) Process and outcome in psychotherapy: noch einmal. In A. E. Bergin and S. L. Garfield (eds), *Handbook of Psychotherapy and Behavior Change* (pp. 270–376). New York: Wiley

Paul, G. L. (1967) Outcome research in psychotherapy. *Journal of Consulting Psychology* 31: 109–18

Pennebaker, J. W. (1990) *Opening up: The Healing Power of Confiding in Others*. New York: Morrow

Perret-Clermont, A.-N., Perret, J.-F. and Bell, N. (1991) The social construction of meaning and cognitive activity in elementary school children. In L. B. Resnick, J. M. Levine and S. D. Teasley (eds), *Perspectives on Socially Shared Cognition* (pp. 41–62). Washington, D.C.: American Psychological Association

Prochaska, J. O. (1995) Common problems: common solutions. *Clinical Psychology: Science and Practice* 2: 101–5

Raskin, N. J. and Rogers, C. R. (1989) Person-centered therapy. In R. J. Corsini and D. J. Wedding (eds), *Current Psychotherapies*, 4th edn (pp. 155–94). Itasca, IL: Peacock

Resnick, R. W. (1980) Foreword. In V. Van De Riet, M. P. Korb and J. J. Gorell, *Gestalt Therapy: An Introduction* (pp. ix–xi). New York: Pergamon

Robinson, L. A., Berman, J. S. and Neimeyer, R. A. (1990) Psychotherapy for treatment of depression: a comprehensive review of controlled outcome research. *Psychological Bulletin* 108: 30–49

Rogers, C. R. (1957) The necessary and sufficient conditions of therapeutic personality change. *Journal of Consulting Psychology* 21: 95–103

Rohrkemper, M. and Corno, L. (1988) Success and failure on classroom tasks: adaptive learning and classroom teaching. *Elementary School Journal* 88: 297–312

Rowan, J. (1994) Do therapists ever cure clients? *Self and Society* 22: 4–5

Scogin, F., Bynum, J., Stephens, G. and Calhoon, S. (1990) Efficacy of self-administered treatment programs: meta-analytic review. *Professional Psychology: Research and Practice* 21: 42–7

Segal, D. L. and Murray, E. J. (1994). Emotional processing in cognitive therapy and vocal expression of feeling. *Journal of Social and Clinical Psychology* 13: 189–206

Selmi, P. M., Klein, M. H., Greist, J. H., Sorrell, S. P. and Erdman, H. P. (1990) Computer-administered cognitive-behavioural therapy for depression. *American Journal of Psychiatry* 147: 51–6

Smith, M. L., Glass, G. V. and Miller, T. I. (1980) *The Benefits of Psychotherapy*. Baltimore: Johns Hopkins University Press

Stein, D. M. and Lambert, M. J. (1984) On the relationship between therapist experience and psychotherapy outcome. *Clinical Psychology Review* 4: 7–42

Stiles, W. B. and Shapiro, D. A. (1989) Abuse of the drug metaphor in psychotherapy process-outcome research. *Clinical Psychology Review* 9: 521–44

Stiles, W. B., Shapiro, D. A. and Elliott, R. (1986) Are all psychotherapies equivalent? *American Psychologist* 41: 165–80

Strupp, H. H. and Hadley, S. W. (1979) Specific versus nonspecific factors in psychotherapy: a controlled study of outcome. *Archives of General Psychiatry* 36: 1125–36

Stubbs, J. P. and Bozarth, J. D. (1994) The dodo bird revisited: a qualitative study of psychotherapy efficacy research. *Applied and Preventive Psychology* 3: 109–20

Svartberg, M. and Stiles, T. C. (1991) Comparative effects of short-term psychodynamic psychotherapy: a meta-analysis. *Journal of Consulting and Clinical Psychology* 59: 704–14

Svartberg, M. and Stiles, T. C. (1994) Therapeutic alliance, therapeutic competence, and client change in short-term anxiety-provoking psychotherapy. *Psychotherapy Research* 4: 20–33

Tallman, K. (1996) Mastery orientation: a common factor in psychotherapy. Paper presented at the Conference of the Society for the Exploration of Psychotherapy Integration, Berkeley, CA, April

Tallman, K., Robinson, E., Kay, D., Harvey, S. and Bohart, A. (1994) Experiential and non-experiential Rogerian therapy: an analogue study. Paper presented at the American Psychological Association Convention, Los Angeles, August

Task Force on the Promotion and Dissemination of Psychological Procedures Division of Clinical Psychology of the American Psychological Association (1995) Training in and dissemination of empirically-validated psychological treatments: report and recommendations. *Clinical Psychologist* 48: 3–23

Wood, J. K. (1995) From the person-centred approach to client-centred therapy: toward a psychology. Keynote address, Third International Conference on Client-Centred and Experiential Psychotherapy, Gmunden, Austria, September

Zimring, F. (1990) Cognitive processes as a cause of psychotherapeutic change: self-initiated processes. In G. Lietaer, J. Rombauts and R. Van Balen (eds), *Client-Centered and Experiential Psychotherapy in the Nineties* (pp. 361–80). Leuven, Belgium: Leuven University Press

28

THE MIRROR AND THE HAMMER: SOME HESITANT STEPS TOWARDS A MORE HUMANE PSYCHOTHERAPY

ERNESTO SPINELLI[†]

Unlike many of my colleagues, I have never considered psychotherapy as being 'my calling'. I cannot remember a time in my youth when, faced with considering the various work options open to me, I gave psychotherapy any serious thought. It was, more accurately, a profession into which I somehow drifted more out of unforeseen circumstance than planned action. While I would not deny that a number of the themes and issues surrounding psychotherapy interested me and, happily, continue to do so; and, equally, while I mainly enjoy and value my encounters with clients, students and colleagues, it remains the case that I can conjure up other areas of interest and enjoyment that equal, if not surpass, the stimulation and pleasure provided to me by psychotherapy.

Although I remain an active, if often critical, exponent of the values and benefits of psychotherapeutic encounters in that I both practise psychotherapy and make attempts to train others to become psychotherapists, I must confess that my own experiences of being in psychotherapy as a client have been on the whole disappointing with regard to both the quantity and quality of insights that they have provoked. Indeed, to speak more plainly, that with which psychotherapy has provided me as a client has been minimal when compared to any number of other exploratory activities in which I have engaged throughout my life. When placed next to my experiences of visiting and living in foreign countries, of socio-political involvement, of reading and writing fiction and poetry, of meditation, of immersion in music and song, of recording and exploring my dreams or watching others' dreams projected on to cinema screens or canvases or chiselled out of rock, and, most of all, of allowing myself to feel love for others and to feel another's love for me, that which I have gained from my personal therapy remains barely significant.

In disclosing this, I do not wish to leave readers with the false impression that, somewhat cynically, I have judged psychotherapy to offer little of worth other than as a means to some degree of personal financial security. Only that my encounters with my therapists have lacked what I can only call that vital 'human' dimension, that 'honest and open meeting of beings' that infuses anything which illuminates and brings meaning to one's life. This is what I have

† Chapter first appeared in Spinelli, E. (2001) *The Mirror and the Hammer: Challenging Orthodoxies in Psychotherapeutic Thought,* London: Continuum, and is reprinted with kind permission of the author and publisher.

sought to offer to my clients and students and which I have been blessed in receiving through my ongoing encounters with them. I can only hope that they have felt something similar in their encounters with me.

I am by no means the first, and will in all likelihood not be the last, to give voice to these views. Indeed, in recent years there has been a groundswell of written accounts by both psychotherapists and clients expressing a wide range of critical views and concerns surrounding the practice of psychotherapy.[1] In the great majority of such instances, the voices raised have been disparaging of any number of theory-derived stances and techniques adopted by psychotherapists in their interactions with clients.

When confronted with such criticisms, the response of many psychotherapists is likely to be: 'But the critic has not understood the need for us to maintain these uncommon attitudes and dispositions if there is to be any hope for the therapy to fulfil its ameliorative possibilities. The psychotherapeutic relationship is like no other and, as such, requires particular forms of intercourse and intervention no matter how unusual or unacceptable these might be in other types of social interaction.' Although I am not convinced by such rationales, let me suppose, for the sake of argument, that they are, in essence, correct at least insofar as they are the necessary underpinnings of a particular, and currently dominant, view of psychotherapy. And let me also concede that this view permits both 'fundamentalist' and 'liberal' interpretations of these necessary underpinnings, of which existential psychotherapy may be its most liberal proponent.

What I want to consider in this chapter, however haltingly (for, on the whole, I consider my own practice to be well within the boundaries of 'liberalism'), is a more radical proposal. In doing so, I am at least in part aware that the views I will put forward may appear to many of my readers to threaten the very possibility of the therapeutic enterprise, and that, as a consequence, I may well be judged as being arrogant, naïve and irresponsible — or, worse, that my very credentials as a psychotherapist may be called into question by at least some of my colleagues. If so, then I suppose I will be placed within a particular circle of disgruntled individuals and, like them, become labelled as one more among the numerous cranks (and the occasional visionaries cohabiting a nearby terrain) who have railed against the parameters of this strange profession.

I recently chanced upon an advertisement for a memoir by Emily Fox Gordon entitled *Mockingbird Years: A Life in and out of Therapy*.[2] My first reaction to it was to suppose that it would be yet another in a developing category of psychotherapeutically focused texts written by ex-clients: the 'Read-about-how-psychotherapy-fucked-me-up-and-how-awful-(or-evil)-it-is' genre. I have read a fair number of such books, yet for reasons that I have yet to ascertain, I experienced an urgent desire to read Ms Gordon's text, and duly ordered it. Having done so, I can state in all honesty that, for me, this was one of those key texts that succeed in provoking a sense of disturbing recognition of their having

---

1. See, for instance: J. Masson, *Against Therapy*, Collins, London, 1989; J. Russell, *Out of Bounds*, Sage, London, 1993; D. Smail, *How To Survive Without Psychotherapy*, Constable, London, 1996; P. Lomas, *Doing Good? Psychotherapy out of its Depth*, Oxford University Press, Oxford, 1999.

2. E. F. Gordon, *Mockingbird Years: A Life in and out of Therapy*, Basic Books, New York, 2000.

captured something felt, but for which no adequate words to give expression to that feeling had been found until now.

Gordon's memoir recounts various meetings with a series of unremarkable men and women who had been her psychotherapist. Interweaved with these often hilarious and harrowing vignettes she writes about incidents in her life with her parents, her friends, her relationship with her husband, and her encounters with institutionalised colleagues who, like her, were forced to 'put up with' the inadequate interventions of those who sought to 'make her better'. As counterpoint to the negligible impact of other psychotherapists, Gordon discusses her encounters with *Dr Leslie Farber*, an altogether different kind of psychotherapist. Although Farber was a respected psychoanalyst and author of a number of highly regarded papers published in specialist journals and textbooks, it is quickly made apparent that he was highly critical of the psychotherapeutic enterprise as understood by his peers, and that his way of working with his clients was, to put it mildly, unorthodox.

Gordon writes that Farber, who greatly admired the writings of the Danish philosopher Søren Kierkegaard, considered psychotherapists to be like

> a man who has spent decades building a splendid mansion, a great multi-storied edifice with wings flung out in every direction. But when the man has finally completed his dream house, he settles contentedly into a shack next door. In Dr Farber's view, the house of psychoanalysis was impressive but unfit for human habitation.
>
> (ibid.: 16)

Gordon tells us that,

> I knew instantly that Dr Farber was a different kind of being from other therapists. His was not the neutral watchfulness I had become so used to; he judged, and revealed his judgement ... I also sensed, if obscurely, that he was a person whose way of looking at the world ... was integrated with, and undetachable from, his self.
>
> (ibid.)

For Farber, the experience of engaging in psychotherapy was inseparable from that of being in a friendship. His stance was focused upon a moral, rather than a technique-dominated and hence safer, professional engagement with his clients. One obvious way of gaining a sense of what Gordon is seeking to convey about Farber's stance can be gleaned from what she tells us of their discussions:

> What did we talk about? We talked of Dr Farber's childhood ... We talked about my childhood ... We talked about his marriages and my boyfriends. We talked about his growing despair at watching ... patients ... loitering in a psychiatric limbo ... We talked about the youth culture ... We talked about movies and TV.
>
> (ibid.: 119)

Just from this brief extract, we can begin to understand that Farber found little value in the maintenance of a psychotherapeutic neutrality and anonymity. But this is but the tip of the iceberg.

Soon enough, Gordon reveals that Farber was willing to meet with her as often as she wished (so long as he was free to do so) and that their sessions could be brief or extend far beyond the 'magical' 50 minutes. Further, Farber saw no reason to limit such meetings to his office and, instead, was willing to go out on walks with her, introduce her to his family, invite her to his home, and provide her with meals and informal, unboundaried discussion. As far as one can tell, Farber did not do this because he had singled out Gordon as being someone 'special' or requiring of unusual degrees of psychotherapeutic attention; instead, this stance towards Gordon was not untypical of his wider stance towards each of his clients. In similar fashion, Farber did not ask or demand anything in particular from Gordon other than that she treat him with a similar kind of human respect and dignity that he sought to embody in his relations with her. As Gordon explains:

> In his practice with patients, Dr Farber was both far humbler than his more conventional colleagues and far bolder: He was humbler because he approached his patients as a whole human being, not as a semianonymous representative of his profession, and because he had abandoned his profession's claims to objectivity and curative power. He was bolder because when he took on a patient, he committed himself to a risky, open-ended friendship and to all the claims of responsibility that friendship entails. It was a brave venture to step from behind the mask of his profession, and a dangerous one ... Many other psychotherapists did something similar in the 1960s, of course, often with disastrous results.
>
> (ibid.: 125)

What was different about Farber, in this last distinguishing respect, was that he seemed to be well aware of the interrelational responsibilities that are required if one is to venture into such perilous territories: 'He was tough-minded, and he held himself very carefully in check. His boundaries were moral, not professional. They were part of his being, not a stifling suit of armor but a flexible skin,' (ibid.: 126).

I would not be surprised if, by this point, the reader may have begun to experience conflicting attitudes towards Farber's 'way of being a psychotherapist'. While there may be some sense of attraction towards Farber's humane attitude towards his relations with his clients, there is also likely to be an opposite niggling concern that his stance breaks all the rules of contemporary psychotherapy. To her credit, Gordon is equally clear-sighted and concludes that 'I can well understand how ... any mainstream psychotherapist ... would have no choice but to judge Farber guilty of serious malpractice', (ibid.: 218).

But then, in response to her (and our) concerns, she challenges her readers with an equally disturbing question: *So what?*

> If Dr Farber's aim had been solely or even principally a therapeutic one, the criticisms ... would have been germane ... [I]n the name of therapy, Farber was doing something quite different. His aim ... was a radical departure from the ordinary goal of therapy: He meant to offer hope to his patients through talk. This was not talk that centered, necessarily, around their problems — it was just the best and most honest talk that he and they were capable of. He meant to break the logic of despair, and his goal in doing so

was not a primarily therapeutic one ... [T]he aim was not so much to restore the patient's health as it was to free him from illusion ... [A]lthough his worldview was tragic, truth was transcendent, and always held a possibility of hope.

(ibid.: 221)

It would seem to me that what Gordon is expressing through these statements is that Farber had shifted the enterprise of psychotherapy away from a set of methodological conditions and, instead, was attempting to replace these with an attitude that expressed a way of being with others that paralleled his broader, more general, way of being with self and the world. He did not merely 'do' psychotherapy; rather, his way of being a psychotherapist could not be separated from his way of being human.

Although an invaluable collection of Leslie Farber's essays has recently been published,[3] I believe that his work has been unjustly neglected by contemporary psychotherapy. He deserves much more attention and consideration and there is a great deal to be learned from him.

Farber, who placed so much import on language and discourse, was unhesitatingly critical of the language of psychotherapy in general and, in particular, of the way in which even the most human-focused psychotherapists chose to write about their clients.

> The people are written about as if they are 'creatures ... [who] ... may bear some resemblance to animals, or to steam engines or robots or electronic brains, they do not sound like people. They are in fact constructs of theory, more humanoid than human; and whether they are based on the libido theory or on the new inter-personal theories of relationships, it is just those qualities most distinctively human which seem to have been omitted.[4]

He argued that it is quite a different matter to ask, 'What is man?', as opposed to 'What is it to be human?'. The former question forces us towards abstraction, removes us from a shared realm of mutual experience and places us in the terrain of clinically detached observation and conceptualisation. This, for him, was the path adopted and advocated by his colleagues. His way, instead, argued for a quite different approach to the understanding of, and meeting with, one's clients.

> Obviously, if meeting is to occur in psychotherapy, it will occur *despite* ... inequalities in position, status, background, education or awareness. Within the therapeutic dialogue, the initiative, hopefully, is the therapist's. It is up to him whether he can forsake the academy in order to address his patient not as an object of knowledge, but as a being engaged in the task [as Kierkegaard puts it] of becoming 'what he is already: namely a human being'.

(ibid.: 590)

---

3. L. H. Farber, *The Ways of the Will*, Basic Books, New York, 2000.
4. L. H. Farber, 'Martin Buber and psychotherapy', in P. A. Schilpp and M. Friedman (eds), *The Philosophy of Martin Buber*, The Library of Living Philosophers, Vol. XII, Open Court, La Salle, IL, 1967, p. 578. Sadly, this brilliant paper has not been included in the above collection (see note 3 above). Interested readers are strongly urged to seek it out.

Farber railed against the adoption of a conventional scientific prose that seeks to disguise, but cannot truly conceal, the 'pathos of two maddened human beings clutching at each other, whatever the pretext' (ibid.: 594).

When I first read this last sentence, I was both deeply shaken and confused. What on earth was Farber attempting to convey? If I have not misunderstood his words, I believe that they seek to capture a crucial awareness which, among other things, paves the way for a radical departure from more ordinary understandings of the therapeutic relationship.

Farber argued that the benefits of a psychotherapeutic relationship begin to emerge only when the client ascertains that the relationship is mutually beneficial to both participants. It is precisely when the client, through this understanding, and something akin to a concomitant concern (or 'pity', as Farber labels it) for the therapist, 'agrees to undertake therapeutic efforts which, although clearly beneficial to himself, have as their primary motive the assuaging of another's pain' (ibid.: 596). It is through the client's connection with the psychotherapist's own confusion and despair of being human and, hence, the acceptance of the uncertainty and wonderment that expresses itself in every facet of his or her life (including, of course, that part of life that constitutes 'being and working as a psychotherapist'), that the client may find the will to recognise and respond in a compassionate fashion to the concern that infuses the therapist's way of being with another (the client).

For Farber, this critical choice on the part of the client to move out of his or her own exclusive and limited self-focused pattern of engagement and, instead, seek to embrace the world of the psychotherapist, serves to confirm the humanity of the participants both to themselves and to one another, and, in turn, permits their encounter to be expressive of its human and humane qualities.

Farber suggests that this 'turn' on the part of the client provides the psychotherapist with the will to be the dedicated, even courageous human being whom he or she is capable of being — and, in the same way, provokes the same felt qualities for the client.

> Pity demands an imagining of the other's particular pain to the degree that the pain is experienced as one's own. In therapy, the paradox is inescapable that the man who is incapable of arousing pity will find it hard to help another.
>
> (ibid.)

When I first began to glimpse the meaning of Farber's assertion, I was both flooded with a new-found understanding of the possibilities of psychotherapy and, as well, was moved to tears. I could see that whatever success I may have had through my therapeutic work with my clients came about not through my skilful interventions, nor even through such qualities of care and respect that I was able to muster forth in my relations with them, but, rather, had emerged through a *mutual* acceptance of our shared powerlessness and uncertainty in the face of the 'impossible dilemmas of being human'. And further that, paradoxically, via this very acceptance, both I and my clients discovered some well-spring of power that permitted us to disclose ourselves to, and be disclosed by, the presence of the other.

Many clients who have either benefited from, or, equally, have been damaged by, psychotherapy have placed the psychotherapist's power, or more advanced (or elevated) way of being, as the source of their experience. While I have been willing to accept that this is what these clients have come to believe, knowing all too well my own and fellow psychotherapists' frailties and conflicting confusions regarding our own lives, I could not conclude the same. But Farber has provided what is to me a far sounder alternative perspective. It may well be that in those instances when both client and psychotherapist turn towards the other and, not in spite of but *because* they permit themselves to ascertain the other's frailties and are willing to embrace them as their own, then, through this very act of human caring, each experiences that necessary empowerment to be, and to be seen to be, the being they both aspire to become. In similar fashion, it may well also be the case that when the client experiences the psychotherapist's authority and power as unhelpful or oppressive, this is an outcome of the psychotherapist's unwillingness to accept the client's frailties as belonging not just to the client alone. As such, no matter how concerned or caring he or she may be towards the client, the psychotherapist's unwillingness to stand revealed as human in turn prevents the possibility of the client's concern being directed towards another (the psychotherapist).

The person who most influenced Farber's approach to psychotherapy was the philosopher and Jewish theologian, Martin Buber. Farber returns again and again to Buber's writings concerning what he called *interhuman relations*.[5] Emily Fox Gordon provides an insightful summary of these views:

> The interhuman is the 'life between person and person'. It is distinct from the social and collective realm. The interhuman is an end, not a means. It has no utility, it is not the foundation on which society is built, and it can be inimical to society's purposes. What happens in life between person and person can carry psychological and sociological meanings, of course, but these are incidental to the fact of meeting itself.[6]

She argues that Farber's psychotherapeutic practice exemplified Buber's interhuman relations. In particular, she suggests, Farber sought to demonstrate these qualities 'through talk, of how talk is to be treated, not as a means to a therapeutic end but as the central source of moral meaning itself', (ibid.: 225). Unlike other psychotherapists who all rely upon 'talk' as their primary means towards ameliorative change, Farber understood, through his study of Buber, that talking cannot be turned into a technique or a 'cure'. For Farber, talk was not a means to a designated end; rather, it was an end in itself in that it was the very expression of interhuman relations. As such, his 'talks' with his clients could be, and were, as Gordon makes so plain, about anything. Their content did not truly matter. Rather, the talk between Farber and his clients served to illuminate the worth and possibilities of open, honest and care-full human encounter.

Gordon writes that,

> In the offices of my earlier therapists, I had understood that the world was to be kept at bay; pieces of it entered the room as carefully prepared

---

5. Various references to Martin Buber's *Between Man and Man* and *I and Thou* appear throughout Farber's paper (ibid.).
6. Cf. Gordon, *Mockingbird Years*, p. 224.

specimens ready for examination and analysis. But in Dr Farber's office, the world flowed in freely and surrounded us ... [and] would take shape between us.

(ibid.: 126)

Farber had seen that interhuman relations require the acknowledgement of the world as their context. And, seeing this, he sought to welcome the world into the encounter between himself and his clients, sometimes through the subject matter of their talks (such as politics, cinema, social events), at others by quite deliberately engaging in talks with his clients outside of the secluded confines of his office (in parks, down city streets, at his home in the company of his family, with significant others in the client's wider world).

In the first and second chapters of my most recent book, *The Mirror and the Hammer*,[7] I argued that while existential psychotherapy has implicitly acknowledged the contextualising presence of the world within the therapeutic relationship, this stance could, perhaps *should*, be made far more explicit. I suggested that one important way by which this could be made more obvious was through the focus upon what I termed the 'they-focused' relations in the client's life. While this may be a sufficient means by which the world can be returned to the therapeutic encounter, Farber's example provides alternative, perhaps more straightforward possibilities.

I realise that the great majority of my psychotherapeutic colleagues (including many of those who label themselves 'existential') would consider it unacceptable, perhaps even potentially abusive, for them to engage in talk with their clients outside of the confines of their offices. What would it mean to the client, and what disturbing impact might there be upon the relationship if, for instance, the talks took place outdoors, in public, or even (a dreadful possibility, this) in the client's home? What price might be paid in this calling forth of, and towards, the world?

In all honesty, I do not know. But if, as existential psychotherapists often claim, their approach stands as being the most sceptically inquiring of all psychotherapeutic stances and, as well, that they are in the forefront of the exploration of the intersubjective, then, surely, we can be sufficiently free and responsible in addressing such questions? After all, Søren Kierkegaard, the philosopher whose writings most clearly anticipated the existential movement, urged his readers to 'say what you mean and to do what you say'.[8] At times, it appears to me, existential psychotherapy, while being bold in 'saying what it means', may well have remained unnecessarily timid in considering what implications there may be in its 'doing what it says'.

Emily Fox Gordon's memoir concludes with what I believe to be one of the most pertinent critiques of contemporary psychotherapy. Taking Buber as her guide, she argues that:

It was clear that when Buber was writing midcentury that a psychotherapeutic ethic was in the ascendancy, and that for this ethic to

---

7. E. Spinelli, *The Mirror and The Hammer: Challenges to Therapeutic Orthodoxy*, Continuum, London, 2001.
8. S. Kierkegaard, *The Diary of Søren Kierkegaard* (edited by Peter Rohde), Philosophical Library, New York, 1960/1990.

prevail, more and more that was heretofore accepted as part of the human condition, to be endured or celebrated or transcended ... would be relegated to the realm of the pathological. There were benefits in this, of course — no sensible person could deny that therapy practiced as an art can be a force for good but in the general progress of therapy, there was also a great and terrible loss of meaning. It was the realm of the interhuman that steadily shrank as therapy advanced ... The world we live in now is one in which nearly all of us ... are so thoroughly indoctrinated in the ideology of therapy that society has remade itself in therapy's image. To one degree or another, nearly every encounter looks like therapy now ... If therapy is all that we can give, or receive, then the possibility of mutuality has all but vanished.[9]

Perhaps foolishly, perhaps because, notwithstanding my reservations, I have invested so much of my life in exploring the potential worth of psychotherapy, I cannot fully agree with her conclusion. And because, while recognising that I have found no argument with which to disprove her contention, still, nonetheless, I continue to disagree, I am obliged to consider radical alternatives such as those posed by Leslie Farber.

I confess, with some all-too-real trepidation, to having begun some cautious explorations along the lines suggested by him. And while I have gained some further clarity (however potentially illusory) through such, I remain, at present, in no position to assert the worth of the enterprise. If anything, in fact, I am suffused with the dreadful concern that I may be profoundly in error and that, if so, it is not I alone, or even principally, who may suffer as a consequence. Nonetheless, perhaps naïvely, I continue to believe that if the meeting point between human beings is approached with all the honesty and respect that one can muster, and that those same qualities are shared by self and other, there will be no critical danger.

'Ah ... but', my colleagues will respond, 'how can you be certain that your clients *are* capable of these very qualities?'. In all honesty, I know that I cannot be certain either of them, or of myself. As a psychotherapist, I share the view that any worthwhile encounter requires *a leap of faith*, a living with uncertainty not only on the part of the client, but of the therapist as well. In the past, I have watched my clients take such leaps from a vantage point of relative security. And while, today, I feel no compulsion to ask anything more of them than that which they are already willing to undertake, I have begun to hear a somewhat insistent voice urging me to find something of their courage in my own stance. It remains to be seen whether this voice is the call of conscience or of hubris.

In asking myself how I might make some sense of my embrace of this uncertain and uneasy path, I am reminded that I have sometimes suggested, not entirely in jest, that the complex workings of psychotherapy might best be likened, at least to some degree, to a number of primary aspects of a model of contemporary physics that has become known as *Chaos Theory*.[10] (Cf. Clarkson's Chapter 7, this volume.) Speaking personally, my attraction to this model lies in its ability to confirm that which in some way I had intuited about the shifting changes and movements in my own life. If I come to a point where I ask myself,

9. Cf. Gordon, *Mockingbird Years*, pp. 228–9.
10. J. Gleick, *Chaos: Making a New Science*, Cardinal, London, 1988.

'How did I ever get to this particular "here"?', I am forced to conclude that no amount of linearly derived 'cause and effect explanation' begins to provide me with a remotely satisfactory solution. Rather, the 'cause' to my being 'here' is so infinitely more subtle and complex than I might like to assume that any attempts I might make to control or predict my future 'being here' experiences become singularly laughable (again, cf. Clarkson's Chapter 7).

The approach taken by existential psychotherapy may be rightfully considered as a sort of 'Chaos Theory of psychotherapy'. For, like Chaos Theory proper, existential psychotherapy enjoins its practitioners to move on and away from their desires to predict and control their clients and, instead, urges them to approach matters from the standpoint of a new proposition — a proposition based, centrally, upon the acceptance of that mutual revelatory disclosure that is the expression of interrelational encounter. These chaos-acknowledging instances of the meeting of *self-with-other* seem to me to be not the predictable 'causes' for change, but rather, serve as embodied confirmations of the actuality of being human and all of the possibilities for freedom and responsibility therein contained and embraced.

Such meetings, like that between a mirror and a hammer, may well be shattering. And yet, through their collision, the human truths that truly matter to us all, and that *are* our humanity, may stand revealed.

Throughout its first century, psychotherapy presented a version of itself that relied upon technological and utilitarian notions. Here a mirror. There a hammer. Now, reflect. Now, smash. Now, rebuild. And reflect once more. The present chapter, in common with the whole of the book from which it is taken, has sought to demonstrate the limits, and the limiting consequences, of this attitude.

In place of such, I have suggested an alternative possibility. It is that which rests upon psychotherapy's exploration of those potentials that may arise when its practitioners come to acknowledge that in their encounters with their clients, they are not the only ones who hold up mirrors and wield hammers.

Even more radically, through the implications of an inter-relational focus upon meeting and encounter, a hint of something far more disturbing — and revealing — has begun to impose itself upon psychotherapeutic consciousness. This 'something' has not yet been sufficiently acknowledged nor suitably identified other than by the tension-provoking label of 'Chaos'.

Perhaps, as I have sought to indicate, it is the task of existential psychotherapy, if not all psychotherapy, to remind us that '"Chaos" is the name we have given to an order that has not yet been understood'.[11]

---

11. H. Miller, *Tropic of Capricorn*, Grove Press, New York, 1961. The actual quotation is as follows: 'Confusion is a word we have invented for an order which is not understood.' My hope is that Mr Miller is too busy up in heaven teaching angels all there is to know about sex for him to be much bothered by my paraphrasing of this great sentence.

29
THE FUTURE OF PSYCHOTHERAPY

DHARMAVIDYA DAVID BRAZIER

Psychotherapy has grown up in particular conditions and is a response to those conditions — conditions which are primarily rooted in the nature of a modern society which has achieved unprecedented material prosperity, but at considerable cost to the human spirit. The culture of an age requires its own particular kind of spiritual and psychological support and, in turn, generates characteristic psychological difficulties for its members. All advanced societies, therefore, also generate methods for helping their members to adjust to, or recover from, the effects of the social conditions resulting from the particular form the civilisation takes. In many cases these methods fall within the province of religion, philosophy or medicine. The degree of independence achieved by the psychotherapeutic profession in modern Western societies is a symptom of the remarkable degree of specialisation of function that has occurred in these societies as well as of the process of secularisation. The possibility of psychotherapy being reabsorbed by one or other of these, its parental figures continues to hover, since the profession is as yet adolescent and not yet fully master of its own house.

The alienation that modern people experience through their participation in working lives in which it is often hard to see any direct connection between effort and intrinsic worth generates much psychological dysfunction. A village in Vietnam that needs a school may have a village meeting and start cutting bamboo to build walls next week. A person working in the head office of the education department of a London borough may be involved in a parallel task, but the structures of sophistication in our society are such that he or she may never experience anything more satisfying than occasionally managing to empty the in-tray, or achieve a few hours of respite from super-ordinate oversight. These structures of sophistication have collective benefits, but they are soul destroying for many of those who operate them.

This situation of alienation has a two-pronged effect upon psychotherapy. On the one hand, it creates the need for particular kinds of repairers of souls. Psychotherapy would not have developed without this need. On the other hand, psychotherapy is itself a structured activity embedded in the same social matrix as all other modern professions, and so there is a constant pressure for psychotherapy itself to adopt and incorporate the very same structures of sophistication from whose pernicious effects it is attempting to deliver others (cf. Kaye's Chapter 24, this volume). Psychotherapy is in constant danger of succumbing to the diseases that it exists to cure.

Psychotherapy may serve to repair those overly damaged by modern society, but it also serves to fit people into that society. What counts as repair or cure may be a function of what a society needs, or it may be some form of liberation from the constraints that the society imposes. Different therapies may work in different directions. Psychotherapy is not, therefore, an inherently unified project, but may encompass a diversity of philosophies that, though sometimes ultimately irreconcilable, are nonetheless allied on account of similarities of technique, medium of operation or arena of concern. In this respect we could make a comparison with politics. All politicians share something in terms of professional identity even when they oppose each other fundamentally on aims.

A society in which economics has achieved virtually religious status needs a workforce in which there are as few obstacles to interchangeability of economic units as possible. By economic units we now mean individuals. Once in history we might have meant families, but no longer. Psychotherapy now helps people to survive as individuals rather than as families or clans. Here we have to face the fact that psychotherapy operates by persuasion. Many psychotherapists like to think that they operate in a value-neutral way, but this is really an insupportable notion. Clients are influenced and tend to adopt values from their therapists, and this ideology-transfer accounts for a major part of psychotherapy's effectiveness.

Psychotherapy is, then, an exercise in faith, and the ideologies of therapy have been significant contributors to the postmodern world-view. In particular, the philosophy of individualism or individuation has tended towards the weakening of family bonds. Seldom in history can the family have been so denuded of function or privacy as it is in the modern world. Psychotherapy has contributed to weakening intergenerational bonds by advancing the notion that parents are responsible for the psychological problems of their offspring. This has introduced resentment between generations where in other cultures gratitude and duty cement closer ties. Again, although marriage counselling and reconciliation have formed a part of the work of psychotherapists, it is probable that there have been a great many more marriages dissolved than saved through the catalyst of therapy. Psychotherapy has not really been good news for families.

The bearing this has on the future of psychotherapy will depend upon how societal attitudes to the family develop, and whether psychotherapy is successful in adapting to whatever changes there may be in this area. Governments tend always to pay lip-service to 'family values', but this does not run very deep. Economic considerations have a stronger pull, and if industry needs people to act as individuals in a fluid market then an anti-family undercurrent is likely to remain powerful. Family ties, after all, are one of the most powerful rigidities hindering the achievement of theoretical maximum labour market fluidity; and as long as it remains a goal to get a larger proportion of the working-age population into employment, family bonds will continue to come under pressure and psychotherapy will have a role in rationalising the resulting ruptures.

At the same time, changes in family life have created conditions for widespread distress. Divorce is common; the nuclear family often cannot cope; larger and larger numbers of people live alone. All this makes work for psychotherapists, helping people to negotiate the painful transitions in life's journey that are now commonplace. Psychotherapy thus both facilitates and profits from social disruption. Further, psychotherapy has taken over some functions from the family. Where, in the past, families were large, now they are small. If one needs a confidante it is much less likely to be found amongst one's kin than was formerly the case. Psychotherapy thus acquires a bridging function, providing on a temporary and usually commercial basis what used to be available within the family for love. Thirdly, just as the former privacy of the family has been increasingly penetrated by the surveillance of the modern state, so too, in psychotherapy, the privacy that once seemed virtually sacred between therapist and client has gradually been eroded so that codes of ethics no longer give the meeting between client and professional anything like the degree of protection it once enjoyed. The demands of an increasingly technological money-orientated society are powerful determinants of the environment within which psychotherapy seeks a meaningful existence.

Then there is the role of religion which, at this point, one would once always have said has declined. However, while it is true that psychotherapists now often fulfil the confessional role that was once the preserve of clerics, it is by no means so obvious that religion is in decline as it once was. Indeed, it could be the case that this trend might gradually be reversing. There are things that religion can offer that psychotherapy will never be able to supply. The very word 're-ligion', however, refers to the re-tying of connections. Religion is a force of social cohesion and, as argued above, cohesion is often valued less highly than mobility, despite the fragmenting effects of economic competition. Surveys tend to show that psychotherapists are a singularly irreligious category, far more so than their clientele.

Religion and psychotherapy may often pull in opposite directions, therefore, though it is also true that there are skills that are transferable between the two domains, and practitioners in each field quite commonly venture into the other in search of enhanced enlightenment or skilfulness. Both domains are concerned with the well-being of the soul, but what 'well-being' is understood to imply in the two cases can be very different. It is not impossible to conceive of psychotherapies that are in harmony with religious values; and were religion once again to become a major force in society these would no doubt become more prominent. At present, however, it seems a more accurate generalisation to characterise psychotherapy as helping people to survive without religion rather than as a course allied to religious purpose and values. The status of religion in society is certainly a significant variable affecting the fortunes of psychotherapy.

Let us also mention the other human relations professions. These exist in a field of constant change. Many years ago, I entered the social work profession, at the time of the Seebohm reorganisation. There was considerable euphoria in the profession and expectations ran high. It was the age of 'social engineering' and the most popular subject at universities was sociology. There was much optimism around about what could be achieved by social change, and social workers felt themselves to be at the cutting-edge of a progressive revolution. There were also many talented people in the profession, and I was fortunate to get a thorough education in what, in effect, was a form of psychotherapy called 'social casework'.

Looking back it seems difficult to believe how rapidly circumstances changed. Social work struggled for full professional status and failed to achieve it. In simple terms we can say that this failure was largely due to the overwhelming weight of state power. Social work gradually ceased to be an intimate therapeutic process and became an arm of state intrusion into family affairs. I became a psychotherapist as a by-product of this process. It became impossible to practise what I had been taught within the framework of the profession within which I had learnt it. Eventually I had to retrain and re-designate myself in order to go on doing what I had been doing. As a psychotherapist in the 1990s I was practising the same art that I had learnt as a social worker in the 1970s. So professional boundaries shift.

In the modern world there is certainly a need for spiritual or psychological help, but that fact in itself in no way determines who will supply that need or what sort of help it will be. Psychotherapy finds itself in competition in various quarters with medicine, nursing, occupational therapy, social work, other paramedical professions, alternative therapies and a host of forms of counselling. There are also always new professions emerging on to the scene. Thus, there is now a certain momentum in coaching. Coaching began as an offshoot of management consultancy, but is rapidly establishing itself and looking to take a slice of the territory that psychotherapy currently occupies.

In addition to these external rivals, we have also to take into account the fact that, as already mentioned, psychotherapy is far from being a unified activity. The many different groups that belong to the UK Council for Psychotherapy do not really have very much in common. There is, consequently, a constant risk of fragmentation. Although psychotherapy has got further than social work did in its project for professionalisation, this project has itself carried a high cost. Regulation inevitably means the setting up of boundaries. Some groups are 'in' and others are 'out'. Those that are 'out' are likely to become hostile competitors seeking a new identity, perhaps, but no less keen to take a share of the work and to advance different perspectives on its meaning, methods and validity. The rapidity with which a group can reinvent itself in modern life is liable to outpace the cumbersome bureaucratic procedures that are necessary to create regulated environments, especially when the activity in question is as difficult to define as psychotherapy. Two people sitting together in a room discussing personal matters could be called by a multitude of names, and any of these is potentially a new professional identity that can be marketed and can inspire loyalty.

A large part of the motivation for professionalisation is financial. A regulated profession has some prospects of being able to charge more highly for its services. A high-cost profession, however, operating in such a competitive arena is also vulnerable to losing its market to those who are outside its fence. Another factor to consider is credibility. If psychotherapy is an art of persuasion, then the credibility of its message is a crucial variable in its success. There was a time when most people in Britain were frightened of psychotherapy. The idea of somebody interfering with one's mind, as it was seen, seemed to many repulsively unattractive. This hurdle has now been surmounted and entering psychotherapy is no longer regarded as a pathological act in itself. Public acceptance has, however, not been unqualified.

Let me digress for a moment into history. Freud analysed a number of women who told him that they had had sexual relations with their fathers. He at first drew the conclusion that this early history of inappropriate sexual activity was causally related to their current neurotic symptoms. Then he encountered a similar case in which it was clear that the woman's account could not be accurate historically. This led him to doubt all the other accounts as well and develop the theory of repressed infantile sexual wishes as a character formative influence in the lives of all people. This theory had enormous influence, as much in stimulating the work, writing and researches of those who disagreed with it as of those who thought it correct. The history of psychotherapeutic theory could, to a large degree, be typified as the history of those who disagreed with Freud and their diverse reasons for doing so.

Although the range of theories advanced by those who disagreed was vast, the question of infantile sexuality came powerfully to the fore once again in the 1970s and 1980s as child abuse — and increasingly sexual abuse — became the focus of attention. The almost universal conclusion was that Freud really had been wrong and here was the evidence. It was suggested that perhaps even as many as a third of all women had been sexually abused in childhood. Suddenly psychotherapy seemed to have found a vital task to perform. A veritable gold rush of interest was stimulated with books, lectures, training courses and media attention. Therapists started to uncover 'lost memories' of sexual abuse in their clients and for a while this seemed to explain all manner of ills.

The gold rush is now over, however. Interest stimulates research, and psychology has now demonstrated just how very easy it is to create 'false memories'. In retrospect, were it ever possible to assess the damage done to family relations and to individual peace of mind by those psychotherapists who were most enthusiastic in support of the repressed memory idea, the indictment would be extremely serious. The pendulum has, therefore, swung back. Psychotherapists now take a more balanced and sober view of client's reports, knowing that sexual abuse is not unknown and that reports of it are not always exactly what they seem, especially when the memory has been 'recovered'. The story of the theory of sexual abuse is an example of the vicissitudes that theories of human psychological pathology and well-being can go through. It demonstrates that the theory base of psychotherapy is unstable. Like dieticians, therapists have had to adapt again and again to changes in data as well as changes in fashion.

Even when they do seem to be on relatively stable ground, they may have to share it with others. Thus, the theory of 'post-traumatic stress disorder' is now regarded as fairly well established, in part because this is one area where the perspicacious observations of Freud have never really been overturned. Nowadays we have more research data, that is all. It has, consequently, become common, and expected, that the authorities will ensure that counselling is available to members of the public in the aftermath of major catastrophes. There is no guarantee that this counselling will necessarily be offered by psychotherapists, however. This demonstrates that in those areas where psychological understanding is fairly well established, it is impossible for any one professional group to monopolise access to, or use of, that knowledge.

So psychotherapy, as a professional grouping, has to manoeuvre between these many cross-currents. In such uncertain waters it is perhaps not surprising that there have been moves towards confederation and regulation. The quest for stability, understandable as it is, may, however, prove to be a Canute-like gesture and could deprive psychotherapy of some degree of the manoeuvrability that has proved essential to its success so far. Psychotherapy conferences have become less concerned with innovation and more with respectability. This may be a sign of maturity, but in a world of short life-spans, maturity soon transforms into senility. All in all, one cannot say that the future of psychotherapy is secure, and the efforts that are currently being made to increase what security there is may hinder essential creativity. What will be crucial will be how the profession responds to changes in public mood and to the less openly acknowledged yet ultimately more coercive and less forgiving demands of the economy.

In the longer term we need to distinguish between psychotherapy as a function and psychotherapy as a profession. As we have seen there is much activity that could fall within a functional definition of psychotherapy that is not performed by psychotherapists, but by other groups in society. The psychotherapy function will be needed for the foreseeable future because it is a function of the societal forces reviewed at the beginning of this chapter. The psychotherapy profession also probably now has sufficient momentum and cohesion to survive and could even prosper, though the forces that will determine whether it does so or not are largely out of its control. There is a tendency for socially successful groups to acquire new functions, however, as the state finds tasks for them to perform, and this can have a depotentiating effect as vitality is traded for security. The dynamics of professionalisation are pushing therapists towards embracing state regulation; but the state is never a passive partner, and what it regulates it also tends to make use of. If psychotherapy wanted to retain its independence it would have a difficult course to steer, but probably it will settle for respectability, limiting as this may prove to be.

30

A CLIENT'S WISH FOR THE FUTURE OF PSYCHOTHERAPY AND COUNSELLING

'ROSIE ALEXANDER'

Ten years ago as I write I was living through the aftermath of a disastrously failed therapy, an experience which had laid waste my life, leaving me in a state of emotional and personal ruin. The straw which I clutched at to survive was the writing of a book, *Folie à Deux* (Alexander 1995), in which I gave a ruthlessly revealing account of what I had been through.

People sometimes ask me how I could have exposed myself in this way. The answer is that it was a book which demanded to be written, dictated by the need to express the torment aroused in the consulting room but which could never be adequately voiced, much less resolved, there. I hoped too that by speaking out publicly I might help to open up a channel for greater communication between service users and providers in a domain where the voices of clients are rarely heard.

This anthology, with the inclusion of chapters written by three former clients (i.e. Chapters 2, 20 and the current one), is proof that this wish is now coming true. The wish has been given added substance by a sustained dialogue which has been taking place for some time between the editors of the book and its client contributors. Our dialogue has been based around articles and interviews for the magazine *ipnosis*, edited by Yvonne Bates and Paula Bentley, and, more generally, on an exchange of ideas about a possible agenda for client/therapist discussion. Further welcome signs are apparent in the greater ease with which clients are now able to get their accounts published and taken seriously, and also in the appearance of therapy websites which serve as a forum for both clients and therapists. And a landmark event in the history of client/therapist relations was surely the invitation to Anna Sands to present a paper at a conference of the British Psychological Society in September 2001.

For far too long the attitude has been that clients should be seen and not heard. Any clients daring to question what was being done to them in the name of therapy risked having their criticisms dismissed as ignorant lay presumption or even as a further indication of their psychological disorder.

Both these assumptions were evident in a review of my book published in *Counselling News* magazine in 1996 and written by therapist Lena Davis. The title itself — 'Rosie in Horrorland' — gives the flavour of the article, a jeeringly flippant piece in which Ms Davis scolded me roundly for giving my therapists a hard time and then for having the temerity to write a book about it.

Even worse than the jibes and the mocking tone of her comments was the impression given that they had been written by someone who was not well acquainted with the basic tenets of analytic psychotherapy. My book *Folie à Deux* is about the aberrant state of mind that can be brought about by transference, the lynchpin of psychoanalysis and related therapies. So necessary did Freud consider transference to be that he believed that patients who remained impervious to the phenomenon could not be treated. And yet, such is the mystery surrounding it that even now those who experience an intense form of it can find little sympathy and understanding, as evidenced by my treatment at the hands of Lena Davis.

My references to being welded to one of my therapists 'by a visceral bond which I couldn't understand or identify and which had no parallel in my conscious experience', to this therapist becoming 'the emotional centre of gravity of my life', to all my emotional energy being 'poured into my relationship with her' are quoted and then dismissed with the sneering comment: 'Etc., etc., etc., in the same infatuated vein' (Davis 1996: 30). She berates me for wanting 'to get directly and deeply involved in a psychodrama-type relationship with [the therapist]' (ibid.), no doubt thinking I should have known better than to try this on with a Neuro-Linguistic Programming practitioner.

Diagnosing me as having problems which fill me with rage, she then claims that this rage is expressed as 'an inappropriate devotion' to psychiatrists or counsellors who become involved with me. She goes on to describe these psychiatrists as 'unfortunate love objects' who are then transported into a fantasy which can only end in upsetting me.

These do not sound like the words of someone who is familiar with transference phenomena or who knows that strong, even excessive, attachment to therapists is a frequent occurrence. Davis does, however, admit that I could have been 'suffering from a very real and painful obsessive illness' (ibid.) without being myself aware of it. If she really believed this, then should she, as a member of a 'caring' profession, have been subjecting me to this public lampooning for the entertainment of a therapist readership? Worst of all, it seems not to have occurred to her that this 'real and painful obsessive illness' was an iatrogenic outcome of the therapy. I had not suffered from this aberrant condition before encountering the therapists, nor have I done so since recovering from the experience.

'Rosie in Horrorland', being the first published response to my book, was, in a sense, the beginning of the dialogue I had hoped to initiate, and it certainly provided grist for much further dialogue as it shocked everyone I presented it to, clients and therapists alike. The review, in fact, epitomises a comment made to me in correspondence by Michael O'Sullivan, a Fellow of the National Council of Psychotherapists and specialist in Post-traumatic Stress Disorder:

> Much of the criticism of your book that I have encountered from within the therapeutic community can fairly be categorised as a 'shoot the messenger response'. This of course allows them to blame anything else other than their own methodologies.

I asked Michael what, specifically, the therapeutic community found in my book to object to. His answer was illuminating.

> I've had therapists describe your book as a tirade against all things therapy — when asked what parts exactly, most of the critics finally admit to not having read your book and express surprise that I would 'waste' my time doing so.

I felt that much of what is wrong in therapy is swept under the carpet, a view supported by Michael:

> The attitude is almost incestuous — problems exist within the family but we dare not talk about it, ignore problems for long enough and they will go away. The therapeutic community demonstrates the kind of insecurities and associated defensiveness which, if present in a client, would lead the average therapist to seek extra supervision.

I wanted to bring these problems out into the light of day and subject them to open debate.

Encouraged by a favourable review of *Folie à Deux* written by a therapist involved in training, I wrote to him proposing some client participation in his courses, possibly question-and-answer sessions with clients giving feedback about what it feels like to be at the receiving end of inappropriate treatment. I received no answer. A similar letter to the author of a book on the subject of erotic transference, in which I suggested contributing some input to his courses on the subject, met with a rebuff. Even a request to POPAN (the organisation which figured prominently, though unnamed, as the support group in my book) to put *Folie à Deux* on its reading-list received only a non-committal reply to the effect that their reviewers were working on a number of books under consideration, a process which would take another four or five months. Eighteen months later *Folie à Deux* has still received no mention anywhere on the POPAN site.

Cruising around the Internet looking for things relating to psychotherapy, I came across the website of a psychiatrist from a leading hospital's medical school. It clearly addressed itself to professionals but it had an approachable face and many promising-looking links. I sent an e-mail explaining that I was trying to carry out some research and that the main stumbling block was that there didn't seem to be any forum in which both practitioners and patients could get together for an exchange of ideas. I outlined the issues I was concerned with — 'the overwhelming dependency which can bind patient to therapist, the very arcane feelings which can be generated in this relationship, and the unwillingness of the profession to deal with or even consider the more negative effects of these'. I asked for some pointers in the right direction:

> It seems to me that most psy sites are geared exclusively towards professionals while the others do little more than provide a mutual support group or chat line for sufferers from various disorders. ... I'm not rabidly anti-therapy, merely keen to set up some kind of constructive dialogue between practitioners and punters. If you have any suggestions as to how this could be achieved, particularly through the Internet, I'd be very grateful.

I received no reply.

I wanted to be able to discuss, on an equal footing, matters of concern to both clients and therapists, to generate an alternative to the present 'us and them' types of discourse which pathologise and infantilise clients and 'cabalise' therapists. I was getting nowhere. Why?, I wondered. Yvonne Bates, co-editor of this anthology and of *ipnosis* magazine, supplied a trenchant answer (personal communication):

Maybe because therapists, these so-called professional listeners, have spent 100 years listening to each other, but not listening to clients. Has there ever been any market research? Has there ever once, anywhere, existed a focus group? It is baffling, ludicrous, outrageous, bewildering that therapists have not asked clients their opinions on therapy in any meaningful way. This has to change, it must change.

Why must it change? Because the fact that a proportion of clients is harmed by therapy is undeniable. One need only attend a meeting of one of the support groups for victims of bad practice or log on to one of the burgeoning websites catering to critics of therapy for evidence of this.

Central to many of the complaints of these victims and critics are problems related to the kind of iatrogenic outcome I mentioned above. This kind of problem is well summed up in the words of Joel Kovel who, in his book *A Complete Guide to Therapy*, balanced the view that therapy 'can touch the human heart and promote freedom' with the observation that it 'can just as likely mechanize, enslave and drive a person crazy'.

I believe it is this 'enslavement' which is at the root of so much that can go wrong in therapy. It manifests itself as a combination of excessive dependency and obsession, the object of both being the therapist. It affects clients to varying degrees, with some people experiencing virtually nothing of such feelings and others finding that their lives and minds have been taken over by them to the exclusion of all else. The pain of unrequited attachment can be intolerable.

The damage can spill over into the lives of other people. The client's feelings for the therapist can dwarf, distort or destroy their feelings for their spouse or other family members. An example of this is the case of Fay Weldon (fictionalised in her novel *Affliction*), who believed her marriage to have broken down as a direct result of the influence of her husband's therapist. 'Harriet', a client interviewed for Rosemary Dinnage's book *One-to-One*, talked of practically hating her children when they were sick and led to her cancelling her appointment, adding that what she resented most when she looked back on her therapy was the fact that her children's lives had been so blighted by the whole business. Similar stories of the breakdown of marital and family relationships appear on the websites devoted to therapy abuse. 'I was so possessed by fantasies of him, the world — family, kids, home — faded into gray', an e-mail correspondent wrote to me. 'Christmas came and went with only a passing resentment that it took energy away from sustaining my non-affair love affair.'

Therapy-induced stress can also cause impaired functioning in the client's work and social environments. In my own case the crazy decisions I took while in this irrational state led to financial disaster. The fall-out in the professional and social domains were equally detrimental to my longer term well-being, and a vicious circle developed with unhappiness breeding even more unhappiness.

The ultimate and irreparable iatrogenic outcome, of course, is suicide. The stories of Paul Lozano, the victim of a reparenting technique gone wrong, and Robert Andrews, whose story is told in *Beware the Talking Cure* by Terence Campbell, are two cases in point. How many others there are we will never know. In his book *Les Jardiniers de la Folie*, French psychiatrist Edouard Zarifian expresses the opinion that psychoanalysis should only be undertaken by the psychologically fit and that for the neurotic it could lead to madness or suicide.

But how far are other therapists prepared to go in recognising the harm which can be done by therapy? In October 1999 the Camden Trust with the Association of Independent Psychotherapists held a conference entitled 'Therapy Hurts?'. Professor Petrûska Clarkson, one of the participants, listed 17 points relating to the conference topics in an article entitled 'Is therapy harmful?' published around November 1999 in Denis Postle's e-journal *Ipnosis* (Independent Practitioners Network 1999). Out of these 17 points, only the following two referred directly to the harmfulness of therapy:

- Evidence exists that there are experiences of psychotherapy by which people feel harmed. One of the most salient facts here is that the harmfulness seems to have to do with the extent to which a psychotherapist entrenches into a theoretical position when challenged or questioned by their client.
- The other major source of harmfulness in psychotherapy is unethical practice such as sexual abuse of clients. POPAN figures show that psychotherapists rank only after doctors as the major perpetrators of abuse.

Nowhere is there any mention of the dramatic harm which can result from the problems of unresolved transference.

In an interview with Bob Mullen for the book *Therapists on Therapy*, Susie Orbach (1996) admitted: 'Some psychotherapy I think is iatrogenic. I think it is damaging.' When asked to be more specific she referred only to a regrettable 'tendency to attack people's defence structures' and to the conduct of a lot of therapists which she described as 'appalling'.

Why this reticence about the potential damage of transference when Freud himself recognised it?: 'It soon becomes evident that this fact of transference is a factor of undreamed-of importance — on the one hand an instrument of irreplaceable value and on the other a source of serious dangers' (Freud 1952).

The state of mind which can be engendered by transference is ill-understood, especially by those who have never experienced it personally. The feelings of extreme dependency are compounded by a regression to an infantile state with the overall result that the client becomes more or less detached from reality. The effect is similar in some ways to that procured by LSD. And just as LSD can have profoundly disturbing effects, so too can transference. Even therapists, for whom it is a working tool, often have little idea of the emotional powder-keg they are handling.

During my first meeting with therapists Mary Edwardes and Jenny Fasal, founders of POPAN, I sought some explanation. 'Why?', I asked. 'Why do I feel like this?' 'We don't know', said Jenny. 'As far as this sort of thing is concerned we're just emerging from the primeval swamp.'

In a recent e-mail discussion with Yvonne Bates in which I raised questions about the nature of transference, Yvonne wrote: 'I really don't know, and I don't believe anyone does, we can only speculate, can't we.' These are refreshingly honest answers which, in their willingness to re-examine the question, are a step towards clarification.

An article I wrote for *The Times* (Alexander 1998), in which I summarised the story of *Folie à Deux*, led to several weeks of discussion in the Letters page, with contributions from both therapists and clients. The question of registration came up, with Philippa Seligman (1998) of the United Kingdom Council for Psychotherapy (UKCP) suggesting that clients wishing to avoid problems should choose only from a list of qualified registered personnel. 'Therapists registered with the UKCP uphold codes of ethics which should prevent the outcome Ms Alexander suffered', she claimed, ignoring the information I had given in the article about my therapist's qualifications (he was a medical doctor, a qualified psychiatrist and a fully trained psychoanalyst). And as a fellow client rightly pointed out in a follow-up letter: 'The issue of competence is not covered by ethical codes and it is one on which therapists will not comment. Accountability is non-existent in this respect.'

Ms Seligman's claim was also contradicted by Pam Whitelaw who chose a UKCP therapist but had experiences 'much the same as Rosie Alexander's'.

A letter from Hilary Dixon (1998) (who found my article 'self-seeking and distasteful, with flashes of crude, topical sensationalism for which she should be ashamed') suggested that I should either see my experience as rooted in the problems which took me into therapy, or complain in the appropriate quarter about my therapist. This allowed me to raise an important point. The problem was not, as Dixon implied, either of my own making or that of an abusive therapist. It lay rather in the force which binds the patient to the therapist — and we should be asking ourselves: What is the nature of this force? What is it about sitting in a room, alone, regularly, with one other person and talking about oneself that can unleash such ungovernable emotions? This is one of the questions which should be on the agenda for further dialogue. Other questions which we might usefully consider are:

- What are the iatrogenic factors that trigger off the excessive dependency and other undesirable psychic phenomena associated with transference?
- What does this mental state signify? Does it contribute in any way to the resolution of one's emotional difficulties or is it merely a side-effect, an associated mental disturbance, like the iatrogenic nausea which accompanies chemotherapy?
- What about the clients themselves? Some are more prone to becoming obsessed and dependent than others. They become serial emotional slaves, going from therapist to therapist and falling into the same dependency trap with each one. Is there something in certain people which predisposes them to this bondage?
- How can prospective clients be made more aware of the potential disruptions to their life before they begin therapy?
- To what extent would therapists agree that these dangers exist?
- To what extent are therapists equipped to deal with the emotional mayhem of a 'transference' gone wrong?
- Finally, given that there will always be a chance of things going wrong even if every effort is made to screen out vulnerable patients and incompetent therapists, what can be done to help those who fall through the safety-net and end up in the state of extreme distress which I and so many others have experienced?

My wish is that by extending the avenues of communication that are beginning to open up between therapists and clients, we will be able to find answers to these questions, thus reducing the harm and promoting the healing done in therapy.

References

Alexander, R. (1995) *Folie à Deux*. London: Free Association Press

Alexander, R. (1998) Life stories. *The Times* magazine, 26th September: 90–1

Campbell, T. (1994) *Beware the Talking Cure*. Boca Raton, FL: Upton Books/Sirs, Inc.

Davis, L. (1996) Rosie in Horrorland: review of Alexander's *Folie à Deux*. *Counselling News* March: 30

Dinnage, R. (ed.) (1988) *One-to-One: Experiences of Psychotherapy*. London: Viking

Dixon, H. (1998) Letter to the editor. *The Times* magazine, 10th October: 103

Freud, S. (1952) *The Major Works of Sigmund Freud*. London: Encyclopaedia Britannica

Independent Practitioners Network (1999) *ipnosis: a journal for the Independent Practitioners Network* — *http://ipnosis.postle.net*

Kovel, J. (1976) *A Complete Guide to Therapy: From Psychoanalysis to Behavior Modification. New York: Pantheon Books*

Orbach, S. (1996) Psychoanalysis. In B. Mullen (ed.), *Therapists on Therapy* (pp. 19–36). London: Free Association Books

Seligman, P. (1998) Letters to the editor. *The Times* magazine, 10th October: 103; 7th November: 95

Zarifian, E. (1988) *Les Jardiniers de la Folie*. Paris: Editions Odile Jacob

FINAL REFLECTIONS

RICHARD HOUSE AND YVONNE BATES

Perhaps ... we will have to do without *any* authority beyond ourselves.
(David Smail, his emphasis)

It is far easier to introduce than it is to conclude an anthology like this one. In this 'conclusion-which-is-not-one', we will attempt selectively to draw out just a few of the central themes that thread themselves through the readings in this book.

FLEXIBILITY

Going right back to the origins of psychoanalysis in the early 20th century, there is a long and distinguished history of practitioner-theorists who have championed a mentality and a practice of *open flexibility* in therapeutic work — Sandor Ferenczi, Georg Groddeck, Franz Alexander, Jacques Lacan and Donald Winnicott, and through to, in the present day, Peter Lomas — and, indeed, several of the practitioners represented in this book. It is no coincidence, of course, that the headlong stampede towards the professionalisation and regulation of the therapy field has been accompanied by a scarcely concealed modernist agenda which includes a creeping (and sometimes rushing) *procedural tightening* of institutional-professionalised practices, a near obsession with abuse and how to legislate against it, a control-fixated holy-grail type pursuance of the 'active ingredients' that constitute a successful therapy 'treatment', an uncritical preoccupation with positivist-empiricist methods of outcome measurement and evaluation... we could go on and on. What all these (essentially un-thought-through) tendencies have in common is their dire effect on spontaneity, innovation and flexibility in therapy work — qualities which, we maintain, are an essential ingredient of effective and empowering practice. Put differently, and with a somewhat grotesque irony, the very attempt somehow externally to guarantee the quality of therapy work ('shrink-wrapped therapy', as Denis Postle evocatively calls it) *routinely brings about the very opposite of its original intention* — that is, creative vision is narrowed and stultified, daring and risk-taking are discouraged (watch out for the law suit), and the 'respectable' freezes out the innovative, the transformative and the maverick. We hope that the essays in this book have demonstrated quite conclusively that openness and reflexivity are essential qualities to nurture and protect if the worst excesses of a soulless, deadening, commonly *defensive* therapy practice are to be avoided.

THE CLIENT'S PERSPECTIVE

One major aspect of such mature flexibility is the urgent need for our field to embrace and learn from our clients and their experience of what therapy offers to them, and how therapy in itself can control, limit and normalise as well as empower and heal. In this volume we are delighted to have included three specially written chapters by ex-therapy clients — 'Rosie Alexander', 'Anna Sands' and 'Natalie Simpson'; and to our knowledge this is the first time that a book of this kind has included such material, on an equal footing with practitioner writings. Of course, it is still far too limited; indeed, we believe it to be a scandal of major proportions that the profession-centred therapy literature has virtually ignored, and continues to ignore, the client view. The editors of this volume recently engaged in an attempt to instigate a substantial and equal dialogue between therapists and clients/ex-clients on the nature of therapy; and while nothing substantive came of this first attempt, we believe that such initiatives are crucial to the mature development of the therapy field as a whole (cf. Rosie Alexander's Chapter 30). The recent published dialogues in the *ipnosis* magazine certainly offer a very useful beginning in this regard; and we are delighted that authoritative noises are indeed beginning to come from within the practitioner domain itself (see references), championing the client viewpoint and the urgent need to incorporate it into our field in a thorough-going way beyond mere cosmetic tokenism.

MODERNITY AND (?)POST-MODERNITY

A number of our contributors have illustrated, some more explicitly than others, the extent to which the modernist *Zeitgeist* is no longer either epistemologically or politically sustainable. The number of therapy publications that challenge the modernist worldview in therapy is continually increasing, and some new university courses are even beginning to reflect these wider *Zeitgeist* changes — one notable example being the 'Clinical psychology in late-modernity' BA degree course at the University of Aarhus, Denmark. We believe that the essays in this book both comprehensively undermine the coherence of 'modernist' therapy as cultural project and clinical practice, and also offer a multiplicity and richness of vision for innovative directions which a viable postmodern, post-professionalised therapy might take.

TO CLOSE...

...it is surely axiomatic that anxiety is constitutive of all human relationships — and it follows that anxiety is a defining feature of all therapy relationships. We can respond to that anxiety in two ways. First, by unwittingly acting out from that anxiety such that the therapeutic community, and therapy itself, become 'dysfunctional'. The alternative is to face, integrate and ultimately transcend these anxieties such that we are enabled to make conscious choices about what a mature 'trans-modern' therapy practice might begin to look like. We feel that the essays in this book offer cutting-edge insights into how this might be achieved; and it is in this spirit that we commend their collective message to you, not least because we passionately believe that the future healthy evolution of 'the therapeutic' depends upon such unity-in-diversity and our honest, unflagging efforts creatively to engage with it.

We leave the final word to Dorothy Rowe:

> The most dangerous people in the world are those who believe they know what is best for others.

REFERENCES

Bates, Y. (2002) Editorial: Listening to our clients. *ipnosis: An Independent Journal for Practitioners* 5 (Spring): 3

Foskett, J. (2001) What of the client's-eye view? A response to the millennium review. *British Journal of Guidance and Counselling* 29 (3): 346–50

Genest, S. (2002) Practical implications, professionals gain from client perspectives on counselling. Symposium paper, 'Linking Research to Educational Practice II', 5–17th July; contact sagenest@ucalgary.ca

House, R. (2003) *Therapy Beyond Modernity: Deconstructing and Transcending Profession-Centred Therapy*. London: Karnac Books

AFTERWORD

IAN PARKER

This book connects concerns over the professionalisation of counselling and psychotherapy with the question of ethics, and of course 'ethics' has been one of the watchwords of the blossoming regulating bodies. But the problem of ethics for us is actually broader and more far-ranging than it seems, for counselling and psychotherapy are embedded in a pervasive professionalisation of ethics that tries to anticipate and shield us from all the different kinds of risk we encounter in contemporary capitalist society. There is one popular narrative about this professionalisation among the therapists. The poor counsellors and psychotherapists are, according to this narrative, trying their best to develop good practice and aim for the good of their clients in a context that is set up to inhibit and frustrate any thorough-going emancipatory personal politics; that is, the self-questioning and challenging of who we are and what keeps us in our place. The book airs this narrative, and there are indeed very serious problems that beset a therapist when they try to follow through the project of therapy in a genuinely radical way, when they refuse to confine their work to the enclosed space of the consulting room and have some vision of how the boundary between the realm of personal politics and social change might be transgressed so that some real transformation becomes possible. But the book does more than this, and a space is opened up by virtue of the inclusion of voices of clients who speak from a different position within this process of professionalisation. This is actually also a position and voice that all good therapists have experienced themselves, of course, but which some of them have allowed themselves to forget.

We need to take from this a second less comfortable narrative about the professionalisation of ethics. Which is, that we do this to ourselves. Well, no, some of us will cry, we always opposed the attempts by wannabe bureaucrats to define and govern how therapy should be done and to lure therapists into the game of state regulation with the promise that this will be for the good of clients. However, the responsibility that we share for the activities of some therapists — those who were keen to set up and sit on the array of registration bodies and ethical committees that pervade therapeutic practice today — runs a little deeper than this. When we do 'therapy' we often transform our images of ourselves in rather pathetic ways, and we are implicated in the construction and representation of forms of self that are fragile and uncertain; much harm is done in therapy, but the path is prepared for much of the harm by our own insistence that human beings are so soft and vulnerable that any act of resistance on their part must be a sign of some kind of pathology. The path is then also laid in a certain direction, so that it seems logical that we must have professional organisations and committees to protect everyone, including ourselves. The voices of some of the powerful clients who have been able to resist are not only testimony to the bad things that have been done but also witness to what it is to be a person who is actually a little less 'therapeutic' than the professional expects them to be. If we follow the implications of that second narrative, then, we might also be able to resist ourselves the seductive safe haven of professionalised 'ethics'.

INDEX

IMPLAUSIBLE PROFESSIONS
Arguments for pluralism and autonomy in
psychotherapy and counselling

Edited by
Richard House and Nick Totton

1997   ISBN 1 898059 17 9   pp. 348   £16.00

At last a book on counselling and psychotherapy that demands to be read. What you get here is a lot of what Virginia Satir once called 'levelling' — telling the honest truth . . . Together [the authors] demonstrate the persistence in many humanistic practitioners of a deep tenacity and groundedness that resist the creeping 'McDonaldisation' of the treatment of contemporary woe that the professionalisation process has ushered in.

David Kalisch, *Self & Society*

I sometimes found this book uncomfortable, for it challenged some of my own beliefs and consistently made me reflect on what I am doing and my own transferential attitudes to these matters. I believe anyone involved in any psychotherapy or counselling regulating body, in training, accreditation, research or practice would benefit from reading this book . . .'

Whizz Collis, *International Journal of Psychotherapy*

IMPLAUSIBLE PROFESSIONS REMAINS AS CHALLENGING TODAY AS IT WAS WHEN PUBLISHED IN 1997. Twenty-eight papers, with contributions from Val Blomfield, Cal Cannon, Jill Davies, Michael Eales, Colin Feltham, Guy Gladstone, Marion Hall, Sue Hatfield, Catherine Hayes, John Heron, Richard House, Juliet Lamont, Peter Lomas, Michael McMillan, Katharine Mair, Richard Mowbray, Denis Postle, Andrew Samuels, Robin Shohet, David Smail, Annie Spencer, Brian Thorne, Nick Totton and David Wasdell.

Buy from www.pccs-books.co.uk
Call for discounts + 44 (0)1989 77 07 07
PCCS Books, Llangarron, Ross-on-Wye, HR9 6PT, UK